# NEW TECHNOLOGY-BASED FIRMS IN THE NEW MILLENNIUM VOLUME VI

*New Technology-Based Firms in the New Millennium Volume V (2007)*
Aard Groen, Ray Oakey, Peter van der Sijde and Saleema Kauser

*New Technology-Based Firms in the New Millennium Volume IV (2005)*
Wim During, Ray Oakey and Saleema Kauser

*New Technology-Based Firms in the New Millennium Volume III (2004)*
Wim During, Ray Oakey and Saleema Kauser

*New Technology-Based Firms in the New Millennium Volume II (2002)*
Ray Oakey, Wim During and Saleema Kauser

*New Technology-Based Firms in the New Millennium Volume I (2001)*
Wim During, Ray Oakey and Saleema Kauser

**New Technology-Based Firms at the Turn of the Century**

*New Technology-Based Firms at the Turn of the Century (2000)*
Ray Oakey, Wim During and Michelle Kipling

**New Technology-Based Firms in the 1990s**

*New Technology-Based Firms in the 1990s Volume VI (1999)*
Ray Oakey, Wim During and Syeda-Masooda Mukhtar

**Previous titles in this series published by Paul Chapman Publishing**

*New Technology-Based Firms in the 1990s Volume I (1994)*
Ray Oakey

*New Technology-Based Firms in the 1990s Volume II (1996)*
Ray Oakey

*New Technology-Based Firms in the 1990s Volume III (1997)*
Ray Oakey and Syeda-Masooda Mukhtar

*New Technology-Based Firms in the 1990s Volume IV (1998)*
Wim During and Ray Oakey

*New Technology-Based Firms in the 1990s Volume V (1998)*
Ray Oakey and Wim During

**Related Journals - Sample copies available on request**

*European Journal of Innovative Management*
*International Journal of Entrepreneurial Behaviour & Research*
*Journal of Enterprising Communities: People and Places in the Global Economy*
*Journal of Small Business and Enterprise Development*
*Social Enterprise Journal*

# NEW TECHNOLOGY-BASED FIRMS IN THE NEW MILLENNIUM VOLUME VI

EDITED BY

**AARD GROEN**

*Nikos, University of Twente, Enschede, The Netherlands*

**RAY OAKEY**

*Manchester Business School, Manchester, UK*

**PETER VAN DER SIJDE**

*Nikos, University of Twente, Enschede, The Netherlands*

**GARY COOK**

*University of Liverpool Management School, Liverpool, UK*

Emerald

United Kingdom • North America • Japan
India • Malaysia • China

Emerald Group Publishing Limited
Howard House, Wagon Lane, Bingley BD16 1WA, UK

First edition 2008

Copyright © 2008 Emerald Group Publishing Limited

**Reprints and permission service**
Contact: booksandseries@emeraldinsight.com

**British Library Cataloguing in Publication Data**
A catalogue record for this book is available from the British Library

ISBN: 978-0-0805-5448-8
ISSN: 1876-0228 (Series)

Printed and bound by MPG Books Ltd, Bodmin, Cornwall

Awarded in recognition of
Emerald's production
department's adherence to
quality systems and processes
when preparing scholarly
journals for print

INVESTOR IN PEOPLE

# Contents

# Contributors

S Jaseem Ahmad          Middlesex University Business School, The Burroughs, London, UK

Alistair Anderson       Centre for Entrepreneurship, Aberdeen Business School, Robert Gordon University, Aberdeen, UK

Frank Cave              Lancaster University Management School, Lancaster, UK

Schaul Chorev           Aberdeen Business School, Robert Gordon University, Aberdeen, UK

Gary Cook               University of Liverpool Management School, Liverpool, UK

Sarah Cooper            Hunter Centre for Entrepreneurship, University of Strathclyde, Glasgow, UK

Kjell de Ruijter        NIKOS, University of Twente, Enschede, The Netherlands

Céline Druilhe          Centre for Business Research, University of Cambridge, Judge Business School, Cambridge, UK

Abby Ghobadian          Henley Management College, Greenlands, Henley-on-Thames, Oxfordshire, UK

Simon Gillespie         Dundalk Institute of Technology, Dundalk, Co. Louth, Ireland

Stephan Golla           Kfw endowed Chair for Entrepreneurship, European Business School (ebs), International University Schloß Reichartshausen, Oestrich-Winkel, Germany

Colette Henry           Centre for Entrepreneurship Research, Dundalk Institute of Technology, Dundalk, Co. Louth, Ireland

| | |
|---|---|
| *Teresa Hogan* | Dublin City University Business School, Glasnevin, Dublin, Ireland |
| *Martin Holi* | Kfw endowed Chair for Entrepreneurship, European Business School (ebs), International University Schloß Reichartshusen, Oestrich-Winkel, Germany |
| *Deirdre Hunt* | Department of Management and Marketing, National University of Ireland Cork, Cork, Ireland |
| *Elaine Hutson* | Department of Banking and Finance, Michael Smurfit Graduate School of Business, University College Dublin, Blackrock, Co. Dublin, Ireland |
| *Tobias Johann* | Kfw endowed Chair for Entrepreneurship, European Business School (ebs), International University Schloß Reichartshausen, Oestrich-Winkel, Germany |
| *Kate Johnston* | Centre for Entrepreneurship Research, Dundalk Institute of Technology, Dundalk, Co. Louth, Dundalk, Ireland |
| *Andrea Kells* | SQW Ltd, Enterprise House, Vision Park, Histon, Cambridge, UK |
| *Paul Kirwan* | NIKOS, University of Twente, Enschede, The Netherlands |
| *Heinz Klandt* | Kfw endowed Chair for Entrepreneurship, European Business School (ebs), International University Schloß Reichartshausen, Oestrich-Winkel, Germany |
| *Magnus Klofsten* | Centre for Innovation and Entrepreneurship (CIE), Linköping University, Linköping, Sweden |
| *Lutz Kraft* | Kfw endowed Chair for Entrepreneurship, European Business School (ebs), International University Schloß Reichartshausen, Oestrich-Winkel, Germany |
| *Andy Lockett* | Nottingham University Business School, Nottingham, UK |
| *William Lucas* | Cambridge-MIT Institute, Massachusetts Institute of Technology, Cambridge, MA, USA |
| *Michael Lynskey* | St John's College, University of Cambridge, Cambridge, UK |

| | |
|---|---|
| *Tim Minshall* | Institute for Manufacturing, University of Cambridge, Centre for Technology Management, Cambridge, UK |
| *Simon Mosey* | Lecturer in Entrepreneurship and Innovation, Institute for Enterprise and Innovation, Nottingham University Business School, Nottingham, UK |
| *Ray Oakey* | Manchester Business School, The University of Manchester, Manchester, UK |
| *Nicholas O'Regan* | Centre for Interdisciplinary Strategic Management Research, Bristol Business School, Bristol, UK |
| *Naresh Pandit* | Manchester Business School, Booth Street West, Manchester, UK |
| *Devang Shah* | Heriot Watt University, Riccarton, Edinburgh, UK |
| *Jelena Širaliova* | Judge Business School, University of Cambridge, Cambridge, UK |
| *Peter van der Sijde* | NIKOS, University of Twente, Enschede, The Netherlands |
| *Ariane von_Raesfeld Meijer* | NIKOS, University of Twente, Enschede, The Netherlands |
| *Anthony Ward* | Department of Electronics, University of York, Heslington, York, UK |
| *Paul Westhead* | Centre for Entrepreneurship, Durham Business School, Durham University, Durham, UK |
| *Bill Wicksteed* | SQW Ltd, Enterprise House, Vision Park, Histon, Cambridge, UK |
| *Malcolm Wilkinson* | Technology for Industry Ltd, St Ives, Cambridgeshire, UK |
| *Kevin Yallup* | Technology for Industry Ltd, St Ives, Cambridgeshire, UK |

Chapter 1

# Introduction

Ray Oakey and Gary Cook

This is the 13th volume of a series of books emanating from the annual International High Technology Small Firms Conference, begun in 1993, which alternates between Manchester Business School (MBS) in the United Kingdom and the University of Twenty in the Netherlands. The 14 papers included below are the best papers to be presented at the conference held at MBS in June 2005. The conference and book series was originally planned to give a higher profile to the problems of High-Technology Small Firm (HTSF) development at a time when government interest was flagging in the early 1900s. However, while this original intention endures by continuing a 'watching brief' on the level of interest in HTSF development exhibited by national governments, the now substantial body of work generated, reflecting trends in HTSF research and policy debates over more than a decade, represents a unique 'time series' record of the evolving interests of a close-knit community of international researchers.

The first decade of the new millennium has been characterised, especially in the United Kingdom and the United States, by a reoccurrence of the trend witnessed in 1993 when this conference and book series was established, in which government support for HTSFs in particular and manufacturing industry in general, has begun to ebb. This decline has been partly caused by a greater government preoccupation with consumption rather than production in a context where 'economic growth' in an economy is judged more by the amount of borrowing (and subsequent spending) that is occurring rather than productive manufacturing output, which continues to steadily decline. Certainly, in the United Kingdom, this attitude represents a strong shift of sentiment from that witnessed during most of the post World War II period until the mid-1990s of the last millennium. Such a consumption oriented approach is symbolised by the fact that, while in the 1970s and 1980s low interest rates were thought beneficial in order to allow productive industry to invest, now they are advocated in order to allow consumer spending to remain high on the basis of cheap credit. Nonetheless, in the medium term, such economic growth based on borrowing will be difficult to sustain, at personal, corporate or national government levels.

Thus, in the future, the governments of Western developed nations *must return* to the business of supporting productive industries that allow us to sell our goods and services to other countries in order to pay for what we buy from them, thus creating a balanced World

New Technology Based Firms in the New Millennium, Volume VI
Edited by A. Groen, R. Oakey, P. van der Sijde and G. Cook

Economic System. Moreover, although new high-technology industries, often founded by HTSF entrepreneurs, will be a major area of potential growth for development in Western nations, the days of their major dominance in this area cannot be assumed. The progress of China and South Korea in electronics and India in software confirms that a form of 'technological colonialism', in which the West dominates 'start of cycle' industries with their high profit margins, while the developing world is consigned to make low value 'end of cycle' products based on cheap labour, is no longer viable. Nonetheless, although successful competition will not be easily achieved, Western nations continue to have considerable intellectual and capital resources and this is a key area of future World Economic Growth *and* competition, where developed countries must successfully compete and not capitulate in order to ensure their economic survival.

Therefore, the question of how best to encourage the formation and growth of HTSFs must remain a key task for any developed national economies. While academics are often primarily concerned with explanatory theory and government development agencies are interested in the more practical goals of economic growth and new jobs, both parties are interested in how often 'naturally occurring' unassisted economic phenomena (e.g. clustering), might most efficiently occur, and in the case of government development agencies, how they might be replicated. On some occasions, the theoretical work of academics has led the thinking of policy-makers. For example, the work of Porter (1998) on clusters has recently triggered worldwide interest in cluster theory as a mechanism for focussed HTSF growth. In other instances such as Science Parks and Academic Enterprise Development, there has been strong policy stimulus provided by governments seeking to gain the maximum local economic benefit from the technical knowledge held in universities in the core and in peripheral regions of nation states.

Ideally, the main role of the academic in the context of HTSF development (or any other economic advisory context) is to perform both research that offers *new* options for the development of policy-makers based on theoretical hypotheses and tested results, and to offer to test the efficiency of the independent actions of government development agencies to ascertain if they have been effective, how they might be improved, and whether they should be replaced by a different approach. However, this relationship is uneasy for a number of reasons. Perhaps the most obvious problem is that government agencies are often the client for academic work, an arrangement in which results are technically confidential. Thus, not only can government set the agenda for any research they fund, they can also suppress its findings if they prove to be politically embarrassing. Notwithstanding these problems, the role of the university researcher should be to take a *completely independent* stance towards his or her work. While an elected government can always ignore advice honestly given on the basis of objective research results, the role of the academic is to always provide such an independent view of policy.

Figure 1, first produced earlier in this series (Oakey & Mukhtar 1997), visually represents an ideal relationship in which, while both academics and policy-makers (practitioners) may work independently on any given problem (e.g. the efficacy of science parks), academics seek to influence the direction of policy at T2 by feeding through theoretical and empirical inputs at T1. Ideally, practitioners take this criticism 'on board' when producing a revised approach at T2, which is again commented on, often involving the suggestion of alternative approaches, by academics, and is further reformed at T3. This 'ideal' pattern of

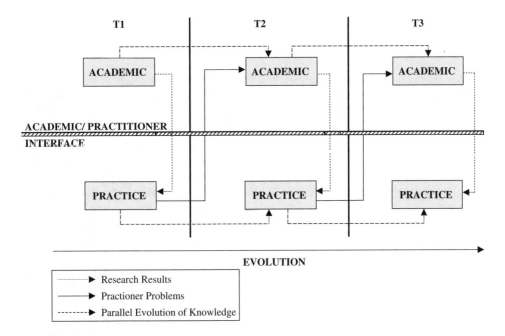

Figure 1: The interaction between academics and practitioners across
the academic/practitioner interface over time.

interaction does not mean that academic and practitioners fully agree on all issues of mutual interest. It is clear that government practitioners have a political dimension to what they do which may not have an economic logic (e.g. the siting of new industrial investment in marginal parliamentary constituencies). However, this interaction is ideal in that constructive dialogue occurs *across* the 'Academic/Practitioner Interface', where the academic is not 'ivory-towerist' and the government practitioner is not totally driven by political dogma and real progress towards solving the development problems of, in this case HTSFs, can occur.

A major motivation here for rehearsing the role of academics in monitoring best practice in HTSF policy development is that, in this volume, the largest group of 5 of the 14 papers below are concerned with policy evaluation. Apart from such scrutiny being, as argued above, a valid and important role for academics, the strong representation in this volume of such evaluations must also partly stem from a number of European-wide initiatives (particularly with regard to academic entrepreneurship) embarked upon at the end of the 1990s, and now at a stage where analysis of their impact is appropriate. Clearly, this is an area of public policies where an independent academic voice can inform public and political debate on what works and how we might improve what we do in terms of *future* policy initiatives.

Apart from evaluation studies, other main themes under which the following chapters are grouped include: 'Clustering/Networking', 'Start-Ups/Spin-Offs' and 'Strategy' and they are introduced below.

## The Papers

*Policy Evaluation*

A broad range of policy evaluations below is begun in Chapter 2 by Kate Johnston, Colette Henry and Simon Gillespie in their evaluation entitled 'Encouraging Research and Development in Ireland's Biotechnology Enterprises'. This investigation critically evaluates Irish government policy towards biotechnology development over a preceding 10-year period. In Chapter 3, Anthony Ward, Sarah Cooper, Frank Cave and William Lucas examine 'The Effect of Industrial Experience on Entrepreneurial Intent and Self-Efficacy in UK Engineering Undergraduates' in a large-scale study that generally produces satisfactory results in terms of raising the profile of entrepreneurship among undergraduates. Deirdre Hunt, in Chapter 4, again focuses on the evolution of strategy in Ireland, this time towards the more general topic of new firm formation with a personal contribution entitled 'Now You See Them — Now You Don't: Paradoxes in Enterprise Development Strategy: The Case of the Disappearing Academic Start-Ups'.

The theme of policy evaluation is continued in a Scandinavian context in Chapter 5 where Magnus Klofsten examines the efficacy of a Swedish scheme set up to support academic 'spin-off' in the region around Linköping University entitled 'Supporting Academic Enterprise: A Case Study of an Entrepreneurship Programme'. In common, with many other investigations of this type, the author finds evidence of both success, and room for improvement. This section on evaluation studies is concluded in Chapter 6 by Simon Mosey, Andy Lockett and Paul Westhead with an investigation entitled 'Building the Foundations for Academic Enterprise: The Medici Fellowship Programme'. This programme, aimed at overcoming attitudinal and operational barriers to university technology transfer by academic entrepreneurs, is found by the authors to be generally worthwhile in ameliorating a process that is often more fraught in practice than in theory.

*Clustering/Networking*

As mentioned earlier in this introduction, the long established principle of clustering advantage (e.g. most famously in Silicon Valley) has lately been resurrected and used as a mechanism for promoting existing and stimulating nascent, HTSF development. This renewed interest has been reflected in recent volumes of this series and is continued here as witnessed by three papers dealing with the related concepts of clustering, networking and spillovers. This sub-section begins in Chapter 7 with a paper by Gary Cook and Naresh Pandit entitled 'An Empirical Assessment of Porter's Clusters Concept Based on London's Media Industries'. This paper assesses how useful Porter's assertions on the development of clusters are in explaining the unique functioning of the media industries of Central London.

While the main mechanism for clustering is inter-firm networking, these connections are not necessarily local. Recently developed Information Technology means that networks can be virtual in nature and maintained over long distances. Chapter 8, jointly written by Peter van der Sijde, Ariane von Raesfeld-Meijer, Kjell de Ruijter and Paul Kirwan, entitled 'Network Differences between Domestic and Global University Start-Ups' examines and compares locally networked firms with those founded on virtual global ties. Finally, this sub-section is concluded in Chapter 9 by Michael Lynskey who, in a paper entitled, 'Knowledge Spillovers from Public Research Institutions: Evidence from Japanese High-Technology Start-Up Firms' traces the role of Japanese public research institutions in creating spillover-based new HTSFs.

### Start-Ups/'Spin-Offs'

A major role of sub-regional, regional and national government development agencies over the past decade has been the encouragement of new HTSF formations in a number of high-technology sectors. This trend is partly reflected in the policy evaluation sub-section above. However, the next set of papers reflects this work in another way by commenting on the success of various attempts at sectoral and/or sub-regional HTSF developments. In Chapter 10, Stephan Golla, Martin Holi, Tobias Johann, Heinz Klandt and Lutz Kraft report on German experience of HTSF nurturing in a paper entitled 'The Development of Venture-Capital-Backed and Independent Companies an Empirical Study among Germany's Internet and E-Commerce Start-Ups', where different sources of capital are analysed to observe their impact on subsequent growth. This comparative theme is continued by Teresa Hogan and Eliane Hutson in comparison from Ireland of 'The High-Technology Pecking order in Spin-Offs and Non-Spin-Offs in the Irish Software Sector' in Chapter 11. This sub-section on start-ups and spin-offs is concluded by Tim Minshall, Bill Wicksteed, Celine Druilhe, Andrea Kells, Michael Lynskey and Jelena Siraliova in Chapter 12 where they investigate how spin-offs impact upon university commercialisation performance in a paper entitled 'The Role of Spin-Outs within University Research Commercialisation Activities: Case Studies from 10 UK Universities'.

### Strategy

In common with any other industrial organisation, HTSFs can benefit or suffer from the quality of the strategic approach they adopt. In complex technical and funding cases, there are many problems that might emerge to thwart an originally sensible growth strategy, thus requiring a new approach. Thus, strategy is a continuing subject of interest, both for HTSF owners and researchers. This first Chapter 13 of this sub-section by Devang Shah, Malcolm Wilkinson and Kevin Yallup entitled 'Analysis of the Factors Leading to Success or Failure of Start-Up Companies in the Field of Micro and Nanotechnology' not only deals with strategic behaviour in a HTSF context, but focuses on the very newest nanotechnology firms as they seek to establish themselves. In Chapter 14, Nicholas O'Regan, Abby Ghobadian and Jaseem Ahmad continue their strong vein of research on strategic issues within HTSF in a contribution entitled 'Drivers of Strategic Direction in High-Technology Small Firms'. This volume concludes with a contribution in Chapter 15 from Israel by Schaul Choreve and Alistair Anderson entitled 'Success Factors for High-Tech Start-Ups — Views and Lessons of Israeli Experts'.

# References

Oakey, R. P., & Mukhtar, S. Y. (1997). High technology small firms development: Bridging the academic–practitioner divide. In: R. P. Oakey & S. Y. Mukhtar (Eds), *New technology-based firms in the 1990s* (pp. 1–6). London: Paul Chapman Publishing.

Porter, M. (1998). *On competition*. Boston: Harvard Business School Press.

Chapter 2

# Encouraging Research and Development in Ireland's Biotechnology Enterprises

Kate Johnston, Colette Henry and Simon Gillespie

## Introduction

Biotechnology is now considered a key emerging sector in Ireland's economic landscape. Defined as the 'application of scientific and engineering principles to the processing of materials by biological agents' (Forfás Report, 2005), biotechnology is now the main high-technology driver affecting industries as diverse as food, agriculture human health and environmental protection. In 2002 it was estimated that over 400,000 people worldwide were employed in biotech (InterTradeIreland, 2002), with the market for biotechnology products worth an estimated €100 billion (European Commission, 2002). However, according to the Technology Foresight Ireland Report (1999), these figures are predicted to increase significantly, with the expectation that, by the end of 2006, the biotechnology sector will be worth an estimated €250 billion and will employ more than three million workers.

With specific regard to Ireland, there are currently 60 bio-enterprises and, while most are micro companies and at an early stage of development, collectively they employ some 5000 people. Their activities range from developing new methods of diagnosing and treating disease to products that assist in remedying environmental damage and the prevention of such issues.

A core objective of the Irish government's current biotechnology strategy is to stimulate growth and development within its emerging indigenous sector (Enterprise Ireland, 2003). To date this strategy has tended to focus on funding investment, building up an industrial profile and on developing a world-class bioresearch base. In some countries, indirect fiscal incentives are being used as a means of stimulating growth within the indigenous biotech sector. Such incentives include taxation credits designed to encourage research and development (R&D) in biotech small- and medium-sized enterprises (SMEs). Indeed, some of the more successful biotech countries already have some form of tax

New Technology Based Firms in the New Millennium, Volume VI
Edited by A. Groen, R. Oakey, P. van der Sijde and G. Cook

incentive in place, which is often seen as a cost-effective means of promoting growth in the indigenous sector by encouraging more R&D.

A key objective of this paper is to provide an overview of the Irish biotechnology sector and examine the government's strategy for promoting the sector to date. By drawing on examples from the UK, France and the USA, and by referring to some of the effectiveness studies conducted to date, the authors also aim to open the discussion surrounding the use of tax credits as a means of promoting the sector by encouraging R&D. In this regard, some issues for further analysis and research are identified.

This paper is structured as follows: firstly, the case for biotechnology and the need to promote the sector are reviewed. Secondly, the current state of Ireland's biotech sector is examined, and the Irish government's strategy in promoting the sector to date is discussed. Thirdly, using examples from three of the world's leading biotechnology countries, the nature of tax credits is considered. Fourthly, the need to further promote Ireland's biotech sector is highlighted, and some of the advantages and disadvantages associated with using tax credit incentives are explored. In this regard, by way of opening the debate on whether tax credits could be used to promote R&D among Ireland's biotech enterprises, the authors suggest that further discussion is merited. Finally, the paper concludes by identifying some of the key issues that require further analysis and research if tax credits are to be given full consideration as potential biotech R&D stimulants.

## Research Context

### *The Case for Biotechnology*

Countries such as the UK, the USA, Australia and parts of continental Europe have already identified biotechnology as a major driver of economic growth in the twenty-first century. In the United States, for example, biotechnology now generates more than $40 billion in annual revenues (Ernst & Young, 2004). Moreover, in Europe the value of products and services using biotechnology is estimated to be worth €250 million, which in turn affects (both directly and indirectly) more than three million jobs (EuropaBio Report, 1997). Increasingly, however, this leading-edge area of technology is not restricted solely to the wealthy nations of Europe and America. India, China, South Africa (and even Cuba) are also moving into the innovative and dynamic realms of biotechnology thus providing a means for these countries to reduce their economic dependency on commodities (e.g. sugar, nickel, tobacco, rum), as well as delivering scientific advancements in high technology, represented by biotechnology (Chen, 2003).

In the broadest sense, biotechnology concerns the use of biological processes or elements to solve technology needs or problems, enabling the application of engineering, technology and science principles, to improve the health, quality and utility of plants and animals. From an economic perspective, the commercialisation of biotechnology is the primary focus, with the technology set to deliver potentially huge gains in all primary industries such as health care, food and agriculture industries, as well as environmental protection. The end result will be new sustainable wealth and knowledge creation, as well as potentially life-enhancing innovations.

However, as with any other sector, the case for supporting the growth and development of biotechnology ultimately must be an economic one. While governments around the world are increasingly keen to stimulate the growth of high-technology industries, biotechnology must compete for economic support with other technology-based industries such as nanotechnology, electronics and telecommunications, as well as traditional industries.

## The State of Biotechnology in Ireland

According to Ernst and Young (2002), Ireland is now recognised among the top 25 global locations for biotechnology. However the biotechnology sector in Ireland is at a very early stage of development. There are currently 59 bio-companies in Ireland of which 41 are indigenous and 18 are multinational, with the indigenous companies consisting of primarily private, early discovery and seed-stage companies (Martin, 2005).

In terms of economic contribution, bio-enterprises currently employ approximately 5000 people in Ireland, with the majority (i.e. 3000 workers) employed in multinational enterprises. Indigenous bio-enterprises account for less than 2000 workers or 40% of total employment of the sector. Most indigenous bio-enterprises are small, with 60% (i.e. 26) in the micro category and employing less than ten people, and less than 10% employing more than fifty (Enterprise Ireland, 2005).

In relation to age distribution, most of Ireland's indigenous biotech businesses are early-stage companies, with an average age of 5 years, reflecting the relatively recent nature of both the technology and the industry. In terms of industrial focus, the majority (i.e. 21) are involved in diagnostics, followed by pharmaceutical biologics (i.e. 16) and agri-food (i.e. 11) with pharmaceutical services and bio-environmental activity making up the remaining 11 companies. The concentration of bio-enterprises in diagnostics, which is primarily concerned with the production of diagnostic kits for use in hospitals and clinics, reflects the low entry barriers for this sub-sector both in terms of manufacturing costs and regulatory controls associated with this type of activity. However, access to R&D expertise and facilities is a major issue for Ireland's early-stage biotech companies, and for this reason most bio-enterprises in Ireland are located close to high-technology centres, such as universities, institutes and hospitals. Forty-six of the fifty-nine technology companies are located in five major concentrations comprising Dublin (16), Belfast (14), Cork (8), Galway (5) and Coleraine (3). This is consistent with comparative analysis that suggests that biotechnology tends to cluster regionally (Prevezer, 1998; Shohet, 1998).

In many cases, biotech companies are spin-offs from universities. Around 25 Irish biotech companies have originated in this way (IntertradeIreland, 2002), while several others are significantly dependent on technologies licensed from universities of other countries.

### Irish Government Policy on Biotechnology

The Irish Government has been aware of the potential of biotechnology for many years. While initial reports were drawn up in the early 1980s, it was not until the 1990s, that a number of significant reports emerged including Forfás Report (1996), 'Shaping Our

Future — A Strategy for Enterprise in Ireland in the 21st Century', which identified biotechnology as a key enabling technology for Ireland's future industrial development. However, it was not until the publication of the Technology Foresight Ireland Report (1999) on health and life sciences that the Irish strategy on biotech was finally established. At this time Ireland was not perceived as an international centre of biotechnology. In fact, after Greece, Ireland had the lowest level of government-supported R&D at less than 1% of total government expenditure (European Commission, 1997). The overall structure of the Irish national biotechnology research programme was weak, outputs were small and the number of top quality biotechnology research groups was limited. Irish biotechnology graduates were leaving the country in large numbers and Irish science students were not encouraged or educated to become science, technology and innovation (STI) entrepreneurs. In the area of commercialisation, there was little funding available for start-up companies, and Irish venture capital funds had little experience of biotechnology investment (Irish Council for Science, Technology and Innovation (ICSTI), 2002).

This 2002 ICSTI Report argued that Ireland could not afford to ignore biotechnology and concluded that:

> [U]nless investment does occur, Ireland will not only fail to benefit from the new biotechnology in terms of a large number of new, high quality, high added-value jobs, but many existing jobs in the pharmaceutical and chemical industries, the food and drink industries and in agriculture will be jeopardised (2002, p. 6).

Since the publication of these early reports, over 12 separate reports on biotechnology related issues have been published in Ireland. Collectively they have resulted in a comprehensive package of measures designed to promote and prioritise biotechnology in Ireland. Table 1 below summaries these measures.

The above measures were complemented by a series of funding programmes administered by the Higher Education Authority (HEA)[1] to boost both capital and recurrent expenditure on university-based research. Life sciences gained more than half of the €600 million that has been disbursed by the HEA, resulting in the creation of new institutes throughout the country's university system designed to focus on areas such as genomics, cellular biotechnology, biomedical engineering, immunology, biopharmaceuticals and molecular medicine, and food and health science.

More recently, the government has announced a €1 million funding initiative targeted at boosting the number of women scientists in Ireland. This initiative consists of three Science Foundation Ireland (SFI)-funded programmes aimed at addressing the under-representation of women in Irish science and engineering research.

Collectively, such initiatives have resulted in five core centres of biotech research located on the campuses of Irish universities. Biotechnology research is predominately carried out at these five centres, along with Teagasc, the national body providing advisory, research, education and training services for agriculture and the food industries.

---

[1]The HEA manages the third-level education sector.

Table 1: Summary of Ireland's biotech measures.

| Measure(s) introduced | Impact on industrial policy |
| --- | --- |
| The development of a quality R&D programme to foster 'leading-edge' research. | The government had set up the National Biotechnology Programme (1987) to develop commercially oriented biotechnology research in Irish universities. In 1995, less than €1.2 million was received in research grants in science and technology in Ireland. In 2000, through the Technology Foresight Fund, over €650 million was invested in technological and scientific research. |
| Additional focus on the commercialisation of research outputs through the creation of BioResearch Ireland (BRI). | BRI is a contract research organisation responsible for commercialising existing biotechnology and developing the expertise and facilities needed for biotech R&D. BRI's principal role is the commercialisation of technologies arising from university research through directly assisting the development and transfer of technology from research facilities to industry. |
| Developing imaginative schemes to foster an indigenous industry while also attracting foreign investors. | In early 2000, Enterprise Ireland (EI) established the first dedicated Biotechnology Start-Up Fund, with €15 million allocated to biotech companies in the early stages of development. |
| Putting in place a communications strategy to increase public awareness and participation. | This was achieved through the publication of several policy documents, including the Irish Council for Science Technology and Innovation (ICSTI) Report on Biotechnology (2002). |
| The establishment of Science Foundation Ireland (SFI) in 2003 to enhance, develop and promote the scale and quality of basic research in Ireland. | SFI's role was to fund research in biotechnology and information and communications technology (ICT) development. To date, SFI has invested over €646 million in academic researchers and research teams working in leading-edge technologies |

*(Continued)*

Table 1: (*Continued*)

| Measure(s) introduced | Impact on industrial policy |
| --- | --- |
| | and competitive enterprises in biotechnology and information and communications technology (ICT). |
| The establishment of a coordinated strategy involving the three main support agencies on the island of Ireland — EI, Industrial Development Authority (IDA) and InterTradeIreland (ITI). | EI launched a number of programmes and initiatives on biotechnology. The IDA promotes Ireland as a location for foreign investment for overseas multinational science and pharmaceutical companies. ITI has published a number of reports and studies mapping biotechnology in Ireland. |

The five leading centres for biotechnology research in Ireland include the National Agriculture and Veterinary Biotechnology Centre at University College Dublin (animal and plant health and reproduction); the National Diagnostics Centre at the National University of Ireland, Galway (immunoassays, diagnostic technology); the National Cell and Tissue Culture Centre at Dublin City University (animal cell culture, MAB production); the National Food Biotechnology Centre at University College Cork (food processing technology, bioremediation); and the National Pharmaceutical Biotechnology Centre at Trinity College Dublin (vaccines, inflammation, neurobiology). In 1995 the Centre for Innovation in Biotechnology (CIB), an associate member of BioResearch Ireland (BRI),[2] was launched in Northern Ireland, presenting a significant opportunity to raise the profile of biotechnology research on the island as a whole (Forfás Report, 2002).

## The Nature of Tax Incentives

In modern economies governments apply various policy instruments to promote R&D in the business sector. Reflecting the link between R&D and productivity, performance, competitiveness, foreign investment and entrepreneurship, the literature has identified a high level of R&D as a crucial factor in maintaining a high and stable growth rate in the economy (Stokey, 1991).

However, both theoretical and empirical evidence indicate that R&D investment is subject to market failure, due to a combination of imperfect information in the market and financing gaps induced by asymmetric information (see, e.g. David, Hall, and Toole (2000) and Hall (1993) for surveys on both topics). However, how best to encourage R&D on an ongoing basis is proving problematic in practice.

---

[2]BRI — part of Enterprise Ireland's development strategy for the development of Irish biotech companies.

Increasingly governments are turning to fiscal incentives in response to this R&D investment market failure. The UK, France and the USA, three of the most successful biotech countries in the world, have all adopted tax as a stimulus for R&D. However, as the discussion below suggests, fiscal policies vary considerably in terms of scope and operation and hence comparison between the various tax-based incentives can be difficult.

Essentially, there are two main types of tax credits for R&D:

1. Tax relief in proportion to the volume (i.e. total amount) of R&D expenditure incurred by the company. This volume basis means that any tax relief will be calculated in proportion to the total amount of R&D expenditure spent in that year.
2. The alternative approach is known as the incremental approach. In this case, the tax relief is based on how much the company increases its R&D expenditure compared to previous years (i.e. on an incremental basis).

The section below briefly discusses the approaches adopted in three of the most successful biotech countries in the world.

### United Kingdom

According to Devereux (2003), promoting innovation and R&D is a fundamental component of the UK government's strategy for improving productivity, performance and competitiveness. The UK had relatively low levels of investment in R&D and, until recently, business spending on R&D as a percentage of GDP actually decreased compared to most other major industrialised countries. To facilitate and influence innovation and to increase R&D, the government announced a new R&D tax incentive package for large companies in the 2002 Budget (effective from 1 April 2002), building on the existing R&D tax credit for small- and medium-sized companies. The UK system adopts a volume approach, i.e. the relief is based on a company's total qualifying R&D expenditure (Devereux, 2003).

Before 2000 virtually all scientific R&D was classed as eligible expenditure. For example, there was a R&D allowance for all firms, allowing plant machinery and buildings to be immediately written-off against profits. However, because capital expenditure was normally only a small percentage of R&D cost (approximately 10%), this was not considered to be a significant factor. In contrast, wages, salaries and current expenditure have no special tax treatment.

In 2000, the government introduced special tax relief (R&D tax credits) for SMEs under the Finance Act (2000). Similar relief was introduced for large companies in the subsequent 2002 Finance Act. Under the Act, SMEs can claim an extra 50% tax relief, and larger businesses can claim 25%, subject to certain restrictions.

In terms of cost eligibility, guidelines issued by the UK Department for Trade and Industry defined eligible R&D costs as expenditure relating to 'creative or innovative work in the fields of science or technology and undertaken with a view to the extension of knowledge and breaking new ground, whether that be through resolving some uncertainty or creating a new or substantially improved product, process or service' (PLASA, 2002).

Under the current system, small- and medium-sized companies are eligible for relief at 150% of the actual expenditure. If the company has no taxable profits, they can in fact obtain cash repayment from the Inland Revenue. Expenditures that qualify for R&D tax relief including:

- Staff directly involved in carrying out R&D.
- Consumable stores used in the R&D work. However, costs of employees providing secretarial, administrative or similar services in support of others' activities do not qualify.
- Software, fuel, power and water.
- 65% of the costs of subcontracting specific elements of R&D work to a third party.
- In addition, where a company incurs capital expenditure on R&D, it is entitled to an immediate 100% tax depreciation allowance in relation to this expenditure.

An interesting feature of the UK system is that there is no requirement for the R&D to be actually carried out in the UK. The benefit of the UK approach is its simplicity and predictability, which is perceived as critical for management and investment decision-making.

*France*

In France a company becomes eligible for certain research incentives when it has incurred expenditure on any technical and scientific research operations. The French system's tax credit is calculated on an incremental basis, thus the current year's expenditure is compared to the average expenditure during the preceding 2 years (adjusted for inflation). The tax credit amounts to 50% of the incremental amount, but is capped at €61 million per year. Costs eligible for this relief include that of personnel assigned to do the research, i.e. scientists or engineers working on the design or invention that is eligible. However, it does not include support personnel, i.e. secretaries, cleaning or physical maintenance of facilities. According to the European Commission (2002), costs eligible for the purposes of calculating the tax credit included:

- Operating costs, calculated as a fixed percentage of 75 or 100% of the research personnel costs, with the particular percentage depending on the relevant qualification of the personnel involved.
- Other consumable types of expenses, including, for example any small tools, apparatus, materials and supplies.
- External research expenditure incurred if the research has been entrusted to other public or private research organisations. Experts approved by the Ministry of Industry and Research were also eligible.
- Depreciation on assets directly assigned to the conduct of the research operations (provided they are located in France).

The benefit of this approach is that, if the tax credit is higher than the tax liability, it can be carried forward in the 3 years that follow. After this, if still not used, it is refunded in cash by the tax authorities. This is considered a very beneficial cash flow feature of the French incentive.

A drawback of this particular method, compared to countries where a volume-based approach is taken, is that, even though the percentage of the credit is higher than most countries, a company will not be eligible for a tax credit if it has spent less on research in the current year compared to the prior 2 years. Commercially, a company's R&D spend might not increase on a year-to-year basis and, if this is the case, it will not benefit from this incentive. Even if R&D spend does increase, it may still not qualify for this benefit, as any 'negative' credits from prior years (amounts corresponding to a decrease in expenditure) must be offset against subsequent research tax credit amounts to ensure the preceding year's deflated basis does not affect the increase unfairly.

### United States

As in most other countries, research eligible for financial relief in the USA has a fairly wide definition and generally includes research undertaken to discover information that is technological in nature and intended to be useful in the development of a new or improved business component, irrespective of where it is undertaken. Furthermore, the research must relate to elements of a process of experimentation that leads to a new or improved function, performance, reliability or quality.

The USA allows a general deduction of research or experimental expenditures during the tax year in which such expenditure is paid or incurred, including any capital expenditure. In addition, for expenditure incurred on R&D, the USA allows a company deduction or credit against its income tax liability on an incremental research basis, i.e. for increased research activities. The calculation of the tax credits is based on a fairly complex formula and depends, among other things, on how many years a company has been involved in R&D activities. A key benefit of the American system is that, if the taxpayer is unable to use all the R&D credits in the year in which they are earned, the unused credit may be carried back to the preceding tax year or carried forward for 20 years (Sarnia-Lambton, 2005).

Research expenses that qualify for this tax credit include expenses incurred in conducting the company's own research, i.e. salaries or wages of employees engaging in or directly supervising or supporting research activities. Other costs included are:

- Consumable supplies, materials and computer use charges.
- 65% of subcontracted expenditure incurred for qualified research that is performed by a person other than an employee of the taxpayer. This percentage increases to 75% of the expenditure if the research is performed by a 'qualified research consortium' (i.e. a tax-exempt organisation whose primary function is to conduct scientific research).

## Discussion

Invariably, the case for further supporting biotechnology in Ireland is based on three related arguments. Firstly, Ireland's industrial profile is well placed to embrace biotechnology. Ireland has, for example successfully attracted a large number of major pharmaceutical manufacturing companies, with nine of the top ten pharmaceutical companies in the world having manufacturing operations in the State (US Department of State, 2005). In addition, Ireland has a major indigenous multinational biotechnology company — Elan — and some of the country's core sectors, such as food, drink and agriculture, offer huge potential for the application of biotechnology.

Secondly, the strong software industry in Ireland offers huge synergistic opportunities through combining health and life sciences with information and communications technology (ICT). In this respect, the Irish government views biotech and ICT as delivering sustainable economic growth, consistent with its policy of creating a competitive knowledge-based economy. Finally, at a wider economic level, the case for further supporting biotechnology is justified in terms of reducing the productivity and innovation gap between Europe and the USA. As highlighted in studies by, for example Fagerbert (1987), Freeman (1995), Lundvall (1992) and Bygrave, Camp, Hey, and Reynolds (1998), Europe was falling behind the USA in science and technology. The USA had a strong science base and was a world leader in the fields of medical research, agricultural bioscience and diagnostics. Thus, investment in European high-technology industries and R&D were seen as crucial to addressing this gap.

By way of further supporting the sector and encouraging R&D among Ireland's indigenous biotechnology enterprises, tax credits as a support mechanism may merit further consideration. Although a thorough analysis of the potential benefits of tax credits in an Irish context is beyond the scope of this paper, in opening this debate, the authors suggest that, from a theoretical perspective at least, tax credits may be more influential than direct grants or other forms of government support. Indeed, tax credits are often preferable, as they have the lowest level of compliance costs. According to the OECD (2002), tax credits are advantageous because they:

- Entail less interference in the marketplace, and thus allow private-sector decision-makers to retain autonomy.
- Require less paperwork and entail fewer layers of bureaucracy.
- Avoid the need to set nebulous and detailed requirements for receiving assistance.
- Have the psychological advantage of achieving a favourable industry reaction.
- Have a high degree of political feasibility.

However, notwithstanding the above, tax incentives may also be disadvantageous because they can:

- Bring about unintended windfalls by rewarding what would have been done without the tax incentive.
- Lead to undesirable inequities.
- Raid the national treasury.
- Represent an ineffective means to achieve focused results.

In assessing the effectiveness of R&D tax credits, supporters cite evidence from empirical studies that have attempted to measure their direct impact on R&D activity (Bloom, Griffith, & van Reenen, 2000). Due to data limitations, the micro-economic evidence regarding the effectiveness of tax credits is restricted. For this reason, most studies to date have examined the macro-economic impact, principally the general effect of government taxation on R&D expenditure (see e.g. Czarnitzki, Hanel, & Rosa, 2005; Hall, & van Reenen, 2000; Klette, Møen, & Griliches, 2000).

Table 2: Effectiveness studies of R&D tax credits.

| Study (date) | Estimated elasticity of R&D to tax credit | Period of study | Country |
|---|---|---|---|
| Bernstein (1986) | −0.13 | 1975–1984 | Canada |
| Mansfield (1986) | −0.35 | 1981–1983 | USA |
| Berger (1993) | −1.0 to −1.5 | 1981–1988 | USA |
| Baily and Lawrence (1992) | −0.75 | 1981–1989 | USA |
| Hall (1993) | −1.0 to −1.5 | 1981–1991 | USA |
| McCutchen (1993) | −0.28 to −0.7 | 1982–1985 | USA |
| Bloom et al. (2000) | −0.16 (short-run) to −1.1 (long-run) | 1979–1994 | G7 plus Australia |
| Hall and van Reenen (2000) | −0.34 | 1990s | USA |
| Lach (2000) | −1.5 | 1996–2000 | Israel |
| Mulkay and Mairesse (2003) | −1.6 | 1995–2001 | France |
| Czarnitzki et al. (2005) | −0.69 | 1990s | Canada |

*Source*: Adapted from Hall and van Reenen (2000).

Table 2 above lists some of the main studies conducted to date, which have examined the amount of R&D induced by the tax credits. These studies have reported the R&D price elasticities associated with tax credit and have sought to measure the additional amount of R&D performed for each dollar decrease in the cost of the R&D. In most cases, the sign of the elasticity is negative, reflecting this inverse relationship.

Table 2 reveals that from the various studies that have estimated the elasticities for R&D tax credits, all have reported negative elasticities, indicating that provision of tax credits increases levels of R&D, although the magnitude of the impact differs significantly from country to country. In some cases, the impact is marginal, while in other studies, tax credits result in a twofold increase. While Hall and van Reenen (2000) report a neutral effect; Lach (2000) and Mulkay and Mairesse (2003) documented a significant positive impact. According to the latter, the long-run increase in R&D is three or four times the budgetary cost.

In interpreting these results, critics point to a number of weaknesses. Firstly, since the majority of the studies are from the USA and Canada, direct comparison with the UK and Europe is problematic. The existing evaluations have been conducted for different countries and cannot be compared due to the use of different types of data, methodologies, scope and time periods. Moreover, as highlighted in this paper, there is little, if any, consistency in R&D fiscal policy internationally. Secondly, there are methodological difficulties in establishing the effect of fiscal incentives. There is a lack of micro-level data, which is necessary to estimate the true impact of such policies. In addition, tax credits can lead firms merely to reclassify current expenditure as R&D expenditure, rather than encouraging firms to raise their level of innovative activity, as this is not measured in many of the current studies. In most cases, studies are based on economic estimates, using highly restrictive assumptions and models. Finally, most of the studies do not estimate the potential externalities (i.e. R&D spillovers), hence it is difficult to evaluate the amount of additional direct and indirect R&D per unit of foregone public revenue due to taxation credits.

## Summary and Conclusions

The authors have examined the current state of Ireland's biotech sector and discussed the Irish government's current strategy in promoting this sector to date. They have reviewed the case for biotechnology and have explored the need to further promote this sector. Drawing on examples from three of the world's leading biotechnology countries, the nature of tax credits as a means of encouraging biotech R&D was considered. The need to further promote Ireland's biotech sector was highlighted, and some of the advantages and disadvantages associated with using tax credit incentives were discussed.

This paper has indicated that, while the Irish biotechnology sector remains at a very early stage of development, its importance in terms of economic contribution is clearly recognised (Enterprise Ireland, 2005). This importance is evidenced in part by the range of reports that have been issued on the sector since the 1980s, the more recent of which have strongly argued for continued investment in the sector (Department of Enterprise, Trade and Employment, 2004). A complex package of funding and support measures focused on developing Ireland's biotech sector has been developed over the past 10 years. However, it might be argued that there is more foreign direct investment (FDI) rather than indigenous evidence of the effectiveness of domestic support measures, as nine of the world's top ten pharmaceutical companies now have manufacturing operations in Ireland (US Department of State, 2005). In this regard, there may be a case for re-thinking support mechanisms to further encourage indigenous biotech enterprises so that the productivity and innovation gap between Europe and the USA does not continue to widen (Bygrave et al., 1998; Freeman, 1995; Lundvall, 1992).

With regard to tax credits, this paper has considered examples from three of the world's leading biotech countries, illustrating how such fiscal policies can vary considerably in terms of scope and operation. The paper has also observed that the actual efficiency of tax credits is difficult to assess, with both advantages and disadvantages (OECD, 2002) being noted. Furthermore, due to data limitations, inconsistencies in the methodological approaches adopted and differing economic contexts, the literature revealed conflicting results in terms of the long-term effectiveness of tax credits (Hall & van Reenen, 2000; Lach, 2000; Mulkay & Mairesse, 2003).

Since, as already acknowledged, a full analysis of the potential benefits or otherwise of tax credits in the Irish biotech context is beyond the scope of this paper, the authors have simply endeavoured to open the discussion surrounding their potential use as R&D stimuli, suggesting that such incentives at least merit due consideration. Given the early stage of development of biotechnology companies in Ireland (Ernst & Young, 2002; Martin, 2005), the use of taxation incentives might well represent an effective mechanism for the Irish government that they might use to stimulate further growth and development. Furthermore, in view of the huge amount of funding invested in the sector to date, tax credits may offer a more economic means of providing ongoing support to indigenous biotech enterprises by actively encouraging and rewarding R&D. Clearly, further investigation is needed.

However, as the authors have already emphasised there is still considerable academic debate regarding the actual impact of tax credits on R&D activity, despite the existence of a number of international studies (Hall & van Reenen, 2000). With regard to Ireland specifically, tax credits may well be capable of playing an effective role in further developing the biotech sector, but it is the nature and extent of that role that needs further investigation. By way of further research, some of the questions that need to be addressed include the following. Firstly, given the early stage of Ireland's biotechnology sector, how cost effective would tax credits actually be? Secondly, what are the practical, legal and compliance costs involved? Thirdly, and perhaps more importantly, given the array of systems adopted in various countries, which type of credit system could be best for Ireland? In attempting to address these questions, researchers and policy makers cannot ignore the successful track record of the UK, France and the USA however they must also be mindful of the need for further effectiveness studies with regard to the actual economic impact of tax credits.

If tax credits are to be given due consideration in the Irish context, then indigenous empirical studies which consider the actual needs of Ireland's fledging biotech enterprises, their capacity for meaningful R&D and their actual R&D capability are urgently required. Only then can a real debate begin.

# References

Baily, M. N., & Lawrence, R. Z. (1992). *Tax incentives for R&D: What do the data tell us?* Washington, DC: Study commissioned by the Council on Research and Technology, January.

Berger, P. G. (1993). Explicit and implicit tax effects of the R&D tax credit. *Journal of Accounting Research, 31*(2), 1312–2171.

Bernstein, J. I. (1986). The effect of direct and indirect tax incentives on Canadian industrial R&D expenditures. *Canadian Public Policy, 12*(3), 23–27.

Bloom, N., Griffith, R., & van Reenen, J. (2000). *Do R&D tax credits work?: Evidence from a panel of countries 1979–1997.* CEPR Discussion Paper DP2415. London: Institute for Fiscal Studies and University College, available from http://www.csmonitor.com/2003/0417/p14s03-stct.html [Accessed 4 July 2006].

Bygrave, W., Camp, S., Hey, M., & Reynolds, P. (1998). *Global entrepreneurship monitor.* Babson Park, MA: Babson College.

Chen, M. Y. (2003). Cutting-edge biotech in old world Cuba. *Christian science monitor*, available at http://www.csmonitor.com/2003/0417/p14s03-stct.html [Accessed 4 July 2006].

Czarnitzki, D., Hanel, P., & Rosa, J. M. (2005). *Evaluating the impact of R&D tax credits on innovation.* Report by the Centre Interuniversitaire de Recherché sur la Science et la Technologie.

David, P. A., Hall, II., & Toole, A. A. (2000). Is public R&D a complement or substitute for private R&D? A review of the econometric evidence. *Research Policy, 29*(4–5), 497–529.

Department of Enterprise, Trade and Employment. (2004). *Building Ireland's knowledge economy: The Irish action plan for promoting investment in R&D to 2010.* Dublin: Government Publications.

Devereux, M. (2003). *Measuring taxes on income from capital.* IFS Working Paper W03/04. London: Institute of Fiscal Studies.

Enterprise Ireland. (2003). *Technology innovation strategy, from knowledge to the marketplace.* Dublin: Government Publications.

Ernst & Young. (2002). *Beyond borders: Ernst and Young's global biotechnology report.* Available for purchase at http://www.ey.com/global/content.nsf/UK/HS_-_Library_-_Beyond_Borders [Accessed 4 July 2006].

Ernst & Young. (2004). *Resurgence: The Americas perspective — global biotechnology report.* Available for purchase at http://www.ey.com/global/Content.nsf/US/Health_Sciences_-_Library_-_Resurgence%3A_Americas_Biotechnology_Report_2004 [Accessed 4 July 2006].

EuropaBio Report. (1997). *Manipulating consent.* Amsterdam: European Summit.

European Commission. (1997). *The second European report on Science and Technology Indicators 1997.* EUR 17639 EN. Brussels: European Commission.

European Commission. (2002). *Biotechnology R&D in Europe.* Brussels: European Commission.

Fagerbert, J. (1987). A technology gap approach to why growth rates differ. *Research Policy, 16*(2–4), 87–99.

Forfás Report. (1996). *Shaping our future — A strategy for enterprise in Ireland in the 21st century.* Dublin: Government Publications.

Forfás Report. (2002). *Baseline assessment of the public research system in Ireland in the areas of biotechnology and information and communications technologies.* Dublin: Government Publications.

Forfás Report. (2005). *From research to the marketplace: Patent registration and technology transfer in Ireland.* Dublin: Government Publications.

Freeman, C. (1995). The "national system of innovation" in historical perspective. *Cambridge Journal of Economics, 19*(1), 4–24.

Hall, B. H. (1993). R&D tax policy during the 1980s: success or failure? *Tax Policy and the Economy, 7,* 1–36.

Hall, B. H., & van Reenen, J. (2000). How effective are fiscal incentives for R&D? A review of the evidence. *Research Policy, 29*(4–5), 449–469.

IntertradeIreland. (2002). *Mapping the bio-island.* Dublin: Government Publications.

Irish Council for Science, Technology and Innovation (ICSTI). (2002). *ICSTI report on biotechnology 2001.* Dublin: Government Publications.

Klette, T. J., Møen, J., & Griliches, Z. (2000). Do subsidies to commercial R&D reduce market failures? Microeconometric evaluation studies. *Research Policy, 29*(4–5), 471–495.

Lach, S. (2000). *R&D policy in Israel: An overview and reassessment.* National Bureau of Economic Research Working Paper no. 7930.

Lundvall, B. A. (Ed.). (1992). *National systems of innovation: Towards a theory of innovation and interactive learning.* London: Pinter Publishers.

Mansfield, E. (1986). The R&D tax credit and other technology policy issues. *American Economic Review, 76*(2), 190–194.

Martin, M. (2005). *Ireland's biotechnology industry is primed for growth.* Speech by the Minister for Enterprise Trade and Employment. Pennsylvania, USA: BIO 2005 Convention.

McCutchen, W. (1993). Estimating the impact of the R&D tax credit on strategic groups in the pharmaceutical industry. *Research Policy, 22*(4), 337–351.

Mulkay, B., & Mairesse, J. (2003). *The effect of the R&D tax credit in France.* Webmeets.com Events: European Economic Association, Seventeenth Annual Congress, available at: http://www.eea.esem.com/papers/eea-esem/2003/2250/RD%20Tax%20Credit%20in%20France.pdf [Accessed 10 October 2005].

OECD (2002). *Tax incentives for research and development — trends and issues*. Paris, OECD: STI Report.

PLASA (2002). *Can I get tax relief for research and development spending? The professional lighting and sound association (PLASA)*. Available at http://www.plasa.org/standards/faq/faq .asp?FAQID=1028718943 [Accessed 10 October 2005].

Prevezer, M. (1998). Clustering in Biotechnology in the USA. In: G. M. P. Swann, M. Prevezer & D. Stout (Eds), *The dynamics of industrial clustering: International comparisons in computing and biotechnology*. New York/Oxford: Oxford University Press.

Sarnia-Lambton. (2005). *Comparison of Canadian and U.S. R&D Tax Incentives*. Sarnia-Lambton Economic Partnership. Available at http://www.sarnialambton.on.ca/main/ns/103/doc/218 [Accessed 10 January 2006].

Shohet, S. (1998). Clustering and UK Biotechnology. In: G. M. P. Swann, M. Prevezer & D. Stout (Eds), *The dynamics of industrial clustering: International comparisons in computing and biotechnology*. New York/Oxford: Oxford University Press.

Stokey, N. (1991). Human capital, product quality and growth. *Quarterly Journal of Economics, 106*(2), 587–616.

Technology Foresight Ireland Report. (1999). *Health and life sciences and the Irish strategy on biotechnology*. Dublin: Government Publications.

US Department of State. (2005). *2005 Investment Climate Statement: Ireland*. US Department of State. Available at http://www.state.gov/e/eb/ifd/2005/42063.htm [Accessed 4 July 2006].

Chapter 3

# How Industrial Experience Affects Entrepreneurial Intent and Self-Efficacy in UK Engineering Undergraduates

Anthony Ward, Sarah Cooper, Frank Cave and William Lucas

## Introduction

The last three decades have witnessed a fundamental shift in the structure of many western economies, which have seen a decline in the number of large enterprises and a marked increase in the number of small- and medium-sized enterprises (SMEs) (Cooper, 1998). In 1999 there were 3.7 million enterprises in the UK, of which 24,000 were medium sized (50–249 employees) and there were only 7,000 large firms (250 or more); SMEs accounted for 38% of national turnover (Hawkins, 2001). There is growing recognition that the future of work for many will lie in SMEs, as small firms play an increasingly important role in economic development and growth, and opportunities for life-long careers in large firms decline (Cooper, 1997). The rate of technological and economic change will also lead to individuals as well as employers having a greater variety of careers; thus, the concept of the portfolio career is likely to become much more common (Henderson & Robertson, 2000). Such trends imply that the world of work, which today's graduates are entering, is very different from that which their counterparts stepped into a decade ago. Today's resource-constrained small firm represents a fast changing, dynamic environment in need of adaptable, flexible and multitasking employees, who are able to contribute and add value to the organisation from a very early stage. The challenge for education is to develop future employees who not only have the right skills but also the ability to learn from experience and adapt to a dynamic and rapidly changing environment.

Today's youngsters are being engaged in enterprise-related activities at an increasingly early age. The vision of Young Enterprise, the national education charity founded in the 1962–1963 curriculum year, is "that all young people will have the opportunity to gain

New Technology Based Firms in the New Millennium, Volume VI
Edited by A. Groen, R. Oakey, P. van der Sijde and G. Cook

personal experience of how business works, understand the role it plays in providing employment and creating prosperity, and be inspired to improve their own prospects, and the competitiveness of the UK" (http://www.young-enterprise.org.uk). The success of Young Enterprise is illustrated by the official engagement figures showing 167,303 young people taking part in Young Enterprise programmes in the year 2003/2004. Initiatives are targeting students at an increasingly early stage; for example the 'P1 to plc programme' in Scotland introduces enterprise into the primary school classroom. Government initiatives have also brought universities into the mainstream of enterprise education and skills development through the Department of Trade and Industry-funded Science Enterprise Challenge Centres which focussed on disciplines in science, engineering and technology and more recently through the Higher Education Funding Council in England (HEFCE)-funded Centres for Excellence in Teaching and Learning in the areas of enterprise and employability. Through such initiatives "the government is keen to encourage programmes of education which focus on raising awareness and understanding of the entrepreneurial sector and help individuals to identify opportunities to engage" with the SME community (Cooper, Bottomley, & Gordon, 2004).

University students derive much of their education and learning from within their principal discipline, directly from the core curriculum where design, content and delivery have key roles to play in influencing the effectiveness of education (Cooper, Bottomley, & Gordon, 2004); however, significant learning will occur outside the classroom, in other environments such as the home, social settings and in the workplace. Increased knowledge and understanding of the SME environment as a workplace should help to ease the transition from education to employment (cf. Pinquart, Juang, & Silbereisen, 2003). The greater the exposure of the entrepreneur to university students, through the provision of temporary part- or full-time employment opportunities, the easier it will be for the entrepreneur to appreciate the potential contribution which graduates can make within the SME. On the part of the university student, the greater their experience in and of the SME environment, the easier it will be for them to envision and understand the types and diversity of employment opportunities likely to be available to them within the SME environment.

Several researchers have sought to quantify graduate employment in SMEs. Connor, Court, and Jagger (1996) found that one in four graduates is employed in small enterprises, and that graduates constitute 8% of employees in enterprises with fewer than 25 employees (Yorke, 1997), while Collinson (1999) revealed that 14% of graduates are employed in enterprises with 26 or more employees.

While the number of graduates leaving the education system and seeking employment is increasing, there remains a significant skills gap between supply and demand (Holden, Jameson, & Parsons, 2002). Research in this area suggests that graduates might be strong in theoretical areas but are weak in practical skills (Middleton & Long, 1990). Other areas where there is a supply/demand mismatch, resulting from either the coverage or approach to teaching, are in project management (Collinson, 1999) and in the ability to transfer knowledge and skills between disciplines (O'Brian & Clarke, 1997). Curran and Stanworth (1987) are critical of the current education system as it makes the general assumption that a small business is simply a smaller version of a large one. Research supports the assertion that small businesses require more multitasking-orientated employees who are able to turn their hand to the wide diversity of problems which occur within the small business operating environment (Collinson, 1999).

The skills required in SMEs are also changing; for example in 1998 there were 380,000 SMEs with an online presence, a figure that had risen to 1.9 million by 2002 (Dixon, Thompson, & McAllister, 2002). Whether the SME management develop this presence from within or outside the organisation is less important than the skill to appreciate the value of a virtual presence to the sustainable competitive advantage of the organisation in its business environment. This also exemplifies the dynamic and changing nature of skills required for the effective management of SMEs.

The UK government has responded to this problem, in part, through the creation of the University for Industry (UFI) and the promotion of continuous education and upskilling of the workforce through Business Link, the Learning Skills Council and the Regional Development Agencies. Dixon, Thompson, & McAllister (2002) noted in his report for the Small Business Service "Government initiatives, consequently, have for some time been aiming to boost new graduate recruitment to SMEs". The report, however, indicates a lack of conviction on the real value which graduates can add to existing SMEs, attributed in part to the reluctance of owner-managers to employ graduates resulting from their skills mismatch. From the higher education perspective, it is important to understand the skills and competencies required within SMEs as well as the influencing factors that will tease out the entrepreneur in those with a latent tendency towards entrepreneurial behaviour.

This paper reports on findings from the Education for High Growth Innovation (EHGI) Research Programme supported by the Cambridge-MIT Initiative (CMI). The EHGI project is a study of the influence of university education on the motivation and capability of graduates to engage in entrepreneurial behaviour, where entrepreneurial behaviour includes entrepreneurship both in its narrow sense of starting new enterprises and in the broader sense of leading innovation in existing companies. The institutions participating in the programme are MIT, the Universities of Cambridge, Strathclyde, Edinburgh, Lancaster, Loughborough, and Sheffield and York (through the White Rose Consortium). This paper explores the impact of industrial experience (in both large and small organisations) on undergraduate students in engineering. Of particular interest is the impact of industrial experience on entrepreneurial self-efficacy and career intent.

## Enhancing Self-Efficacy and the Value of Experiential Learning

The level of confidence and self-belief that an individual has in his/her abilities to undertake a whole range of activities is important in their decision to engage in a wide range of behaviours (Bandura, 1997). Thus, the likelihood of a student engaging in innovation and entrepreneurial actions will be influenced in part by their levels of confidence with respect to certain abilities. Bandura's (1997) concept of self-efficacy is founded on 'people's judgement of their capabilities to organise and execute courses of action required to produce given attainments' and is central to an individual's willingness to engage in activities. For example behaviours such as innovation, opportunity identification and entrepreneurship have been linked to self-efficacy (Ardichvili, Cardozo, & Ray, 2003) and self-efficacy has been shown to influence career persistence (Mau, 2003).

Thus, an individual who perceives that they have capabilities in a certain area will be more likely to initiate new behaviours in that field and persist in those activities. However, a realistic sense of one's abilities is important if the danger of failure and its negative impact on self-efficacy is to be avoided. At the other end of the spectrum, a person who does not fully appreciate their strengths and abilities may be inclined to act within their capabilities, thus, foregoing the opportunity to enhance their self-efficacy through stretching, acting successfully a little beyond the bounds of their known abilities. Enhanced self-efficacy may be developed through self-efficacy, authentic mastery, failure, vicarious experience, success of others and the appraisal of an individual's skills (Bandura, 1997). While in some situations failure will have a negative impact, learning from the failure of others or through modest levels of personal failure does have the potential to influence authentic mastery. Work experience within the small firm environment may provide the opportunity to see how an individual is able to contribute to innovation within the firm and influence the development and growth of an enterprise and may stimulate an individual's interest in and confidence to engage in such activities in their future career.

An individual develops new understanding and frames of reference through learning from multiple sources and in multiple ways. Ausubel (1968) identifies four forms of learning which range from 'rote', where the learner is passive and there is a right answer, to 'discovery' learning, which is firmly within the experiential domain. In the lecture context the student has little scope for interaction, whereas they assume a more active learning position in the analysis of case studies, which explore the SME environment (Krebner, 2001). Observation of entrepreneurs who have first-hand experience of the innovation and venture creation process, as guest speakers (Cooper, Bottomley, & Gordon, 2004) or via video profiles (Robertson & Collins, 2003), can provide effective observational learning environments. Arguably, however, "the most powerful learning situation is achieved where experiential learning, through active involvement with an entrepreneurial company, enables students to acquire knowledge about the business environment, and develop questioning and problem-solving skills in a real-life setting" (Cooper, Bottomley, & Gordon, 2004). Work experience, thus, provides opportunities to engage in observational, vicarious and direct experiential learning to build subject mastery.

In conceptualising the value of experiential, work-based learning, Kolb's (1984) learning cycle is valuable in highlighting the four critical phases: (1) experience, which leads to (2) observation and (3) reflection and then to the development of new ideas, which results in (4) experimentation, and then further (1) experience. Train and Elkin (2001) believe strongly that the most effective learning is grounded in experience, which can play a central role in developing self-belief and self-efficacy (Ndoye, 2003), while others emphasise the importance of reflection in consolidating lessons (Barclay, 1996; Cope & Watts, 2000; Krebner, 2001; Loo & Thorpe, 2002).

With increasing numbers of students working on a full- or part-time basis over vacations and/or during the academic year, there are increased opportunities for them to accumulate a portfolio of work experiences against which to reflect. The value is likely to be most marked where work experience is in an area closely related to the student's field of study, where they have the opportunity to see the practical application of theoretical and conceptual constructs in the work place. Students have opportunities to learn explicitly or implicitly from their experience in work. Some educational programmes integrate periods of work experience, in particular undergraduate masters programmes, which seek to develop a level of professional practice alongside the programme of academic study. Even within the taught part of degree programmes the integration of professional practice modules is becoming increasingly common. Courses are also making increasingly extensive use of company-based projects. Work that is closely related to a student's area of study is likely to enhance learning and the development of skills related to the business environment or the applications of analytical techniques in practice rather than in theory. Such work is also likely to influence self-efficacy beliefs with regard to capabilities to succeed in innovation and entrepreneurship (Stajkovic & Luthans, 1998).

In the context of student learning from work experience, asking students to reflect on their experience in the context of an assessment may deepen learning (Kolb, 1984), thus, asking a student to draw upon experience will engage them in the reflective learning cycle, particularly where the experience is closely related to the area of study (Krebner, 2001). Direct experience may lead to the development of enhanced self-efficacy through subject mastery within specific task-domains (Bandura, Reese, & Adams, 1982; Gecas, 1989; Pajarcs, 1996), while the opportunity to observe others in positive behaviours associated with the business world/environment not only acts as a source of vicarious learning but also provides role models which may stimulate a sense of desirability for the working environment (Scherer, Adams, Carley, & Wiebe, 1989).

Much of the emphasis in this discussion has focused on learning within the small firm; however; many individuals will undertake work within large firms where they will gain valuable work experience. It raises a question as to whether learning will differ within and between the two environments, and if so, how it will differ. The perspective and skills may differ: research in the high technology small firm arena suggests that the small firm environment is one which arguably stimulates more spin-outs than the large firm (Cooper, 1973) as the employee gains a product/market focus rather than a narrower functional focus which is more common in the large firm context where skills within a narrower domain are well developed but reflect lower levels of integration with other parts of the business. This raises the question as to whether the student working in the small firm will develop a broader business perspective but less depth within a task-specific domain, whereas the student in the large firm may develop task-specific skills in a narrow domain, more closely associated with the large firm functional approach, at the expense of the broader business perspective. A focus on the development of task-specific versus domain skills (Gecas, 1989) linked to a broader sense of capability suggests the potential for these contrasting environments to have interesting influences and impacts upon outcomes. Thus, the student from the small firm may develop an entrepreneurial perspective associated with a greater appreciation for and understanding of the 'big picture', whereas the student from the large firm will develop task-specific, analytical skills which are closely aligned with the needs of the functionally-oriented, large firm. Large firms may be better able to accommodate the student worker and yet the small firm will increasingly need to draw upon graduate talent to drive innovation and help maintain a technological edge.

It is suggested that the longer the duration of the work situation the deeper the level of learning that will occur. Thus, prolonged periods of employment are likely to lead to the development of higher levels of self-efficacy with respect to relevant skills and abilities than shorter periods of employment, where the opportunity to learn either through direct experience or observation will be reduced. Having said that, a period of work which is closely related to the student's discipline, where the individual will be inclined to reflect and consolidate upon their learning, is likely to have more impact than a job of longer duration which is not related. Individuals learn from the experience and formulate new views and opinions and attitudes, which will influence future behaviours and actions. The level of feedback during or at the end of a period of the work experience will again enhance learning and the development of attitudes of mastery and the observation of an individual who acts as a positive role model will again provide a stimulus to enhance attitudes towards the enterprise environment (Scherer, Adams, Carley, & Wiebe, 1989).

## Method

Survey research is used to determine the nature of student industrial experiences, and how those experiences relate to undergraduate self-confidence in their skills and ability to perform tasks central to innovation, and to interest and intentions to work in innovative industry environments. The measures used in this study were first tested in spring 2004 in a pilot study of 150 UK undergraduates when significant relationships were found between aspects of industry work experience. Additional questions were added in a subsequent study conducted at five universities using both classroom distribution of paper surveys and e-mail invitations that led students to an on-line questionnaire. Because our view is that the experience of summer work is different for students who have some science and engineering knowledge to build upon, the study includes only undergraduates in science and engineering courses of study, and excludes first-year students who would be reporting on summer work before they had begun their university studies.

### Work Experience

Of the total UK science and engineering students in the original survey, after excluding first-year students, there were 800 engineering and science undergraduates. Of these second- through fourth-year students, 74.1% had one or more work experiences in the previous year, and 65.7% had taken on full-time work during the recent summer of 2004. Only 3.2% had worked full time for the entire previous academic year; 3.4% reported that they had worked full time for a term or some other part of the academic year; and 58.1% had at one time or another worked part time. To be sure that any results can be attributed to a particular work experience, students were only retained in the data set used for this study if they only had one work experience, and that experience was in the summer and at a company. The concern of this paper then becomes a subset of 158 surveyed students who are UK undergraduates in their second or a subsequent year of their studies, who worked in industry during the preceding summer 2004, and who had no other work experience in the preceding year.

The students were asked three questions in an attempt to capture the concepts of relevance, challenge and performance key to the above discussion of the causes of enhanced self-confidence in skills. For each reported work experience, the students were asked how closely it was related to their course of study and 42.6% of the science and engineering students studied here reported that it was closely related to their studies. Only 14.6% felt that the difficulty of the work had been above their level, and only 1.9% felt they had performed less than adequately. (See Table 2 for more detail.)

## Self-Confidence in Skills

Following Bandura and others as discussed above, self-confidence in skills was determined by specifying a series of tasks that each had some quality that suggested a level of difficulty, with attention to making them representative of the tasks in two domains: technical skills and business innovation skills. Eight items focused on tasks related to business skills ranging from tasks that related to opportunity, business planning, estimating value, costing a venture, sales, marketing and hiring. It should be stressed that the language was intended to refer to new business ventures, with the expectation that the responses would evoke answers from both those interested in entrepreneurship and those more interested in innovation in the established firm. The technically-oriented tasks ranged from more academic skills like defining a hypothesis and understanding articles, to practical skills like translating user requirements into technical specifications.

These were intermingled as a set of items and students were asked how confident they were that they could perform each task on a scale of 0–100%. The responses varied widely, with all tasks having a range with a low of 1, or 10% confidence, and a high of 10. The average difficulty (see Table 1) ranged from 45.4% for knowing what steps one would take to determine the financial value of a venture, to a high of 62.7% who could design something and build it so the result came close to the design specifications.

To test the assumption that these items were measuring two distinct forms of task self-efficacy, they were first put through a factor analysis. The results confirm that there are two factors corresponding to venturing, and science and technology skills. Using the items with a loading of 0.6 on one dimension and not over 0.4 or the other, two scales were created. For example, picking the right marketing approach for a new service loaded most heavily on the business innovation dimension (0.814), but translating user needs into requirements seems split across business (0.557) and technical skills (0.538), and was not used.

The selected items were then tested for reliability using a Cronbach's $\alpha$. The technical scale consisted of six items that included both more academic and applied tasks had an $\alpha$ of 0.899. The business self-efficacy scale is made up of eight items that include tasks that involve finance, sales, marketing and hiring and had an $\alpha = 0.688$.

## Entrepreneurial Intent

An additional outcome of interest is the entrepreneurial intention of the students, and how that might relate to work experience and self-efficacy. A scale originally developed in 2002 in an internal study of MIT students has been used in a variety of CMI assessments, and has proven to perform consistently in a variety of studies with Cronbach's $\alpha$ in the range of 0.78–0.81, and in one instance of 0.68. It is made up of four items that ask the individual to agree or disagree on a seven-point scale whether the 'idea of a high risk/high pay-off venture appeals' to them; whether if they see an 'opportunity to join a start-up company in the next few years', they will take it; whether they often think about ideas and ways to start a business: and whether they feel that 'at least once in my life I will take a chance and start' their own company. These items have repeatedly fallen on a single dimension in factor analysis. For the 158 students in this study, the $\alpha$ was 0.77.

Table 1: Factor analysis of self-efficacy items.

| | Average % confidence | Component | |
|---|---|---|---|
| | | 1 | 2 |
| Pick the right marketing approach for the introduction of a new kind of service. | 52.8 | **0.814** | 0.224 |
| Know the steps you would take to place a financial value on a new business venture. | 45.4 | **0.790** | 0.316 |
| Estimate accurately the costs of running a new project or venture. | 53.8 | **0.768** | 0.222 |
| Work with a supplier to get better prices that help a new venture become successful. | 51.8 | **0.764** | 0.201 |
| Convince a customer or client to try a new product for the first time. | 59.9 | **0.746** | 0.171 |
| Recognise when an idea is good enough to support a major business venture. | 55.4 | **0.740** | 0.341 |
| Hire the right employees for a new project or venture. | 56.3 | **0.682** | 0.369 |
| Write a clear and complete business plan. | 46.1 | **0.600** | 0.331 |
| Translate user needs into requirements for a user-friendly design. | 60.3 | 0.557 | 0.538 |
| Follow lab procedures and use a notebook in a way that protects ownership of a discovery. | 57.1 | 0.517 | 0.329 |
| Develop your own original hypothesis and a research plan to test it. | 53.2 | 0.141 | **0.806** |
| Design and build something new that performs very close to your design specifications. | 62.7 | 0.275 | **0.779** |
| Lead a technical team developing a new product to a successful result. | 60.5 | 0.302 | **0.769** |
| Convert a useful scientific advance into a practical application. | 55.1 | 0.185 | **0.763** |
| Grasp the concept and limits of a technology well enough to see the best ways to use it. | 58.1 | 0.290 | **0.751** |
| Understand exactly what is new and important in a ground breaking theoretical article. | 56.5 | 0.411 | 0.689 |
| Conduct tests to establish values of a property or parameter under specified conditions. | 52.9 | 0.338 | **0.632** |
| Create a process to produce low cost copies of a physical prototype for field testing. | 48.1 | 0.518 | 0.633 |

The items which load on the separate factors are shown in bold.

# Results

The plan of analysis is dictated by the central hypothesis that the relationship between the nature of the summer work experience is related to technical and business innovation self-efficacy differently in smaller and larger business units. The question is not the total size of a company, but rather the size of the local business unit that provides the social context for the student's work experience.

One might first note (see Table 2) that undergraduates working in the larger business units are more likely to find the work closely related to their course of study, reflecting the tendency of large technology-dependent companies to hire substantial numbers (depending on the prevailing economic conditions) of science and engineering undergraduates during the summer. There seems to be little difference, however, between the level of difficulty the students encountered. Perhaps most importantly, very few of the students in either size

Table 2: Characteristics of work experience by company size.

| | Number of employees in company | | |
|---|---|---|---|
| | **1–50** | **51 or more** | **Total** |
| Relationship to course of study | | | |
| Not related | 44.0% | 26.9% | 32.3% |
| Somewhat related | 26.0% | 25.0% | 25.3% |
| Closely related | 30.0% | 48.1% | 42.4% |
| Total | 100.0% | 100.0% | 100.0% |
| $\tau_B = 0.181$, significant at 0.015 | ($N = 50$) | ($N = 108$) | ($N = 158$) |
| | | | |
| How difficult was the work? | | | |
| Well below my level | 24.0% | 22.2% | 22.8% |
| Somewhat below my level | 20.0% | 27.8% | 25.3% |
| About right for my level | 36.0% | 37.0% | 36.7% |
| Above my level | 18.0% | 13.0% | 14.6% |
| Well above my level | 2.0% | 0.0% | 0.6% |
| Total | 100.0% | 100.0% | 100.0% |
| $\tau_B = -0.052$, not significant | ($N = 50$) | ($N = 108$) | ($N = 158$) |
| | | | |
| How well did students perform? | | | |
| Poor job | 0.0% | 0.9% | 0.6% |
| Less than adequate job | 2.0% | 0.9% | 1.3% |
| Adequate job | 12.0% | 14.8% | 13.9% |
| Good job | 58.0% | 54.6% | 55.7% |
| Excellent job | 28.0% | 28.7% | 28.5% |
| Total | 100.0% | 100.0% | 100.0% |
| $\tau_B = -0.011$, not significant | ($N = 50$) | ($N = 108$) | ($N = 158$) |

*Note*: $\tau_B$, Kendall tau-b statistical test.

company felt they were challenged well beyond their capabilities (2.0 and 0.0%), and roughly the same proportions (24.0 and 22.2%) thought the work was well beneath their capabilities. Self-rated performance was also similar, for when one sums those who felt that they had done poorly, or a less than adequate job, only 2.0 and 1.8% believed they had performed below par. Over a fourth (28.0 and 28.7) felt they had done an excellent job.

One interim conclusion is that other differences between the two sizes of business units found elsewhere in this study cannot be attributed to differences in the difficulty of work or student views of their performance. One does need to note that work was in general found more closely related to student course of study in the large companies.

### Work Experience, Self-Efficacy and Intent

One final adjustment is now made to the sample before calculating the strength of the relationships among the variables being studied. Because the underlying theory of self-efficacy predicts that self-confidence in skills increases with the over-coming of difficulty, those who felt they had performed less than adequately (only three students) are dropped from the calculations. Work difficulty for all students studied here was met with at least adequate performance.

A close relationship between the nature of the work and the technical course of study being pursued by these science and engineering students appears to be quite important when it is correlated with other factors. Consistent with the tabular data in Table 2, for both small ($r = 0.617$) and larger ($r = 0.461$) business units, the closer the nature of the summer work was to the student's current science and engineering course of study, the more difficult they found the work. This result suggests that these science and engineering students employed in work more closely related to their course of study were pressed to perform technical work that challenged their skills somewhat more. One then sees a classic condition that should predict higher self-efficacy with technical skills: stretched skills and satisfactory performance.

### Technical Self-Efficacy

As seen in Table 3, this closeness to the students studies to their work is strongly related to technical self-efficacy at both smaller and larger locations. In small business units, both closeness ($r = 0.457, p < 0.001$) and difficulty ($r = 0.355, p < 0.001$) predict enhanced self-confidence in one's ability to perform technical tasks. In business units with over 50 local employees, relative similarity of student area of studies is also related to technical self-efficacy ($r = 0.416, p < 0.001$). Here difficulty is not significantly related (0.126) with confidence and technical skills and difficulty are related somewhat less strongly ($r = 0.461, p < 0.001$). The closer the relationship between the company work and the student's course of study, the higher the technical self-efficacy ($r = 0.434, p < 0.001$).

### Venturing Self-Efficacy

In contrast, the results for the relationship between summer experiences in smaller and larger business units and student confidence in business skills is strikingly different. In small facilities, there is a strong tie between a closer relationship between the summer

Table 3: Relationship among industry work experience, self-efficacy and career attitudes.

| | Small Companies (50 employees or less) | | | Larger Companies (51 employees and more) | | |
|---|---|---|---|---|---|---|
| | Closeness to studies | Difficulty of work | How well performed | Closeness to studies | Difficulty of work | How well performed |
| Difficulty of work | 0.618*** | | | 0.474*** | | |
| (N) | (49) | | | (106) | | |
| How well performed | −0.302* | −0.276 | | 0.052 | −0.107 | |
| (N) | (49) | (49) | | (106) | (106) | |
| Technical self-efficacy | 0.457*** | 0.355* | −0.185 | 0.416*** | 0.126 | 0.104 |
| (N) | (46) | (46) | (46) | (93) | (93) | (93) |
| Venture self-efficacy | 0.409*** | 0.211 | −0.017 | 0.106 | −0.076 | 0.129 |
| (N) | (46) | (46) | (46) | (91) | (91) | (91) |
| Entrepreneurial intent | 0.495*** | 0.462*** | −0.215 | 0.001 | −0.125 | 0.165 |
| (N) | (47) | (47) | (47) | (94) | (94) | (94) |

Level of statistical significance, $p^* < 0.05$; $p^{**} < 0.01$; $p^{***} < 0.001$.

work and the course of study and confidence in business skills needed for new ventures ($r = 0.409, p < 0.001$). Here also, difficulty encountered and met with satisfactory or better performance is associated with venture self-efficacy. No meaningful relationship appears between these two factors in larger locations.

### Entrepreneurial Intent

The business skills used here are those focusing on tasks necessary for the development of new ventures, with the statements silent on whether the venture is inside the established firm or part of starting a new company. One might expect self-confidence in performing these tasks to relate at least to some degree with entrepreneurial intention. The results show that the closer the work was to the student area of studies, the higher the entrepreneurial intent ($r = 0.495, p < 0.001$). Similarly, the greater the difficulty that was met, the higher the intent ($r = 0.462, p < 0.001$) in small business units. In contrast, these factors did not relate to entrepreneurial intent for students employed in summer work in larger facilities ($r = 0.001$ and $r = -0.125$, neither of them significant). There is no evidence that intention to pursue entrepreneurship is related to summer work in larger locations.

Looking across both forms of self-efficacy and the entrepreneurial intent variable, in small business units at all levels it is the strength of the relationship with 'closeness to studies' and 'difficulty of work' in each case that is stronger than self-rated performance.

It is the difficulty that is met, not the level of performance that is key for these students, a prediction consistent with the general theory of self-efficacy.

## Discussion

A note of caution should be offered before the implications of the results are considered. For survey data of this kind, one must be very cautious about making any assumptions about the direction of causality. While it would appear that small company experience produces higher self-confidence in business skills, the fact of a stronger correlation between technically-relevant small company experience and venture confidence could also be argued that those confident in their venture skills and interested in entrepreneurship seek out summer employment in smaller firms. Of course one can also assert that both forces are at play and that the prior attitudes and small company experience are reciprocally reinforcing: self-confident undergraduates with business interest seek employment in small firms, but once they are working in those environments, their confidence and attitudes are strengthened further. This ambiguity strongly suggests the need for a test–retest study of the impact of work in industry to clarify the interpretation that should be offered, but whatever view is taken, it remains that there is a relationship of some importance here.

Another consideration is that it seems likely that the longer the duration of the work situation the deeper the level of learning that will occur. Thus, prolonged periods of employment are likely to lead to the development of higher levels of self-efficacy with respect to relevant skills and abilities than shorter periods of employment, where the opportunity to learn either through direct experience or observation will be reduced. Having said that, a period of work which is closely related to the student's discipline, where the individual will be inclined to reflect and consolidate upon their learning, is likely to have more impact than a job of longer duration which is not related. Individuals learn from the experience and formulate new views and opinions and attitudes, which will influence future behaviours and actions. The level of feedback during or at the end of a period of the work experience will again enhance learning and the development of attitudes of mastery, while the observation of an individual who acts as a positive role model will again provide a stimulus to enhance attitudes towards the enterprise environment (Scherer, Adams, Carley, & Wiebe, 1989). Regrettably, the number of students in this study with longer work experiences in the academic year was not sufficient to explore this possibility.

## Conclusions

The implications of this work are that self-confidence in skills and entrepreneurial intention for undergraduates, including technically-educated students, relate to the types of work they experience, closeness of the work to the content of their science and engineering courses of study. The relationship found between self-confidence and skills and the difficulty of the work supports a central premise that self-confidence is increased by performing adequately or well in the face of difficulty, providing a lens for the assessment of summer work programmes. Further, it appears that the work environment of the smaller business units is associated with higher levels of confidence in business venturing skills, but not in larger organisations, suggesting that the nature of undergraduate work experiences may have varied and defining impacts on both their technical and business venture self-confidence, which one knows in turn predicts their future career paths.

# References

Ardichvili, A., Cardozo, R., & Ray, S. (2003). A theory of entrepreneurial opportunity identification and development. *Journal of Business Venturing, 18,* 105–123.

Ausubel, D. P. (1968). *Educational psychology: A cognitive view.* Winston: Holt.

Bandura, A. (1997). *Self-efficacy: The exercise of control.* New York: Freeman.

Bandura, A., Reese, L., & Adams, N. (1982). Microanalysis of action and fear arousal as a function of differential levels of perceived self-efficacy. *Journal of Personality and Social Psychology, 43,* 5–21.

Barclay, J. (1996). Learning from experience with learning logs. *Journal of Management Development, 15*(6), 28–43.

Collinson, E. (1999). The entrepreneurial curriculum — Equipping graduates for a career in the SME sector. *Research in marketing and entrepreneurship, 1*(1), 18–23.

Connor, H. P. R., Court, G., & Jagger, N. (1996). *University challenge: Student choices in the 21st century.* Brighton, University of Sussex: The Institute for Employment Studies.

Cooper, A. C. (1973). Technical entrepreneurship: What do we know? *R&D Management, 3*(2), 59–64.

Cooper, S. Y. (1997). *You take the high road and I'll take the low road: contrasting routes to entrepreneurship in high technology small firms.* Paper presented at IntEnt97, the 7th International Entrepreneurship Conference, Monterey, California, 25–27 June.

Cooper, S. Y. (1998). Entrepreneurship and the location of high technology small firms; implications for regional development. In: R. P. Oakey & W. During (Eds), *New technology-based firms in the 1990s* (pp. 247–267). London: Paul Chapman.

Cooper, S., Bottomley, C., & Gordon, J. (2004). Stepping out of the classroom and up the ladder of learning: an experiential learning approach to entrepreneurship education. *Industry and Higher Education,* 11–22.

Cope, J., & Watts, G. (2000). Learning by doing: An exploration of experience, critical incidents and reflection in entrepreneurial learning. *International Journal of Entrepreneurial Behaviour and Research, 6*(3), 104–124.

Curran, J., & Stanworth, J. (1987). The small firm — A neglected area of management. In: A. G. Cowling, M. J. K. Stanworth, R. D. Bennett, J. Curran & P. Lyons (Eds), *Behavioural sciences for managers.* London: Edward Arnold.

Dixon, T., Thompson, B., & McAllister, P. (2002). *The value of ICT for SMEs in the UK: A critical review of literature.* Report for Small Business Service Research Programme, The College of Estate Management, Reading.

Gecas, V. (1989). The social psychology of self-efficacy. *Annual Review of Sociology, 15,* 291–316.

Hawkins, L. (2001). *Fundamental productivity improvement tools and techniques for SME* (Vol. 33). Loughborough: Pera Knowledge.

Henderson, R., & Robertson, M. (2000). Who wants to be an entrepreneur? Young adult attitudes to entrepreneurship as a career. *Career Development International, 5*(6), 279–287.

Holden, R., Jameson, S., & Parsons, D. J. (2002). Making a difference — The contribution of graduates to small business success. *Small Business Service Report,* URN 03/868.

Kolb, D. A. (1984). *Experiential learning.* Englewood Cliffs, NJ: Prentice Press.

Krebner, C. (2001). Learning experientially through case studies? A conceptual analysis. *Teaching in Higher Education, 6*(2), 217–228.

Loo, R., & Thorpe, K. (2002). Using reflective learning journal to improve individual and team performance. *Team Performance Management: An International Journal, 8*(5/6), 134–139.

Mau, W. C. (2003). Factors that influence persistence in science and engineering career aspirations. *The Career Development Quarterly, 51*(3), 234–243.

Middleton, B., & Long, G. (1990). Marketing skills: Critical issues in marketing education and training. *Journal of Marketing Management, 5*(3), 325–342.

Ndoye, A. (2003). Experiential learning, self-beliefs and adult performance in Senegal. *International Journal of Lifelong Education, 22*(4), 353–366.

O'Brian, E. M., & Clarke, D. (1997). Graduates — Their entrepreneurial role in the small firm. *Marketing Education Review, 7*(3), 29–37.

Pajares, F. (1996). Self-efficacy beliefs and mathematical problem-solving of gifted students *Contemporary Educational Psychology, 21,* 325–344.

Pinquart, M., Juang, L. P., & Silbereisen, R. K. (2003). Self-efficacy and successful school-to-work transition: a longitudinal study. *Journal of Vocational Behavior, 62,* 329–346.

Robertson, M., & Collins A. (2003). The video role model as an enterprise teaching aid. *Education and Training, 45*(6), 331–340.

Scherer, R. F., Adams, J. S., Carely, S. S., & Wiebe, F. A. (1989). Role model performance effects on development of entrepreneurial career preference. *Entrepreneurship, Theory and Practice, 13*(3), 53–71.

Stajkovic, A. D., & Luthans, F. (1998). Self-efficacy and work-related performance: a meta-analysis. *Psychological Bulletin, 124*(2), 240–261.

Train, B., & Elkin, J. (2001). Branching out: A model for experiential learning in professional practice. *Journal of Librarianship and Information Science, 33*(2), 68–74.

Yorke, M. (1997). The skills of a graduate — A small enterprise perspective. *Capability, 31*(1), 27–32.

Chapter 4

# Now You See Them — Now You Don't: Paradoxes in Enterprise Development Strategy: The Case of the Disappearing Academic Start-Ups

Deirdre Hunt

A series of research experiences provoked this paper. In the spring of 2003, I was asked to act as an assessor, for the Island of Ireland Seed Corn competition.[1] There I came across academic start-ups (ASUs), directly linked to Irish public sector science and technology (S&T) funding. Several of the competition teams consisted of young scientists, who presented business plans. Probing demonstrated that the teams appeared to possess little understanding of the business concepts these contained. Another consistent finding was that any market reference made was focused on multinational corporation (MNC) subsidiaries already located in the country. Intrigued by this, together with a colleague, we then began looking at ASUs, university-based funded S&T research centres and the activities of the newly created Science Foundation of Ireland (SFI).[2]

We were interested to learn about routes to commercialisation. The more we looked the more puzzled we became. Here were post doctoral researchers, independently funded by the SFI, based in third-level institutions, launching ASUs with apparently little or no business input, gaining seed corn funding and focused on MNC buyers. This model did not appear to fit the literature as we knew it on enterprise economies and ASUs as product champion creators.

What we thought we knew fell into three propositions; that to grow, developed economies need to move from a corporate to an enterprise economy (Audretsch & Thurik, 2001), that high-technology small- and medium-sized enterprises (HTSMEs) were central

---

[1] Inter-Trade Ireland Seed Corn Competition 2002. This competition was an offshoot of one of the first all island agencies and aimed to develop an all island approach to high-tech start-ups.

[2] SFI is charged with developing and funding S&T reference in all third-level institution in the Republic of Ireland.

**New Technology Based Firms in the New Millennium, Volume VI**
**Edited by A. Groen, R. Oakey, P. van der Sijde and G. Cook**

to the creation of enterprise economies[3] (Caree & Thurik, 2003) and, that the University sector provided the most likely source for the most potentially dynamic of HTSME, the ASU.[4] We knew that the evidence for ASUs incorporation was widespread and growing. Numerous studies beginning in the 1990s had highlighted a significant increase in the number of new ventures developed from universities and other public funded research institutes across a number of different countries.[5] At government level across Europe we were aware that a range of enabling legislation and grant and fiscal packages had been created to support ASUs. These included removing regulatory constraints, to allow full-time academics to create companies, setting up enterprise funding competitions to allow focusing of investment capital and mentoring support for promising ASUs and the creation of incubators and specialised venture capital funds to support start-ups (Audretsch, Thurik, Verheul, & Wennekers, 2002).

Nor were we, exempt from many of the common underlying assumptions contained in a literature that sees ASUs as a universal, necessary and transformational good, providing the initial essential building blocks for the development of product champions (Chiesa & Picaluga, 2000; Mustar, 2001). The ASU model we ourselves subscribed to, therefore contained assumptions around economic good, sectoral position, independent growth and persistence over time.

Above all, it assumed the existence of a creative entrepreneur at the core of all ASUs, acting as prime creator and driver. In this model, government and public sector policy support, as promulgated via a range of policy initiatives, proceeded on the assumption that economic change is driven by the individual academic/entrepreneur (Franklin, Wright, & Lockett, 2001). This was not the model that emerged in our analysis of ASU development in Ireland. We were aware of the economic success of the Irish economy in the preceding two decades, having lived through the experience. On all counts the Irish model over the last 20 years has been transformational, with GDP growth rates of ca. 6% per year and increasing exports and private consumption running at more than 7.5% per annum between 1990 and 1997. This put Ireland among the top ten of the world's fastest growing economies during the 1990s.[6] We were also aware, however, that in terms of the SME economic development models, Ireland had for some time been seen as theoretically challenging.

In the SME development literature, economic growth, wealth creation and the ability to respond to change are strongly linked to SME growth. In this respect the Republic of Ireland presents strong contrasts. To quote Clarysse and Duchene (2000) "economic growth

---

[3] See Caree and Thurik (2003) for an overview of studies investigating the link between entrepreneurship and economic growth.

[4] In Europe increases in the number of spin-offs from academic institutions has been noted in the United Kingdom, Germany, France, Italy, Portugal, Spain, Finland, Belgium and Sweden. Fostering Entrepreneurship (OECD Paris, 1998).

[5] The annual study of the American Association of University Technology Managers (ATUMS) of 200 universities, hospital/university start-ups per academic institution shows a sustained growth starting at a level of 0.6 between 1980 and 1993, 1.5 in 1994 and 2.1 at the end of 1990s. In Canada five firms were founded by academics in the 1970s, 20–30 during the 1980s, 60–70 during the 1990s.

[6] Government economic stats of success.

at the end of the eighties, beginning of the nineties was primarily the result of a climate that attracted foreign investments. These foreign enterprises were traditionally multinationals, especially from the US, which established large production plants in Ireland. In Ireland, multinational subsidiaries were seen as the engines of transformation and economic growth, to be attracted to the State through the development of clear fiscal, locational and training packages aimed in particular at the US. Inward investment policy was overwhelmingly focused on the large, for which read MNC. By the late 1990s 2/3 of public sector support consisted of classical technology policy instruments. Capital subsidies and R&D subsidies for middle-sized and large companies made up in total 68% of the whole financing budget in 1997. Only 6% of companies availing of such supports in 1997 were R&D active SMEs".

These figures in turn reflect the reality that SMEs were not the main drivers of the Irish economy in the late 1990s and that economic growth was strongly tied to large foreign-owned subsidiaries. For public sector figures, both civil servants and politicians, their experience of success, did not stem from the SME sector, let alone the ASUs. Given this, it is not surprising that the subsequent development of an enterprise economy in Ireland was not centred on the promotion of HTSMES/ASUs.

A further characteristic of the Irish economy, as noted by Clarysse and Duchene (2000), was that only a very small proportion of State aid was focused on innovation: "only 11% of all financing goes to newer forms of innovation support. About a half, 5%, is provided in the shape of investment capital. A similar amount is spent on management development and support. 1% finally goes to 'in-company training' of personnel".

This picture was to persist into the 2000s. "Investment in R&D remained low at 0.88% of GDP. Ireland's business expenditure on R&D stood at only 73% of the EU average and 57% of the OECD average".[7] Furthermore, what R&D that existed, was focused on a small number of companies. As the Foresight Report (2000) noted "Fifty companies account for half of all our exports and only 13 of the 50 do any R&D. Firms which have no strategic roots i.e. R&D function, in a location are particularly susceptible to international mobility" (ICSTI, 2000).

So if there was no public sector or government experience of SMEs as drivers of economic growth at the end of 1990s, there was also little or no understanding of innovation in any setting. Overall, the economic model that had produced exceptional growth had created a highly reactive, passive economy. As the report, "Ahead of the Curve" Report[8] commented "until now, Ireland's principal enterprise strengths have been in the operational aspects of manufacturing and services, rather than in market and product development. This is particularly true of the foreign owned sector which accounts for most of our exports and which, for the most part, produces goods that were designed elsewhere, to satisfy market requirements that were specific elsewhere, and sold by other people to customers with whom the Irish operation has little contact and over whom it has little influence". The final characteristic of the 1990s model, which in itself followed earlier

---

[7] The Irish Action plan for promoting Investment in R&D to 2010 Report to the Interdepartmental Committee on Science Technology Innovation, July 2004.
[8] The Enterprise Strategy Group (ESG) report 'Ahead of the Curve, Ireland's Place in the Global Economy' 2004.

iterations, was the degree to which changes were brought about in the public sector, as opposed to entrepreneurially driven.

Central government via the relevant departments has long played a dominant role in Irish economic development (see IBEC, 1952), thinking and policy implementation. In the move to the enterprise economy, the Department of Trade, Enterprise and Employment continued to call the tune. It was against this background that this paper attempts to address the questions, how did Ireland move towards an enterprise/knowledge based economy? What policy followed? And what was the role of ASUs, if any, in such moves?

Aware of faltering economic statistics in the late 1990s, as well as the wider European debates that led to the Lisbon[9] framework, it was the senior civil servants in the Department of Enterprise, Trade and Employment who instigated a series of reports and business consultations on emerging technological trends and the opportunities facing Ireland.[10] These reports concluded that the primary need was to "recreate the economy as a knowledge economy and that this demanded a major shift away from the existing dependency model". But at no point did the reports grasp the nettle and address what issues arise from the need to develop a more independent enterprise stance. For instance, there was no discussion in any of the papers as to the role of HTSMEs or ASUs, and on from this, no discussion as to what strategies would need to be developed around this agenda. What happens in the reports early on is the separation of the concept of the Knowledge economy from the concepts of the Enterprise economy; the latter concept is largely parked. What was clear was that the reviews believed that if the Irish economy was to continue to grow, it would need to radically shift its existing economic base towards high knowledge content commercial activities. This shift in its turn would demand significant strategy changes.

In revolutionary-founded societies such as Ireland, radical change and the recreation of the society is legitimised, by foundation myths. Such societies carry within themselves, both the understanding of the benefits of radical social transformation and possess mechanisms that support further such radical change. The presentation of revolution as a legitimate and achievable occurrence, in this instance, in relationship to the creation of the Knowledge society in Ireland occurs repeatedly in government and departmental pronouncements from 2000 onwards. To cite one such example, in the Irish government action plan for R&D investment "Building Ireland's Knowledge Economy" (Forfas, 2004) the executive summary uses the phrase "the vision herein would represent a transformation of Irish society" and there are many more such phrases.

Post civil war societies are equally aware of the need for consensus and of strong rule from the centre. Reflecting this, Irish public sector policy has been characterised by the development of strong consensual political mechanisms, in particular the creation of strategy platforms, consisting of leading players from industry to the unwaged, meeting

---

[9] The Lisbon strategy, March 2000.

[10] (These reports for the first time presented an estimate of business and public sector R&D investment as a separate item) ERA 3% initiative — Review of Industrial Potential to Increase R&D to 2010 PA Consulting Group report to Forfas Public Procurement for Increased Innovation Jacobs and Associated report to Forfas (Forfas, 2003).

with government to agree achievable economic goals over agreed time spans.[11] These consensual approaches were also apparent in the attempt to buy into the strategies needed to roll out the Knowledge society in Ireland. But in the end, as in the 1990s economic growth model, it was the public sector, which acted as the initiating agent for economic change, not the entrepreneur.

These three cultural aspects centred around change, consensus and central public sector control are apparent in all the policy initiatives surrounding the creation of a knowledge-based economy in Ireland. As Clarysse and Duchene (2000) noted. "The current institutions which are responsible for the implementation of innovation policy show in Ireland a high degree of integration in comparison with other countries like, for instance, Flanders or France. This integration is the result of a complex evolution since 1970 from a classic science and technology policy towards a broad centralised innovation policy, servicing a wide and strong diversified range of products". Though their review appears too overly positive in retrospect, it does highlight the strongly integrated and public sector driven nature of economic policy in the Republic.

Change began with the creation of a new entity tasked with defining and responding to emerging trends. As early as 1994, the government established its own technology foresight think tank, FORFAS. Its remit was to advise on policy issues relating to science, technology and innovation. Located in the Department of Enterprise, Trade and Employment, the new think tank reported directly to the Minister.[12] This was a radical move that broke the existing dominance of the pre-existing Industrial Development Agency (IDA) and positioned the department as the initiator of subsequent change. In 1994 following advice from Forfas, the department established the Irish Council for Science, Technology and Innovation (ICSTI, 1997). The President of the new University of Limerick, Dr. Walsh, known for his mould-breaking opinions and out-spokenness, was appointed as council chair. He used his position to push for the development of new thinking in the area of S&T support, "there is a strong argument that Government should use the fruits of the current performance of the economy to reinvest in areas which will ensure that its development potential remains strong, when the current period of exceptional growth comes to an end — as inevitably it must. Science, Technology and Innovation (STI) are one such area".[13] The statement is curious in several ways; in its assumption that the growth being experienced was not sustainable, was a one-off, yet at the same time, it contains the assumption that further future public sector investment would have to occur to ensure positive future economic development. Here we see several of the themes that were to reappear and animate subsequent development strategy in Ireland, firstly that future economic growth was tied to investment in S&T and secondly, the inevitability of slow growth if nothing was done. There is no mention of HTSMES, ASUs or research uptake capacity let alone the entrepreneur in this vision; all the emphasis

---

[11] See agreement for equity and fairness (Stationary Office, 2004).

[12] Forfas statue dated 1994.

[13] Press statement issued by Forfas (9 November 1998) to accompany Walsh's appointment as Chair of Irish Council Science and Technology and prior to launch of the report Mechanisms for Prioritisation of Public Expenditure on Science and Technology 1998.

is on the role of the government. Dr. Walsh added "the Government constantly faces multiple demands for investment in a wide range of areas and in the circumstances there is a need to demonstrate clearly the sectors, technologies and structural areas where STI investment will pay high social and economic dividends. There is also a need to achieve greater clarity in relation to the priorities". Here one sees the third dominant theme that was to reappear in subsequent government S&T policy development, the need to prioritise funding and identify and fund sectors that showed economic promise. How such prioritisation was to be identified was not addressed but the assumption was that this would come from government not from the private sector.[14]

The initial need as seen by Forfas was to create amid the unprecedented affluence, an understanding of the potential of these emerging technologies. As the civil servant heading up Forfas, John Travers commented.[15] "It would be ordinarily naive to believe that more of the same in policy terms will lead to the same commensurate results in economic and social terms over the next 20 years as it has done over the past 20 years".

The next task was to achieve buy-in from both industry and the third-level sector to support further radical change. Here at least, there was a hint that the government or at least the civil service realised that they might not be able to implement the proposed changes themselves and that other agents, in this case the universities, might have a more central role to play in the economic development. The vision put forward for accomplishing continuing progress was three pronged and not primarily private sector driven. As Travers went on to say "You may well infer my belief that the traded goods and services sector provides the dynamic for social and economic transformation in Ireland. Such an inference is correct but it is not the full story". He went on to argue that the craft that drives that progress forward is not single-engined. Rather it is a four-engined craft in which the three other engines of technology, the socio-cultural environment and public sector capacity are also of major importance. Having listed the efforts made by the government to accelerate technological change, Travers went on to provide the justification for the government decision to prioritise public sector funding for only certain niche areas in the emerging sciences by referring to the 1997 study of the US team Coates, Mahaffie, and Hines (2005). This had identified five areas of new technological developments that would shape the evolution of social and economic development around the world over the next 25 years. These were: Information Technology, Genetics Technology, Materials Technology, Energy Technology and Brain Technology. Only the first two were to become the sectors to receive funding under the new initiatives.

It would be my contention that it was Coates et al. (2005) who's work provided the vision, as well as the selection criteria, which was to inform the radical new policy initiatives in the areas of S&T from 1999 to the present. Public and business buy-in to the

---

[14] It was Forfas' good fortune that the minister appointed to the department responsible for science and technology policy funding was the head of the coalition minority party, needed a differentiating agenda and was particularly committed and able. She gave Forfas the political support at cabinet that was needed to drive through Walsh's agenda.
[15] In a speech entitled 'The Forfas Enterprise 2010 Strategy Report: The Underlying Requirements of Rapid Socio-Technical Progress' summarised the longer publication, which had served as basis for the negotiations between the social partners and government (Enterprise 2010: A New Strategy for the Promotion of Enterprise in Ireland in the 21st Century).

creation for the first time of an integrated and funded public sector S&T policy was addressed by initiating a series of consultation processes. Consultations with defined out-come agendas set by Forfas would perhaps be a better description of the process. Drawing on models derived from elsewhere (New Zealand, etc.) in 2000 Forfas, under the chair-manship of Brian Sweeney the deputy chairman of ICSTI, (the CEO of Siemens Ireland), launched a Foresight exercise aimed at informing, accessing know how and gaining support from Irish industry. To quote from the subsequent report[16] (ICSTI, 1999) that was drafted by Forfas, the Technology Foresight exercise concluded, "the Irish economy should be repositioned, to be widely recognised internationally as a knowledge-based economy. To do this, the knowledge framework can be visualised as a pyramid where industry, the higher education sector, Government and society are the four interlinked faces forming a partnership at all levels. However, a gap at the apex of the pyramid has been identified; the need for a world-class research capability of sufficient scale in a number of strategic areas within our universities and colleges, research institutes and industry. The gap identified will only be filled if the partnership of Government, industry, the higher education sector and society can combine to deliver the knowledge framework, which will in the future realise":

- Research and Technology Development (RTD) intensive and advanced technology-based and overseas companies, using high-level expertise.
- A vibrant, cohesive, durable and internationally recognised competitive RTD base involving industry, universities and colleges and research institutes, which provides an attractive career structure for researchers to work in Ireland.
- An environment conducive to innovation.
- Investment in the physical and human infrastructure.
- Citizens well informed on scientific issues in the context of an innovation culture.[17]

Efforts should now be concentrated, the report concluded, on developing the apex of the pyramid where the gap in world-class research activity has been identified. Continuing the current incremental approach to STI investment will not achieve, it argued, world-class research capability on the scale required. "To accelerate this development, Ireland needs to take a quantum leap in investment by anticipating the areas of strategic opportunity and investing ahead of demand" (ICSTI, 1999). Here again we see the affirmation of the need for a revolutionary commitment to change.

---

[16] The sector areas covered by the Technology Foresight Ireland exercise were: Chemicals and Pharmaceuticals; Information and Communication Technologies; Materials and Manufacturing Processes; Health and Life Sciences; Natural Resources (Agri-food, Marine, Forestry); energy; Transport and Logistics; Construction and Infrastructure; few of these areas were dominated by SMEs and even fewer SMEs participated. Each sector was asked to nominate participants. In all 180 people were directly involved as members of the eight panels, 60% from industry; 430 more were involved in consultative workshops; 115 organisations made submissions; 3000 hits were recorded on the web site participants made use of 'scenarios', or pictures of where future markets and technological opportunities might lie. These had been created by Forfas prior to the meetings and formed the basis of the subsequent report.

[17] Unless one can assume that ASUs are included as part of the indigenous there appears to be no thinking about transfer to start-up mechanisms in this model that appears to assume that existing typologies of industry will remain.

This development report stands in sharp contrast to its predecessors. Prior to this report, economic development discussion had been dominated by macro economic and business perspectives (Culliton, 1992). The report prioritised scientific and emerging technology perspectives themselves derived from earlier American-based research. These perspectives were to drive the subsequent national development, determine funded changes in the third-level institutions in the S&T areas and dominate policy making, with all Government departments and agencies being required to utilise the Foresight findings in future planning and funding exercises.

Of great significance to the subsequent roll out, and lost in the hype surrounding it's launch, the report chose to marginalise the sectoral reports and the subsequent SFI executive involved no business leaders. This had major implications. As it developed there was no mechanism for industry feed back and no voice to raise issues as to relevance and implementation and for whom.

During the 1990s, the Irish development agency, Enterprise Ireland, had focused on the creation of a niche development policy, targeting pharmaceutical and ICT manufacturing plants as well as niche players in the medical support areas. This had worked well. In this new phase, a niche approach was again taken. The Foresight report argued that there existed "a need for a substantial increase in national capability in niche areas of information and communication technologies and biotechnology. These are widely identified in the Panel reports as representing, for the future, the engines of growth in the global economy". The degree to which the panel reports did indeed prioritise these sectors, appears to me to be questionable.

The nod in the direction of indigenous firms in the Foresight appears to me to assume at best, continual dependency and at the worst is flannel. It fails to grapple with the transformational needs of existing indigenous sectors such as food and construction, and offers no discussion of reach, readiness or research uptake capacity. As importantly, it presents no agenda for the creation of high tech SMEs and fails to discuss the implications of commercialisation and therefore ASUs for the university sector. At best indigenous companies it appears to assume could hope to learn from incoming MNC.

There was no conception in the report of the ability of existing firms to initiate and respond to new developments in the area of S&T. The development of a world-class S&T base was, it is interesting to note, at best seen as a marketing tool "in the context of the development of existing indigenous firms, the attraction of a new phase of multinational companies to Ireland and the creation of new technology-based enterprises, the Irish economy must develop a credible base of knowledge and activities in these key technologies. Competing in these technologies means competing with the best in the world. A world-class research capability in selected niches of these two enabling technologies is an essential foundation for future growth" (ICSTI, 1999).

The dependency theme, which runs throughout the report, is continued in the discussion of sources for new skills particularly in the area of S&T. Despite the evidence of massive transformational capability in the education and training sectors since the 1970s, many supported by EU funded programmes, this was downplayed and the report commits to a strategy of external sourcing of new knowledge including people. As the report states, "these key technologies (Bio and ICT) require new skills, and in particular the development of a cadre of world-class S&T personnel. Attracting international expertise into Ireland in key technology areas (it argued) will be necessary" (ICSTI, 1999).

There are five aspects of these reviews that require comment; the shift in intellectual perspective, the lack of esteem for native innovation, the shift in geographical focus away from Europe to the USA, the centralised planning framework and the ensuing enhancement of dependency, all coupled with revolutionary imagery. Up to this point, economic change reports in Ireland had been dominated by macro/business paradigms (Culliton, 1992). With these three exercises, this approach was relegated to the past and one sees the emergence of scientism as the guiding development perspective. More in line with past thinking was the emphasis on importing best practice from abroad, to be incorporated into home-based development strategies as part of a continuing neglect of native talent.

This is particularly curious post-1973, as Irish scientists had been especially active from their first launch in the EU S&T framework programmes and had become signifi-cant players in the network activities embedded in these programmes developing robust research links across Europe. The EU framework programmes have had as one of their major goals the creation of European-based, world-class, leading edge science as a basis for the development of global product champions. The Framework programmes, seeing such product champions developing from ASUs, sustained a strong focus on SMEs, which became more pronounced as the programmes developed. But Europe figured little in the Foresight deliberations; rather the emphasis was on American S&T as prefiguring the future. The SFI vision was itself later highly critical about the inadequacies of the European programmes and their development over time.[18] The reason for this remains obscure unless one speculates that far from developing on the European model, a S&T strategy from which ASUs might emerge, the Irish strategy was more intent on sustaining an existing MNC attraction and retention policy with particular emphasis on the attraction and retention of American MNC.

The effects of the Foresight report were transformational; the Minister, and thus the government, did not only accept the report but also received massive funding to implement its main conclusions. In 2000, the Government established a Technology Foresight Fund of IR£647 million over 5 years which was to be administered by Forfas. At this point, Forfas was acting as both policy initiator and as executive and administrative director. The new fund had several goals, these being "well focused and significant investment in upgrading the technological infrastructure of the economy (which) will enable Ireland to develop world-class research capability in strategic technologies for the future competi-tiveness of indigenous industry, facilitating the undertaking of R&D in this country by

---

[18] Prior to the allocation for RTDI under the NDP 2000–2006 researchers in Ireland were dependent largely on the EU Framework programmes, the Welcome Trust and other European initiatives for the larger grants necessary to support research activities. Such grants typically won sporadically do not foster the emergence of a sustained critical mass of research competence. This lack of core research funding left researchers in Ireland with inadequate opportunities to establish for a globally competitive research programmes *ibid* Vision 2003–2008 people ideas and Partnerships for a globally competitive Irish research system SFI 2003.

multinational companies and attract more high-tech companies to Ireland in the future".[19] There is only one passing reference to the new industries in the whole report. The role of universities and ASUs are not mentioned.

It forms a central plank of this paper to suggest that the formulation of the Foresight exercise and in particular the report that followed lead to the exclusion of any discussion of the need for, desirability of, or possibility of ASUs being seen as a part of this publicly funded development agenda. I would argue that in terms of implementation that the report at best represents a generalised magic view of the ability of S&T to create new sector industry.[20] So on from the establishment of a budget, the Fund, and plethora of reports and consultation[21] what emerged was a highly focused substantially funded S&T product champion with no implementation strategy. At this point the champion was called the National Strategic Research Foundation. This was quickly to change.

It is interesting to examine the public statements that accompanied the creation of this change agent and the gradual shifts in both title and emphasis that occurred subsequently. The creation of the Foundation was announced by An Tánaiste, Ms. Mary Harney, in March 2000. "Its role is to direct and fund world-class Irish research programmes in the fields underpinning two main areas, Biotechnology and ICT. Its budget is £500 (€635) million in states funding available to support this work under provisions in the National Development Plan 2000–2006".[22] There is no mention in her speech about existing Irish Industry. The head of Forfas John Travers saw the new champion as justifying its existence because

---

[19] The rapid nature of the Foresight exercise followed by the immediate implementation of certain aspects of the report suggests that the Foresight exercise was more of a window dressing exercising than sustained consultation.

[20] How the Foresight fund was to be actualised required further input and by-in by local players. In March 2002, the Minister for Enterprise, Innovation and Employment charged ICSTI to develop an organisational framework for an overarching national policy for research and technological development. It also requested the Council to convene a high-level Commission (chaired by the Chairman of ICSTI, the same Brian Sweeney who had chaired the Foresight exercise) to assist it in bringing forward these proposals. The high-level Commission of national and international experts) reported to the Council in November of that year. In December, the Chairman presented the Council Report to the Tánaiste and Minister for Enterprise, Trade and Employment, Ms. Mary Harney, T. D. The terms of reference tell much about assumptions around change. The functions of the Commission were: To examine the current situation in Ireland relating to the structures, policies and implementation mechanisms for Research and Technological Development that underpin innovation for economic and social development; to analyse the structures, policies and implementation mechanisms for Research and Technological Development in other relevant countries with a view to the identification of the most appropriate 'best practice' for Ireland; to consult widely in Ireland, with industry, government departments, government agencies, the higher education sector, research and technological institutes and other relevant organisations. With a view to underpinning innovation for economic and social development in Ireland, to make recommendations for improving the structures and mechanisms for the formulation and implementation of national policy for Research and Technological Development including co-ordination, synergy and linkages across the sectors and activities in the National Development Plan and securing appropriate funding balance.

[21] Between 1999 and 2003, Forfas alone issued four pertinent reports (Forfas 2003) (These reports for the first time presented an estimate of business and public sector R&D investment as a separate item) ERA 3% initiative — Review of Industry Potential to Increase R&D to 2010 PA Consulting Group report to Forfas. Forfas 2003. In addition the higher education authority issues its own report The Programme for Research in Third-Level Institutions (PRTU) Transforming the Irish Research Landscape Dublin HEA 2003.

[22] Press announcement of creation SFI M Harney Minister of State Department Trade Enterprise and Innovation, Noel Tracey Junior, Minister State Science and Technology, March 2003.

"the investment involved, the knowledge generated and the skills that will become available from this initiative will provide an essential building block in the new strategy for the promotion of industry and enterprise in Ireland set out in the Forfás Report Enterprise 2010 — launched by the Tánaiste in recent weeks. It will greatly strengthen the capacity of both Enterprise Ireland and IDA Ireland to promote a new generation of high technology, high-productivity industrial projects deeply rooted in the knowledge base of Ireland's economy. Forfás will work closely with the Implementation Group and the Department of Enterprise, Trade and Employment to establish the new National Strategic Research Foundation as quickly as possible".[23] In this one speech one can see the beginnings of shift that was to accelerate away from sectoral involvement, in sharp contrast to the preceding comprehensive inclusive consultation process. IDA (2000) Ireland the main NGO involved in attracting and retaining MNCs to Ireland also welcomed the initiative, though their interpretation had a marketing emphasis "the IDA welcomes today's announcement by the Tánaiste and Minister for Enterprise, Trade and Employment that leading researchers world wide are being invited to submit proposals under the £500 million Technology Foresight Fund to be administered by SFI. A fundamental element of IDA Ireland's policy is to achieve greater embeddedness in the wide range of advanced technology companies now operating from this economy. A critical part of this involves IDA Ireland in securing the highest level of research alongside these production and services operations. This major R&D initiative is specifically targeted at leading researchers in Ireland and overseas and is the key to the creation within the country of the highest level of skills in the technologies of the future. The establishment of SFI will substantially enhance Ireland's profile and status in the world of R&D and strongly support IDA Ireland's strategy to secure more high-level R&D within the overseas companies in Ireland" (IDA, 2000).

This statement encapsulates what was to become the IDA strategy in the early 2000s, the marketing of Ireland Inc. as an R&D location. This would have two aims, the relocation of R&D activities from overseas MNC to Ireland and the creation in Ireland of R&D activities in subsidiaries already operational in Ireland. Having derived the future vision from the US, it is scarcely surprising that the overall organisational cultural perspectives, norms and appointments were also North American. True to the view that Ireland lacked talent in this sphere, the three science administrators appointed were all US citizens, Dr. Alistair Glass and Dr. John Atkins as Directors of ICT, and Biology and Biotechnology, with Dr Bill Harris as director. From this point onward it followed that the development models and selection processes that were rolled out were all based on US models related to the appointee's experience.

Initially the location of SFI as part of a government department was distinctive. That was rapidly changed. In 2002 SFI was established by a parliamentary act as an independent institution in its own right[24] and moved outside the control of Forfas who had created it.

Harris as director reinforced the US influence at both executive and operational levels. Analysis of the make up of the executive Board of SFI shows the dominance of US input

---

[23] Forfas John Travers, 8th March 2000.
[24] SFI Parliamentary Act.

with 5 out of the 12 members based in the US, plus a further UK member, with the balance made up of public sector Irish representatives. The gaps were also significant. The committee contained no representatives from the business or from the small business sector either at an organisational or individual level. Furthermore, of the Irish participants, two were retired public sector appointees, one a civil servant carrying a brief for the Minister and one a private consultant. As a whole, the Irish participants with the exception of Travers, the retired head of Forfas, who now reappears as a private consultant, lacked either the relevant experience or positional power to act as a counterweight to the US appointees.[25]

Harris had been appointed as an authority on university-based S&T commercialisation. SFI systems around funding selection and a diffusion mimicked this US experience.[26] In a tactic borrowed from the US, Harris was to introduce a funding system that provided funding not just for science programmes but also for individual scientists to conduct research — what Harris, speaking in (2004) calls creating a "market system for science based on creativity". He explains "the genius of the US system was that it allowed young people to have grants and to be free from superiors or senior leaders". Introduction of this system radically altered the power base of existing scientific departments in the State through the introduction of individually accessed research budgets aimed at young research post docs. According to Harris "this broke the existing culture thing in which senior professors made the decisions". Bringing this into the Irish system, where until this point professorial departmental heads held all funding and promotion power, was to say the least a radical break from the existing situation. It served, I would argue, to significantly reduce the dominance of Irish science by existing senior scientists in the third-level departments, who excluded from the SFI executive board, had already been marginalised in terms of S&T strategy and funding. The funding of only two areas of science further created a two-tiered scientific community.

But curiously, at the end of the all the scenarios and meetings and with funding committed, the specific targets of the SFI remained unclear. There were a plethora of general statements that glissaded from R&D to commercialisation, but beyond feel good statements about the general economic good, there was no discussion of actual implementation practicalities.[27] A good example of this can be seen in relationship to R&D transfer capacity.

How the massive public funding into R&D in the areas of Biotechnology and ICT was to translate into enhancement of existing industry, both indigenous and MNC, as had been defined in the foundation statement, remained unclear.[28] If there was no

---

[25] See p. 19 for list of SFI Board members in SFI Vision Document 2004–2008 SFI 2003.

[26] Before taking up his position with the STI in September 2001, Harris a New Yorker of Irish extraction, held a number of senior positions in US universities and research institutes. One of these was director for mathematical and physciences at the National Science Foundation (NSF) in Washington, DC, where he was responsible for national research policy and a budget of US$700m.

[27] We can move quickly from basic research into commercialisation as opportunities arose Professor Eoin O. Reilly, SFI on line presentation 2003.

[28] The underlying assumptive framework was that S&T policy is acultural and could be transposed without modification.

discussion of commercialisation mechanisms within the third-level sector, there was clearly no discussion of ASUs as forming part of that transfer process. Nor were there discussions of R&D take up capacity. Yet this issue was critical, particularly to the indigenous sector.

Examination of R&D capacity in early 2000 shows an almost non-existent level of such activities in indigenous companies. Overall R&D in Ireland had increased threefold during the 1990s. BERD had reached 917 m in 2001 but for the most part this was generated by foreign affiliates. As the Irish action plan on R&D 2003 states "one third of foreign affiliates in Ireland (300 enterprises) are active in R&D. These firms account for two thirds of all business R&D. Of these, 50% spend less than 500 K annually; 119 spend more than 5 m annually and account for two-thirds of all R&D performed by Irish foreign affiliates in Ireland. Of the indigenous enterprises, only one third have some expenditure on R&D with 85% spending less than 500 K per annum. Only 26 of the indigenous enterprises have expenditure of more than 2 m annually. Overall, if the EU at 1.9 GDP lagged behind the US 2.7 GDP and Japan 3.1 GDP in R&D Ireland was well below the EU average of 1.42".[29]

The questions that arise from this are never addressed in the SFI literature. There appears to have been no public SFI discussion as to the need to create differing transfer and support mechanisms for the differing recipients of the R&D funding and it follows, no mention of the particular potentialities and vulnerabilities of ASUs. The reasons for these lacunae are not fully understood.

But the absence of defined operational goals did not lead to paralysis. In one of his initial moves, Harris announced plans to develop a network of science, engineering and technology centres in Ireland (CSETS), which, he announced, would be co-funded by the SFI (80%) and industry (20%). Each centre was to focus on a particular scientific area such as semiconductors, food science or software. "They will be in a whole variety of areas that will have a strategic value to Ireland", announced Harris, who saw the centres as the engines for gaining critical mass in a range of scientific areas. He described this as "the Irish system trying to learn the lessons from the US in order to get a leg up the learning curve" and nonetheless "as a bold experiment for Ireland to try to do". So in three years Ireland shifted its Science R&D strategy away from European models and networks that emphasised networking collaboration and the potentiality of ASUs to an individually based market system for science funding, to quote Harris "a market system for science based creativity based on the individual and not programmes".[30] Presented as supporting

---

[29] (These reports for the first time presented an estimate of business and public sector R&D investment as a separate time) ERA 3% initiative — Review of Industry potential to increase R&D to 2010 PA Consulting Group report to Forfas Public Procurement for Increased Innovation Jacobs and Associated report to Forfas (Forfas, 2003).

[30] Evidence of the pervasiveness of US models can be seen in minutes of working party "Funding of Overheads for Research". A subgroup chaired by C. O'Carroll, was established to investigate the current situation as regards overheads in Ireland and the practice in other countries. The subgroup presented its report on 18th January 2002. It was agreed that this subgroup will continue its work focusing on the system used in the US and report back in March. C.H.I.U. Review January 2002 for C.H.I.U. on 28th January 2002 in University College Dublin.

the future, the model was not only based on prior practice without the jurisdiction but also based on US based future trend speculation almost ten years out of date at the point at which it was implemented.[31]

By 2003, SFI had gained control of Irish public sector science research funding. By expanding its remit to take over the basic science budget from Enterprise Ireland, SFIs gained a monopoly on Science R&D funding. With this move, SFI took over all basic science research and programmes for individual researchers as well as funding for the creation of the themed science centres (CSETS) that it had already announced. It was envisaged that approximately 30% of the overall funding of SFI would be expended on such centres. Temporary secondments of Irish academic scientists to SFI were to occur as well as the establishment of internships for post-graduate S&T students.

In the first 2 years the SFI notched up some notable achievements. It funded the work of almost 80 scientists in Irish universities and committed almost €160 m in research support to CSETS. The individually successful candidates were chosen by a process of international peer review using what was claimed to be an objective system of appraisal, pioneered by the NSF in the US. This approach further emphasised the groundbreaking nature of what was happening, it drew a line under previous experience and further increased dependency on externally derived models of selection.

The third goal that of attracting external talent, was also met. SFI attracted a dozen top researchers from around the globe to base their research in Ireland. SFI defined its target as scientific groups belonging to the American academy of sciences, the Royal Academy, and other such world class authorities in one of the two defined fields of strategic interest, ICT and Biotechnology. Those appointed included non-nationals such as Chris Dainty from Imperial College London, who moved to the National University of Ireland, Galway, and Dr. David Parnas, who moved to the University of Limerick from Canada, as well as Irish-born scientists such as Professor John Boland, returned from North Carolina to Trinity College Dublin.[32] All of these plus their teams were funded by the SFI's competitive research grant system. In addition, via the Science University funding initiative, the teams were presented with custom-built labs. These moves could be seen to increase feelings of marginalisation and inferiority among existing science teams. In particular, scientists in the fields of mathematics, physics and chemistry experienced the development of a two tiered science research system in which some were more equal than others.

By 2003 the SFI appeared to be in pole position. It had moved outside the control of Forfas, marginalised business interests, had taken control of all S&T R&D funding and upturned existing academic power structures. Harris was even involved in overseas trade missions with the IDA.

In 2003, 3 years after its foundation, SFI published its first vision statement. The title itself excluded all reference to economic signals, a further shift away from the initial foundation visions of the Foresight exercise. As one reads the 2003 speeches and

---

[31] It was not until 2003 that SFI set out an initial vision statement "People ideas and Partnerships for a globally competitive research system". Why this emerged so late is a puzzle.

[32] Announcement of teams appointed see SFI achievements 2003 Press release SFI.

interviews with Harris, the justification for the creation of SFI narrows down to two areas, the creation of a science spine and the linking of this to support knowledge intensive MNCs. And all of this with little or no reference to other economic NGOs such as the IDA or Enterprise Ireland. Overall, the emerging reality could well be summarised as scientists talking to scientists being seen as the main drivers of Irish-based S&T research in whatever setting.[33] The publicly stated goal, the "development of a strong science spine", also appeared curiously detached from the body politic by 2003, and from any external economic planning regime and again there are no specifics. It contains no discussion of transfer strategies or spin-offs, nor does it mention the need for accompanying support strategies.

The main vertebrae in the construction of the spine were the establishment of CSETS. By 2003, five such centres had been established all but two headed up by and staffed by overseas teams.[34] But analysis of wider press statements suggests that in parallel to the creation of a science spine, another agenda was emerging. Implicit in the foundation statements of SFI was the idea of upgrading S&T capacity across all sectors by 2003, this had been refocused. The focus now was solely on MNCs, either existing on the ground or as potential relocators. This is clearly seen in SFI press releases, which from 2002 onwards, highlight SFI achievements in terms of joint collaborative research activities involving existing MNC subsidiaries. In the 2003 report SFI cites CETS funded related work linking HP, Server, Surgeon/Aventis, Protagen, Allegro Technologies, Alimentary Health, Procter and Gamble and Teagasc, Ireland's agriculture and food development authority. Earlier there had been announcements of a €69 million investment programme agreed between Lucent Technologies, Bell Labs, IDA Ireland and SFI and funding of €10 million for a new SFI Centre for Science, Engineering and Technology (CSET) at TCD in partnership with UCC and UCD. To be known as The Centre for Research on Adaptive Nanostructures and Nanodevices (CRANN) this had as its main industry partner Intel Ireland Ltd. In strong contrast to the initial vision of Forfas, R&D policy as it unfolded appeared focused on relationships with Irish-based MNC subsidiaries. One effect of this

---

[33] The only wider support that Harris acknowledges is the need to ensure an increased supply of new recruits to the areas of science that he is promoting. This he came to argue requires a shift in cultural bedrock in Ireland away from Joyce and towards hitherto unknown Irish scientific luminaries. Commentators highlight this mainstreaming of science as a key theme pursued by Harris in his role as director general of Science Foundation choose one of these two quotes. Between 2001 and 2004 Harris presented the same theme repeatedly "throughout history, Irish researchers have made significant contributions through seminal achievements in science and engineering. Those of us who appreciate the value of research have a responsibility to share the awareness so that one day every Irish child will recognise the contributions of Sir Francis Beaufort, Lord Kelvin and Sir William Rowan Hamilton. They are hardly household names now but they were back in 19th century Ireland when their respective achievements in the fields of meteorology, physics and mathematics catapulted them to fame, and others in much the same way the great Irish writers and artists are recognised as an integral and illustrious part of Ireland's traditions". The fact that these names do not appear to be mainstream themselves appears to have missed Harris. It is also a curious speech as it for the first item raises the cultural components surrounding S&T take up without at the same time examining how his perspective reflects on the acultural transposition models behind SFI.
[34] How this affected career paths of existing Irish scientific teams and how such centres related to the governance structures of the universities remains unclear.

was to strengthen enterprise dependency rather than reduce it. This contrasted sharply with the aspiration contained in the Foresight exercise.

The strategy chosen by Harris, as it exists, pushes the time lag between R&D and independent commercialisation via ASUs ever further into the future. I will quote at length to give the flavour of what was emerging. This quotation could be replicated many times over.

> The West of Ireland has built up a strong medical industry base and it is now attracting a matching research base with backing from Science Foundation Ireland. This should help in the process of anchoring manufacturing activity in the area while providing an impetus to key research.

The Regenerative Medicine Institute has just opened its doors (in January) with the assistance of a grant of fifteen million Euros from Science Foundation Ireland. The grant is for a 5-year period. Its Director, Professor Tim O'Brien, spent 14 years at the prestigious Mayo Clinic in the US and the Assistant Director, Frank Barry, returned to Ireland, in recent weeks, having also spent fourteen years in the US.

The Centre's main areas of focus are gene therapy and adult stem cell research. "Our goal is to combine the two, with the object of regenerating new tissue so that we can avoid having to replace organs", according to Tim O'Brien.

Initially, the Institute will be concentrating on the regeneration of heart muscle damaged as the result of heart attacks and on the regeneration of cartilage in joints affected by osteoarthritis.

The Institute has linked up with two companies; Medtronic a US-based medical devices company and Chondrogene, a Canadian biotech firm, which is exploring the association between cartilage problems and defective genes.

Medtronic already has a large manufacturing plant in Galway and while substantial engineering research is carried out there, the idea is that activity in the biotechnology area could be added through the association with the new centre. "Frank has a strong background in product development. He is an industry-academic whereas I am a clinician-scientist", said O'Brien.

The whole area of regenerative medicine is developing fast, though Tim O'Brien is wary when it comes to promises of imminent, dramatic, medical breakthroughs. "Things have started to move quite quickly in the field. There have been some early, small, preliminary studies. A lot of basic research is required. We are looking at a ten to fifteen year time horizon before current innovations become accepted, standard practice. I don't want to give patients false hope". Not surprisingly, he regards Science Foundation Ireland as a "hugely significant undertaking. A number of researchers have returned, or have arrived from other countries. There will be a time lag before this translates into real delivery. I am not concerned that the Government will lose interest, though one can never know what might transpire over a ten to fifteen year time frame".

He also has warm words for the Higher Education Authority and its Programme for Research in Third Level Institutions. "Over a billion Euros has been invested in buildings and equipment under the Programme. It has laid the foundations over the past six years or so in the area of capital infrastructure. We are working in a PRTL funded building". Now, the human infrastructure is being assembled so that the capital infrastructure can be put to best use. The Institute has just started recruiting. "There will be around thirty to thirty-five people working for us in Galway. NUIG have committed themselves to hiring eight additional permanent members of faculty in areas of relevance to regenerative medicine such as polymer chemistry and biomedical engineering research with a US company", Osiris. SFI's goal is to see products developed.

In the Irish context this is what I now think that I have been looking at, a two headed policy initiative involving the reinvention of locally positioned overseas MNC subsidiaries drawing on and working with the SFI to move their activities up the knowledge chain and the creation/provision and marketing of world class research labs as a tool to attract research-based MNC activities to Ireland. If I am right, then my colleague and I in 2003 were asking the wrong question to the wrong people. Or perhaps we were asking the right questions based on our own optimism about the possibility of small states' ability to develop independent product champions spun out from locally created ASUs. But at the moment the new S&T strategy in Ireland is not focused on this goal. SFI, I would argue, as it stands, is not about the creation and development of ASUs as the building blocks for product champions but the upgrading and extension of an existing attraction and retention strategy for MNC subsidiaries.[35]

Despite neglect in a system focused on other goals, ASUs have appeared but not as the creatures of potential growth that exist in the literature. The possibilities for the post-doc teams I encountered seem at best to be the development of incorporated vehicles for recently patented discoveries. The defined goal then becomes not long term growth but short-term existence before sale of either the patent and/or the patent plus team. The ASU in Ireland therefore exists at most, I would argue, to provide a platform for financial gain for both the post-docs and their institutions before being absorbed into the R&D activities of locally based MNCs.

So finally, it became possible to understand the logic behind the apparent arrogant neglect of enterprise learning as it appeared in the post-doc teams I encountered. If such teams and their companies are but short term phenomenon, vehicles for enhancing the viability of existing MNC in Ireland by moving them up the value chain or for strengthening the ability of Ireland Inc to attract more knowledge intensive MNC[36] subsides, ASU teams do not need to acquire enterprise skill.

Once one knows that, then everyone is happy — the development authorities, the MNC and even the enterprise researchers who can now stop looking for new product champions and have discovered a new ASU model, the Mayfly ASU.

---

[35] This is well illustrated by assessment of the value of the participation of Harris and glass in trade missions to the States. Harris and Glass regularly visit the US with colleagues from the other agencies to persuade US companies to invest in research and development in Ireland. Both Harris and Glass are so well acquainted with the US scientific community that one can only imagine the enormous credibility that their presence must lend any trade mission.

[36] The belief that indigenous companies were innately inferior to incoming large business, which alone was capable of innovation, is a long held belief in Ireland.

## References

Audretsch, D. B., & Thurik, A. R. (2001). What is new about the new economy: Sources of growth in the managed and entrepreneurial economies. *Industrial and Corporate Change, 10*(1), 25–48.

Audretsch, D. B., Thurik, A. R., Verheul, I., & Wennekers, S. (2002). *Entrepreneurship: Determinants and policy in a European — US comparison*. Boston: Kluwer Academic Publishers.

Caree, M. A., & Thurik, A. R. (2003). The impact of entrepreneurship on economic growth. In: Z. J. Acs & D. B. Audetsch (Eds), *Handbook of entrepreneurship research* (pp. 437–471). Boston: Kluwer Academic Publishers.

Chiesa, V., & Piccaluga, A. (2000). Exploitation and diffusion of public research: The general framework and the case of academic spinoff companies. *R&D Management, 30*, 329–340.

Clarysse, B., & Duchene, V. (2000). *Innovation policy in Ireland from FDI to competitive indigenous companies*. IWT Observatium.

Coates, J. F., Mahiffie, J. B., & Hines, A. (2005). *Scenarios of US and global society reshaped by science and technology*. New York: Midpoint Trade Books Inc.

Culliton, F. A. (1992). *A Time for change: Industrial policy for the 1990s*. Dublin: The Stationery Office.

Forfas. (2003). BERD 2001, Dublin Forfas State Expenditure on Science and Technology, 2001. Vol. 2: *The research and development element of the science and technology budget*. Dublin.

Forfas. (2004). Building Irelands knowledge economy: The Irish action plan for promoting investment in R&D to 2010. *Report to the Interdepartmental Committee on Science, Technology and Innovation*.

Franklin, S. J., Wright, M., & Lockett, A. (2001). Academic and surrogate entrepreneurs in University spin out companies. *Journal of Technology Transfer, 26*, 127–141.

IBEC. (1952). *Technical services corporation an appraisal of Ireland's industrial potential*. Stacey May Report. New York.

Mustar, P. (2001). Spinoffs from public research trends and outlooks STI. *Science Technology and Industry, 26*, 165–172.

Chapter 5

# Supporting Academic Enterprise: A Case Study of an Entrepreneurship Programme

Magnus Klofsten

## Introduction

There is growing worldwide interest in entrepreneurship and new business development. This has become particularly widespread in Sweden during the last 10 years. We see more and more professorships in entrepreneurship at our universities, new credit-bearing courses on entrepreneurship are emerging and different training programmes for those who want to start new firms are being developed. Among established firms, we are also seeing much activity, for example Swedish firms such as Ericsson, Telia and Saab have in recent years instituted activities to stimulate fresh ideas through intrapreneurship and take advantage of the energy and ideas of individuals involved in the day-to-day operation of their businesses. The trend is clear — the number of initiatives aimed at stimulating the entrepreneurial behaviour of individuals is growing.

However, a big challenge today is how to develop efficient activities designed to promote such entrepreneurial behaviour and minimise the barriers involved. One way to achieve this could be to arrange entrepreneurship training programmes. The aim of this paper is, through a case study, to find out how efficient entrepreneurship training can be, and what the actual success factors are.

The data analysed below comes from the entrepreneurship and new business programme (ENP), for training individuals to start new technology-based or knowledge-intensive businesses. The model was developed at the Centre for Innovation and Entrepreneurship (CIE) at Linköping University, with the help of a network of local enterprises. This programme has now spread in many districts of Sweden and has, in recent years, also been internationalised. Since the beginning of 1994, over 50 programmes have been carried out, which have resulted in more than 500 new businesses as well as a dozen or more new business areas within established organisations. Today, these firms and organisations employ over 2000 people.

New Technology Based Firms in the New Millennium, Volume VI
Edited by A. Groen, R. Oakey, P. van der Sijde and G. Cook

In the introduction of this paper, entrepreneurs and entrepreneurship are thoroughly defined, together with the implications that these definitions have for the training of individuals. Thereafter, the programme itself is presented, followed by feedback from participants and what characterises a successful entrepreneurship programme. The paper concludes with a summary where a number of conclusions are drawn.

## On Entrepreneurs and Entrepreneurship

Different aspects of entrepreneurs and entrepreneurship have been frequently discussed over the years. The literature in this field supports the argument that there is no universal definition of entrepreneur or entrepreneurship. The attempts that have been made to differentiate, for example entrepreneurs from small business leaders and business executives in general have not been able to make a clear distinction between the two (Brockhaus, 1982). In an oft-quoted article, Gartner (1988) directly states that the question "Who is an entrepreneur?" is simply the wrong question. Moreover, he advocates a behavioural outlook where it is the creation of new organisations that is the central issue in entrepreneurship. With this premise, what differentiates entrepreneurs from non-entrepreneurs would be that entrepreneurs create organisations, while non-entrepreneurs do not. Entrepreneurship is, accordingly, in its most basic form, the creation of new organisations.

What is attractive about Gartner's definition is the broad scope for interpretation that it allows. The creation of organisations can, logically, mean the start of, for example new firms as well as the initiation of a project or a business area in an established organisation. By focusing on activities rather than personal characteristics, the complicated discussion on whether one is born to be an entrepreneur or not is avoided. With the view that entrepreneurship instead is dependent on different activities and courses of action by individuals, conditions are created under which entrepreneurship can flourish in society. The big challenge is then to develop activities that promote this effect, such as training programmes in entrepreneurship.

## Stimulating Entrepreneurship

Garavan and O'Cinneide (1994) have conducted an interesting discussion on the differences in activities that devise for training or stimulating entrepreneurs. They are of the opinion that each training activity should have a unique purpose and pedagogical design. In this paper it is suggested that three basic activities should be undertaken at universities and colleges:

* The creation of an entrepreneurial culture throughout the university. From this point of view, entrepreneurship should permeate all activities at the university: its research, the curriculum and external activities.
* The teaching of specific courses where entrepreneurship is the main subject of study.
* Specific training programmes for individuals who intend to start their own businesses.

It would be most productive to allow all of these instruments to work together in parallel and enrich each other. For example an entrepreneurial university culture and a selection of courses in entrepreneurship would most likely to influence attitudes positively towards starting businesses and, hopefully, their quality. Training entrepreneurs can provide a valuable contribution to courses in the form of case studies and lectures given by entrepreneurs who have participated in previous programmes and activities.

## Barriers and Opportunities in the Training of Entrepreneurs

There exist many obstacles and opportunities, both on the supply side (the one who trains) and the demand side (the one to be trained), in entrepreneurship training. On the supply side, many studies have found a resistance to entrepreneurship education at our universities. This can be explained by the fact that, traditionally, universities often lack sufficient expertise of their own (both theoretical and practical) to be able to design anything other than the three instruments described above (Curran & Stanworth, 1989; Klofsten & Mikaelsson, 1996). In the last decade, however, entrepreneurship as an academic discipline in its own right has developed, and there is a growing acceptance of conducting research, education and training in entrepreneurship in our university systems. There is, however, more to do if entrepreneurship is to become a natural part of a university's activities, for example to integrate entrepreneurship training into the academic structure in general for the purpose of creating an entrepreneurial university (Etzkowitz & Klofsten, 2005; Klofsten & Spaeth, 2004).

To deliver effective training in different situations is a difficult task. This usually has to do with a discrepancy between what entrepreneurial content is desired and what actually reaches the one to be trained (Gibb, 1990). Why this is so is associated with many factors, such as the participant's time and economic ability to participate, ignorance about what types of training there are on the market and a generally negative attitude to training by potential providers and its contribution to a business's development. Other studies show, that entrepreneurs, depending on their experiences and degree of success, have differing attitudes to training. Klofsten and Mikaelsson (1996) found that the further entrepreneurs had progressed in their development, and the more successful it was, the more positive was their attitude towards training. These entrepreneurs also spent more time looking for different alternative training programmes on the market, which at last resulted in finding the right one. Similar results in studies on general management training were found in Davidsson (1989) and Ylinenpää (1997). They maintained that business leaders who are ready to invest in the firm's long-term development — where immediate results are unlikely — have a more entrepreneurial attitude compared with those who prefer to set aside resources for more short-term, quantifiable results.

Critical voices have also been raised against the training of firms in general. Westhead and Storey (1996) maintained that the link between management training and work performance in firms that provide training is weak. In this study, however, no distinction between general management training and training in entrepreneurship was made. The authors are, however, in favour of focused programmes that take into account heterogeneity in the needs of different types of firms represented by, for example size and stage of development.

# The ENP Case Study

The ENP programme began in the spring 1994, and it was the last part of a more comprehensive programme of support activities for technical- and knowledge-intensive university-derived firms. At that time, Linköping University, together with the Foundation for Business Development (SMIL), had already amassed a great deal of experience in the support of established firms. A high level of respect had also been built-up for their ability to encourage university spin-offs. Since the late 1970s, a large number of firms had spun off, mainly in connection with the technical university (e.g. IFS, Intentia and Sectra). It was thought important, however, to build support for 'younger' entrepreneurs who would accelerate the frequency of new start-ups; raise the quality of the companies, and help to create a highly entrepreneurial university. This goal was not, at that time, clearly expressed in the university's formal policy. The university's administration neither hindered nor supported the establishment of the programme. It was rather a question of individual academics at the university combining with SMIL to ensure that the programme was launched.

During the first programme in the late 1990s, which was more of a pilot approximately 10 people representing five potential firms participated. The programme evaluation was very positive, and we were encouraged to continue. Interest in the programme has since then grown considerably. In the subsequent two programmes that were conducted in 2000, 52 people participated and 40 new firms were created. The programme has in recent years also grown nationally and internationally. The first programme outside of the Linköping region took place in 1999 at Teknikbyn in Västerås, and since then it has spread to other university towns, such as Kista (Kista Innovation and Growth), Skara (Liveum), Trollhättan (Innovatum), Umeå (Uminova) and Örebro (NetCity). In 2003 a programme was conducted in Moldavia, and in 2004, a new programme was started in Russia — in the Kaluga region. The ENP is currently also part of the European Commission (EU)-funded project 'Unispin', which aims to support regions in Europe that are attempting to build an infrastructure for entrepreneurial development.

### The Programme's Content and Execution

The start-up of a new business requires knowledge in many different areas, and it was therefore considered important that the nature of the programme be holistic with a broad content, spanning everything from business development, funding and leadership to legal matters and presentation techniques. Participants were required to be progressive in their entrepreneurship with future business growth in their objective. In the programme, only 'soft' resources in the business development process, such as experience, knowledge, guidance and networks were provided. Resources of a 'hard' nature, such as money, premises and equipment were the responsibility of the participants.

Specifically, the ENP contains the following activities:

- *Business plan:* Each participant was required to develop a simple business plan where the purpose was to structure and clarify the idea.
- *Workshops:* In these, the most important components in the business development process are explained with emphasis placed on the ability of participants to present their ideas.

- *Mentoring*: Each participant was given a mentor who had been or was a senior entrepreneur.
- *Supervision*: The participants regularly met a supervisor who checked progress, and from whom they received coaching.
- *Networking*: Each participant was given membership of SMIL free of charge for the year in which the programme took place.

Another important aspect of the programme was access to a good network (e.g. SMIL), SMIL is comprised of not only numerous experienced entrepreneurs, but also financiers and members of other supporting organisations. There is also close co-operation with the local science parks, not only concerning available premises, but also with regard to recruitment of participants to the programmes and the execution of on-site workshops. Another aspect of this programme was the distinction between mentoring and supervision. The former has more to do with the transmission of actual experiences of business from the mentor to the participants, while the role of the latter is that of following-up (i.e. making sure that the work of the business plan is carried out), auditing and coaching.

In the beginning, the programme lasted approximately 1 year, beginning in the early spring and finishing in November or December. It soon became clear that this time span was far too drawn out, mainly because most participants were able to start their firms before the programme concluded. Put simply, the programme required a shorter time span. It was therefore decided to shorten the programme considerably, and today it spans from 4 to 6 months period. This shortening had a positive impact and the participants were more engaged than previously in the duration of the programme.

### Target Group and Recruitment

The ENP programme is marketed by advertisements in the university's in-house newspaper, through leaflets distributed primarily to the students in their last year of undergraduate study, and also to graduate students. Firms and other organisations, which are members of SMIL, are invited via e-mail, fax or regular mail. Perhaps the most important marketing instrument is direct communication with students through the courses given in entrepreneurship or by the 'word-of-mouth', of satisfied participants on earlier programmes.

The ENP has two main target groups (see appendix for examples):

- Students, researchers and teachers at Linköping University
- Technology-based or knowledge-intensive firms and organisations in the region

The criteria used, to recruit people from these target groups is very simple. Participants should have a communicable idea (which need not be fully articulated), and they should be enthusiastic. Each of the applicants is interviewed by the programme management to ensure that they fulfil these two criteria and that they have understood that the aim of the programme is for the participants to start new businesses, and that the programme is not the usual credit-bearing university course. This relatively simple and informal recruiting procedure was chosen based on the following:

- It is almost impossible to assess whether in the early stages of an idea, it is economically sound. Moreover, it is not at all certain that the first idea will be the idea for the future of the company (Davidsson, Hunter, & Klofsten, 2006; Klofsten, 2005; Timmons, 1994).

- The entrepreneurial process itself is distinguished by the active and achievement-oriented behaviour of people in the form of being able to develop different business opportunities (Bygrave, 1994; McClelland, 1961).

Consequently, the programme emphasises the entrepreneur (or the entrepreneurial team) rather than the idea. To develop an idea into a business is a process that can take long time. It is wholly dependent on the persons behind the firm and their ability to take advantage of business opportunities on the market. Consequently, active participation in the programme is expected, where participants must be responsible for the relationship with their mentor, take advantage of the networks that are offered and exploit the relations that are created during the programme.

That which is offered can be compared to an arena of activities or opportunities where the participant is responsible for taking advantage of these as effectively he or she can. An ethos for this programme therefore, is the ability of participant entrepreneurs to set aside enough time for both the programme's content, and their own development work.

### Funding the Programme

There is no fee for participating in an ENP programme, a decision that was taken before the programme was initiated. The reason was that the target groups, largely expected to be students, lack the ability to pay and it would therefore not be suitable to demand a fee that might cause individuals with entrepreneurial characteristics to miss this opportunity. However, a deposit of SEK 500 is required from each participant when he or she produces a participating idea (project) at the beginning of the programme. This fee is returned on the condition that the participant is committed, turns in an evaluation and presents his or her business plan at the end of the programme. It was also considered whether some form of ownership of any new firm activities could be a long-term source of funding for the ENP programme. However, this option was not pursued primarily because the university and SMIL wanted to remain neutral partners and avoid becoming an investment company.

The programmes are financed through public money from the Nutek and the Technology Bridge Foundation. The costs of running a normal-sized programme at the university (with 10–12 firms) are reported to be approximately 450,000 SEK (50,000 Euro).

### Feedback from the Participants

Continuous follow-ups are made to check on this progress of alumni, and participants have responded that the programme gave them the following:

- A better structure to their new business because of a more thorough business plan.
- Support and pressure to achieve.
- The network that we were given access to has stimulated our development.
- I feel more secure on what is required and have been given a good foundation to stand on.
- It has meant that I have a more professional view of entrepreneurship.
- Analyse the business idea and business plan. Had it illustrated in different ways.
- A good start and probably a contributing factor to why I kept at it.
- Have become more secure in my role as a business leader.

Without exception, three factors were felt to be the most valuable result of participation. Firstly, the network with which the participants came into contact through their mentors and SMIL; secondly, the forced pace that the programme exhorts on the participants' own development and thirdly, the structured business model that the participants develop for the business they intend to develop.

Of the number of participants who participated in the programme, an average of 75% started firms during the course of the programme, 3 years later, 75% of these newly started companies have survived. After 3 years, 20% of the surviving companies had more than five employees. Those who did not complete the programme, stated primary causes, such as the splitting up of the founding team, a lack of time, family circumstances or a business idea that did not turn out well. However, lack of time was the most common reason why researchers (i.e. doctoral candidates) dropped out of the programme.

## Success Factors in Entrepreneurship Training

From the start we have regularly evaluated the programme in order to continually improve their structure and process. Based on this work, the following success factors have been identified:

- *The establishing of a holistic approach:* The contents of the programme should be broad, so that many conceivable aspects of starting new businesses are dealt with.
- *Ensure that the supply of competence is suited to the situation:* Early business development is dynamic and requires continual adjustments of the programme to meet the needs of circumstances in which the participants find themselves.
- *Define actual needs:* It is not certain that the participants are best at defining their actual needs. The supervisor or the mentor can help, based on the experienced need, to define the actual need and then to assist with a solution.
- *Link the programme to a network of firms:* The participants seldom have an established network and are usually in great need of coming into contact with other business leaders, not only to get advice, but also to form business contacts.
- *Increase the participants' self-confidence as business leaders:* Many of the participants lack experience in entrepreneurship, and it is important to begin to view them as business leaders as soon as possible and get them to grow into this role.
- *Emphasise commitment:* Before the start of the programme, it is important that the participants understand that results are completely dependent on whether they are able to set aside enough of their own time for the programme's activities and for their own on-going project work.
- *Demand distinct and measurable results:* The participants' progress in the programme must be able to be documented in some way, for example through a business plan, a project specification, work performance or visits made to customers.
- *Use a tried and proven set of tools:* Because the programme is largely practical, success will, to a large extent, depend on which tools are used in, for example the programme's workshops. Engage people, for example experienced entrepreneurs, who have skills that, from experience, have proven to be functional and successful.

- *Plan mentoring*: It is our experience that taking time to carefully choose a group of mentors is worth the effort. Factors that are important to consider are, for example personal chemistry, age and the student competency profile.
- *Include some theory alongside the practical:* The programmes should be practically oriented, but it is often advantageous that certain steps are set in a theoretical context.
- *Focus the programmes on target groups*: An important ingredient to programmes is a strong commitment by the participants and their mutual contribution to each others' activities. The ENP is designed for technology-based and knowledge-intensive activities where the majority of the participants have a common academic background.
- *Build credibility*: One requirement for being able to carry out a programme effectively is that the participants are frank with each other. Business development, however, is often associated with secretiveness, and it is hardly suitable to write secrecy agreements between everyone who is involved in a programme. Therefore, a working climate based on confidence must be quickly established, both among the participants, and with programme management, to create an air of frankness.
- *Find a balance between the formal and informal*: Entrepreneurship is associated with activity, drive, flexibility and frankness. This must be reflected in the organisation of the programme at all levels. At the same time, there must also be orderliness.

The above success factors are all of a 'soft' nature. It is important under these circumstances not to be blinded by how many firms have been started or how many participants have dropped out. Instead, what is important is the quality of the activities and the qualitative development that the individuals go through during the programme.

For society, the number of new firms or the number of new jobs created is a natural measure of success. This way of evaluating success must, however, be used with some caution. With experience from studies made at, for example Chalmer's Innovationcentrum, we know that the increase in employment through new business development can be expressed as an exponential function (Wallmark & Sjösten, 1994). This means that the strong employment effect appears first 7–10 years or later following the start of a new business. We must therefore have a long-term perspective on the benefits of initiatives, such as the ENP.

## Discussion and Conclusions

In this paper a programme for training individuals to act entrepreneurially was described and analysed. Arguments were made that entrepreneurship is behaviourally conditioned. This is closely associated with many factors, such as the ability to act, levels of commitment and the driving force of the individuals who create the ideas. Previous studies on entrepreneurship training have shown that individuals who are ambitious, well-motivated and willing to take risks often run up against barriers that inhibit them from letting loose their energies (Kent, 1990; Rabbior, 1990).

These barriers are associated with internal goals and the setting of priorities among prospective entrepreneurs as well as the requisite expertise and credibility of those who offer training in entrepreneurship. Thousands of universities in the international arena have developed some form of training programme in entrepreneurship, not only to stimulate growth and development on the societal level, but also to offer alternative career paths to students, researchers and teachers. An important conclusion for a sustainable development of these initiatives is that acceptance of this type of activity must be quickly created, both in universities for example, support from the university's administration, as well as from the target group of entrepreneurs for which the programmes are designed. It is important, as in other contexts, to be aware of the success factors, examples of which have been given above.

It has become evident that the growing institutionalisation of entrepreneurship in our universities has generated new implications both for research and practice. Entrepreneurship has become discipline with a breadth that touches on philosophy, business economics, history, psychology and sociology. Although the field is complex, it is important to understand what new business development is about and especially what happens during the early business development processes (Klofsten & Spaeth, 2004). These factors, although not the same, are probably similar to those found in traditional management development of established firms — save for those dissimilarities that emanate from differences in size, maturity and credibility. The individual or individuals who are setting up new business are often inexperienced, have no employees, lack sufficient funds or a developed network. The business ideas that such individuals have are usually vague, but the driving forces are strong.

One of the most important aspects of all entrepreneurship training is to attempt to minimise the previously mentioned barriers by encouraging individuals to take the step to become entrepreneurial, increase their self-confidence and at the same time give them professional aid to realise these goals. These aspects are prominent in the evaluations that have been made of the ENP. The participants emphasise not only the academic aspects of their programmes, but also that they were better able to structure their business development work, had access to a network of experienced entrepreneurs, and were given professional treatment and feedback on their ideas. Programme management has also witnessed with great satisfaction how individual participants were able to grow as entrepreneurs during the course of a programme.

Rabbior (1990) and Klofsten and Spaeth (2004) maintain that entrepreneurship training should not be evaluated on quantities, such as numbers of newly started businesses or growth in these. This does not mean that such measures are uninteresting when they, for example provide information on the efficiency of the training among trainees. But in many cases individual participants in the programme will not be starting new businesses, neither in the short nor in the long-term. Instead, insights that are generated by a programme can hopefully be used in other contexts, for example in association with business development in established firms. Results of training programmes are best evaluated using distinct aims formulated in advance, and there are no hard and fast rules for what these are or ought to be. In the meeting with participants, we learnt more about the needs of potential entrepreneurs and about how we can meet these needs — and that we who train entrepreneurs must probably be something of an entrepreneur ourselves. The use of experienced entrepreneurs and entrepreneurial supervisors, with this premise, is naturally something that paves the way for success in a training programme. In an evaluation of the number of newly started firms, it should also be kept in mind that the results in part depend on the admission criteria for the programme used and the initial requirements placed on the participants.

When regions seek new opportunities for economical development through, for example increased new business development, entrepreneurship training will not only involve the university, but also other levels in the educational system such as the 9-year compulsory school and upper-secondary school programmes. The ENP was primarily developed to stimulate the establishment of technique-based and knowledge-intensive activities in the Linköping region. Most probably, however, the programme and its work methods have a more general relevance in that the ENP model could be used in a wide variety of contexts, where it is desirable to stimulate the start of new businesses that are not necessarily technology-based or knowledge-intensive. The spread of the ENP model to other areas of Sweden, (e.g. the strong and rapid development of Teknikbyn in Västerås) and internationally, is proof that the model can be used in other contexts.

It is, however, important to realise that it takes time to create growth businesses and generate employment through new business development. In this connection, the ENP is an important instrument for supporting these processes, but as discussed above, the results should be judged over a 7–10-year period. Teknikbyn in Västerås, which was founded in 1998, is today undergoing substantial growth in both the number firms and the employment they provide in the region.

There are several initiatives today that aim to be the catalysts for economic development in a region. Included here, among other things, are incubators, science parks, different organisations for the development of networks and other forms of business development support. Substantial resources are being invested today in the creation of different types of physical infrastructure. This paper has instead focused on entrepreneurs and the development of entrepreneurship and emphasised the importance of using a process-oriented outlook (see also Autio & Klofsten, 1998). We can build the most spectacular buildings, and draw up the most generous budgets and thorough organisation charts. But based on the perspective presented in this paper, our work will come to nothing without motivated entrepreneurs of high-quality, produced through practically oriented training able to meet the real needs of these entrepreneurial individuals.

## Acknowledgement

Many thanks to Mr. Staffan Öberg for valuable contribution on the article. The author also wants to thank Technology Link for the financial support of this study.

## Appendix

## Examples of New Firms that have Participated in ENP

### Calluna AB

The firm was founded in 1992 by five students at Linköping University and two of the founders participated in an ENP in 1999. Activities are oriented towards environmental impact descriptions, environmental management practices (landscaping, conservation planning) and environmental restoration.

## Dynamics Code AB

The company was founded in 2001 by two researchers at Linköping University. The firm's business idea is to create tailor-made services and products in the field of DNA that are based on the firm's expertise in genetics, molecular biology and bioinformatics.

## Kreatel Communications AB

The company was founded by two students in 1996. At present, activities are to develop products for digital TV via broadband, either via an ADSL modem or via a fibre-based network.

## Licera AB

The company was founded in 1999 by two people who were previously active in another high-technology firm in Linköping. The company produces products capable of automatic monitoring and communication with mechanical equipment, so-called M2M applications.

## Mathcore Engineering AB

The company was founded in 1998 by three researchers at Linköping University. The company develops, among other things, modelling and simulation tools.

## Meqon Research AB

The firm was founded in 2003 by three students at Linköping University. The company develops physics generators for the simulation of realistic movements in three-dimensional, virtual surroundings.

## Micromuscle AB

The company was founded in 2000 by three researchers at Linköping University. The company develops microsurgical instruments based on electroactive polymer components.

## Nescit Systems AB

The company was founded in 1999 by two students at Linköping University. Activities are concentrated in the area of software and information services, including the development of programmes and services for terminology management.

## Optimal Solutions AB

The company was founded in 1997 by two researchers at Linköping University. The firm's business idea is to develop optimisation systems for complex decision processes.

# Development of New Business Areas in Established Firms

*Telia Prosoft AB*

The management in charge of electronic trade and information services participated in an ENP in 1998 to develop the business area.

*Enea Epact AB*

Two of the firm's people in charge of business areas participated in an ENP in 1999 to develop the firm's business in telecom and system validation.

*NIRA Dynamics AB*

Management participated in an ENP in 2001 to develop the firm's business area in advanced systems and technical solutions for different vehicle dynamics applications.

*Bluelabs East AB*

Two staff members participated in an ENP in 2002 to develop the firm's business area of software solutions for built-in systems.

# References

Autio, E., & Klofsten, M. (1998). A comparative study of two European business incubators. *Journal of Small Business Management, 36*(1), 30–43.

Brockhaus, R. H. (1982). The psychology of the entrepreneur. In: C. A. Kent, D. L. Sexton & K. H. Vesper (Eds), *Encyclopaedia of entrepreneurship* (pp. 39–57). Cambridge, MA: Ballinger.

Bygrave, W. D. (1994). *The portable MBA in entrepreneurship.* Toronto: Wiley.

Curran, J., & Stanworth, J. (1989). Education and training for enterprise: Some problems of classification, evaluation, policy and research. *International Small Business Journal, 7*(2), 45–58.

Davidsson, P. (1989). *Continued entrepreneurship and small firm growth.* PhD thesis, Stockholm School of Economics, Stockholm.

Davidsson, P., Hunter, E., & Klofsten, M. (2006). Institutional forces: The invisible hand that shapes venture ideas. *International Small Business Journal, 24*(2), 115–129.

Etzkowitz, H. E., & Klofsten, M. (2005). The innovative region: Toward a theory of knowledge-based regional development. *R&D Management, 35*(3), 243–255.

Garavan, T. N., & O'Cinneide, B. (1994). Entrepreneurship education and training programmes: A review and evaluation — Part 1. *Journal of European Industrial Training, 18*(8), 3–12.

Gartner, W. B. (1988). Who is an entrepreneur? Is the wrong question. *American Journal of Small Business,* 11–32.

Gibb, A. A. (1990). Design effective programmes for encouraging the small business start-up process. *Journal of European Industrial Training, 14*(1), 17–25.

Kent, C. A. (Ed.) (1990). *Entrepreneurship education: Current developments, future directions.* New York: Quorum Books.

Klofsten, M. (2005). New venture ideas: An analysis of their origin and early development. *Journal of Technology Analysis and Strategic Management, 17*(1), 105–119.

Klofsten, M., & Mikaelsson, A.-S. (1996). Support of small firms: Entrepreneurs views of the demand and supply side. *Journal of Enterprising Culture, 4*(4), 417–432.

Klofsten, M., & Spaeth, M. (2004). Entrepreneurship training for regional growth and innovation: A Swedish case study and ten year retrospective. Paper presented at the ICSB 49th world conference, Johannesburg, South Africa, June 20–23.

McClelland, D. C. (1961). *The achieving society.* Princeton, NJ: Van Nostrand.

Rabbior, G. (1990). 4 elements of a successful entrepreneurship/economics/education program. In: C. A. Kent (Ed.), *Entrepreneurship education: Current developments, future directions* (pp. 53–65). New York: Quorum Books.

Timmons, J. A. (1994). Opportunity recognition: The search for higher potential ventures. In: W. D. Bygrave (Ed.), *The portable MBA in entrepreneurship* (pp. 26–54). Toronto: Wiley.

Wallmark, T., & Sjösten, J. (1994). Stability and turbulence among spin-off companies from Chalmers University. Paper presented at the 8th Nordic Congress on Small Business Research, Halmstad, June.

Westhead, P., & Storey, D. (1996). Management training and small firm performance: Why is the link so weak? *International Small Business Journal, 14*(4), 13–24.

Ylinenpää, H. (1997). *Managing competence development and acquisition in small manufacturing firms.* Ph.D. thesis, Luleå Technical University, Luleå.

Chapter 6

# Building the Foundations for Academic Enterprise: The Medici Fellowship Programme

Simon Mosey, Andy Lockett and Paul Westhead

## Introduction

Despite a recent increase in government funded intervention schemes a number of attitudinal and operational barriers continue to constrain university technology transfer in the UK (Wright, Birley, & Mosey, 2004). A recent report commissioned by the UK government (Lambert, 2003) asserts that the inability of some universities to develop links with industry is a key barrier to the commercialisation of research. Moreover it is argued that academics focus exclusively upon their research due to the explicit link to career progression (Slaughter & Leslie, 1997). As a result academics, in the main, remain reluctant to explore the potential for commercialising their research. This paper considers a novel fellowship scheme aiming to overcome these barriers by retraining academics and encouraging them to interact with their peers and with industry practitioners to help commercialise research within their schools.

Traditionally the debate about the impact of such intervention initiatives has focused on the skills, or rather the skills shortages, of the universities. In this paper we seek to add to this debate by examining the role of networks. We propose that networks are an important determinant of university success in commercialising their research. For instance, academics seeking to commercialise a radical innovation need to accumulate some broader legitimacy (Delmar & Shane, 2004) to ensure the technology is pursued and exploited in the market. Information, advice and financial resources from actors, external to the university may, therefore, need to be sought.

If the network of a university (or academic) is to provide any potential benefit to commercialisation, then it is important that the network is able to access important resources. In this paper we focus on two principal types of network. Our arguments are stylised for simplicity thus: (i) the academic network and (ii) the practitioner network (which includes customers, suppliers, financiers, legal experts, etc.). These different networks are, to a

New Technology Based Firms in the New Millennium, Volume VI
Edited by A. Groen, R. Oakey, P. van der Sijde and G. Cook
© 2008 Emerald Group Publishing Limited. All rights reserved.

greater or lesser degree, distinct from each other and exhibit very different structural characteristics.

Within the UK, many science-based academics are solely engaged within a peer review research networks, which are primarily concerned with publication of research evidence. This leads to the development of scientific elites, which are aided by the peer review process in scholarly publications, and also the distribution of research grants. Consequently, individual academics tend to be 'locked in' to the peer review system that is explicitly linked to career progression through the Research Assessment Exercise (RAE). As such they have little incentive to look or engage outside this network or attempt to make use of practitioner knowledge as it appears to have little value or relevance (Seashore Louis, Blumenthal, Gluck, & Stoto, 1989). Academics can utilise their ties within the scientific academic networks to identify technical opportunities but not necessarily commercial opportunities. The reluctance (or inability) of most academics to develop ties with several actors positioned in practitioner networks may retard the commercialisation process.

Practitioner networks (i.e. financiers, lawyers, accountants, etc.), in comparison to academic networks, are less inward looking. They can provide academics with the resources and for broader expertise they need to convert a technical idea into a new commercial business. Practitioners can provide expertise related to several issues (i.e. opportunity identification, pursuit and exploitation, idea protection, resource assemblage, organisation governance and appropriate strategic orientation to deal with dynamic and hostile external environmental conditions). The information, knowledge and expertise provided by practitioners can enable academic entrepreneurs to address the 'liabilities of newness' (Schoonhoven, 2005) associated with new technical ventures. Academics who develop broader network ties may therefore more quickly address several barriers to the commercialisation of knowledge from universities.

However even if ties exist between the networks, the actors involved may have difficulties in communicating with one another. Davidsson (2002) argues that such difficulties in communication between actors may be due to fundamental differences in knowledge, goals and assumptions of those involved. We propose that these differences can be overcome through the appropriate development of academics' network ties. Academics, for example may have close or strong ties with other team members in their department. Repeated collaboration between academics in the same department may lead to mutual trust and thereby closer working relationships. In contrast, many academics may only have loose or weak ties, (Alder & Kwon, 2002), that is, to say social linkages, with actors located outside their department. However, Granovetter's (1973) weak ties concept suggests that the dissemination of novel information, resources and opportunities can be facilitated by weak ties that integrate otherwise disconnected/actors (Burt, 1992). Cooper and Yin (2005, p. 99) have asserted, "Weak ties generate opportunities for entrepreneurs by bridging contacts between different groups and circles". An academic seeking to address an operational barrier to commercialisation may, therefore, seek to develop these loose or weak ties to gain access to valuable information that would otherwise be difficult and costly for them to obtain (Baron, 2005). Academics who 'get through the door' and talk to industrial actors may subsequently develop their social and entrepreneurial skills, which can ensure mutually successful relationships, with a variety of non-academic actors. Their individual entrepreneurial attributes and capabilities may, therefore, be subsequently enhanced by focusing on loose or weak ties with industrial actors. Moreover, "over time, loose ties can sometimes develop into strong ones, in which case they would lead to relationships based on mutual trust" (Baron, 2005, p. 225).

In this paper we examine whether a fellowship scheme can help academics build appropriate ties and thereby encourage commercialisation. By participating in the scheme the fellow, being able to understand both the science and the business side of commercialisation, themselves may build new ties and encourage others to follow. Moreover, through their actions they may well act as an agent of change to promote wider commercialisation and hence change the attitudes of academics. Building upon existing research into network theory we specifically address two questions:

- What impact will commercialisation fellowships have upon the development of ties between academic and practitioner networks?
- What impact will commercialisation fellowships have upon the nature of resources exchanged between academic and practitioner networks?

This paper is structured as follows. In Section 2 we outline our methodology and data collection techniques a while. Section 3 presents the findings of the case-study. The fourth section discussion builds upon the case-material to develop a theoretical framework and provide propositions to guide future research. Finally, in Section 5 conclusions and implications are presented.

## Methodology and Data Collection

This paper utilises the logic of inductive inquiry to investigate a complex process in which the interaction between the phenomena and contexts are unclear (Glaser & Strauss, 1967). In this section we first outline the Medici Fellowship programme, on which the case-study is based. We then comment on the data collection methods employed in a case-study.

### *The Medici Fellowship Scheme*

The Medici fellowship was selected for study as it provides a specific and novel intervention within a wide variety of contexts. It was implemented within five research intensive universities located in the midlands of England. Each university had a strong tradition in biomedical research, yet exhibit a diverse record on commercialisation.

The aim of the scheme is to engender a culture of change within biomedical faculties towards the commercialisation of their research. The scheme is unusual among intervention schemes due to the provision of formal structured training, in conjunction with experiential learning, and the financial resources to 'buy out academics' (i.e. the fellows) time. In total 50 annual fellowships were established across the 5 universities over a 2-year period between September 2002 and September 2004. In this study, we examine the outcomes associated with the first cohort of 20 fellows who were in post between

September 2002 and September 2003. All fellows had considerable academic research experience within the biosciences, and were required to demonstrate a personal desire to learn about the theory and practice of commercialisation.

Fellows were provided with local training at their host institution. Typically this involved participation in Business School teaching modules related to finance, marketing, intellectual property and business strategy. In addition, fellows participated in workshops, where the full cohort of 20 fellows were brought together to reflect upon each others learning experiences, and engage with practitioners from the biomedical business community including the University Technical Transfer Officers (TTOs) as well as representatives from the legal, regulatory and finance professions. These events are summarised in chronological order in Table 1.

Following the induction workshop, the task of the fellow was to respond to the commercialisation needs of a participating school during the year in post. To help them put their training into practice they were provided with a mentor, which was typically a Business Development Officer (BDO). Within each Institution a host of other intervention initiatives were conducted in parallel. Notable examples include networking events, staff training days and business plan competitions.

Table 1: Global training workshops for first cohort of medici fellows.

| Course title | University facilitators | External network representatives |
|---|---|---|
| Residential Induction Workshop | TTMs, TTOs, Business and Biomedical Academics | Psychologist and Biomedical Entrepreneurs |
| IP and regulatory | TTOs, Business and Biomedical Academics | Legal and Biomedical Industry |
| Technology Audit | TTMs, TTOs, Business and Biomedical Academics | Biomedical Entrepreneurs |
| Commercial Audit | TTOs, Business and Biomedical Academics | Finance Industry |
| Business Strategy | TTOs, Business and Biomedical Academics | Biomedical Entrepreneurs and Biomedical Industry |
| Finance | TTOs, Business and Biomedical Academics | Finance Industry, Biomedical Entrepreneurs and Biomedical Industry |
| Masterclass | TTMs, TTOs, Business and Biomedical Academics | Finance Industry and Biomedical Entrepreneurs |
| Showcase Event | TTMs, TTOs, Business and Biomedical Academics | Finance Industry, Biomedical entrepreneurs, Biomedical Industry and Government Agencies |

*Notes*: TTM, technology transfer office manager; TTO, technology transfer officer.

## Data Collection

We selected six Medici fellows from diverse contexts to enable theory building through cross case comparison (Eisenhardt, 1989). This variance can be seen in Table 2 and includes the academic position of the fellow, their role in terms of commercialisation activities within the school, and the overall level of commercialisation activity within the school.

Data were collected using in depth face to face and telephone interviews with the 6 fellows and 20 other key actors having direct experience of the differing intervention initiatives underway between 2002 and 2004 within the host schools. The respondents therefore included: 6 senior academics with direct experience of a number of commercialisation initiatives; 6 technology transfer staff members with direct responsibility for commercialisation within the host biomedical research schools and 6 Medici fellows from the first cohort of 20 fellows, interviewed 6 months after completion of their year in post. Within each interview we asked a series of structured and semi-structured open-ended questions to establish the respondent's views regarding the impact of Medici fellows upon interactions between academic and industrial networks (including the actors involved), the perceived value of these interactions and the nature of the resources exchanged.

Interview transcripts were analysed separately for each case through consideration of the research questions. Subsequently, cross case analyses were made to help highlight exceptions from the norms (Miles & Huberman, 1984). In this way theoretical insights were gained through an iterative process of comparative analysis. Triangulation was aided through the collection of numerous secondary data (Yin, 1993). These data included records of the commercialisation performance of the participating schools and feedback forms completed by the fellows following each training event. Three researchers took part in the inquiry. The interviews and subsequent analysis was deliberately isolated (Yin, 1993). To help minimise confirmatory bias one researcher conducted the interviews while the remaining researchers explored the collected data. Throughout the analysis the validity of the emerging insights were checked by discussion with key actors and the managers of the scheme (Strauss & Corbin, 1990).

## Findings

As highlighted above we structured our data collection and analysis to focus on two specific issues. Firstly, the impact of the Medici fellows upon the interactions between the academic and practitioner networks. Secondly, the impact of the Medici fellows upon the information exchanged between the academic and practitioner networks. This section considers each of these perspectives in turn and considers the empirical evidence gathered by making comparisons between the different fellows and host schools investigated.

### Interactions between Academic and Practitioner Networks

Respondents were first asked questions regarding the awareness and use of network actors by Medici fellows within their schools. They were provided with the 17 types of network actors (Wright, Binks, Lockett, & Vohora, 2003) summarised in Table 3. The potential

Table 2: Characteristics of the interview respondents.

| Respondent | Academic position | Commercialisation role | School (university) | Level of tech transfer within school 2002–2003 inclusive[a] |
|---|---|---|---|---|
| Medici Fellow 1 | Post Doctoral | Exploring commercialisation of research within school | BioScience (1) | Low |
| Technology Transfer Officer 1 | IP Exec | Intellectual property management university wide | BioScience (1) | Low |
| Senior Academic 1 | Professor | Facilitates tech transfer within the school | BioScience (1) | Low |
| Medici Fellow 2 | Lecturer | Exploring commercialisation of research within group | Medicine and BioSciences (2) | Moderate |
| Technology Transfer Officer 2 | Head of IPR | Intellectual property management university wide | Medicine and BioSciences (2) | Moderate |
| Senior Academic 2 | Head of School | Strategic management of I.P within school | Medicine and BioSciences (2) | Moderate |
| Medici Fellow 3 | Senior Lecturer | Exploring commercialisation of research within group | School of Electronic Engineering (3) | Moderate |
| Technology Transfer Officer 3 | Tech Transfer Officer | Intellectual property management within school | School of Electronic Engineering (3) | Moderate |

| | | | School | Rating |
|---|---|---|---|---|
| Senior Academic 3 | Professor | Manages I.P. within research group | School of Electronic Engineering (3) | Moderate |
| Medici Fellow 4 | Lecturer | Exploring commercialisation of research within group | BioScience (4) | Moderate |
| Technology Transfer Officer 4 | Head of IPR | Intellectual property management university wide | BioScience (4) | Moderate |
| Senior Academic 4 | Head of School | Strategic management of I.P. within school | BioScience (4) | Moderate |
| Medici Fellow 5 | Post Doctoral | Exploring commercialisation of research within group | Pharmacy (3) | High |
| Technology Transfer Officer 5 | Tech Transfer Officer | Intellectual property management within school | Pharmacy (3) | High |
| Senior Academic 5 | Professor | Manages I.P. within research group | Pharmacy (3) | High |
| Medici Fellow 6 | Lecturer | Exploring commercialisation of research within group | Life and Health Sciences (5) | High |
| Technology Transfer Officer 6 | Head of IPR | Intellectual property management university wide | Life and Health Sciences (5) | High |
| Senior Academic 6 | Senior Lecturer | Manager of research group | Life and Health Sciences (5) | High |

[a] A technology transfer rating of high means >1 U.S.O. or licensing deal, a rating of medium means between 0 and 1 U.S.O. or licensing deals, a rating of low means 0 U.S.O. and licensing deals.

*Source*: Adapted from Wright et al. (2003).

Table 3: Awareness and usage of network actors by medici fellows (number of respondents = 17).

| Network actors used by medici fellows | Aware of actor | | Actor used | |
|---|---|---|---|---|
| | No. | % | No. | % |
| (p) Intellectual property/legal firms | 17 | 100.0 | 16 | 94.1 |
| (p) Large firms/industry | 17 | 100.0 | 15 | 88.2 |
| (i) Regional development agencies | 17 | 100.0 | 14 | 82.4 |
| (i) University challenge/proof of concept funds | 17 | 100.0 | 14 | 82.4 |
| (p) Small and medium-sized enterprises (SMEs) | 16 | 94.1 | 14 | 82.4 |
| (i) Government grants (e.g. SMART awards) | 17 | 100.0 | 13 | 76.5 |
| (a) Medical schools | 17 | 100.0 | 12 | 70.6 |
| (a) Other universities | 17 | 10.00 | 12 | 70.6 |
| (p) Venture capital firms | 17 | 100.0 | 11 | 64.7 |
| (i) Business link (or regional equivalent) | 16 | 94.1 | 11 | 64.7 |
| (p) Management consultants | 17 | 100.0 | 10 | 58.8 |
| (i) Science parks | 17 | 100.0 | 9 | 52.9 |
| (p) Business angels | 16 | 94.1 | 8 | 47.1 |
| (i) Business incubators | 17 | 100.0 | 7 | 41.2 |
| (p) Private laboratories | 17 | 100.0 | 5 | 29.4 |
| (i) Surrogate entrepreneurs/interim managers | 11 | 64.7 | 4 | 23.5 |
| (i) Professional venture management firms | 13 | 76.5 | 3 | 17.6 |

*Note*: (p), practitioner network; (i), potential intermediary and (a), academic network.

actors were categorised as belonging to the practitioner network, for example large firms, venture capitalists, the academic network, for example medical schools, other universities or as potential intermediaries, for example surrogate entrepreneurs and regional development agencies.

According to the respondents the fellows were aware of 12 of the 17 network actors. However, less than 95% of fellows were aware of the following potential intermediaries: Business Link (or regional equivalent) (94%), surrogate entrepreneurs/interim managers (65%), professional venture management firms (77%) or the following industry actors: small and medium-sized enterprises (SMEs) (94%), and business angels (94%).

Respondents reported the usage of the network actors the fellows were aware of. Considerable variability in the reported usage of the network actors is summarised in Table 3. At least three quarters of the fellows had used the following practitioner network actors: intellectual property/legal firms (94%), large firms/industry (88%), SMEs (82%) and/or the following potential intermediaries: University challenge/proof of concept funds (82%), and Government grants (e.g. SMART awards) (77%). Conversely, the following practitioner actors were used by less than half of fellows: professional venture management funds (18%), private laboratories (29%) and business angels (47%) and the following intermediaries were used by less than half of fellows: surrogate entrepreneurs/interim managers (24%) and business incubators (41%).

Table 4: Usefulness of network actors used by medici fellows (number of respondents = 17)[a].

| Usefulness of network actors used by medici fellows | No. | Mean | Standard deviation |
|---|---|---|---|
| (p) Intellectual property/legal firms | 15 | 4.60 | 0.51 |
| (p) Large firms/industry | 15 | 3.63 | 0.61 |
| (i) Regional development agencies | 14 | 3.32 | 1.59 |
| (i) University challenge/proof of concept funds | 12 | 4.33 | 0.65 |
| (p) Small and medium-sized enterprises (SMEs) | 13 | 3.58 | 1.19 |
| (i) Government grants (e.g. SMART awards) | 12 | 3.92 | 1.51 |
| (a) Medical schools | 12 | 4.04 | 0.92 |
| (a) Other universities | 11 | 3.82 | 0.75 |
| (p) Venture capital firms | 9 | 2.94 | 1.01 |
| (i) Business link (or regional equivalent) | 10 | 2.50 | 1.35 |
| (p) Management consultants | 10 | 3.20 | 1.14 |
| (i) Science parks | 9 | 3.56 | 1.33 |
| (p) Business angels | 7 | 2.43 | 0.98 |
| (i) Business incubators | 7 | 3.86 | 1.21 |
| (p) Private laboratories | 5 | 2.20 | 1.10 |
| (i) Surrogate entrepreneurs/interim managers | 3 | 2.67 | 1.53 |
| (i) Professional venture management firms | 3 | 2.67 | 1.53 |

*Note*: (p), practitioner network, (i), potential intermediary and (a), academic network.
[a]The following scale was used: (1) not at all useful, (2) not useful, (3) neither not useful nor useful, (4) useful and (5) very useful.

Respondents were then asked to rank the usefulness of the actors the fellows had used. A five point scoring system was employed, where a score of 1 suggested 'not at all useful', a score of 3 suggested 'neither not useful nor useful', while a score of 5 suggested 'very useful'. Table 4 shows that the following four actors had mean scores of 4 or higher: intellectual property/legal firms (4.6), University challenge/proof of concept funds (4.3) and medical schools (4.0). In contrast, the following actors had mean scores of 3.5 or lower: private laboratories (2.2), business angels (2.4), business link (or regional equivalent) (2.5), surrogate entrepreneurs/interim managers (2.7), professional venture management firms (2.7), venture capital firms (2.9), management consultants (3.3) and regional development agencies (3.3). 'External' private and public sector actors were, therefore, widely perceived to be useful. In summary, the most useful practitioner actors were seen to provide legal advice. Moreover the most useful academic actors provided medical research knowledge and the most useful intermediaries provided early stage funding. By contrast, the practitioner actors offering equity finance were found less useful. Equally, the potentially useful intermediaries of surrogate entrepreneurs and management consultants were also considered less useful.

### *Nature of the Resources Exchanged between the Networks*

To gain more insight into these interactions, respondents were presented with 12 specified statements relating to how the Medici fellows impacted upon the resources exchanged

Table 5: Impact of the medici fellows on the resources exchanged (number of respondents = 15).

| Impact of the Medici fellows on the resources exchanged | No. | Mean | Standard deviation |
|---|---|---|---|
| 1. Encouraging academics to exploit the IP generated from their research | 15 | 4.60 | 0.63 |
| 2. Access to market information | 15 | 4.33 | 0.72 |
| 3. Working with other HE or research institutes | 14 | 4.07 | 0.83 |
| 4. Access to potential partner firms | 14 | 4.07 | 0.62 |
| 5. Working with other departments within University | 14 | 4.07 | 0.73 |
| 6. Access to potential customers | 15 | 4.00 | 0.53 |
| 7. Availability of proof of concept funding | 14 | 4.00 | 0.78 |
| 8. Access to management skills | 15 | 3.93 | 0.70 |
| 9. Ability to obtain finance from industrial partners | 14 | 3.71 | 0.47 |
| 10. Ability to obtain finance from venture capital firms | 15 | 3.60 | 0.63 |
| 11. Attracting commercial management to spin outs | 14 | 3.36 | 0.63 |
| 12. Ability to obtain finance from business angels | 13 | 3.31 | 0.48 |

*Note*: The following scale was used: (1) strongly impeded, (2) impeded, (3) no effect, (4) promoted and (5) strongly promoted.

during these interactions (adapted from Wright et al., 2003). With regard to each statement a five point scoring system was employed, where a score of 1 suggested 'strongly impeded', a score of 3 suggested 'no effect', while a score of 5 suggested 'strongly promoted'. Eight out of the 12 specified statements had mean scores of 3.9 or higher suggesting the Medici fellows were associated with several beneficial resource exchanges. Table 5 shows that the following six statements/outcomes had mean scores of 4 or higher: encouraging academics to exploit the Intellectual Property (IP) generated from their research (4.6), access to market information (4.3), working with other higher education (HE) or research institutes (4.1), access to potential partner firms (4.1), working with other departments within the University (4.1), access to potential customers (4.1) and availability of proof of concept funding (4.0). Only two out of the specified statements had mean scores of 3.5 or lower; these were attracting commercial management to spin-outs (3.4) and ability to obtain finance from business angels (3.4).

The above presented evidence suggests that the fellows developed strong ties with academic actors when considering the broader issues associated with the process of technology transfer, particularly the disclosure of intellectual property both within and between schools. TTO (6), for example asserted:

> The Medici scheme had most impact via technology audits — establishing what the Academics are doing and then encouraging them to bring their ideas forward and develop them.

Moreover, a Head of school (2) claimed that the:

> Medici fellows had the most impact by identifying IP in people who didn't think they had it.

By developing new weak ties to industry actors fellows were seen to provide market research and potential partners firms for academics. TTO (1) claimed:

> The impact depended on the stage of the project that the fellow was working on — some instances it was raising money, doing market research, writing of business plans. It was project dependent but fellows because of their skill base were able to assist on any aspect.

Forming new ties also provided benefits to the fellow, as argued by a Fellow (5):

> I benefited by generally learning about the technology transfer process, being able to objectively see if what you've got is as good as you think it is. I gained team-working skills. I learnt to network and it provided ways of working with industry. And it provided contacts. I now look at new projects in a different way. I would try and commercialise rather than creating a one off.

This was supported by another Fellow (4), who asserted:

> I gained leadership, financial acumen and business understanding and benefited from networking and a pool of people who you can call on for advice.

The fellows also built new weak ties between academic and financial actors, particularly with proof of concept funders who focus upon early stage projects. One academic for example, claimed:

> The fellow provided the ability to get things done — going forward with ideas. If I was aware of awards the Medici Fellow could find out about the award, start to draft the proposal, have input from myself and then make a success of it.

Ties between academics and business angels and venture capitalists were, however, less frequently established. Demand and supply issues may account for the latter pattern. The pecking order hypothesis of Myers (1984) suggests that many smaller firms choose to use sources of finance in this order of precedence: internal equity, short-term debt, long-term debt and then external equity. Further, some venture capitalists assert that many owners of firms seeking funding for novel and technologically sophisticated products and/or products do not provide them with sufficiently reliable information to make adequate risk and return decisions. Additional attention appears to be required to address the asymmetric information flow between academic actors and external formal and informal venture capitalists.

## Discussion

In this section, we draw together the evidence presented above to develop a theoretical model of the impact made by fellowship schemes. In doing so we generate propositions to guide future research into the effectiveness of fellowship schemes. The framework is presented in Figure 1.

### *Enhancing Interaction between Academic and Practitioner Networks*

It is argued the commercialisation of research is by necessity a collaborative activity (Murray, 2004; Oliver, 2004; Zucker, Darby, & Armstronget al., 2002). It requires a combination of technical know-how (which is typically contained within the University) with financial resources and commercial management capabilities, which are typically widely dispersed outside the University (Audretsch & Feldman, 2003; Powell, Koput, Bowie, & Smith Doerrs, 2002). Within the Midlands of the UK it is argued that the former is present within the Universities, yet the latter is either not present or not being fully utilised (Lambert, 2003).

To consider this phenomenon we employ a network perspective. Hoang and Antoncic (2003) propose that the characteristics of networks can be considered from three perspectives. Firstly, the network content, defined as the nature of the content exchanged between actors in the network. Secondly, the network governance, defined as the mechanisms that govern relationships between actors. Thirdly, the network structure, defined as the pattern of relationships between actors (Amit & Zott, 2001). We observed the Medici scheme to have a positive impact upon each of these perspectives. The fellows were seen to encourage interaction between academic and industry actors to exchange market information, legal information and to identify potential customers. In addition the fellows increased the number of ties within the academic network, through an increase in technical and commercial exchanges between departments and between universities. Moreover, the fellows formed new ties with other public sector actors to gain proof of concept funding.

These activities were observed to affect the governance within the academic network as an increasing number of academics saw a potential benefit in engaging outside their peer review network. Benefits realised included improved financial resources and also increased technical resources through new academic interactions. This provided an unforeseen benefit whereby commercialisation could provide research benefits to the academic network. Here we propose that fellowship schemes can provide a potential advantage over other intervention schemes, such as business plan competitions, public venture funds or public sector advisors. If fellows are drawn from within the academic network, they are considered as more credible advisors and potential role models. As a result the information

Figure 1: The proposed impact of commercialisation fellowship schemes.

they disseminate regarding the financial benefits of commercialisation are more likely to be given more credence among academics and result in attitudinal changes. This leads to our first finding.

- Fellowship schemes have a positive impact upon attitudinal barriers to commercialisation of research.

Furthermore, the fellowship scheme was seen to affect the network structure since it increased the number of weak ties to industry actors based within the legal profession and within large and small firms. Medici fellows were seen to create these ties personally and then to transfer them to academic colleagues. Similarly new weak ties were formed with public sector bodies where financial benefits were recognised. These arguments lead to our second finding.

- Fellowship schemes encourage increased interaction between academic and practitioner networks.

It must be acknowledged, however, that the fellows, we studied, tended not to form ties with some types of actors. In particular, fellows rarely formed ties with surrogate entrepreneurs or venture management firms. Equally they infrequently engaged with equity funding sources. Arguably both these sources are required to provide the knowledge and resources required to realise the value of radical new technologies (Lockett, Siegel, & Wright, 2005). Within the Medici fellowship two constraints may explain this deficiency: firstly, the focus of the majority of fellows upon developing nascent research towards the proof of concept stage and secondly, the geographic limitations on the provision of equity funding within the midlands of the U.K.

## Conclusions

In this paper we have examined the impact of the Medici Fellowship scheme on commercialisation behaviour across a number of biomedical departments from different universities. The above findings suggest that such fellowship programmes may have an important role to play in terms of: (i) encouraging fellows to act as intermediaries between the different networks involved in the commercialisation process and (ii) encouraging attitudinal change within biomedical departments.

The findings reported here are based upon the opinions of individuals who have, in the main, been positively affected by the Medici scheme. We feel that it is important, however, to note that the same individuals have also reported participation with a range of other intervention initiatives. There was, however, a remarkable degree of consensus relating to the advantage of the fellowship schemes over other initiatives, in particular in relation to encouraging academics to exploit the IP within their research and engage with industry networks.

Nevertheless it must be noted that within the departments studied barriers remained. Ties remained to be built between academic networks and external actors, such as surrogate entrepreneurs and private equity financiers, necessary for the sustained development of nascent ventures (Lockett et al., 2005). We conclude that such fellowship schemes therefore provide a necessary intervention, but that additional support is required to further improve the technology transfer process.

Moreover, our findings also have implications for the design of technology transfer performance metrics that form the basis for funding allocation decisions by government. In addition to the traditional quantitative metrics such as number of ventures created, we propose a consideration of network related output metrics such as attitudinal change and the development of network ties is required to fully evaluate the impact of fellowship schemes.

Finally the applicability of the findings of this study is limited to the schools investigated. However, due to the efficacy of the scheme upon such a diversity of schools, the implication is that such a scheme would offer similar benefits were it applied to other universities and academic disciplines. This remains to be established through further research.

# References

Alder, P., & Kwon, S. (2002). Social capital: Prospects for a new concept. *Academy of Management Review, 27*, 17–40.

Amit, R., & Zott, C. (2001). Value creation in e business. *Strategic Management Journal, 22*, 493–520.

Audretsch, D. B., & Feldman, M. P. (2003). Small firm strategic research partnerships: The case of biotechnology. *Technology Analysis and Strategic Management, 15*, 273–288.

Baron, R. A. (2005). Social capital. In: M. A. Hitt & R. D. Ireland (Eds), *The Blackwell encyclopedia of management entrepreneurship* (2nd ed., pp. 224–226). Oxford: Blackwell Publishing.

Burt, R. (1992). *Structural holes*. Cambridge, MA: Harvard University Press.

Cooper, A. C., & Yin, X. (2005). Entrepreneurial networks. In: M. A. Hitt & R. D. Ireland (Eds.), *The Blackwell encyclopedia of management Entrepreneurship* (2nd ed., pp. 98–100). Oxford: Blackwell Publishing.

Davidsson, P. (2002). What entrepreneurship research can do for business and policy practice. *International Journal of Entrepreneurship Education, 1*, 5–24.

Delmar, F., & Shane, S. A. (2004). Legitimating first: Organizing activities and the survival of new ventures. *Journal of Business Venturing, 19*, 385–410.

Eisenhardt, K. M. (1989). Building theory from case study research. *Academy of Management Review, 14*(4), 532–550.

Glaser, J., & Strauss, A. (1967). *The discovery of grounded theory*. Chicago: Aldine.

Granovetter, M. S. (1973). The strength of weak ties. *American Journal of Sociology, 78*, 1360–1380.

Hoang, H., & Antoncic, B. (2003). Network based research in entrepreneurship a critical review. *Journal of Business Venturing, 18*, 165–187.

Lambert, R. (2003). *Lambert review of business–university collaboration*. London: HMSO.

Latour, B. (1987). *Science in action: How to follow scientists and engineers in society*. Cambridge, MA: HBS Press.

Lockett, A., Siegel, D., & Wright, M. (2005). University spin-outs. In: M. A. Hitt & R. D. Ireland (Eds.), *The Blackwell encyclopedia of management entrepreneurship* (2nd ed., pp. 241–244). Oxford: Blackwell Publishing.

Miles, M. B., & Huberman, M. A. (1984) *Qualitative data analysis: A sourcebook of new methods*. London: Sage.

Murray, F. (2004). The role of academic inventors in entrepreneurial firms: Sharing the laboratory life. *Research Policy, 33*, 643–659.

Myers, S. C. (1984). The capital structure puzzle. *Journal of Finance, 39,* 575–592.

Oliver, A. (2004). Biotechnology entrepreneurial scientist and their collaborations. *Research Policy, 33,* 583–597.

Powell, W., Koput, K., Bowie, J., & Smith Doerrs, L. (2002). The spatial clustering of science and capital: Accounting for biotech firm-venture capital relationships. *Regional Studies, 36*(3), 291–305.

Schoonhoven, C. B. (2005). Liability of newness. In: M. A. Hitt & R. D. Ireland (Eds), *The Blackwell encyclopedia of management Entrepreneurship* (2nd ed., pp. 171–175). Oxford: Blackwell Publishing.

Seashore Louis, K. Blumenthal, D., Gluck, M. E., & Stoto, M. A. (1989). Entrepreneurs in academe: An exploration of behaviors among life scientists. *Administrative Science Quarterly, 34,* 110–131.

Slaughter, S., & Leslie, L. L. (1997) *Academic capitalism, politics, policies and the Entrepreneurial University.* Baltimore: The Johns Hopkins University Press.

Strauss, A., & Corbin, J. (1990). *Basics of qualitative research: Grounded theory procedures and techniques.* Newbury Park, CA: Sage.

Wright, M., Binks, M., Lockett, A., & Vohora, A. (2003). *Survey on university commercialisation activities, Financial Year* 2002. Nottingham: NUBS.

Wright, M., Birley, S., & Mosey, S. (2004). Entrepreneurship and University Technology Transfer. *Journal of Technology Transfer, 29,* 235–246.

Yin, J. (1993). *Case study research.* London: Sage publications.

Zucker, L. G., Darby, M. R., & Armstrong, J. S. (2002). Commercializing knowledge: University science, knowledge capture, and firm performance in biotechnology. *Management Science, 48*(1), pp. 138–153.

Chapter 7

# An Empirical Assessment of Porter's Clusters Concept Based on London's Media Industries

Gary Cook and Naresh Pandit

## Introduction

Within academic literature, there has been a burgeoning of literature in the field of economic geography which has centred on the nature of local concentrations of economic activity, with particular interest on those which are most dynamic, variously styled as clusters (Porter, 1990; Swann, Prevezer, & Stout, 1998), innovative milieux (Camagni, 1991), industrial districts (Piore & Sable, 1984), new industrial spaces (Scott, 1988) and nodes (Amin & Thrift, 1992). Such intense interest among geographers stands in contrast to the relatively more muted impact within the management, and more specifically, the strategy field (Audretsch, 2000). What makes this particularly odd are firstly, the intense interest of policy makers that has been stimulated by the seminal work of Porter (1990), and secondly the manifest claim and implication of much of the extant literature that the existence of dynamic clusters is at once both a result of corporate strategies and also a vital consideration which should inform strategic thinking. This chapter assesses the extent to which one of the UK's most successful clusters behaves in ways which are consistent with Porter's positive statements about the nature of clusters. In doing so, the chapter will consider insights which the wider literature offers on how and when concentrations of economic activity will give rise to superior performance, at least among some of the firms located there, which do not feature prominently in Porter's thinking. In particular, it will explore Martin and Sunley's (2003) critique of Porter's clusters concept and its utility as a basis for regional development policy. It will also consider recent contributions which claim that the resource-based theory (RBT) of the firm offers a superior framework for thinking about the strategic implications of clusters for corporate strategy, rather than the more industrial organization-based lens through which Porter views this issue. This chapter concludes that a synthesis is warranted rather than an attempt to claim that one view is correct and the other wrong.

New Technology Based Firms in the New Millennium, Volume VI
Edited by A. Groen, R. Oakey, P. van der Sijde and G. Cook

## Literature Review

### Cluster Benefits and Costs

The basic Porter diamond is well known and is briefly rehearsed here in order to provide a theoretical context against which to evaluate the empirical evidence presented later in this paper. Porter's basic framework has remained little altered since it was first articulated (Porter, 1990, 1998a, 1998b, 2000). The fundamental idea of the diamond is that there are four basic sets of conditions which interact in successful clusters, and which are all necessary to sustain world class performance among the firms located therein: firm strategy and rivalry; factor (input) conditions; related and supporting industries and demand conditions. Table 1 lists the specific examples Porter (2000, p. 258) provides of the components of each of these four elemental conditions, which is a useful *aide-memoire* for later discussion.

According to Porter (1998a, 1998b, 2000), there are three main advantages of industrial clustering, to which the above factors in concert contribute:

1. Increased productivity (see also Best, 1990; Henderson, 1986; Piore & Sable, 1984). This arises due to better sourcing of inputs such as labour and suppliers of local goods and services, which includes lower search and transaction costs in recruiting. A specialised supplier base develops and proximity brings additional benefits of lower transport costs, common culture which aids communication and co-ordination, trust, speed, greater responsiveness and can enable firms to carry less stock. Firms may also benefit

Table 1: Elements of the Porter diamond.

| Context for firm strategy and rivalry | Factor (input) conditions | Related and supporting industries | Demand conditions |
|---|---|---|---|
| A local context that encourages appropriate forms of *investment* and *sustained upgrading* | Natural resources Human resources Capital resources Physical infrastructure | Presence of capable, locally based *suppliers* | *Sophisticated and demanding* local customers Unusual local demand in *specialised segments* that can be served globally |
| Vigorous competition among *locally based rivals* | Administrative infrastructure Information infrastructure Scientific and technological infrastructure | Presence of competitive *related industries* | Customer needs that *anticipate* those elsewhere |

from access to specialised information both regarding technology and demand. Moreover, the trust which develops more easily in closer proximity supports a freer flow of such information. Firms within a cluster may benefit from a variety of complementarities, such as symbiotic relationships between different types of leisure facilities in a tourist resort or a common marketing or standards setting agency. Porter places some importance on the benefits of local rivalry in stimulating intense competition, and underpins the point by arguing that firms within the same cluster are likely to compete in similar ways with similar resources and will be able to benchmark more effectively against each other.

2. Improved innovation (see also Audretsch & Feldman, 1996; Jaffe, Trajtenberg, & Henderson, 1993). Some of the same factors that enhance productivity can also enhance the ability to innovate. Supplying demanding customers will help cluster members see the directions in which they should innovate and specialised suppliers and labour may provide such firms with the resources they need to effect innovation. Competitive pressure is a further spur to innovate.

3. Clusters experience a positive feedback loop of dynamic growth as cluster firms grow faster and new entry is easier. Opportunities are easier to spot and necessary resources can be assembled more easily. Moreover, there is a positive externality in so far as the manifest success of the cluster signals that it is a good place to do business. As Porter points out, clusters are not a panacea for new firms and some will fail. Nevertheless, the churn of new entries adds to cluster dynamism.

Porter pays heed to the fact that social institutions can provide the 'glue' that holds clusters together. Transaction costs are lowered as trust and norms of reciprocity develop. Furthermore, these make it easier for firms to form short-term alliances as demand conditions dictate. In short, geographic proximity contributes to a greater flexibility that strategic networks may offer over formal vertical integration, while mitigating the contractual risks of dealing with third parties.

### *Alternative Perspectives on the Strategic Importance of Clusters*

**The Economic Geography Perspective**  Although the economic geography literature is far from a unified body of thought (Markusen, 2003), much of it has been critical of Porter and also of the economic approach of Krugman (1991). Morgan (2004) criticises Porter's view of clusters as being too simplistic and failing to appreciate the differing types of local concentrations, which may or may not involve the dense interaction among firms that Porter implies. Economic geographers have made more progress in developing typologies of different kinds of geographic concentrations of economic activity (McCann & Sheppard, 2003). Markusen (1996), who has proposed one of the most widely applied frameworks, argues that these different types have different implications for the success, variously defined, of the cluster and for its sustainability. Gordon and McCann (2000) propose another compact and useful typology, which has recently been applied to a series of city case studies and comparisons in the UK (Boddy & Parkinson, 2004). These are important frameworks that arguably provide a more robust basis for policy intervention than Porter's more generic concept.

Another general objection to economics-based approaches is that they pay insufficient attention to social institutions, and their local constitution and reproduction which underpin the networks and interactions that are associated with cluster dynamics (Amin & Thrift, 1995; Marchionni, 2004), as exemplified, for example in the *innovative milieu* approach (Camagni, 1991). Economic geographers are generally much more careful in articulating how such institutions arise and reproduce themselves in particular locations at particular times. Boggs and Rantisi (2003) identify some important aspects of the 'relational turn' in economic geography, considerations that exemplify the more sophisticated way in which economic geographers treat social relations between economic agents. The essence here is the focus on relationships between firms and individuals as prime sources of regional capacity to produce, innovate and develop over time. This includes a sophisticated appreciation of structure–agency interactions wholly absent in Porter. Another important aspect of the relational approach is to eschew methodological individualism. Individual agents derive their power to act in part due to their relations with other agents in the social and economic system. Finally, it acknowledges the reality of power in the system of relations, feature given insufficient attention in the Porter framework. Gertler (2003, p. 91), in his careful exposition of the nature of tacit knowledge, argues that effective creation and sharing of tacit knowledge "... depends on institutional proximity — that is, the shared norms, conventions, values, expectations and routines arising from *commonly experienced frameworks of institutions*". Such institutions will be in part locally and in part nationally constituted.

A particularly trenchant critique of Porter has been advanced by Martin and Sunley (2003). While their 'fire' is aimed squarely at Porter, much of what they say is also applicable to some degree to the panoply of work in economic geography (see Markusen's (2003) critique of contemporary economic geography). The issues identified are ones which have generally been more carefully considered by economic geographers, but for which no definitive answers have emerged. Their key criticisms may be summarised as follows:

1.  The cluster concept is sufficiently vague and indeterminate enough to be applicable to a wide range of different industrial groupings. Specifically Porter does not pin down what range of related activities should be included in a cluster, nor how specialized the group of activities should be, nor how strong the linkages between firms have to be.
2.  Porter is vague about the spatial scale at which cluster dynamic operate (Martin, 1999).
3.  Porter advocates that delineation and identification of clusters needs to be based on detailed industry knowledge and judgement of the researcher. Martin and Sunley argue that this is a *carte blanche* for anyone to make it up as they go along.
4.  Porter's cluster concept is so vague, particularly when including potential or embryonic clusters, that any firms could be conceived as belonging to some type of cluster, albeit often a very weak one.
5.  Porter, along with others, ignores the internal structure of the firm and the firm's ability to learn from knowledge flows, which may be available within the cluster.

Martin and Sunley (2003) round their critique off with a trenchant discussion of the shortcomings of the cluster concept as a guide to regional development policy. Firstly, they bemoan the lack of convincing empirical evidence to prove that clustering brings increased economic prosperity. Secondly, they criticise the standard cluster development policies of encouraging network formation, collective marketing (including place marketing), provision of generic services such as financial, marketing and design advice targeted to particular sectors and attracting inward investment to parts of the cluster value chain perceived to be weak. These policies are not necessarily wrong in themselves, but rather their straight-jacketing into a cluster framework.

In a seminal article, Amin and Thrift (1992) argue persuasively that the emphasis on local production complexes is overdone for several reasons. Models that are locally based do not recognise the importance of emerging global corporate networks. Industrial districts and local complexes are often outgrowths of a world economy, which is still rapidly inter-nationalising and is still a world of global corporate power in which many industries increasingly function on an integrated global scale through the medium of global corporate networks. They argue that centres are needed within which the dissemination of dis-courses, collective beliefs, stories about what world production filières are like and to develop, track and test innovations might be generated. Within such centres, emerging entrepreneurs need contacts with numerous knowledgeable people to help spot gaps and find new uses for technologies.

**The Resource-Based Theory of the Firm**  RBT has rapidly become influential in the strategy and international business literatures and is also becoming important within the entrepreneurship field (Barney, 1991, 1996; Schoemaker & Amit, 1994; Shrivastava, Huff, & Dutton, 1994; Wernerfelt, 1984, 1995). In a series of recent articles (Pinch, Henry, Jenkins, & Tallman, 2003; Tallman, Jenkins, Henry, & Pinch, 2004), an important attempt has been made to merge insights from strategic management and economic geography to explain how membership of key clusters can be the foundation for sustained competitive advantage. This group of authors emphasise the challenge, by providing an account of how and why some firms in clusters will outperform others, despite the intensive sharing of knowledge within the cluster. This work is not only rooted in the RBT of the firm, but also claims to provide an underpinning for the insights of Porter on the nature of superior per-formance of clusters and their strategic implications. Nevertheless, Tallman et al. (2004) note that the research stream within which their work is based, emphasises on the impor-tance attached to competition as opposed to the cooperation implied in Porter. While not gainsaying the importance of other types of resource, these authors place particular empha-sis on knowledge-based resources, in tune with the current emphasis on the knowledge-based economy (e.g. Audretsch, 2000; DTI, 1998). In so doing they point out that the RBT is a rich vein of research in the field of strategic management which has been relatively neglected by economic geographers in their quest to understand the durability and supe-rior performance of certain regional agglomerations.

As Tallman et al. (2004) point out, a recent strand of literature has pointed out that competitive advantage typically rests on the particular ways in which tacit and codifiable knowledge are combined. Therefore, although codifiable knowledge may be ubiquitous, it is nevertheless an important ingredient in corporate success. A particularly important type of knowledge Pinch et al. (2003, p. 379) define is architectural knowledge, which relates to understanding of an entire system and the structures and routines used in organ-ising component knowledge for productive uses. Architectural knowledge, they argue, is the most firm-specific form of knowledge and therefore an essential underpinning of sus-tained competitive advantage, not least because architectural knowledge is held to be a crucial determinant of the firm's *absorptive capacity* to assimilate and make use of new knowledge (Cohen & Levinthal, 1989; Zahra & George, 2002). The link with spatial clusters is made by arguing that there exist cluster level architectural knowledge systems. This cluster level knowledge system enables knowledge to be shared among firms in the cluster, an idea which finds echoes in the literature on innovative milieux, albeit expressed in a much different way (Capello, 1999). Similarly, the idea that competencies are dynamic and need to be augmented over time (Bozner, Maloney, & Thomas, 1998; Teece, Pisano, & Shuen, 1997) is cognate with the emphasis in the innovative milieux literature on collective learning.

## Conclusion

Porter's framework is very general and incorporates issues regarding social institutions and local and regional governance structures, which have been examined far more convincingly in the economic geography literature. Its potential strengths relative to the economic geography literature are the much greater emphasis it gives to productive efficiency, the strength and sophistication of local demand and the significance of local rivalry. Its major weaknesses are the lack of insight into how the significance of particular types of positive externality within clusters will differ between industries of different type, a failure to differentiate between different types of cluster and a failure to deal adequately with the issue of processes operating at different spatial scales. In addition, Porter provides little insight as to why there will be marked differences in the success of different firms within particular clusters, an area where the RBT holds some promise. Curiously, there is a lacuna in the literature regarding the ways in which the significance of particular cluster benefits may be contingent on the strategy a firm is pursuing. This is particularly surprising with regard to Porter, famed for his generic strategy work.

## Methodology

The findings reported below are based on a questionnaire survey conducted between January and April 2004. The questionnaire used was subject to extensive pre-testing and was mailed to a stratified random sample of 1500 companies drawn from a bespoke database built-up from the FAME financial database and the Broadcast Production Guide, the leading industry trade directory. The largest 300 firms in the database were 100% sampled, subject to the proviso that the sample was split *pro rata* to the numbers of advertising and broadcasting firms. The reason for this is that advertising firms are larger on average than broadcasting firms, therefore in order not to have a disproportionate number of advertising firms in the final sample; their number within the sample of the largest 300 firms was capped. At the opposite end of the spectrum there was under-sampling of freelance operators, since clearly a number of questions on the questionnaire were not relevant to them. Nevertheless it was felt important to include at least some freelance operators since they make up a very important constituency of the industry.

In all 204 usable questionnaires were returned, an apparent response rate of 13.6%. Around 50 nil-responses were received which shed some light on the genuine response rate. The majority of these nil-responses related to either firms that had gone out of business, an important feature of the industry which has a high churn of firms, and firms which had been incorrectly classified as belonging to the broadcasting industry in the FAME database. These latter firms remained in the sample despite a lengthy effort to clean up the database. Taking these factors into account the response rate among live firms in broadcasting and advertising was closer to 16%.

The overall importance of the range of factors asked about in the questionnaire was measured in two ways. The first was the total score received by a factor which adds up all the individual ratings it receives, from a low of 0 indicating the factor was not relevant to 5 indicating it was highly important. The minimum score any factor could receive was 0, where all respondents indicated it was not at all relevant, to 1020 (204 respondents each giving a rating of 5, highly important). On this criterion, the scores for the 67 factors asked about ranged from a high of 777 for the importance of being located close to other firms in London due to the ability it offered to have face-to-face contact with other people, to a low of 256 for the importance of support from local government as being a general benefit of being located in London. The mean score was 562.

The authors' previous econometric work concluded that the main positive spillovers within the cluster emanate from the broadcast programme production and post-production (e.g. editing, sound, special effects) sectors. Collocation within these sectors fosters both faster growth of firms within those particular lines of activity and also encourages entry from a wide range of broadcasting and broadcast-related firms. These facts are important to bear in mind when considering the results that follow.

# Results

## *Demand Conditions*

Figure 1 gives an impression of which sectors are most closely inter-related, based on evidence from the questionnaire survey. The figure was constructed by first, classifying each firm to a sector on the basis of what it classed as its most important line of activity. The next step was to examine which sectors those firms stated was the most important with which it had inter-relationships. The arrowheads show the direction of the relationship with the arrowhead entering the sector rated as most important. The thickness of the lines gives a crude indication of the percentage of each sector's number one rankings being accorded to each sector as per the key provided. It is essential to bear in mind that the diagram conveys no information about the number of rankings, for example there were only seven valid rankings made by the broadcasters.

A number of features stand out. Firstly, the broadcasters appear to be at the hub of the cluster, which was to be expected. It is also intuitively correct that broadcast production should value being close to broadcasters, who are their clients. In this respect, it is important to note that other broadcast activities include a number of freelance production managers and directors. Advertisers also emerge as being an important part of the

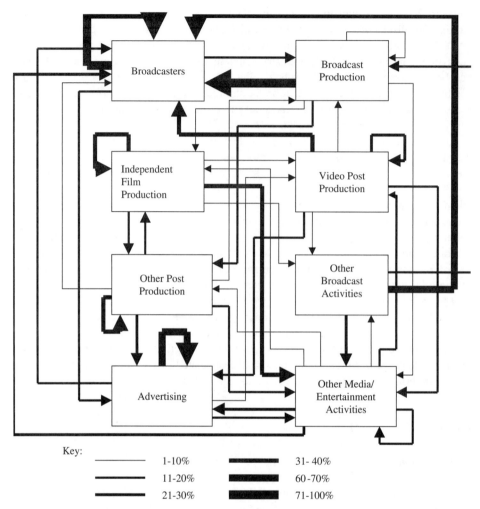

Figure 1: Importance of collocation among sectors.

cluster, unsurprising given that they are high-budget clients of broadcasters and parts of the post-production community. Post production itself emerges as being quite central to the cluster, providing essential services to all forms of production, some of whom are subsumed in the other media category (corporate and commercials production). Figure 1 provides some indirect evidence of the importance of demand. Both broadcasters and advertisers are important sources of demand for media services. Also, and particularly, so in the case of advertisers, they are sources of sophisticated demand, demanding both high quality and innovative work. This provides an important dynamic impulse to the London cluster.

The importance of proximity to customers, a factor by which Porter sets great store and being easily located by customers varies by line of activity. The ability to be found by customers external to London and subsequently to interact with them is seen to be of moderate importance overall. Nevertheless it is of high importance to particular firms. As with many other factors, it is firms in W1 and in post-production, and especially post-production firms in W1 who particularly rate this as being a particular advantage. There is more work commissioned from outside London going to London-based post-production houses. London is an important centre for international demand for high quality post-production work in both film and advertising and this finding is consistent with sophisticated demand being an important influence on cluster strength. This demand for very high quality and innovative work keeps London at the 'cutting edge' of the industry and also brings the revenues that support continuous innovation and capital investment. These advantages, initially garnered by the leading firms, eventually diffuse more widely through the cluster.

Regarding the importance of a 'credible address', there is a sharp differentiation among firms, some of whom see it is as highly important while others do not. At first glance having the right address may seem an almost frivolous reason for choosing a given location. Insights from the economics of information, however, provide important support for such significance. This factor is above all important to firms located in Soho, an area where firms also have to pay very high rents. Production and post-production are both highly creative activities, notwithstanding the fact that there are elements of 'commodity' production in both sectors. They are also activities where a lot of money and reputation is often at stake, and where outcomes are seen as being inherently unpredictable in terms of ultimate success. Just as a Harley Street address would be taken by many as a reliable signal of the quality of the physicians who operate from there, so a Soho address is an important signal of the quality of the firms who locate there.

### The Importance of Factor (Input) Conditions

A pool of talented labour with relevant skills stands as the pre-eminent *local* factor helping firms innovate. This is the third highest ranked factor across the whole questionnaire and is significantly more important to large firms. The formation of a dense labour pool is a classic advantage of a cluster or industrial district, although in the traditional Marshall's (1920, 1927) conception this is seen as being a source of static efficiency in production as opposed to a dynamic advantage in terms of superior innovation. Nevertheless, the density of the labour pool and the cluster more generally, may support innovation in a range of ways. As Adam Smith so astutely observed, the division of labour is limited by the extent of the market, and the finer the division of labour the greater will be the gains in terms of both static production efficiencies and innovation. Smith observed that more highly specialised labour would pursue improvements in products and processes in their area of specialisation, which would escape the interest and attention of a 'jack of all trades'. A dense labour pool also supports more rapid labour turnover, which helps disseminate and cross-fertilise ideas. Thirdly, a denser labour market will act as a magnet to the most talented labour to migrate to the cluster.

Labour market flexibility was generally viewed as being a source of advantage in a variety of ways. The most important advantage was seen as the ability to recruit good people at short notice, which stood apart from the other advantages of a flexible labour market. This is clearly important in media businesses that have a predominantly project-based mode of operation. Much importance is also given to the fact that a fluid labour market is important in attracting good staff. There are several dimensions to this factor. Most people in the industry understand the short-run nature of many employment engagements; therefore it is important that there are many opportunities to gain employment to provide a reasonable chance of securing continuity of employment, albeit with a variety of different firms. This is also important because it gives individuals the incentive to acquire highly specialised skills, which might be required only occasionally by any individual firm, but the general demand for which across firms in the cluster may be reasonably strong and consistent. This fine-grained division of labour has several benefits. Firstly, it multiplies the range of possibilities for production in London. Related to this, secondly, it is a source of advantage to the London cluster, since it can provide specialised services which are not available elsewhere in the UK and possibly at very few locations globally. Thirdly, it contributes to innovation as has already been explained. Finally, it is likely to lead to higher levels of skills within particular occupations or crafts within the industry. It is important to underscore that the attraction of London to those who seek a career in the industry is a highly important dynamic source of enduring cluster advantage. London is the best place to work for many individuals because of the possibility of doing the most interesting work and to secure the attendant financial and professional rewards (i.e. professional status). Therefore, the best talent tends to be drawn to London that has the opportunities and the incentives to attract and develop high levels of skill. This reinforces the pre-eminent standing of the cluster and so the 'magnet' exerts a more powerful attraction. The benefits of London's ability to draw in good staff are particularly seen in companies located in W1, and in post-production and independent broadcast production companies.

The fluidity of the labour market is also often mentioned as a source of advantage because it helps to spread a network of contacts. Again this factor tends to be more highly rated by broadcast production firms and post-production firms in W1, although the relationship is generally just outside conventional levels of statistical significance. Why is a network of contacts important? In some cases it can be a useful source of advice. For example a production company shooting at a particular location overseas will benefit if it can have a chat with someone who has already worked in that country for advice on what contingencies to plan for, and how to smooth the path by eliciting the names of good local contacts. Good contacts can also facilitate other forms of cooperation which are beneficial to the cluster, such as the sharing of personnel, and sometimes, sharing of equipment.

**Local Institutions**   A range of other factor inputs emerge as being of far less importance. For all that the importance of local institutions is vaunted as being important, particularly in respect of innovation, the evidence from this meagre study offers support to such a claim. The higher rating accorded to trade associations in supporting innovation in broadcasting compared to a parallel study of financial services may reflect, in part, the traditional importance of the Royal Television Society as an engineering forum and the Moving

Image Society which has also had a traditional role in supporting technological innovation. Local government and academic institutions hardly feature.

### Firms in Related Industries

Local customers and suppliers are noted to be important sources of help with innovation by Porter (1990) and many other writers (e.g. von Hippel, 1988). Customers may demand innovation, a spur for both broadcast production and post-production companies competing for business against strong rivals. Moreover, customers may themselves be important innovators who are able to guide their suppliers to innovative solutions. Post-production companies in Soho have produced a stream of innovations in hardware and software over recent years, sometimes alone and sometimes in collaboration with equipment and software suppliers. Another commonly held belief regarding innovation is that, typically, it requires many strands to be drawn together, and the ability to find suppliers of required, sometimes novel, inputs is an advantage of leading clusters.

The importance of being close to firms with complementary expertise and the ability to draw together multidisciplinary teams quickly did not emerge as being particularly important, despite the highly flexibly-specialised nature of the production systems in broadcasting and independent film making. Nevertheless, Figure 1 does indicate that co-location with the post-production sector, which services the broadcasting, film and advertising industries, is generally held to be important.

### The Importance of Local Rivalry

The importance of competitive rivalry within a cluster has been emphasised most strongly by Porter (1990), although many other writers (e.g. Jacobs, 1972; Malmberg & Maskell, 2002; Saxenian, 1994) have pointed the importance of competition allied to cooperation. Among these factors, relatively more importance is given to London being the best location for taking market share from rivals. This factor is significantly more likely to be stressed by post-production companies in W1, which fits in with their perception that having the right address is important to being perceived as credible. This factor resonates with the importance attached to being close to market leading customers. However, the benefit of being near market leading competitors is not rated as being particularly important, although the reasons why this should be true are unclear. Being near leading competitors is significantly more likely to be rated important by post-production companies and companies located in W1 (indeed these two categories overlap substantially). The competitive spur of rivalry and the ability to benchmark against rivals are given somewhat lesser importance among this group and fall well below the mean score for all factors. Again both these factors are significantly more likely to be rated important by post-production companies and companies in W1 and central London locations around W1. The relative importance to post production stems from the fact that they are much more often in direct competition for particular projects. Competition is seldom direct between production companies, who only rarely become involved in competitive tenders. Their primary focus is on convincing commissioning editors they have an idea for a commercially successful programme, and this is not generally perceived as being in competition with specific rivals.

Rivalry among post-production firms in particular is a stimulus to innovation in the way Porter suggests. It is also important to note that there is a highly competitive fringe of small firms and freelance operators servicing the core firms in the media industries, again consistent with Porter's framework.

### The Importance of Face-to-Face Contact and Personal Relationships

Face-to-face contact is significantly more highly rated than maintaining personal contacts and emerges as the pre-eminent factor. Maintaining personal contacts in turn is significantly more highly rated than building relationships of trust. Why should these two things be so important? In large part it is due to the fact that what is being communicated is, most importantly, an image and sound that will convey meaning. These are cultural artefacts whose most important qualities are the extent to which they convey meaning, emotion and information. This makes it of paramount importance that those who are engaged in their production understand the meaning, which is to be conveyed. In order to come to that understanding, communication with the maximum 'bandwidth' is required, that is face-to-face contact. It is no accident that producers and editors in broadcast, film and advertising media often work hand in glove as the final product is fashioned during post-production. Here there can be long and intense days where, by a process of verbal and non-verbal communication, the desired end result is fashioned. This behaviour also sheds light on why building and maintaining personal contacts is so important. In respect of efficient production it allows convergence on the desired look, sound and feel to be achieved more quickly. It is also important for allowing a frank exchange of views to take place without lasting offence or a breakdown in relations occurring. In terms of effective production it is more likely that the end product will be as conceived.

A network of personal contacts smoothes the path of creative production in a variety of ways. It allows teams to be assembled quickly in order to carry out what, by most industry standards, is a short-term project with the assurance that those engaged will be able to understand and produce what is required. Where direct personal contacts cannot fill all the required places in the production team, then often producers and directors will have trusted personal contacts to whom they can go for a recommendation, be it for someone to work on sound, camera or some other function. Personal contacts are also important in getting the job done by the ability to quickly negotiate concessions on a 'give-and-take' basis. A common scenario which was often repeated during the course of the interviews was where, for example, an independent production company would be 'strapped for cash' to fund post-production work, and would be able to arrange for a 'special fee' from a post-production company with the promise that on some future occasion the favour would be returned by paying a little over the odds. Such behaviour is underpinned by trust, a system for establishing and maintaining reputations and norms of reciprocity. These relationships are all easier to create and reproduce in a more compact geographic space.

The advantage of physical proximity in promoting trust and cooperation with other companies was highly rated. Trust is very important within the production system in broadcasting, film and advertising due the tight time and money constraints, which attend most projects. What adds to the importance of trust is the inherent uncertainty surrounding the quality of the ultimate output. The quality of a television programme or advertisement is not something that can be controlled in the same way a more physical process. There is no precise formula for arriving at a successful product. To reduce this uncertainty, people tend to work with those whom they can trust in order to 'get it right', both in terms of doing what they say, will do and doing it when they are expected to. There is no high degree of differentiation among firms as to whom trust is especially important. It does tend to be emphasised more by firms in W1 or close to W1, with the possible exception of film, commercial and corporate production companies outside the centre. This makes sense given the very close juxtaposition of firms in W1, which allows denser interaction to take place. Much the same can be said of personal contacts, the importance of which is claimed more frequently by firms in W1, particularly post-production firms.

The importance of coming to a common understanding of what the ultimate product should be also helps explain why proximity is seen to have a strong advantage in terms of making communication easier, because firms and individuals in London have a common understanding of the business. A strong theme in the important literature of *innovative milieux* is that one of the keys to superior innovation in regional innovation systems is the ability for firms, who may do quite different things, to share ideas through the ability to talk a common, or at least common enough, language. What goes for innovation also goes for production. The production system in broadcasting, film and advertising, notwithstanding the existence of some large firms who can and do most things (even all things) in house, is generally fragmented down the value chain and for efficient and effective production it is important that firms performing different functions are able to contribute to the whole. This requires a common language and a common understanding. The biggest premium on this again seems to be placed by post-production companies in W1.

**Where and How is Information Exchanged?**   The two most highly rated factors in this 'where' and 'how' context were firstly, mixing with industry colleagues in social settings and secondly, with virtually the same score, contact by telephone or e-mail for short-term problem solving. These two methods were followed by contact by telephone for specific information. It may appear at first glance that the importance of contact by telephone and e-mail undermines the argument that physical proximity is necessary or particularly beneficial. What gives the lie to this is the supreme importance of face-to-face contact indicated elsewhere in the questionnaire. The point is that people are more likely to telephone or e-mail someone with whom they have a direct personal relationship.

The importance of meeting in social settings and of the benefits of hearing things of interest were significantly more likely to be rated as important by firms located in central London, particularly W1 (see Table 2). This makes sense given the high density of broadcast, film and advertising companies in and around this location, and in addition the plethora of bars, restaurants, pubs and clubs where people can meet both inside and outside the hours of work.

Comparing post-production and production firms, post-production companies were roughly twice as likely to mention informal meetings in pubs as production companies. Although the average number of mentions is low, production companies are significantly more likely to mention meetings in clubs than post-production companies (roughly four times as likely). One plausible reason for this difference is that contact with commissioning editors

Table 2: Where does informal interaction take place?

| Venue | Number of times rated in top three |
|---|---|
| By telephone | 86 |
| By e-mail | 82 |
| Within the firm | 58 |
| Wine bars/pubs | 56 |
| Restaurants | 56 |
| Seminars/conferences | 49 |
| Professional bodies | 40 |
| In the street | 26 |
| In clubs | 11 |
| At sport clubs or events | 1 |

and other key broadcasting personnel in important clubs such as the Soho club and the Groucho club is far more important to production than to post-production companies. Firms in W1 and central London were significantly more likely to cite meetings in the street among their three most important types of informal interaction (over seven times more likely to cite if in W1 and four times more likely to cite if in central London compared to firms outside these areas.) Firms in W1 and central London were also significantly more likely to cite meetings in restaurants, wine bars and pubs than firms outside such areas. On the other hand, firms outside central London were significantly more likely to cite interaction via telephone, e-mail and professional bodies. Thus the general pattern is that the closer firms are to Soho, the more likely it is they will find exchanges with colleagues at informal social settings or simply meeting by chance in the street to be beneficial. By contrast, firms further away from Soho tend to rely on more remote and formal channels of interaction.

### *The Influence of Strategic Posture on Perceived Benefits of Location in the London Cluster*

Firms were asked to rate the importance of competition over a range of dimensions: cost/price; product differentiation; service differentiation; innovation and ability to serve customers across borders. An analysis was undertaken to explore whether the relative importance of each of these competitive dimensions was associated with the perceived importance of different types of cluster benefit.

Firms who rated competition on cost and price highly were significantly more likely to see benchmarking against competitors and having the best location to take market share from rivals as being highly important. Although they were not significantly more likely to see location next to leading competitors as being an important advantage of location, they were the only group to be very close to statistical significance in this regard. This resonates with Porter's (1998a, 1998b) emphasis on the importance of local rivalry as being a benefit of location in a dense cluster. They also placed most emphasis on the 'softer' benefits of being physically close to other firms such as the ability to establish relationships of trust, ease of communication, being able to maintain a network of personal contacts and the ability to meet face-to-face. It is well known from a variety of other industry studies, most especially those of new industrial districts in the 'Third Italy', that these factors support productive efficiency by making it easier to form and maintain working linkages with customers and suppliers in networks of 'flexibly specialised' firms (Piore & Sabel, 1984).

Those firms giving the highest importance to product differentiation emerge as showing the least amount of differentiation on cluster benefits and disadvantages, relative to other strategic dimensions. This group is the only one which is significantly more likely to rate support from local government as being an important benefit, reflecting the disproportionate number of independent film companies in their number. They are also the only group significantly more likely to view the support of industry associations as being highly important to their innovation efforts, as well as customers and a talented labour pool, which are also stressed by firms rating service differentiation and innovation as being particularly important. In general this group placed large emphasis on the benefits of being able to access a deep, talented and mobile labour pool.

Firms giving a high rating to service differentiation and those giving a high rating to innovation showed a highly similar pattern of responses. This group, along with those emphasising the ability to serve customers across borders, were the only ones to rate as important or very important both the ability to be located near to customers external to London and to interact with them. They were also highly significantly more likely to rate their location as being an important or highly important benefit in terms of developing new services. They rated all the 'soft' benefits of their location — the ability to establish relationships of trust, having complementary expertise with other firms, ease of communication, being able to maintain a network of personal contacts, being able to assemble multidisciplinary teams quickly and the ability to meet face-to-face — as being important or very important benefits. These groups see all the potential advantages of a flexible labour market as being important benefits of their location — the fact that a fluid labour market attracts good staff, ease of recruiting labour with appropriate skills at short notice and the ability to quickly tailor staffing levels to the volume of work, and the fact that labour market mobility both helps spread good practice and creates a network of personal contacts.

Those firms which gave the highest rating to the ability to serve customers across borders found the widest range of other factors (46 out of 62) to be important. They were the only group, to rate proximity to professional bodies as being important. They were also the only group significantly more likely to rate international transport links as being an important threat to the future success of the London cluster. This is a very important detriment in the principle of a globally networked industry where some companies have forged new overseas markets by dint of considerable effort. Heavy emphasis is placed on the ability to forge good links, based on trust, ease of communication and complementary expertise, with other local firms and exchange information in a variety of settings.

## Conclusions

The broadest thrust of the evidence presented here is that there are indeed many sources of advantage to firms located in their respective industry clusters in London. None of the individual broad-brush findings really contradicts what is felt to be known either in the strategy or the economic geography literatures. Above all, access to a strong, skilled labour supply and the ability to engage in high 'bandwidth' communication and build and maintain relationships of trust and cooperation are of paramount importance. Despite these obvious conclusions, the evidence does raise some question marks about the adequacy of existing frameworks, and taken together with the literature review, suggests that a formidable research agenda confronts scholars in this field. One aspect in particular is the general tendency in the literature to place heavy emphasis on innovation. The evidence here is that clusters have important benefits for efficient production, including factors such as trust and information exchange, which have been especially strongly associated with innovation by many writers.

Porter's framework, the workhorse of the strategy literature and policy-makers around the globe, stands up well, as might be expected given its empirical antecedents and its generality. The importance of information and knowledge and labour inputs, the role of leading customers and high quality specialised suppliers are all attested to, as are the importance of trust and easy communication. The evidence does cast some doubt on the importance of rivalry as opposed to cooperation within the cluster. There are just a few hints that process at a range of spatial scales matter; more would probably have been discovered if the questionnaire had been directed at them. There is clear evidence that the identity and nature of particular firms, including their strategic posture, matter to a greater extent than the emphasis given to them in the Porter framework. This is also true of the importance of industry-specific influences on the perceived importance of particular cluster benefits.

What of the other frameworks identified in the literature review? The importance of intensive interpersonal interaction and high bandwidth communication is entirely consistent with both the work of Amin and Thrift (1992) (and much other work in economic geography) and also the newer literature linking cluster benefits with RBT. Both are consistent with Porter's framework, but they appear to provide a welcome emphasis on these softer issues, as well as a firmer theoretical rationale as to their importance. It is also noteworthy that firms emphasising competition across borders identify the broadest range of advantage from location in the cluster. This may well relate to the ongoing search for any kind of advantage in a world of remorseless global competition. More speculatively, it may hint at the fact that such firms have greater 'absorptive capacity' to extract benefits that less experienced and less sophisticated firms cannot. Finally, Amin and Thrift's emphasis on physical propinquity seems borne out by the higher salience of cluster advantages to broadcasting firms located in Soho, the geographic heart of the cluster. The importance of such interaction in terms of global strategy formulation is given much clearer articulation in this strand of literature than in Porter (see also Castells, 2000). The emphasis given on local and regional governance and 'institutional thickness' receives very little support in the evidence reported here.

The various strands of literature briefly considered here each provide important insights into the phenomenon of geographically concentrated production and there would appear to be scope for a fruitful synthesis. None seems to reflect adequately the 'microclimate' within the cluster, with precise location and line of activity being more important than any extant literature suggests. For policymakers, the implication is that clusters need to be taken seriously. They are highly complex systems and in a profound sense idiosyncratic, therefore 'off-the-peg' policy prescriptions are not warranted. What underscores this conclusion is that the benefits of cluster membership depend on who the firm is, what they do, where exactly they are located and what strategy they are pursuing.

# Acknowledgement

The authors acknowledge the support of the British Academy grant number SG-36816.

# References

Amin, A., & Thrift, N. (1992). Neo-Marshallian nodes in global networks. *International Journal of Urban and Regional Research, 16*, 571–587.

Amin, A., & Thrift, N. (1995). Globalization, institutional 'thickness' and the local economy. In: P. Healey, S. Cameron, S. Davoudi, S. Graham & A. Madanipour (Eds), *Managing cities: The new urban context*. Chichester: Wiley.

Audretsch, D. B. (2000). Corporate form and spatial form. In: G. L. Clark, M. P. Feldman & M. S. Gertler (Eds), *The Oxford handbook of economic geography* (pp. 333–347).

Audretsch, D. B., & Feldman, M. P. (1996). R&D spillovers and the geography of innovation. *American Economic Review, 86*, 630–640.

Barney, J. B. (1991). Firm resources and sustained competitive advantage. *Journal of Management, 17*, 99–120.

Barney, J. B. (1996). The resource-based theory of the firm. *Organizational Science, 7*, 469.

Best, M. (1990). *The new competition*. Cambridge, MA: Harvard University Press.

Boddy, M., & Parkinson, M. (Eds), (2004). *City matters competitiveness, cohesion and urban governance*. Bristol: The Policy Press.

Boggs, J. S., & Rantisi, N. M. (2003). The 'relational turn' in economic geography. *Journal of Economic Geography, 3*, 109–116.

Bozner, W. C., Maloney, J. T., & Thomas, H. (1998). Paradigm shift: The parallel origins, evolution and function of strategic group analysis within the resource-based theory of the firm. In: J. A. C. Baum (Ed.), *Advances in Strategic Management, 15*, 63–102.

Camagni, R. (1991). Local 'milieu', uncertainty and innovation networks: Towards a new dynamic theory of economic space. In: Camagni, R. (Ed.), *Innovation networks: Spatial perspective* (pp. 121–142). London: Belhaven.

Capello, R. (1999). Spatial transfer of knowledge in high technology milieux: Learning versus collective learning processes. *Regional Studies, 33*, 353–365.

Castells, M. (2000). *The rise of the network society* (2nd ed.). Oxford: Blackwell.

Cohen, W. M., & Levinthal, D. A. (1989). Innovation and learning: The two faces of R&D. *The Economic Journal, 99*, 569–596.

DTI. (1998). *Our competitive future: Building the knowledge driven economy*. (Cmnd. 4176.) London: HMSO.

Gertler, M. S. (2003). Tacit knowledge and the economic geography of context, or the undefinable tacitness of being (there). *Journal of Economic Geography, 3*, 75–99.

Gordon, I. R., & McCann, P. (2000). Industrial clusters, complexes, agglomeration and/or social networks? *Urban Studies, 37*, 513–532.

Henderson, J. V. (1986). Efficiency of resource usage and city size. *Journal of Urban Economics, 19*, 47–70.

Jacobs, J. (1972). *The economy of cities*. Harmondsworth: Penguin.

Jaffe, A. B., Trajtenberg, M., & Henderson, R. (1993). Geographic localisation of knowledge spillovers as evidenced by patent citations. *Quarterly Journal of Economics, 108*, 577–598.

Krugman, P. (1991). *Geography and trade*. Cambridge, MA: MIT Press.

Malmberg, A., & Maskell, P. (2002). The elusive concept of localisation economies: Towards a knowledge-based theory of spatial clustering. *Environment and Planning A, 34*, 429–449.

Marchionni, C. (2004). Geographical economics versus economic geography: Towards a clarification of the dispute. *Environment and Planning A, 36*, 1737–1753.

Markusen, A. (1996). Sticky places in slippery space: A typology of industrial districts. *Economic Geography, 72*, 293–313.

Markusen, A. (2003). Fuzzy concepts, scanty evidence, policy distance: The case for rigour and policy relevance in critical regional studies. *Regional Studies, 37*, 701–717.

Marshall, A. (1920). *Principles of economics.* London: Macmillan.

Marshall, A. (1927). *Industry and trade.* London: Macmillan.

Martin, R. (1999). The new 'geographical turn' in economics: Some critical reflections. *Cambridge Journal of Economics, 23*, 65–91.

Martin, R., & Sunley, P. (2003). Deconstructing clusters: Chaotic concept or policy panacea? *Journal of Economic Geography, 3*, 5–35.

McCann, P., & Sheppard, S. (2003). The rise, fall and rise again of industrial location theory. *Regional Studies, 37*, 649–663.

Morgan, K. (2004). The exaggerated death of geography: Learning, proximity and territorial innovation systems. *Journal of Economic Geography, 4*, 3–21.

Pinch, S., Henry, N., Jenkins, M., & Tallman, S. (2003). From 'industrial districts' to 'knowledge clusters': A model of knowledge dissemination and competitive advantage in industrial agglomerations. *Journal of Economic Geography, 3*, 373–388.

Piore, M., & Sabel, C. (1984). *The second industrial divide: Possibilities for prosperity.* New York: Basic Books.

Porter, M. E. (1998a). Clusters and the new economics of competition. *Harvard Business Review,* 77–90.

Porter, M. E. (1998b). *On competition.* Boston, MA: HBS Press.

Porter, M. E. (1990). *The competitive advantage of nations.* London: Macmillan.

Porter, M. E. (2000). Locations, clusters and company strategy. In: Clark et al., *The Oxford handbook of economic geography* (pp. 253–274) (op. cit.).

Saxenian, A. (1994). *Regional advantage: Culture and competition in silicon valley and Route 128.* Massachusetts: Harvard University Press.

Schoemaker, P. J. H., & Amit, R. (1994). Investment in strategic assets: Industry- and firm-level perspectives. In: P. Shrivastava et al. (pp. 3–33) (op. cit.).

Scott, A. (1988). *New industrial spaces: Flexible production, organization and regional development in North America and Western Europe.* London: Pion.

Shrivastava, P., Huff, A., & Dutton, J. (1994). *Advances in strategic management* (Vol. 10). Greenwich, CT: JAI Press, Inc.

Swann G. M. P., Prevezer M. & Stout, D. (Eds), (1998). *The dynamics of industrial clustering: International comparisons in computing and biotechnology.* Oxford: Oxford University Press.

Tallman, S., Jenkins, M, Henry, N., & Pinch, S. (2004). Knowledge, clusters and competitive advantage. *Academy of Management Review, 29*, 258–271.

Teece, D. J., Pisano, G., & Shuen, A. (1997). Dynamic capabilities and strategic management. *Strategic Management Journal, 18*, 509–533.

von Hippel, E. (1988). *The sources of innovation.* Oxford: Oxford University Press.

Wernerfelt, B. (1984). A resource-based view of the firm. *Strategic Management Journal, 5,* 171–180.

Wernerfelt, B. (1995). The resource-based view of the firm: Ten years after. *Strategic Management Journal, 16*, 171–174.

Zahra, S. A., & George, G. (2002). Absorptive capacity: A review, reconceptualisation and extension. *Academy of Management Review, 27*, 185–203.

Chapter 8

# Network Differences between Domestic and Global University Start-Ups

Peter van der Sijde, Ariane von_Raesfeld Meijer, Kjell de Ruijter and Paul Kirwan

## Introduction

Over many years people have tried to understand the entrepreneurial process (e.g., Hayek, 1945; Kirzner, 1973; Shane & Venkataraman, 2000; Schumpeter, 1934). Van der Veen and Wakkee (2004) reviewed the literature and introduced the role of the entrepreneur and the environment in this process. An environment can have two roles: as a stimulus for opportunity (Burt, 1992; Gaglio, 1997; Shane, 2000; Vesper, 1989), and as a resource for pursuing that opportunity (Brush, Greene, & Hart, 2001). The view emerging from the research by Shane and Venkataraman (2000) and Van der Veen and Wakkee (2004), is that the entrepreneurial process is not merely a series of decisions, but more a sequence of events the entrepreneur goes through as a result of the environment and previous actions taken.

Although entrepreneurs may start from comparable situations, the companies that are eventually established may come in many different shapes and sizes. In this research, we explore networks at the earliest stages of global (high-tech) start-up companies and compare them to the networks of domestic (high-tech) start-up companies. These global start-up companies are companies which from inception seek to recognize and exploit opportunities by combining resources from and selling outputs in multiple regions around the world (Kirwan, Van der Sijde, & Groen, 2006; Oviatt & McDougall, 1994; Wakkee, Kirwan, & van der Sijde, 2004). Oviatt and McDougall (1994) made a distinction between the different degrees of international entrepreneurship, based on the number of value chain activities undertaken abroad and the number of countries involved. Only companies with many activities undertaken abroad, as well as a significant number of countries involved, qualify as being a truly global start-up.

The term *global start-up* is not used by many authors; most prefer to use the terminology *born global*, defined by Knight (1997). A combination of these has been the contribution of

New Technology Based Firms in the New Millennium, Volume VI
Edited by A. Groen, R. Oakey, P. van der Sijde and G. Cook

Knudsen and Madsen (2002), who have applied the framework of Oviatt and McDougall (1994), but limited the activities considered. Instead of considering the entire value chain, Knudsen and Madsen (2002) focused on only the sales and sourcing activities.

Oviatt and McDougall (1994) stated that the International New Venture relied on alternative means to secure its resources. In order to explore this, the environment of companies in terms of the network surrounding the entrepreneur has been chosen. Hite and Hesterly (2001) and Elfring and Hulsink (2003) have explored the use of networks in start-up firms, the latter aiming their research at the high-tech businesses. Both concluded that, in different situations a different configuration of the actors and ties in the networks are present.

In this study, the network configurations of global high-tech start-up companies and domestic high-tech companies are compared. The Entrepreneurship in Networks (EiN) model (Groen, 1994, 2005; Groen, de Weerd-Nederhof, van Drongelen-Kerssens, Badoux, & Olthuis, 2002; Kirwan, Van der Sijde, & Groen, 2006) will be used to explore this issue. In this model, the entrepreneurial process (opportunity recognition, opportunity exploitation, and value creation) is influenced by four different "capitals": the social, cultural, economic, and strategic capitals. These capitals are drawn from four different mechanisms, respectively: (1) interaction between actors as *social* capital; (2) maintaining patterns of culturally shared symbols which can be found in organizations' values, knowledge, skills, experience, and technology, the *cultural* or human capital; (3) optimization of processes, having an efficient organization of entrepreneurial processes with money as the basic resource for the *economic* capital; and (4) striving for goal attainment as *strategic* capital. In this contribution the emphasis is on analyzing network configurations, thus focusing on the social capital dimension. However, the four capital model is also used to indicate the type of capitals or resources acquired by the firms investigated.

In order to explore the differences in network configurations of global versus domestic high-tech start-up companies, we start with looking at similarities in partner characteristics. Madsen, Neergaard, Fisker, and Ulhøi (2004) distinguished three different roles that can be played by actors (actor-roles): the roles of buyer, supplier and advisor. Further, they stated that for every company these roles are identical, though the actual organization of these may vary from one company to the next. This leads us to believe that:

*Hypothesis 1:* *When looking at the type of relationships, there is no difference between a global start-up and a domestic high-tech start-up with regard to the roles of the actors present.*

Not only should the actors be considered but also their contributions. Elfring and Hulsink (2003) considered three different benefits to be gained from a network and its actors; opportunity, resources, and legitimacy. The first two are directly related to the findings of Wakkee (2004). She stated that for starting global, the sources and the opportunity should be global. This leads to an additional proposition.

*Hypothesis 2:* *Global start-ups have more global actors in their network.*

Groen (2005) argues that for companies to be successful, all four capitals need to be fulfilled. This applies to any type of company, both global as well as domestic. The starting company will have to secure the required capitals through its network and the partners already present. We argue that, this would apply to all the capitals (Groen, 2005) and that either directly or indirectly, all capitals can be acquired.

*Hypothesis 3:  When looking at the providers of capital, there is no difference between global start-ups and domestic start-ups with regard to the four capital providers present.*

Apart from the actor characteristics, the network configuration can also be described by the ties between the focal firm and its counterparts (Burt, 1992; Granovetter, 1992). Shane (2000) indicated that companies' prior experience will influence the type of entrepreneurial choices made. A similar argument is made for global start-ups (Oviatt & McDougall, 1994; Zahra, Korri, & Yu, 2005). Such entrepreneurial capabilities are a combination of proprietary resources, knowledge, and skills held by the entrepreneurs, their companies and actor ties in their network. As we expect that global start-ups will have less proprietary resources, which could be used in the global setting, we expect that:

*Hypothesis 4:  Global start-ups will acquire more resources/capitals from external sources compared to domestic start-ups who acquire their resources more from internal sources.*

# Method

## Selection of Cases

The selection of the cases has been made on several criteria:

- A clear link with a university.
- The companies should be relatively young.
- Active in technology based industries.

Further, global start-up companies are considered to be those that from inception seek to recognize and exploit opportunities by combining resources from and selling outputs in multiple regions around the world (Oviatt & McDougall, 1994). The domestic start-ups are to be considered was companies that do not fulfill the above definition. The final selection of the cases was made by the manager of the University of Twente spin-off program.

Effectively, all but D5 were companies that participated in the University of Twente spin-off support program, TOP (Van der Sijde, Karnebeek, & Van Benthem, 2002). But nonetheless, the backgrounds of the entrepreneurs vary from case to case (see also Table 1). Eight companies were founded by Twente alumni and all the entrepreneurs had an academic background; the two non-alumni started their company with the support of the University of Twente. All the companies were relatively small: 8 companies had less than 10 employees, 2 had less than 20. The companies were spread all over the Netherlands, but with a higher concentration in the Twente region.

Table 1: Characterizations of the domestic (D) and global (G) start-up companies.

| Company | Industry | Foundation | Origin |
|---|---|---|---|
| D1 | Software Development | 2002 | Business |
| D2 | Mechanical Engineering | 2001 | University |
| D3 | Electrical Engineering | 2003 | Business |
| D4 | Software Development | 1999 | University |
| D5 | Bio-pharmaceutical | 2002 | University |
| G1 | Communication | 2002 | University |
| G2 | Bio tech. | 2001 | University |
| G3 | Communication | 2003 | Business |
| G4 | Mechanical Engineering | 2000 | University |
| G5 | Electrical Engineering | 1998 | University |

Table 2: Differences between domestic and global start-ups with regard to the size of the network (number of actors).

| | Size of the network at time of foundation | | Size of the network at time of measurement | |
|---|---|---|---|---|
| | MWU value | *p* value | MWU value | *p* value |
| Actors: Capital providers | 3.5 | $p < 0.10$ | 7.5 | n.s. |
| Actor-roles | 1.5 | $p < 0.05$ | | |
| Advisors | 10.5 | n.s. | | |
| Knowledge providers | 4.5 | $p < 0.10$ | | |
| Finance providers | 0 | $p < 0.01$ | | |
| Product suppliers | 10 | n.s. | | |
| Buyers | 10 | n.s. | | |

Each of the 10 companies was individually interviewed using a semi-structured protocol. The interviews took place in February and March, 2005.

## Results

We distinguish between actors who are in the role of buyers, suppliers, and advisors (actor-roles), and actors that provide "capitals" (in the sense of the EiN model). The results in the Annex (Tables A.1 and A.2) show that, the networks of global start-ups are substantially larger than those of domestic start-ups. Global start-ups do have significantly more actors that provide "capitals" (MWU = 3.5; $p < 0.10$) and that fulfill the aforementioned roles (MWU = 1.5; $p < 0.05$) than domestic start-ups (see Table 2).

Global start-ups have larger networks from the start (i.e., more actors in their networks) than domestic start-ups. The networks of both types of companies grow but neither of the types of company shows more substantial growth in the size of their network than the other. Nevertheless, the networks of global start-ups contain significantly more global actors at the time of foundation (MWU = 4.5; $p < 0.10$) as well as at the time of the study (MWU = 2.5; $p < 0.05$) than those of the domestic startups. However, the increase in global partners is not significant (MWU = 6; $p$ = n.s.) compared to the increase of domestic partners (MWU = 5.5; $p$ = n.s.). At the time of their foundation, global startups have more capitals acquired via external partners than domestic start-ups (MWU = 3.0; $p < 0.10$), although at the time of the study there was no difference (MWU = 8, $p$ = n.s.). The difference at the time of foundation is caused by the fact more external parties contribute to the economic capital (MWU = 0, $p < 0.01$). At the time of the study, global start-ups have more external parties that provide them with networks (social capital: MWU = 3, $p < 0.10$). All types of actor-roles are fulfilled in both types of companies. Global start-ups, however, do have more actors that provide knowledge, as well as financial means (see also Table 3).

Table 3: Differences between domestic and global start-ups with regard to the number of capital providers and the number of domestic and global actors in the network at the time of foundation and of measurement.

| | Capital providers at the time of foundation | | Capital providers at the time of measurement | | Increase of capital providers from foundation to time of measurement | |
|---|---|---|---|---|---|---|
| | MWU value | *p* value | MWU value | *p* value | MWU value | *p* value |
| Social capital | 9.5 | n.s. | 5.5 | n.s. | 7 | n.s. |
| Economic capital | 0 | $p < 0.01$ | 8.5 | n.s. | 9.5 | n.s. |
| Network capital | 9.0 | n.s. | 9.0 | n.s. | 5.5 | n.s. |
| Strategic capital | 6.5 | n.s. | 9.5 | n.s. | 6.7 | n.s. |

| | Domestic and global actors providing capitals at the time of foundation | | Domestic and global actors providing capitals at the time of measurement | | Increase of domestic and global actors providing capitals from foundation to time of measurement | |
|---|---|---|---|---|---|---|
| Domestic actors | 10.5 | n.s. | 7 | n.s. | 5.5 | n.s. |
| Global actors | 4.5 | $p < 0.10$ | 2.5 | $p < 0.05$ | 6 | n.s. |

With regard to the four types of capital, it appears from the data that the number of actors that participate in the economic capital of the global start-up is larger than the number that participate in the domestic start-up (MWU $= 0$; $p < 0.01$).

## Discussion

There is no difference in the types of actors present (Hypothesis 1). However, there is a difference in the number of actors in general; there are less global actors in the case of the domestic firms. This does, to a certain extent, fail to support the hypothesis of Danskin Harveston, Wakkee, Kirwan, Groen, and Ridder (2004) who found that born globals (global start-ups) had no more global a mindset than gradual internationalizers. This research indicates that there are more global actors involved. Both in domestic and global start-ups the roles are performed by external actors and by the entrepreneur himself/herself. The actor-roles of advisor, financier as well as knowledge supplier are performed in all of the cases. The supplier of products is virtually absent probably since many of the organizations are not yet on the market selling their products, but are still in the stage of developing.

Madsen, Neergaard, Fisker, and Ulhøi (2004) found that firms who can rely on a broad and diverse network are more successful. In the same article they do make a distinction between the personal and professional network and it is argued that in the earliest stages of the firm these are identical. The network of a global high-tech start-up is more extensive than the network of a domestic high-tech start-up.

The network of global start-up companies is significantly larger than that of domestic start-ups. Both at the time of foundation and the study, global start-ups have more global actors in their networks than domestic start-ups. Domestic start-ups do have actors with a global network, but the use of those actors is, in our opinion, primarily for "domestic" use. Global start-ups, however, need the global networks of these actors in their networks. The number of global actors is larger at the start as well at the time of the study. The data show that the increase in the number of global actors is not significantly different for either type of start-up companies. Both types of start-up companies do need domestic actors — both types of companies have established themselves in a local area and need their contacts for many operational affairs. Nevertheless, this confirms our second hypothesis.

Both types of companies have each of the four types of capitals available, either via the company itself or via external parties. This confirms Groen's hypothesis (Groen, 2005) that every company needs at its start a certain amount of "capital," it also concords with results of previous work (Kirwan, Van der Sijde, & Groen, 2006) that at the start, access to each of the four capitals should be guaranteed. Our hypothesis (Hypothesis 3) that there is no difference in capital providers is confirmed for three of the four types of capital. Economic capital for global start-ups is provided by a significantly greater number of partners than in the case of domestic start-ups (the same is indicated with respect to the number of finance providers). The economic capital (financial needs) of global start-ups is, more often than not, larger than that of domestic start-ups. This leads to a partial confirmation of the fourth hypothesis: global start-ups acquire more resources than domestic start-ups: this is confirmed for economic capital at the time of foundation (economic capital is provided by more actors than in the case of domestic start-ups), but not for the other types of capital. At the

## Annex

Table A.1: Role of actors in domestic and global start-ups.

| | Advisors | | Suppliers: Knowledge | | Suppliers: Finances | | Suppliers: Products | Buyers | |
|---|---|---|---|---|---|---|---|---|---|
| **Domestic start-ups** | | | | | | | | | |
| D1 | USP | D | Department | G | Own | | – | – | |
| | Mentor from previous start-up | | | | | | | | |
| D2 | USP | D | Own | D | USP | D | – | From previous employer | D |
| D3 | USP | D | Department | G | USP | D | – | – | |
| | GSP | D | | | | | | | |
| | Spouse | D | | | | | | | |
| D4 | Network group | D | Own | D | Own | | – | – | |
| | Network group coordinator | D | | | | | | | |
| D5 | New partner | G | Institute | G | GSP | D | – | – | |
| | Institute director | G | | | | | | | |

(*Continued*)

Table A.1: (*Continued*)

| | Advisors | | Suppliers: Knowledge | | Suppliers: Finances | | Suppliers: Products | | Buyers | |
|---|---|---|---|---|---|---|---|---|---|---|
| **Global start-ups** | | | | | | | | | | |
| G1 | Business coach producer | G | Producer | D | Business coach | G | Producer | D | – | |
| | USP | D | | | Informal investors | G | | | | |
| | GSP | D | | | USP | D | | | | |
| G2 | Business coach | G | Former employer | D | Government support grant | D | – | | – | |
| | Investor in previous venture | D | | | Former employer | D | | | | |
| G3 | Colleagues from former employer | D | Former Employer | G | Former employer | G | – | | – | |
| | | | | | USP | D | | | | |
| G4 | GSP | D | University professor | G | Bank | D | – | | Customer | G |
| | USP | D | Previous company | D | USP | D | | | | |
| G5 | University professor | G | Research position | D | New partner | G | – | | User of technology | G |
| | | | New partner Institute | G | Research fund | D | | | | |
| | | | | G | | | | | | |

*Abbreviations:* GSP, government support program; USP, university support program.

Table A.2: Capitals at time of foundation and at the time of the study.

| | Social capital | | Economic capital | | Cultural capital | | Strategic capital | |
|---|---|---|---|---|---|---|---|---|
| **Capitals at the time of foundation** | | | | | | | | |
| D1 | USP | D | Own | | Previous start-up | D | Previous start-up | D |
| | Mentor | D | | | Department | G | Department | D |
| D2 | Previous employer | D | USP | D | Education | D | Education | D |
| | Customer | D | | | Traineeship | G | | |
| D3 | USP | D | USP | D | Research experience | G | Own | D |
| | GSP | D | | | Department | G | | |
| | Department | G | | | | | | |
| D4 | Network club | D | Own | | Previous employer | D | Own | D |
| | Club co-ordinator | D | | | | | | |
| D5 | Institute | G | Government grant | G | Institute | G | Venture capitalist | G |
| | | | | | New partner | G | New partner | G |
| | | | | | Research position | D | Government grant | D |
| G1 | Business coach | G | Business coach | G | Producer | D | Business coach | G |
| | GSP | D | Informal investors | G | Trainee experience | G | Previous start-up | D |
| | Network clubs | D | USP | D | Previous start-up | D | Family | D |
| | Family | D | | | Family | D | | |
| G2 | Colleagues | D | Former employer | D | Former employer | D | Business coach | G |
| | Business coach | G | Government support grant | D | Research institute | G | Former employer | D |

(*Continued*)

Table A.2: (Continued)

| | Social capital | | Economic capital | | Cultural capital | | Strategic capital | |
|---|---|---|---|---|---|---|---|---|
| G3 | Colleagues | D | Former employer | G | Former employer | G | Former employer | G |
|  |  |  | USP | D |  |  |  |  |
| G4 | Customer | G | USP | D | Other company | D | Other company | D |
|  | Other company | D | Bank | D |  |  | University professor | G |
|  | University professor | G |  |  |  |  | USP | D |
|  | GSP | D |  |  |  |  |  |  |
| G5 | University professor | G | New partner | G | New partner | G | New partner | G |
|  | Customer | G | Research grant | D | Institute | G | Institute | G |
|  | New partner | G | University | G |  |  |  |  |
| **Capitals at the time of measurement** | | | | | | | | |
| D1 | Customers | D | Own | | Leading developer | G | Customers | D |
|  | Reseller | D |  |  | Customers | D | Previous start-up | D |
|  | Mentor | D |  |  | Previous start-up | D |  |  |
| D2 | Network club | D | Own | | Supplier | D | Business Coach | D |
|  | Supplier | D |  |  |  |  |  |  |
|  | Customers | D |  |  |  |  |  |  |
| D3 | Department | G | GSP | D | Department | G | Hired advisor | D |
|  | Neighbor | D |  |  | Health care providers | D |  |  |
|  | Network club | D |  |  |  |  |  |  |
| D4 | Design firm | D | Design firm | D | New partner | D | New partner | D |
|  | Department (2) | G | USP | G | Hired consultant | D | Customers | D |
|  | Research institute | D | GSP | D | Department (2) | G |  |  |

| | Contact | | Contact | | Contact | | Contact | |
|---|---|---|---|---|---|---|---|---|
| D5 | Internet | G | High-tech supplier | D | Customers | D | New partner | G |
| | Club coordinator | D | Venture capitalist | D | Institute | G | | |
| | Advisory board (4) | D | Institute | D | New partner | G | | |
| | Network groups | D | | | | | | |
| | Producer | D | | | | | | |
| | Supplier | D | | | | | | |
| | Institute | G | | | | | | |
| G1 | Business coach | G | Business coach | G | Producer | G | Business coach | G |
| | Entrepreneur competition | D | Informal investor | D | | | | |
| | Customer (2) | G | Share holders (6) | G | | | | |
| | Network clubs | D | | | | | | |
| | Suppliers (2) | G | | | | | | |
| G2 | USP | D | USP | D | Former employer | D | Courses | D |
| | New venture | G | Government grant | G | Research institute | G | Business coach | G |
| | Researchers | G | Former employer | G | | | | |
| | Colleagues | D | | | | | | |
| | Business coach | G | | | | | | |
| | Marketing firms | G | | | | | | |
| G3 | Network club | D | Government grants | D | Supplier | G | — | |
| | Universities (2) | G | | | | | | |
| | Seminars | G | | | | | | |

*(Continued)*

Table A.2: (*Continued*)

| | Social capital | | Economic capital | | Cultural capital | | Strategic capital | |
|---|---|---|---|---|---|---|---|---|
| G4 | Customers (3) | G | USP | D | Customers | G | University | D |
| | Patent expert | D | | | Other company | D | Other company | D |
| | Other company | D | | | | | | |
| | Fairs | D | | | | | | |
| | Insurer | G | | | | | | |
| G5 | Academic community | G | New partner | G | Trainees | D | New partner | G |
| | Fairs | G | | | Joint research | G | Institute | G |
| | New partner | G | | | New partner | G | | |
| | Producers | G | | | Institute | G | | |
| | Distributors | G | | | | | | |

*Abbreviations*: GSP, government support program; USP, university support program.

time of the study, the social capital for global start-ups is provided by more actors than for domestic start-ups, thus Hypothesis 4 is also partly confirmed.

Further research should investigate the relationship between the size of the network as either as a factor or a determinant in the success of a venture and the importance and use of global actors in global start-ups.

# References

Brush, C. G., Greene, P. G., & Hart, M. M. (2001). From initial idea to unique advantage: The entrepreneurial challenge of constructing a resource base. *Academy of Management Executive, 15*(1), 49–80.

Burt, R. S. (1992). *Structural holes: The social structure of competition.* Cambridge, MA: Harvard University Press.

Danskin Harveston, P., Wakkee, I. A. M., Kirwan, P. M., Groen, A. J., & Ridder, A. (2004). Born global versus gradually globalising firms: A cross cultural comparison. In: P. C. van der Sijde, A. Ridder & A. J. Groen (Eds), *Entrepreneurship and innovation: Essays in honour of Wim During.* Enschede: Nikos.

Elfring, T., & Hulsink, W. (2003). Network in entrepreneurship: The case of high-technology firms. *Small Business Economics, 21,* 409–422.

Gaglio, C. M. (1997). Opportunity identification: Review, critique and suggested research direction. In: J. A. Katz (Ed.), *Advances in entrepreneurship, firm emergence and growth* (pp. 139–202, Vol. 3).

Granovetter, M. S. (1992). Problems of explanations in economic sociology. In: N. Nohria & R. Eccles (Eds), *Handbook of economic sociology* (pp. 453–475). Boston: Princeton University Press.

Groen, A. J. (1994). *Milieu en MKB: Kennis en Kennissen, milieuinnovatie in de grafische industrie: Modelmatig verklaard. (Environment and SME; environmental innovation in printing industry quantitatively explained).* Groningen: Wolters Noordhoff.

Groen, A. J. (2005). Knowledge intensive entrepreneurship in networks: Towards a multi-level/multi dimensional approach. *Journal of Enterprising Culture, 13*(1), 69–88.

Groen, A. J., de Weerd-Nederhof, P. C., van Drongelen-Kerssens, I. C., Badoux, R. A. J., & Olthuis, G. P. H. (2002). Creating and justifying research and development value: Scope, scale, skill and social networking of R&D. *Creativity and Innovation Management, 11*(1), 2–15.

Hayek, F. (1945). The use of knowledge in society. *American Economic Review, 35,* 19–530.

Hite, J. M., & Hesterly, W. M. (2001). Research notes and commentaries. The evolution of firm networks: From emergence to early growth of the firm. *Strategic Management Journal, 22,* 275–286.

Kirwan, P., Van der Sijde, P., & Groen, A. (2006). Assessing the needs of new technology based firms (NTBFs): An investigation among spin-off companies from six European universities. *International Entrepreneurship and Management Journal, 2,* 173–187.

Kirzner, I. M. (1973). *Competition and entrepreneurship.* Chicago: University of Chicago Press.

Knight, G. A. (1997). *Emerging paradigm for international marketing: The born global firm.* Unpublished doctoral thesis, Michigan State University.

Knudsen, T., & Madsen, T. K. (2002). *Small "born global" firms: An empirical study of basic economic characteristics.* Paper presented at a Research Seminar Born Globals — What's the meaning. Denmark: Copenhagen Business School.

Madsen, H., Neergaard, H. Fisker, S., & Ulhøi, J. P. (2004). *Entrepreneurship in the knowledge-intensive sector: Influential factors at the start-up and early growth phase.* Paper presented at NCSB, 13th Nordic Conference on Small Business Research, May.

Oviatt, B. M., & McDougall, P. P. (1994). Towards a theory of international new ventures. *Journal of International Business Studies*, *25*(1), 45–64.

Schumpeter, J. (1934). *Capitalism, socialism, and democracy*. New York: Harper & Row.

Shane, S. (2000). Prior knowledge and the discovery of entrepreneurial opportunities. *Organization Science*, *11*(4), 448–449.

Shane, S., & Venkataraman, S. (2000). The promise of entrepreneurship as a field of research. *Academy of Management Review*, *25*(1), 217–226.

Van der Sijde, P. C., Karnebeek, S., & Van Benthem, J. (2002). The impact of a university spin-off programme: The case of NTBFs established through TOP. In: R. Oakey, W. During & S. Kauser (Eds), *New Technology-based firms in the new millenium* (Vol. 2). Amsterdam: Pergamon.

Van der Veen, M., & Wakkee, I. (2004). Understanding the entrepreneurial process. In: D. Watkins (Ed.), *ARPENT, annual review of progress in entrepreneurship research* (Vol. 2, pp. 114–152). Brussels: EFMD.

Vesper, K. H. (1989). *New venture strategies*. Englewood Cliffs, NJ: Prentice-Hall.

Wakkee, I. (2004). *Starting global: An entrepreneurship in networks approach*. Ph.D. thesis, University of Twente, Enschede.

Wakkee, I., Kirwan, P., & van der Sijde, P. C. (2004). *An empirical exploration of the Global Startup Concept in an Entrepreneurship Context*. Paper presented at the Academy of Management Conference "Creating Actionable Knowledge", New Orleans, August 6–11.

Zahra, S. A., Korri, J. S., & Yu, J. (2005). Cognition and international entrepreneurship: Implications for research on international opportunity recognition and exploitation. *International Business Review*, *14*, 129–146.

Chapter 9

# Knowledge Spillovers from Public Research Institutions: Evidence from Japanese High-Technology Start-Up Firms

Michael Lynskey

## Introduction

It is widely recognised that universities and other research institutions (hereinafter, PRIs) are sources of knowledge in their regional and national economies. They have a broad impact on economic growth through several activities, including educational partnerships, industry-sponsored research, job placement, technical assistance to industry and the creation of start-up firms. This is essentially an issue of knowledge transfer from PRIs to industry, which may take several forms and be either *direct* or *indirect* in nature.[1]

One form of *indirect* transfer of knowledge is commonly known as 'knowledge spillovers'.[2] These externalities are a central element of theories of innovation and capture

---

[1] For example, one *direct* means of knowledge transfer is the flow of researchers to industry (e.g., Ehrenberg, 1992).

[2] Accurately speaking, this is one type of R&D spillover. *Knowledge spillovers* occur because knowledge created by one organisation is typically not contained within that organisation and thereby creates value for other organisations. Another type of R&D spillover, *network spillovers*, result from the profitability of a set of interrelated and interdependent technologies that may depend on achieving a critical mass of success, so that each firm pursuing one or more of these related technologies creates economic benefits for other firms and their customers. Griliches (1992) also makes a distinction between two types of spillovers: *embodied and disembodied*. The former relate to the purchase of equipment, goods and services. They can be defined as rent spillovers to the extent that improvements — which are the results of a firm's efforts — in the products that are sold to other firms are not fully absorbed by a concurring price increase. Embodied spillovers are generally measured through input-output or flows of international trade. Disembodied or pure knowledge spillovers-the type we consider here-are more significant than embodied spillovers. According to Griliches (1992), however, the main problem with calculating knowledge spillovers is an accurate definition of the technological proximity or closeness between firms, as an inverse relationship between spillovers and technological distance may be expected.

---

**New Technology Based Firms in the New Millennium, Volume VI**
**Edited by A. Groen, R. Oakey, P. van der Sijde and G. Cook**
© 2008 Emerald Group Publishing Limited. All rights reserved.

the idea that economic benefits resulting from R&D are shared by organisations other than the R&D performer. For example, a citation on a patent by firm X to university Y's patent suggest that X's technology builds on knowledge from Y (e.g. Bernstein & Mohnen, 1998; Griliches, 1992; Los & Verspagen, 2000). Such involuntary flow of knowledge indicates that "the productivity achieved by one firm or industry depends not only upon its own research efforts but also on the level of the pool of general knowledge accessible to it" (Griliches, 1995, p. 64). Grossman and Helpman (1991, p. 16) describe the attributes of spillovers as follows:

> By technological spillovers, we mean that (1) firms can acquire information created by others without paying for that information in a market, and (2) the creators (or current owners) of the information have no effective recourse, under prevailing laws, if other firms utilize information so acquired.

There are several channels through which knowledge might spread in this manner: it may seep into the public domain in publications or public presentations; it may travel with individuals who change employment or establish new firms of their own; and it may be uncovered through reverse engineering and other purposive search procedures. The extent to which knowledge is diffused through these different channels depends on several factors, including the absorptive capacity of the recipient firm, the nature of the knowledge itself (e.g. whether it is codified or tacit) and the distance it has to traverse.

Much of the scholarship on knowledge spillovers from R&D has been directed at the level of aggregate industries or at inter-firm transactions within industries. Other approaches have examined individual industries in isolation (e.g. Almeida & Kogut, 1997; Link, 1998; Stolpe, 2002; Zucker, Darby, & Armstrong, 1994, 1998). Relatively few studies have also been conducted in Japan, and these generally investigate the relationship between spillovers and R&D productivity improvements in manufacturing firms (e.g. Goto & Suzuki, 1989; Griliches & Mairesse, 1990; Odagiri & Iwata, 1986). They demonstrate that the effects of R&D expenditure on productivity improvements are significantly positive. Goto and Suzuki (1989), for example, ascertain that the impact of R&D in Japanese electronics industries on the productivity growth of other Japanese manufacturing industries can be attributed more to knowledge diffusion than to the transaction of goods; and that the diffusion from electronics industries to other more technologically diverse industries is greater the closer those industries are to the electronics industries. This implies that Griliches (1992) was correct in identifying knowledge spillovers are being more significant than rent spillovers. More recently, Murakami (2007) showed that the presence of foreign-owned firms has a positive effect on the productivity of Japanese firms as a result of technology spillovers.

The remainder of this paper is organised as follows. In the next section, we review some of the salient points in the literature on knowledge spillovers from PRIs. In Section 3, we introduce the econometric model and methodological framework, and describe the data used in the study. The results of our empirical analysis are presented in Section 4 and interpretations are discussed in Section 5. We conclude the paper in Section 6 by commenting on the policy implications of knowledge spillovers from our findings, and refer to some limitations of the study.

# Knowledge Spillovers from PRIs

Several seminal studies (e.g. Jaffe, 1986, 1989; Jaffe, Trajtenberg, & Henderson, 1993; Mansfield, 1991, 1995, 2000; Nelson, 1986, 1993) demonstrate the effects of academic research on industry and innovation. Jaffe (1989) argued that knowledge spillovers from universities to firms exist because universities have few incentives to keep research a secret; and Nelson (1986) found that such spillovers are an important source of innovation in high-technology industries. Although universities now attempt to appropriate the results of their research and retain ownership of their intellectual property, there is evidence that knowledge spillovers from PRIs are particularly important to firms in strategic industries, such as biotechnology, computing, and new materials (Klevorick, Levin, Nelson, & Winter, 1995).

Studies also indicate that knowledge spillovers from PRIs are geographically bounded (Acs, Anselin, & Varga, 2002; Acs, Audretsch, & Feldman, 1992; Autant-Bernard, 2001; Jaffe, 1989). There are several explanations for this localisation (Breschi & Lissoni, 2001). The most probable reason is the presence of tacit knowledge (Krugman, 1998). The marginal costs of transmitting such knowledge increase with distance (Audretsch, 1998), which favours proximity to the spillover pool. Another explanation is that firms select the most accessible source of knowledge, which is usually geographically close, and seek other sources of knowledge only when the first selection is deemed a failure (Beise & Stahl, 1999). Nooteboom (1999) argues that the extent to which knowledge is targeted by firms affects the significance of geographical proximity between firms and the spillover pool. Searching for less targeted knowledge enables firms to establish contact with relatively accessible sources of knowledge, whereas searching for more targeted knowledge requires them to expand the geographical range of the search, since they must access the source of knowledge despite where it is located.

A number of studies have investigated who best utilises knowledge spillovers to achieve industrial innovations. These indicate that small technology-based firms have an advantage in exploiting the knowledge of PRI scientists (Acs, Audretsch, & Feldman, 1994; Audretsch & Vivarelli, 1996; Link & Rees, 1990; Piergiovanni, Santarelli, & Vivarelli, 1997), owing to their size and relatively scarce internal resources. Such firms are able to utilise linkages with universities and other PRIs more efficiently than large firms, since they have more to learn from external sources of knowledge and greater potential for growth than their large counterparts, which often have sufficient internal resources for innovation by themselves (Acs & Audretsch, 1988; Feldman, 1994; Link & Rees, 1990; Sakakibara, 1997). Acs et al. (1994, p. 337) found "spillovers from university research laboratories are more important in producing innovative activity in small firms", and proposed that small firms have a comparative advantage over large firms in exploiting such spillovers.

The literature also suggests that technology-based small firms exploit knowledge spillovers from PRIs by means of less-interactive (e.g. formal connections mediated by a third party) channels for immediate problem solving in core areas and that they require less absorptive capacity for the assimilation of such knowledge than the larger firms do (Santoro & Chakrabarti, 2002; Schartinger, Rammer, Fischer, & Fröhlich, 2002).

Most of the empirical studies on knowledge spillovers, from PRIs to private firms, use data from the USA (e.g. Acs et al., 1992; Anselin, Varga, & Acs, 1997; Feldman, 1994; Jaffe & Trajtenberg, 1996, 2002; Mansfield, 1995; Mansfield & Lee, 1996; Rosenberg & Nelson,

1994; Zucker et al., 1994) or Europe (e.g. Audretsch & Vivarelli, 1996; Autant-Bernard, 2001; Beise & Stahl, 1999; Blind & Grupp, 1999). All these spatial-economic approaches stress the influence of spatial clustering. However, an important aspect of knowledge development is the geographical context and institutional framework in which innovation occurs. Since Japan has a distinct national innovation system different from that in the USA and Europe (Nelson, 1993; Goto, 2000), the question arises whether results similar to these studies, suggesting that the proximity of firms to PRIs is positively correlated with innovation in firms, also holds true for Japan. The question is important because industrial policy in Japan is partly based on the assumption that proximity is imperative for the promotion of innovation.[3] However, very few studies — an exception being Kenney and Florida (1994) — discuss the issue of knowledge spillovers from the public to the private sector in Japan, using indigenous firm-level data. Those studies that have been conducted are confined to inter-firm or inter-industry spillovers (e.g. Goto & Suzuki, 1989; Odagiri & Kinukawa, 1997; Suzuki, 1993), and do not treat knowledge spillovers from PRIs to industry.

Against this background, and with the intention of filling a gap in the literature, we undertook to examine empirically the relationship between knowledge spillovers from PRIs and industrial innovation in Japanese high-technology start-up firms, or, as they are referred to generally in the literature, Japanese new technology-based firms (NTBFs). We assumed *a priori* that spillovers occur in Japan because of the nature of public scientific research and the extant literature in support of their presence elsewhere. Nevertheless, we wished to confirm this and we were motivated by the following questions:

1. Are knowledge spillovers from PRIs localised in Japan?
2. If so, what is the extent to which geographical location restricts such knowledge spillovers?
3. Does the type of tool we use to measure the effects of spillovers have a bearing on our results? Is there, for example, any difference if we measure knowledge spillovers by patents or by scientific publications?
4. What can we discern about the degree of such knowledge spillovers and the innovative activities of NTBFs?

## Empirical Analysis

### Model Development

In order to examine the effect of knowledge spillovers, one needs:

(a) An observable measure of performance, which is likely to be affected by (and thus register the size of) such spillovers.
(b) A means to determine which producers or users are 'close' to one other.

---

[3] One chapter of Japan's Third Science and Technology Basic Plan, which covers the period FY 2006 through to FY 2011, is to reform the nation's science and technology system. One aspect of this is the creation of research hubs to revitalise regional communities through the use of local university resources in order to stimulate innovation.

To address point (a), we adopt the knowledge-production function approach introduced by Griliches (1979) and subsequently modified by Jaffe (1989).[4] Following the methodology used in Acs et al. (1994) and Autant-Bernard (2001), we consider the following simple knowledge production function:

$$I_j = (RD_j)^\alpha (PUB_1)^\beta (PUB_2)^\gamma \qquad (1)$$

The dependent variable $I_j$ denotes the results of innovation in firm $j$. One indicator of innovation that is frequently used, despite its limitations, is the number of patents granted. The incentives to patent vary greatly, however, as does the private and social values of the associated research results.[5] The majority of patents are of little or no real value, while a small fraction of them is associated with large economic returns.[6] Since new firms generally do not have issued patents, because of the time lag for a technology to be patented, we use instead the number of patent *applications* made by firms.[7] Patent applications are an accepted indicator of innovation because "they are representative of innovations which are the sources of productivity gains" (Autant-Bernard, 2001, p. 1072); and the use of patent data in a knowledge production function can be justified by empirical results obtained elsewhere (e.g. Acs et al., 2002). Thus, we define the dependent variable as the total number of patent applications made by firm $j$ in 1998. For a NTSF this is likely to take the value zero or one (or two) in a given year (Branstetter, 1996, p. 19), confirming the observation by Lotka (1926), which was re-examined and corroborated by Narin and Breitzman (1995), that research is driven mainly by a few productive scientists.

The independent variable $RD_j$ denotes the R&D expenditure of firm $j$ in 1997.[8] A firm's RD is a proxy for its technological capability (e.g. Lach, 2000), and it is reasonable to assume that private effort in R&D is proportional to R&D expenditure (Autant-Bernard, 2001). Technological capability is the capacity of firms to "undertake a set range of productive tasks aimed at improving their ability to operate specific functions and compete in specific markets and industries" (Lynskey, 1999, p. 318). It provides the basis for in-house innovation and competitive advantage (Cohen & Levinthal, 1990; Coombs, 1996; Figueiredo, 2002). Firms with superior technological capability can secure greater efficiency gains by pioneering process innovations and can achieve higher differentiation by product innovations in response to the changing market environment (Teece & Pisano,

---

[4] These are of the general deductive model of the production function, such as the Cobb–Douglas form.

[5] A consequence of this is that there is a gap between patents and innovations: all innovations do not lead to the registration of a patent and conversely all patents do not result in an innovation (Autant-Bernard, 2001, p. 1072).

[6] A classic example of huge economic returns garnered from a patent is that of recombinant DNA. Cohen of Stanford University and Herber Boyer of UCSF applied for a patent on recombinant DNA technology in 1974; it was granted in 1980. The Cohen–Boyer patents eventually had more than 200 licensees — biotechnology and pharmaceutical companies — and earned Stanford and UCSF more than $100 million in royalties.

[7] Hall, Jaffe, and Trajtenberg (2001) argue that the patent application date should be used to date inventive activity as the lag between patent application and patent grant dates reflects administrative policies at the US Patent Office.

[8] We recognise the need to take into account time lags between patents and R&D before defining the variable RD as R&D investment in 1997. The independent variable RD takes the value of flow of R&D. Some studies use 'knowledge capital' instead of flow of R&D. We were unable to construct such knowledge capital, however, due to insufficient data.

1994; Verona, 1999). We expect that firms with a higher technological capability will make a larger number of patent applications and hence we predict the coefficients of this variable to be positive in our analysis.

The independent variable $PUB_i$ ($i = 1, 2$) denotes the knowledge created by PRIs. This public knowledge PUB is divided into two sub-categories, $PUB_1$ and $PUB_2$. The variable $PUB_1$ represents knowledge from PRIs that are located within the *same* geographical area as firm $j$. Conversely, variable $PUB_2$ designates knowledge created by PRIs that are located in the *neighbouring* geographical areas to where firm $j$ is located. If there are any geographical restrictions on knowledge spillovers from PRIs to industry, the power of $PUB_1$ (i.e. $\beta$) should be greater than that of $PUB_2$ (i.e. $\gamma$) in Eq. (1).

Since 'knowledge' is an abstract concept, we select a proxy for it that permits quantitative analysis. Here, we measure the variable PUB in the following three ways:

i. The total amount of R&D expenditure in the PRIs.
ii. The total number of scientific papers published by the PRIs.
iii. The total number of patents owned by the PRIs.

To address point (b), about which producers or users of knowledge are 'close' to one another, we conceived a total of 47 geographical units. Each of these corresponded to a Japanese 'prefecture' and its 'neighbouring prefectures'.[9] Here 'neighbouring prefectures' are defined as the group of prefectures adjacent to the target prefecture. For example, in the case of Tokyo, the neighbouring prefectures comprise the four prefectures that border Tokyo: Chiba, Kanagawa, Saitama and Yamanashi. We then calculated each of the three types of public knowledge (R&D, papers and patents) for each geographical unit. Finally, we eliminated Hokkaido and Okinawa from the samples because these two prefectures are island prefectures, which have no land border with their nearest prefectures (see Figures 1 and 2).

*Methodology*

As mentioned above, the dependent variable is the number of patent applications made by a firm, which is a non-negative integer. Branstetter (1996, p. 19) contends that:

> Patent data are "count data" — non-negative integers — and in any given year a number of firms perform R&D but generate no patents. The distribution of patents is highly skewed with most firms generating far fewer than the mean number of patents in a given year. The liner model was not designed to handle such data.

Hence, it is reasonable to conclude that the number of patents applied for by NTBFs take the value zero or one (or two). Previous studies have employed TOBIT, Negative Binomial

---

[9]A prefecture in Japan is the local administrative equivalent to a state in the USA or to a county in Great Britain. Prefectures were used because they are easy to identify and the data are accessible and more reliable than at more local levels. Jaffe (1989) employed a similar formulation where the geographic unit was at the state level in the USA; and Autant-Bernard (2001) used the department in France. Some previous studies (e.g. Anselin et al., 1997; Breschi & Lissoni, 2001) have measured spatial lag in metric distances. In the case of the Japanese prefectures, typical distances inside these units exceed 100 km.

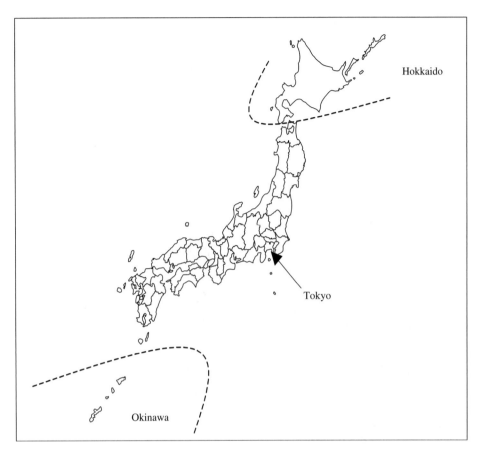

Figure 1: Japan's prefectures. The prefectures of Hokkaido and Okinawa were excluded from our analysis since they do not have a land border with their neighbouring prefectures.

Regressions or Poisson Regressions to estimate equations that include these kinds of variables as dependent variables (Greene, 1997).[10] Here we estimate Eq. (1) by using the TOBIT and the Poisson Regression models, as shown in Eqs. (2) and (3), respectively.[11] When estimating Eq. (2) by TOBIT, we transform the dependent variable from $I_j$ into $\ln(10(I_j+1))$.[12]

$$\ln I_j = \text{const} + \alpha \ln RD_j + \beta \ln PUB_1 + \gamma \ln PUB_2 + \delta X_j + \theta Z_j + u_j \text{ (TOBIT)} \qquad (2)$$

$$I_j = \text{const} + \alpha \ln RD_j + \beta \ln PUB_1 + \gamma \ln PUB_2 + \delta X_j + \theta Z_j + u_j \text{ (Poisson)} \qquad (3)$$

[10] Negative binomial regressions did not provide meaningful results, and so we report only the results of the TOBIT and Poisson Regression models.
[11] The multiplication equation is transformed into a linear function by expressing variables in terms of their logarithms.
[12] See Acs et al. (1994).

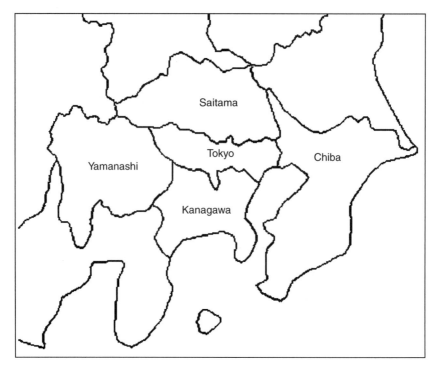

Figure 2: The Kanto area: Tokyo and its adjacent prefectures.

The variables $X_j$ and $Z_j$ in Eqs. (2) and (3) represent several firm-level and managerial-level characteristics of NTBFs, as explained below.

### Firm-Level Characteristics

The innovative activities of NTBFs might be influenced by factors other than R&D expenditure (Lynskey, 2004a, 2004b). To account for this, we introduce the variable $X_j$ in Eqs. (2) and (3) to capture firm-specific characteristics other than R&D expenditure. These include the size of the firm (SIZE), its annual growth rate of sales (SG) and the age of the firm (F_AGE).

### Firm Size

Several researchers (e.g. Acs & Audretsch, 1988; Link & Rees, 1990) have examined the rate of innovation in small firms compared to large firms, and why smaller firms are more innovative than larger firms relative to their size. Link and Rees (1990) hypothesise that smaller firms that utilise university research are more efficient in their internal R&D and are not prone to bureaucratic impediments that hinder R&D in larger firms. They surveyed 209 firms and found that smaller firms devote a larger percentage of their sales to R&D and use university researchers for problem solving in their operations. They also confirmed that small firms are able to transfer knowledge gained from their university research relationships more effectively compared to large firms. Although larger firms have more university contact than smaller firms, the latter are able to use their university relationships to leverage their internal R&D to a greater degree. Here, the variable SIZE is defined as the natural logarithm of total employees in 1998; and the size effects on innovative activities will be eliminated through SIZE.

## Sales Growth

Sales growth is widely considered as the key indicator of the market's acceptance of an NTBF's products (Autio et al., 2000). The variable SG is defined by the formula: (sales in 1998 – sales in 1997)/(sales in 1997). This variable controls for the effects of demand on innovative activities (Cohen & Klepper, 1996a, 1996b).

## Firm Age

The final firm-level variable, F_AGE, is defined as the number of years that have elapsed since a firm was established. We consider firm age because research suggests that firm growth and the probability that a firm will fail decrease with age (Evans, 1987). This variable partly reflects the macroeconomic conditions prevailing in the year when a firm is founded. Highfield and Smiley (1987) suggest that macroeconomic factors are one of two factors (the other being microeconomic factors) that influence the rate of creation of new firms. One of the incentives for an entrepreneur to establish a NTBF and engage in research is to commercialise the results of R&D and thereby to seek rents from doing so (Kirzner, 1973; Lynskey, 2002). The macroeconomic conditions prevailing in the year when a firm is established have some effect, however, on the rent-seeking activities of the firm and influence its subsequent development and R&D expenditure.[13] Since such effects might bias the regression results, we control these macroeconomic effects by using the variable F_AGE.

## Managerial-Level Characteristics

In addition to these firm-specific variables, we also take into account managerial characteristics and introduce the variable $Z_j$ in Eqs. (2) and (3) to capture such characteristics. Our reason for doing so is that it is plausible to assume that some qualities of the chief executive officer (CEO) of a NTBF influence the performance of the firm. We consider two managerial characteristics that we assume to have a bearing on the innovative potential of such firms: the educational background and the occupational experience of the CEO (see Romijn and Albaladejo, 2002).

## Educational Background

Regarding the first of these, it is conceivable that a CEO's tertiary-level education has a *direct effect* on the innovative activities of NTBFs because the development of new products or the management of R&D requires specialised knowledge acquired in higher education. Studies (Hitt & Tyler, 1991; Wally & Baum, 1994) suggest that more educated managers have greater cognitive complexity. It is generally assumed that such cognition provides greater ability to

---

[13] Such economic conditions include, for example the interest rate, the unemployment rate, and the growth rate of demand.

absorb new ideas and recognise innovations. Studies also indicate a positive effect between education and self-employment (Robinson & Sexton, 1994; Reynolds, 1997). Bates (1995) controlled for differences in industry when examining the role of education, and also found a positive relationship between education and self-employment. Indeed, in the USA, many entrepreneurs launch firms based on the knowledge acquired in graduate schools.[14]

Studies suggest that education is a key differentiating factor between high-technology entrepreneurs and the general population of entrepreneurs, since the former exhibit higher academic credentials (Klandt & Szyperski, 1988; Roberts, 1991; Westhead & Storey, 1994). Studies also found that CEOs with higher education lead more innovative firms (Bantel & Jackson, 1989; Kimberly & Evanisko, 1981; Thomas, Litschert, & Ramaswamy, 1991). Klandt and Szyperski's (1988) study in Germany found that 88% of the founders of NTBFs had attended university, compared to 32% of founders in general and 7.5% of employees. In a UK study, Westhead and Storey (1994) revealed that 84% of high-technology entrepreneurs had a degree and 48% had a higher degree, while only 20% of entrepreneurs in general were educated to degree level and only 2% had a postgraduate qualification. A later study by Bhidé (2000) of 500 firms founded by entrepreneurs in the USA revealed that more than 80% of the founding entrepreneurs had a university education. Thus, education appears to have a positive impact on self-employment, at least in some (knowledge-intensive) industries.

Studies also report a positive relationship between education and firm growth (e.g. Almus & Nerlinger, 1999; Jo & Lee, 1996; Roberts, 1991; Van de Ven, Hudson, & Schroeder, 1984; Wilbon, 2000), although this does not appear to be straightforward. Van de Ven et al. (1984) and Jo and Lee (1996), for example find a direct and linear relationship between education and performance. The relationship between performance and education beyond degree level is not supported, however, in Almus and Nerlinger (1999); and Roberts (1991) does not find a relationship between performance and education beyond master's degree level. Almus and Nerlinger (1999) examine the impact of the type of degree on performance in NTBFs in Germany, and find that those established by entrepreneurs, with technical degrees, grow more rapidly than those with other qualifications. This may be because such degrees create managers with a more positive attitude to innovation (Tyler & Steensma, 1998). Almus and Nerlinger (1999) also affirm that neither postgraduate business education in the form of an MBA, nor the combination of an MBA and a technical degree, impact on growth. This supports earlier findings that MBA programmes do little to develop innovative or risk-taking skills in students (Finkelstein & Hambrick, 1996; Hambrick & Mason, 1984). Stuart and Abetti (1990) find a negative, though not significant, relationship between education and performance, resulting primarily from the relatively poor performance of PhDs: "advanced education beyond the bachelors degree did not help but was negatively related to performance" (Stuart & Abetti, 1990, p. 151). Likewise a study by Roberts (1991) in the USA reveals that education beyond master's degree level is negatively linked to success. In other words, while entrepreneurs with degrees generally outperform those without degrees, entrepreneurs with PhDs, do not perform as well as those with master degrees. Roberts (1991) suggests that

---

[14] In 2000 alone, some 454 start-up firms were formed from universities in the US, and some 430,000 people were employed in firms stemming from university-industry collaboration. Also, the notion of 'star scientists', and academic entrepreneurs, generally, are examples of research-productive university scientists whose management of, or collaboration with, start-up firms has assisted innovation (Darby & Zucker, 2001; Zucker & Darby, 1998a, 1998b, 1999 ).

the association between education and success in high-technology firms is most likely to represent an 'inverted "U" relationship' rather than any statistically significant direct relationship. In this study, we considered a CEO's tertiary-level education to be a determining factor in the innovative potential of NTBFs. Since the proportion of CEOs with first degrees is very high in Japan, we examined how many CEOs have postgraduate degrees.[15]

In addition to this *direct effect*, educational background also has an *indirect effect* on the R&D management of NTBFs. Bates (1990), for example, shows that entrepreneurs with higher qualifications can raise money from capital markets more easily and can survive in the market longer. Similarly, Scherer and Huh (1992) make a link between senior managers' education and the level of R&D investment. In such cases, qualifications appear to signify the entrepreneur's potential in managing a successful firm. Here, EDU is a dummy variable that takes the value 1 when a CEO has graduated from a postgraduate programme, and is otherwise zero. We expect this variable to be positively related to the results of innovative activities.

### Prior Experience

In an early study on the influence of managers' career experiences, Dearborn and Simon (1958) argued that experience of a particular business function in a firm causes managers to perceive and interpret information in ways that are consistent with and replicate their functional training. More recent studies suggest that CEOs with significant career experience in output functions (i.e. R&D/engineering and marketing/sales) favour innovation strategies because these functions emphasise growth through discovering new products and markets (Finkelstein & Hambrick, 1996; Hambrick & Mason, 1984). Consequently, CEOs with output function career experience are likely to emphasise innovation. Indeed, Thomas et al. (1991) found that firms in the computer industry pursuing strategies of product and market innovation had CEOs whose primary career experience was in output functions.

Thus, the innovative activities of a NTBF may require a CEO to have practical knowledge gleaned from business experience in an R&D function. In contrast to the explicit knowledge gained through formal education, and accounted for above, this type of knowledge is tacit in nature (Polanyi, 1958). It may be evident, for example, in the expertise needed to allocate appropriate resources to R&D, to manage research projects, and in other 'hands-on' tasks. Hills, Shrader, and Lumpkin (1999) suggest that between 50% and 90% of start-up ideas derive from prior work experience. Such findings lend support to Stinchcombe's (1965) notion of the 'liability of newness', and the argument that firms tend to be established in those fields of previous relevant experience to the founder. Therefore, a CEO's prior experience in an R&D capacity will impact on a NTBFs ability to innovate and may substitute for its lack of a track record. We assume that this prior experience is essential in conducting R&D efficiently in NTBFs and in determining the appropriate level of R&D investment in such firms. Here, EXP_RD is a binary dummy variable that is set to one when a CEO has such prior experience before founding his own firm, but is otherwise zero.

---

[15] There were 649 universities and junior colleges in Japan in 2000, which accepted 599,747 high school leavers into undergraduate education, representing 49.1% of the school leavers' population. All of these undergraduates leave university with a degree. Therefore, since the minimum qualification of a CEO of a technology-based firm is more than likely to be a first degree, we examined how many CEOs have postgraduate qualifications.

Finally, all the sample firms in this empirical study belong to technology-based industries. These industries cover a broad spectrum, ranging from the chemical industry to manufacturers of precision instruments. Thus, it is reasonable to expect that unobservable differences exist among these industries, and consequently we introduce six industrial dummies to eliminate these differences.

## Data

We employed two sets of data in this empirical study: one on NTBFs and one on Japanese PRIs. Both were compiled from responses to questionnaire surveys conducted under the auspices of the National Institute of Science and Technology Policy (NISTEP) in Tokyo.[16]

The data on NTBFs were obtained from a questionnaire survey we conducted at NISTEP in 1999. This survey was administered by post to 4958 firms selected from a database provided by Tokyo Shoko Research (TSR).[17] It was sent to firms in the following sectors: (1) chemical (482 firms), (2) metalworking machinery (606 firms), (3) special industrial machinery (329 firms), (4) electrical machinery (2332 firms), (5) motor vehicles and associated parts (492 firms) and (6) precision instruments (394 firms). An identical follow-up survey was sent to firms in the information and communications technology (ICT) and biotechnology sectors (323 firms), from which 111 firms in the ICT sector and 49 firms in the biotechnology sector responded. Thus, our sample firms (replies were received from 1384 firms, representing a response rate of 27.9%) were respondents that are classified into one of eight sectors, and which were founded after January 1989, and hence had been established for 10 years or less at the time of the survey in 1999.[18] Regarding the distribution of the ages of the firms, 36.2% of the firms were formed in the three years 1989–1991, but this ratio declined later; only 6.9% of the firms were formed in the three years 1997–1999. The survey asked the managers of these NTBFs questions on various topics, including their educational backgrounds, managerial experience, motivations for establishing start-up firms, financial status, innovative activities and technology partnerships. Considering the availability of a complete data set for all the variables in which we were interested, we have reduced the number of sample firms to 168.

The data on Japanese PRIs were obtained from a questionnaire survey conducted at NISTEP in 1998. In Japan, PRIs include the following five types of institutions: national universities, municipal universities, private universities, national research institutes and municipal research institutes. In 1998, there were 99 national universities, 61 municipal public (prefectural and city government) universities and 444 private universities. Most of the national universities are considered 'research universities'.[19] The 'private universities' are not wholly 'private', since they receive financial assistance from the government, either in national subsidies or from local tax allocation to support their running costs.

---

[16] The National Institute of Science and Technology Policy (NISTEP) is a government policy research institute that is part of the Ministry of Education, Culture, Sports, Science and Technology (MEXT) in Japan.

[17] The TSR Database is one of the most comprehensive and credible sources of firm information in Japan.

[18] The NISTEP questionnaire was administered by post to 4,958 firms selected from a database provided by TSR, and based on technology or manufacturing start-up firms established within 10 years. The survey contained 343 questions. Replies were received from 1384 firms. For more details (see Sakakibara, Koga, Honjo, & Kondo, 2000).

[19] 80% of Grants-in-Aid for Scientific Research was distributed to national universities in FY 1999 (Asonuma, 2002, p. 110).

In addition to the universities, there are a large number of other PRIs in Japan, such as, national and municipal research institutes. At the national level, for example the Ministry of Economy, Trade and Industry (METI), has some 13 national research institutes under its domain. Selecting just one of these, the National Institute of Advanced Industrial Science and Technology (AIST), has under its organisation some 32 research centres (e.g. the Tissue Engineering Research Center, the Research Centre for Advanced Manufacturing on Nanoscale Science and Engineering); 21 research institutes (e.g. the Neuroscience Research Institute, the Ceramics Research Institute); 2 special divisions (e.g. Special Division of Human Life Technology) and 8 research initiatives (e.g. Single-Molecule Bioanalysis Laboratory, Laboratory for Membrane Chemistry). About 80% of Japanese R&D is performed in industry. Of the 20% of R&D performed in the public sector, universities play the key role.[20]

This survey asked 1473 PRIs a series of questions on a range of topics concerning their role and innovative activities, including R&D expenditures, the number of patents granted, the number of researchers and the number of published scientific papers. This study is based on data from 932 respondents to the PRI survey (representing 63.27%) and represents information as of 1997.

Table 1 shows the definition of the variables and Table 2 reports the summary statistics.

Table 1: Summary descriptions of the variables.

| Variable | Definition |
| --- | --- |
| PT | The number of patents applications in 1998 |
| PTL | The natural logarithm of PT (defined above) |
| RD | The natural logarithm of firm R&D expenditures in 1997 |
| $PUB_1$ | Public knowledge created by PRIs located in the *same* prefecture as the recipient firms of such knowledge |
| $PUB_2$ | Public knowledge created by PRIs located *outside* the prefecture where recipient firms of such knowledge are located |
| Firm-level | |
| SG | The annual growth rate of sales during the year 1998, calculated by: (Sales in 1998– Sales in 1997)/ (Sales in 1997) |
| SIZE | The natural logarithm of total employees in 1998 |
| F_AGE | The number of years a firm has been in business |
| CEO-level | |
| EXP_RD | Experience in R&D function. A dummy variable set to 1 if a CEO has prior experience in an R&D role |
| EDU | Educational background. A dummy variable set to 1 if a CEO holds a postgraduate degree |

[20] The Ministry of Education, Culture, Sports, Science and Technology (MEXT) was responsible for 64% of government R&D expenditure for 2002. METI is responsible for the second-largest budget of 16.9% (Asonuma, 2002).

Table 2: Summary statistics.

| Variable | OBS | Mean | SD | Min | Max |
|---|---|---|---|---|---|
| PT | 168 | 3.619 | 19.06 | 0 | 242 |
| PTL | 168 | 3.038 | 0.908 | 2.303 | 7.796 |
| RD | 168 | 2.308 | 1.783 | 0 | 8.78 |
| $PRD_1$ (measured by Public R&D expenditure) | 168 | 11.24 | 1.27 | 9.075 | 13.12 |
| $PRD_2$ (measured by Public R&D expenditure) | 168 | 11.75 | 0.7 | 10.13 | 13.31 |
| $PRD_1$ (measured by Public Papers) | 136 | 11.3 | 1.311 | 9.22 | 13.12 |
| $PRD_2$ (measured by Public Papers) | 136 | 11.87 | 0.681 | 10.6 | 13.31 |
| $PRD_1$ (measured by Public Patents) | 154 | 11.31 | 1.249 | 9.22 | 13.12 |
| $PRD_2$ (measured by Public Patents) | 154 | 11.83 | 0.657 | 10.6 | 13.31 |
| SG | 168 | 0.205 | 1.225 | $-0.74$ | 14 |
| SIZE | 168 | 2.763 | 1.087 | 0.693 | 7.011 |
| F_AGE | 168 | 5.756 | 2.572 | 1 | 9 |
| EXP_RD | 168 | 0.571 | 0.496 | 0 | 1 |
| EDU | 168 | 0.06 | 0.237 | 0 | 1 |

## Estimated Results

### Basic Results

Table 3 reports our results for the extent of the effects of public knowledge on the innovative activities of Japanese NTBFs. Columns (1) and (2) show our estimations for public knowledge as measured by R&D expenditures by PRIs.

The coefficients of $PUB_1$ are significantly positive in both columns (1) and (2), indicating that PRIs provide positive externalities to the innovative activities of NTBFs. Furthermore, our results show that the coefficient of $PUB_2$ is insignificant in column (2), suggesting that those knowledge spillovers from PRIs to NTBFs that occur strictly within the borders of a prefecture have much greater impact on the innovative activities of a firm than knowledge spillovers from adjacent prefectures. In other words, knowledge spillovers are geographically localised, such that an NTBF located in Tokyo receives more knowledge spillovers from PRIs located in Tokyo than from PRIs located in other prefectures. These findings concur with those of several empirical studies using patents and bibliometric data (e.g. Jaffe, 1989; Jaffe et al., 1993; Katz, 1994), which conclude that knowledge spillovers are geographically bounded and that they dissipate quickly with distance. However, this result may not be robust. The public knowledge generated by PRIs located in adjacent prefectures turn out to have a positive impact on firm innovation that is significant at the 5% level, according to the TOBIT estimation. The measured contribution of R&D expenditure by PRIs does not allow us to state unequivocally that proximity matters for

Table 3: Estimated results (1).

| | R&D | | Papers | | Patents | |
|---|---|---|---|---|---|---|
| | **(1) TOBIT** | **(2) Poisson** | **(3) TOBIT** | **(4) Poisson** | **(5) TOBIT** | **(6) Poisson** |
| RD | 0.3320*** | 0.3744*** | 0.3497*** | 0.3900*** | C.3367*** | 0.3825*** |
| | (0.0588) | (0.0551) | (0.0634) | (0.0571) | (C.0627) | (0.0566) |
| $PUB_1$ | 0.2573*** | 0.2604*** | 0.2287*** | 0.2645*** | 0.1282** | 0.1827*** |
| | (0.0823) | (0.0870) | (0.0950) | (0.0977) | (0.0618) | (0.0637) |
| $PUB_2$ | 0.2675** | 0.1198 | 0.2433 | 0.2414 | 0.1265 | 0.0471 |
| | (0.1478) | (0.1577) | (0.1738) | (0.1730) | (0.0838) | (0.0675) |
| SG | 0.0070 | 0.0383 | -0.0513 | -0.0000 | -0.0148 | 0.0050 |
| | (0.0920) | (0.0848) | (0.0988) | (0.0992) | (0.0964) | (0.1002) |
| SIZE | 0.2644*** | 0.5243*** | 0.2899*** | 0.5221*** | 0.2893*** | 0.5252*** |
| | (0.0946) | (0.0701) | (0.1031) | (0.0712) | (0.1007) | (0.0709) |
| F_AGE | -0.0292 | 0.0544 | -0.0676 | 0.0285 | -0.0523 | 0.0331 |
| | (0.0403) | (0.0522) | (0.0445) | (0.0503) | (0.0424) | (0.0510) |
| CONST | -3.262 | -5.858*** | -0.7644 | -5.248*** | 1 798 | -2.305*** |
| | (2.243) | (2.380) | (1.942) | (1.803) | (1 272) | (0.5959) |
| Industry D | Yes | Yes | Yes | Yes | Yes | Yes |
| Pseudo $R^2$ | 0.148 | 0.727 | 0.158 | 0.751 | 0.146 | 0.737 |
| No. of observations | 168 | 168 | 136 | 136 | 157 | 154 |

*Note*: The dependent variable is the number of patents applications in the Poisson regression and the natural logarithm of the number of patent applications in the TOBIT regressions, respectively. The standard error is shown in parentheses. *, ** and *** indicate statistical significance at the 10%, 5% and 1% level, respectively (two-tailed *t*-test).

knowledge spillovers from PRIs in the innovative output of NTBFs. Knowledge spillovers — embodying some type of knowledge — appear to occur from other prefectures, or they may attenuate slowly with distance.

Next, we report our results for the measurement of public knowledge by the total number of published papers and the total number of patents granted, respectively. An important question here is whether any change in the tool used to measure public knowledge — papers or patents — will produce an estimated result different from each other. Also, with which of the outcomes mentioned above will these results agree?

We have already considered the case where public R&D expenditure was used to measure public knowledge. Since a large proportion of public R&D expenditure covers the expenses of researchers, the knowledge captured by public R&D strongly reflects the interests and expertise of the researchers who develop it.[21] Inevitably, the knowledge measured by public R&D includes a component of tacit knowledge, such as the know-how embodied in the experience of the researchers themselves (Polanyi, 1958; Ryle, 1946, 1949). This kind of knowledge is 'sticky' (Szulanski, 1996) and is difficult to transfer and utilise without the assistance and guidance of its inventors (Nonaka, 1994). Contrary to the idea of knowledge as a public good, tacit knowledge does not spill over inexpensively (Nelson, 1992; Teece, 1992) and such knowledge spillovers are geographically bounded. Thus, firmed located within close geographic proximity to researchers have an advantage in utilising such public knowledge.

On the other hand, unlike tacit knowledge bound up in individual PRI scientists, the knowledge expressed in published papers and patents is codified and overt. Firms attempting to utilise this kind of knowledge do not usually seek direct interactions with the researcher(s) who created or developed it. As a result, geographic proximity would not be expected to lend an advantage to those firms located close to the sources of such explicit knowledge. Instead, the more tacit knowledge is, the more that knowledge spillovers would tend to be geographically localised.

If geographical limitations on spillovers of explicit knowledge are considerably less significant than limitations on spillovers of tacit knowledge, the coefficient of $PUB_2$ should be larger than that of $PUB_1$ in Eqs. (2) and (3). Columns (3) and (4) of Table 3 report the estimated results for published papers. Both columns show that the coefficient of $PUB_1$ is significantly positive, but that of $PUB_2$ is not. Similar findings appeared when we measured public knowledge according to patent applications by PRIs, as shown in columns (5) and (6). These results suggest that knowledge spillovers from PRIs are geographically restricted, irrespective of the kind of proxies (scientific papers or patent applications) we employ for public knowledge.

### Firm-Level Characteristics

The variable RD, which represents R&D expenditure and is a proxy for the technological capability of a firm, is significantly positive in all columns of Table 3. This suggests that technological capability is an important determinant of innovation in NTBFs. According

---

[21] In Japanese public research institutes, the average share of researchers' expenditure to the total R&D budget is 59.7%.

to Cohen and Levinthal (1989), technological capability plays two roles in innovation: it enables the absorption of knowledge from outside the firm, and it enables the creation of new knowledge and technology. Cohen and Levinthal (1990) also suggest that R&D expenditure creates a capacity — 'absorptive capacity' — to assimilate and exploit new knowledge. This is particularly important for NTBFs because they often lack sufficient internal resources to further such knowledge by themselves (Link & Rees, 1990).

The coefficients of the variable SG, which is a proxy for demand, do not show significant signs in any columns of Table 3. Cohen (1995) maintains that demand is an important determinant of innovation, as exemplified, for example in the 'demand-pull' aspect of the linear model of innovation, and patenting is a way to increase sales. We were unable to find this relationship between demand and patents. That is, the demand-side conditions do not appear to influence the number of patent applications made by a firm. This may have been the result of the time lag between patenting and sales. Instead, 'technology-push' aspects, such as, R&D expenditure and knowledge spillovers appear to determine patent applications. This is not surprising if one considers for example the case of new biotechnology firms, which have R&D timescales extending to many years and whose patent portfolio is the result of access to knowledge from universities and other PRIs (e.g. Audretsch & Stephan, 1999; Zucker & Darby, 1996).

The coefficients of the variable SIZE are significantly positive in all columns of Table 3, implying that R&D expenditure, published papers and patent applications are proportional to the size of the firm (see Cohen, 1996). As one would expect, a NTBF will have to reach a critical size before it has sufficient R&D resources to produce papers and products that merit patent protection. Firms bear various costs in preparing and filing patent applications, the average cost of which will decrease as the number of applications increases. Under such circumstances, the propensity to file more patent applications clearly goes with NTBFs that have surpassed a certain size. Owing to the cost of initial patent application, NTBFs below this size may hesitate to apply for patent rights to protect their ownership interests in their inventions, and choose alternative means instead to secure their returns from innovation (Teece, 1986, 1987).

### *Managerial Characteristics*

We focussed on two managerial characteristics thought to influence the innovative activities of NTBFs: the prior R&D experience and the educational background of a firm's CEO. Both characteristics can be considered as knowledge embodied in the CEO and we wished to evaluate the relationship between these kinds of knowledge and the public knowledge from PRIs. Table 4 shows the estimated results for the CEO's prior experience in an R&D role. The coefficients of the variable EXP_RD show significantly positive signs in columns (2), (3) and (6) of Table 4. These results confirm that a firm where the current CEO has worked in an R&D role tends to achieve a high degree of innovative activities. In addition, the significance of the variable $PUB_1$ does not change, even after the variable EXP_RD in the equations is introduced. This suggests that the knowledge captured by EXP_RD may be a *complement* to the knowledge from PRIs, so that tacit knowledge from prior R&D experience enables one to absorb and use effectively the knowledge from PRIs.

Table 5 shows the estimated results for the educational background of the CEO. The coefficients of the variable EDU show significantly positive signs in columns (1), (2), (4)

Table 4: Estimated results (2): R&D experience.

| | R&D | | Papers | | Patents | |
|---|---|---|---|---|---|---|
| | (1) TOBIT | (2) Poisson | (3) TOBIT | (4) Poisson | (5) TOBIT | (6) Poisson |
| RD | 0.3321*** | 0.3897*** | 0.3455*** | 0.4086*** | 0.3343*** | 0.3945*** |
| | (0.0584) | (0.0583) | (0.0629) | (0.0603) | (0.0623) | (0.0603) |
| $PUB_1$ | 0.2438*** | 0.2364*** | 0.2130** | 0.2420*** | 0.1165** | 0.1699*** |
| | (0.0824) | (0.0842) | (0.0941) | (0.0945) | (0.0617) | (0.0624) |
| $PUB_2$ | 0.2390 | 0.0954 | 0.2299 | 0.3086* | 0.1186 | 0.0625 |
| | (0.1488) | (0.1571) | (0.1729) | (0.1745) | (0.0834) | (0.0656) |
| SG | -0.0048 | 0.0004 | -0.0722 | -0.0408 | -0.0295 | -0.0278 |
| | (0.0924) | (0.0969) | (0.1003) | (0.1222) | (0.0969) | (0.1182) |
| SIZE | 0.2652*** | 0.4627*** | 0.2869*** | 0.4558*** | 0.2921*** | 0.4721*** |
| | (0.0939) | (0.0742) | (0.1018) | (0.0764) | (0.0997) | (0.0765) |
| F_AGE | -0.0305 | 0.0666 | -0.0701 | 0.0337 | -0.0531 | 0.0428 |
| | (0.0401) | (0.0540) | (0.0441) | (0.0523) | (0.0422) | (0.0531) |
| EXP_RD | 0.2409 | 0.5503** | 0.0479* | 0.6146 | 0.3204 | 0.5069** |
| | (0.2088) | (0.2372) | (0.2327) | (0.2677) | (0.2213) | (0.2431) |
| CONST | -2.800 | -5.278 | -0.4984 | -5.448*** | 1.876 | -2.248 |
| | (2.260) | (2.339) | (1.927) | (1.827) | (1.263) | (0.6177) |
| Industry D | Yes | Yes | Yes | Yes | Yes | Yes |
| Pseudo $R^2$ | 0.0151 | 0.734 | 0.166 | 0.758 | 0.0151 | 0.743 |
| No. of observations | 168 | 168 | 136 | 136 | 154 | 154 |

*Note*: The dependent variable is the number of patent applications in the Poisson regression and the natural logarithm of the number of patent applications in the TOBIT regressions, respectively. The standard error is shown in parentheses. *, ** and *** indicate statistical significance at the 10%, 5% and 1% level, respectively (two-tailed *t*-test).

Table 5:  Estimated results (3): educational background.

| | R&D | | Papers | | Patents | |
|---|---|---|---|---|---|---|
| | (1) TOBIT | (2) Poisson | (3) TOBIT | (4) Poisson | (5) TOBIT | (6) Poisson |
| RD | 0.3111*** | 0.3427*** | 0.3487*** | 0.3610*** | 0.3351*** | 0.3529*** |
| | (0.0578) | (0.0448) | (0.0627) | (0.0448) | (0.0619) | (0.0454) |
| PUB$_1$ | 0.2668*** | 0.1556** | 0.2343*** | 0.1241 | 0.1382** | 0.0892 |
| | (0.0814) | (0.0849) | (0.0940) | (0.0936) | (0.0613) | (0.0596) |
| PUB$_2$ | 0.2808 | 0.1992 | 0.2372 | 0.1817 | 0.1270 | 0.0344 |
| | (0.1456) | (0.1418) | (0.1713) | (0.1682) | (0.0825) | (0.0694) |
| SG | 0.0089 | 0.0154 | -0.0510 | -0.0405 | -0.0131 | -0.0260 |
| | (0.0909) | (0.0793) | (0.0982) | (0.0934) | (0.0956) | (0.0868) |
| SIZE | 0.2551*** | 0.4052 | 0.2828*** | 0.4149*** | 0.2809*** | 0.4115*** |
| | (0.0933) | (0.0746) | (0.1020) | (0.0751) | (0.0995) | (0.0761) |
| F_AGE | -0.0302 | -0.0148 | -0.0690 | -0.0341 | -0.0530 | -0.0339 |
| | (0.0395) | (0.0438) | (0.0439) | (0.0487) | (0.0417) | (0.0451) |
| EDU | 0.7018* | 1.255*** | 0.5472 | 1.156*** | 0.6463 | 1.214*** |
| | (0.3936) | (0.2742) | (0.3980) | (0.27221) | (0.4040) | (0.2606) |
| CONST | -3.465 | -4.700** | -0.7257 | -2.743 | 1.794 | -0.9607 |
| | (2.215) | (2.090) | (1.917) | (1.561) | (1.254) | (0.4717) |
| Industry D | Yes | Yes | Yes | Yes | Yes | Yes |
| Pseudo $R^2$ | 0.155 | 0.754 | 0.163 | 0.776 | C.152 | 0.764 |
| No. of observations | 168 | 169 | 136 | 136 | 154 | 154 |

Note: The dependent variable is the number of patent applications in the Poisson regression and the natural logarithm of the number of patent applications in the TOBIT regressions, respectively. The standard error is shown in parentheses. *, ** and *** indicate statistical significance at the 10%, 5% and 1% level, respectively (two-tailed *t*-test).

and (6) of Table 5. The significance of the variable PUB$_1$ decreases in columns (4) and (6) when the variable EDU in the equations is introduced. Why this might be is uncertain. One suggestion is that the knowledge captured by EDU may *substitute* for the knowledge transferred from PRIs. It is assumed that these kinds of public knowledge will primarily benefit those CEOs without a postgraduate education. Such CEOs could acquire various kinds of knowledge necessary to assist the development of their NTBF through knowledge spillovers from PRIs. However, a careful examination of those firms (especially their location) whose CEO has a postgraduate degree may reveal why introducing EDU leads to a non-significant coefficient of PUB.

It is possible to infer from these results that managerial characteristics do potentially have a positive effect on the innovative activities of NTBFs. We have found evidence, moreover, that the characteristics of recipients may also affect the extent of knowledge spillovers.

## Interpretation and Discussion

This paper examined several firm-level and managerial determinants of innovative activity in Japanese NTBFs, using original data from questionnaire surveys conducted in Japan. We took NTBFs as those firms that were classified into one of several technology sectors and that had been established for less than 10 years at the time of the survey.

Our empirical analysis led to the following findings. Firstly, we found evidence using Poisson regression on R&D expenditures that knowledge spillovers from PRIs to NTBFs do occur in Japan, and that there is a significant localisation effect in a firm's innovation activities and in spillovers associated with them. This is in agreement with the results for other countries (e.g. Adams, 2001; Autant-Bernard, 2001; Jaffe, 1989). However, we also found evidence that spillovers from PRIs in neighbouring prefectures are significant at a 5% threshold in the TOBIT estimation. This indicates that knowledge spillovers from Japanese PRIs are not geographically localised or do not dissipate quickly, which is at variance with results from studies elsewhere. Whether this indicates, for example, that some aspect of knowledge (e.g. explicit knowledge) used by the NTBFs is not contingent on geographic proximity to PRIs, or that the relevance of knowledge externalities differs according to industry, requires further investigation.

The result of the Poisson regression is not surprising when one considers that researchers account for a large proportion of public R&D expenditure in Japan and the knowledge captured by public R&D reflects the accumulation of tacit and explicit knowledge in these researchers. The transfer of tacit knowledge to NTBFs is difficult because it "is hard to articulate or can only be acquired through experience" (Hansen, 1999, p. 87), and direct collaborative work is often the only way to transfer such knowledge (Lynskey, 2001, 2006a). Thus, firms located in close geographic proximity to PRIs, and with access to their researchers, have a clear advantage when utilising such public knowledge (Florax, 1992). On the other hand, the result of the TOBIT estimation might be explained by the mobility of researchers between public institutions, or even to firms, and their public engagements to disseminate research results.

Secondly, we demonstrated that the extent to which knowledge spillovers are contingent on geographic location does not depend on the type of tool or proxy (papers or patents) used as a substitute variable to measure public knowledge. Moreover, although one might suppose that these codified forms of knowledge are not susceptible to localisation effects, there is a tendency for them to be localised, concurring with the Poisson regressions for public R&D expenditure.

How can one interpret these results? The information provided in published papers and patents are a codified form of knowledge. In theory, then, everyone has equal ease of access to this type of public knowledge and one might expect that geographical remoteness should not be a constraint on knowledge spillovers. The availability of resources such as the Internet and knowledge-based tools makes it much cheaper, easier and faster to obtain codified information. It must be remembered, however, that the mere ability to acquire public knowledge is different from the capacity to interpret it and utilise it in innovation (which is what we are assessing here). While the cost of transmitting information may be increasingly invariant to distance, the cost of transmitting tacit knowledge rises with distance. In practice, the knowledge provided in published papers and patents may be complex and difficult to decipher and apply. Simple access to such knowledge does not ensure that recipients will be able to replicate the results (Lynskey, 1999).

The recipient of such knowledge may not be able to employ it fully without some collaboration or consultation with the PRI in which it was developed. For example, a patent document generally provides the minimum novel information on a new technology and simply cites references to 'prior art' — previous patents and publications — on which the technology is based. Under such circumstances, potential users of the patented information may not be able to utilise this knowledge without direct assistance from the patentee. Our finding, that knowledge spillovers, irrespective of the type of tools used to measure public knowledge, is geographically bounded, supports the idea that firms are unable to make full use of certain types of public knowledge without maintaining close contact with the PRIs from where they obtain such knowledge. Moreover, intuitively, it is reasonable to expect that spillovers from PRIs do not happen simultaneously with firm innovation. One can expect long-term lags in the relationship between the emergence of public-generated knowledge and innovation in firms, and that the effect on innovation would decrease steadily as knowledge becomes more dispersed and commonly known. These results correspond to those of Jaffe et al. (1993) who compare the geographic localisation of patent citations with that of the cited patents, as evidence of the extent to which knowledge spillovers are geographically localised. They find that, although localisation fades slowly over time, a US patent tends to be cited more frequently within the state in which it was filed than outside the state. Moreover, Feldman (1994) finds that product innovations also exhibit a pronounced tendency to cluster geographically, and concludes that the geographic clustering of product innovation at the state level is related to the level of university R&D expenditure in the state, which is consistent with earlier findings of Jaffe (1989).[22]

Thirdly, we found that the managerial characteristics we considered — prior experience in an R&D role and the educational background of the current CEO — have an effect on

---

[22] Feldman's (1994) study also suggests that the clustering of product innovation at the state level is related to other innovative inputs, including the presence of related industry and specialised business services (see King et al., 2003). The presence of these complementary activities promotes information spillovers that lower the cost of developing new innovations for firms located within these areas.

firm's innovative activities and there is a relationship between public knowledge from PRIs and different types of knowledge embodied in a firm's CEO. Knowledge acquired by a CEO through prior experience in R&D appears to serve as a *complement* for the knowledge from PRIs. On the other hand, the knowledge captured by formal postgraduate education appears to be a *substitute* for such public knowledge.

## Conclusion

What are the policy implications of the results of this empirical study? Firstly, the presence of knowledge spillovers justifies the current policy in Japan of strengthening the relationship between industry and PRIs, particularly universities. Various initiatives, such as the creation of technology licensing offices and start-up incubation units at universities (Lynskey, 2004c, 2006b), and government-backed consortia comprising firms and PRIs, have been introduced to promote knowledge transfer from PRIs in order to grow the number of NTBFs and strengthening Japan's economy. Our findings suggest that such measures are a legitimate support to innovation in NTBFs. Indeed, a recent study suggests that small firms in Japan are more likely to initiate interactions with university-based scientists on the basis of formal intermediaries such as technology transfer offices than large firms (Fukugawa, 2005).

Secondly, the existence of geographical boundaries to knowledge spillovers makes a case for further decentralisation of PRIs. Japan is a highly centralised society, with large numbers of PRIs concentrated in the Kanto (centred on Tokyo) and the Kansai (centred on Osaka) regions (OECD/IMHE, 1999): "Japan seems to be very much centralised in terms of higher education policies and funding as well as governance of science and technology policies" (Kitagawa, 2003, 2005, p. 12); "R&D related activities have been heavily concentrated in the area around Tokyo" (Kitagawa, 2005, p. 23). This concentration of research intensity — and public R&D expenditure — in a few prefectures may account for spillover effects across prefectures in one of the regressions. There may be merit in decentralisation, by establishing PRIs as anchors (see Agrawal & Cockburn, 2002; Feldman, 2003) of innovation and economic activity in provincial regions. Related to this point, since PRIs play a number of important roles in providing knowledge to local NTBFs, they should be open to local firms and industries and concentrate their knowledge-transfer resources at the prefectural level. Firms may make more use of public knowledge if they can maintain close contact with the researchers in their near-by PRIs.

Thirdly, since some NTBFs may hesitate to apply for patent rights to protect their intellectual property, due to the high cost of initial patent application, the patent law may need to be modified so that different levels of application fees are charged in accordance with the firm size. Such revision would be a remedy for the current situation and accommodate the needs of NTBFs.

Fourthly, the findings on CEOs' education and prior experience suggest that those CEOs with insufficient prior R&D experience may be less able to benefit from knowledge spillovers. This is not because they lack knowledge — indeed, they may have formal postgraduate education — but because they require the tacit knowledge and absorptive capacity to benefit from such knowledge.

Finally, we refer to three limitations of this study that might serve to guide future research. Firstly, the use of patents as an indicator of innovation has its flaws because not all innovations are patented and because patents differ widely in their economic impact. Acs et al. (1992) suggest that instead of measuring innovative output using patents, another measure is to count numbers of innovations, as listed, for example in science and technology news reports, official statements and trade periodicals in each industry. We used patent applications because the firms in question were NTBFs and it seemed likely that they would have applied for patents on their innovations, irrespective of whether the innovations were referenced in journals. Moreover, the findings of Acs et al. (1992) are broadly similar to those of Jaffe (1989) using patent data, except that the impact of spillovers is greater for innovation counts than for patents, and the impact of geographical proximity also appears greater.

A second limitation is that it is not clear if Japanese prefectures are the most appropriate unit for seeking geographical coincidence effects. The Tokyo region, for example, has about one-fifth of Japan's population and concentrates many of Japan's firms and much of its public research activity. Further estimations should be performed to include a dummy variable for firms that belong to this region.

Another drawback is that a national institute administered the questionnaire survey. Thus, those firms having stronger relations with public research institutions may have been more inclined to fill in the questionnaire correctly and this would have introduced a bias in the data.

Finally, production function approaches, as used here, assume, to varying degrees, invariant production techniques among firms. This is clearly an over-simplification, which, although helpful for empirical purposes, is difficult to maintain in the face of research on firm behaviour (which shows that such behaviour is heavily dependent on the firm's history and context). Production function representations of firms' behaviour are therefore simply 'mental models' of the way in which the world works: "It has not been proven that such production functions exist or take the form assumed by economists". Nevertheless, despite these limitations, it is hoped that this study represents a useful start in exploring the phenomenon of spillovers from PRIs in Japan.

# References

Acs, Z. J., Anselin, L., & Varga, A. (2002). Patents and innovation counts as measures of regional production of new knowledge. *Research Policy, 31*(7), 1069–1085.

Acs, Z. J., & Audretsch, D. B. (1988). Innovation in large and small firms: An empirical analysis. *American Economic Review, 78*(4), 678–690.

Acs, Z. J., Audretsch, D. B., & Feldman, M. P. (1992). Real effects of academic research: Comment. *American Economic Review, 82*(1), 363–367.

Acs, Z. J., Audretsch, D. B., & Feldman, M. P. (1994). R&D spillovers and recipient firm size. *Review of Economics and Statistics, 76*(2), 336–340.

Adams, J. D. (2001). *Comparative localization of academic and industrial spillovers.* NBER Working Paper 8292. National Bureau of Economic Research, Cambridge, MA.

Agrawal, A., & Cockburn, I. (2002). *University research, industrial R&D, and the anchor tenant hypothesis.* NBER Working Paper W9212. National Bureau of Economic Research, Cambridge, MA.

Almeida, P., & Kogut, B. (1997). The exploration of technological diversity and the geographic localization of innovation. *Small Business Economics, 9,* 21–31.

Almus, M., & Nerlinger, E. A. (1999). Growth of new technology-based firms: Which factors matter? *Small Business Economics, 13*(2), 141–154.

Anselin, L., Varga, A., & Acs, Z. (1997). Local geographic spillovers between university research and high technology innovations. *Journal of Urban Economics, 42,* 422–448.

Antonelli, C. (1994). Technological districts localized spillovers and productivity growth: The Italian evidence on technological externalities in the core regions. *International Review of Applied Economics, 8*(1), 18–30.

Asonuma, A. (2002). Finance reform in Japanese higher education. *Higher Education, 43,* 109–126.

Audretsch, D. (1998). Agglomeration and the location of economic activity. *Oxford Review of Economic Policy, 14,* 18–29.

Audretsch, D., & Vivarelli, M. (1996). Small firms and R&D spillovers: Evidence from Italy. *Small Business Economics, 8*(3), 249–258.

Audretsch, D. B., & Stephan, P. E. (1999). Knowledge spillovers in biotechnology: Sources and incentives. *Journal of Evolutionary Economics, 9,* 97–107.

Autant-Bernard, C. (2001). Science and knowledge flows: Evidence from the French case. *Research Policy, 30*(7), 1069–1078.

Autio, E., Sapienza, H. J., & Almeida, J. G. (2000). Effects of age of entry, knowledge intensity, and imitability on international growth. *Academy of Management Journal, 43*(5), 909–924.

Bantel, K. A., & Jackson, S. E. (1989). Top management innovations in banking: Does the composition of the top team make a difference? *Strategic Management Journal, 10*(Special Issue), 107–124.

Bates, T. (1990). Entrepreneur human capital inputs and small business longevity. *Review of Economics and Statistics, 72*(4), 551–559.

Bates, T. (1995). Self-employment entry across industry groups. *Journal of Business Venturing, 10*(2), 143–156.

Beise, M., & Stahl, H. (1999). Public research and industrial innovations in Germany. *Research Policy, 28*(4), 397–422.

Bernstein, J. I., & Mohnen, P. (1998). International R&D spillovers between U.S. and Japanese R&D intensive sectors. *Journal of International Economics, 44*(2), 315–338.

Bhidé, A. V. (2000). *The origin and evolution of new businesses.* Oxford: Oxford University Press.

Blind, K., & Grupp, H. (1999). Interdependencies between the science and technology infrastructure and innovation activities in German regions: Empirical findings and policy consequences. *Research Policy, 28*(5), 451–468.

Branstetter, L. (1996). *Are knowledge spillovers international or intranational in scope? Microeconomic evidence from the U.S. and Japan.* NBER Working Paper 5800. National Bureau of Economic Research, Cambridge, MA.

Breschi, S., & Lissoni, F. (2001). Knowledge spillovers and local innovation systems: A critical survey. *Industrial and Corporate Change, 10*(4), 975–1005.

Cohen, W., & Levinthal, D. A. (1989). Innovation and learning: The two faces of R&D — Implications for the analysis of R&D investment. *Economic Journal, 99,* 569–596.

Cohen, W., & Levinthal, D. A. (1990). Absorptive capacity: A new perspective on learning and innovation. *Administrative Science Quarterly, 35,* 128–152.

Cohen, W. M. (1995). Empirical studies of innovative activity. In: P. Stoneman (Ed.), *Handbook of the economics of innovation and technological change.* Oxford: Blackwell.

Cohen, W. M., & Klepper, S. (1996a). Firm size and the nature of innovation within industries: The case of process and product R&D. *Review of Economics and Statistics, 78*(2), 232–243.

Cohen, W. M., & Klepper, S. (1996b). A reprise of size and R&D. *Economic Journal, 106*(437), 925–951.

Coombs, R. (1996). Core competencies and the strategic management of R&D. *R&D Management, 26*(4), 345–354.

Darby, M. R., & Zucker, L. G. (2001). Change or die: The adoption of biotechnology in the Japanese and U.S. pharmaceutical industries. In: R. A. Burgelman & H. Chesbrough (Eds), *Comparative studies of technological evolution* (pp. 85–125). Amsterdam and Oxford: Elsevier Science.

Dearborn, C. C., & Simon, H. A. (1958). Selective perception: A note on the department identifications of executives. *Sociometry, 21*, 140–144.

Ehrenberg, R. G. (1992). The flow of new doctorates. *Journal of Economic Literature, 30*(2), 830–875.

Evans, D. S. (1987). The relationship between firm growth, size, and age: Estimates for 100 manufacturing industries. *Journal of Industrial Economics, 35*(4), 567–581.

Feldman, M. (2003). The locational dynamics of the US biotech industry: Knowledge externalities and the anchor hypothesis. *Industry and Innovation, 10*(3), 311–328.

Feldman, M. P. (1994). *The geography of innovation*. Boston, MA: Kluwer Academic Press.

Figueiredo, P. N. (2002). Does technological learning pay off? Inter-firm differences in technological capability: Accumulation paths and operational performance improvement. *Research Policy, 31*(1), 73–94.

Finkelstein, S., & Hambrick, D. C. (1996). *Strategic leadership: Top executives and their effects on organizations*. St. Paul, MN: West Publishing Company.

Florax, R. (1992). *The university: A regional booster? Economic impacts of knowledge infrastructure*. Aldershot, Hants, UK: Avebury.

Fukugawa, N. (2005). Characteristics of knowledge interactions between universities and small firms in Japan. *International Small Business Journal, 23*(4), 379–401.

Goto, A., & Suzuki, K. (1989). R&D capital, rate of return on R&D investment and spillover of R&D in Japanese manufacturing industries. *Review of Economics and Statistics, 71*(4), 555–564.

Goto, A. (2000). Japan's national innovation system: current status and problems. *Oxford Review of Economic Policy, 26*, 103–113.

Greene, W. H. (1997). *Econometric analysis* (3rd ed.). Upper Saddle River, NJ: Prentice Hall.

Griliches, Z. (1979). Issues in assessing the contribution of research and development to productivity growth. *The Bell Journal of Economics, 10*(1), 92–116.

Griliches, Z. (1992). The search for R&D spillovers. *Scandinavian Journal of Economics, 94*(Suppl.), 29–47.

Griliches, Z. (1995). R&D and productivity. In: P. Stoneman (Ed.), *Handbook of industrial innovation*. London: Blackwell Press.

Griliches, Z., & Mairesse, J. (1990). R&D and productivity growth: Comparing Japanese and US manufacturing firms. In: C. Hulten (Ed.), *Productivity growth in Japan and the United States* (pp. 317–348). Chicago: University of Chicago Press.

Grossman, G. M., & Helpman, E. (1991). *Innovation and growth in the global economy*. Cambridge, MA: MIT Press.

Hall, B. H., Jaffe, A. B., & Trajtenberg, M. (2001). *The NBER patent citation data file: lessons, insights and methodological tools*. NBER Working Paper 8498. National Bureau of Economic Research, Cambridge, MA.

Hambrick, D. C., & Mason, P. A. (1984). Upper echelons: The organization as a reflection of its top managers. *Academy of Management Review, 9*(2), 193–206.

Hansen, M. T. (1999). The search-transfer problem: The role of weak ties in sharing knowledge across organization subunits. *Administrative Science Quarterly, 44*(1), 82–111.

Highfield, R., & Smiley, R. (1987). New business starts and economic activity: An empirical investigation. *International Journal of Industrial Organization, 5*(1), 51–66.

Hills, G. E., Shrader, R. C., & Lumpkin, G. T. (1999). Opportunity recognition as a creative process. In: Babson College, *Frontiers of entrepreneurship research*. Wellesley, MA: Babson College.

Hitt, M. A., & Tyler, B. B. (1991). Strategic decision models: Integrating different perspectives. *Strategic Management Journal, 12*(5), 327–351.

Jaffe, A. B. (1986). Technological opportunity and spillovers of R&D: Evidence from firms' patent, profits, and market value. *American Economic Review, 76*(5), 984–1001.

Jaffe, A. B. (1989). Real effects of academic research. *American Economic Review, 79*(5), 957–970.

Jaffe, A. B., & Trajtenberg, M. (1996). *Flows of knowledge from universities and federal labs.* NBER Working Paper 5712, 1–18. National Bureau of Economic Research, Cambridge, MA.

Jaffe, A. B., & Trajtenberg, M. (2002). *Patents, citations, and innovations: A window on the knowledge economy.* Cambridge, MA: MIT Press.

Jaffe, A. B., Trajtenberg, M., & Henderson, R. (1993). Geographic localization of knowledge spillovers as evidenced by patent citations. *Quarterly Journal of Economics, 108*, 577–598.

Jaffe, A. B. (1996). Economic analysis of research spillovers: implications for the Advanced Technology Programme. Economic Assessment Office, The Advanced Technology Program, National Institutes of Standards and Technology, US Department of Commerce.

Jo, H., & Lee, J. (1996). The relationship between an entrepreneur's background and performance in a new venture. *Technovation, 16*(4), 161–171.

Katz, J. S. (1994). Geographical proximity and scientific collaboration. *Scientometrics, 31*(1), 31–43.

Kenney, M., & Florida, R. (1994). The organization and geography of Japanese R&D: Results from survey of Japanese electronics and biotechnology firms. *Research Policy, 23*(3), 305–322.

Kimberly, J. R., & Evanisko, M. J. (1981). Organizational innovation: The influence of individual, organizational and contextual factors on hospital adoption of technical and administrative innovations. *Academy of Management Journal, 24*(4), 689–713.

Kirzner, I. M. (1973). *Competition and entrepreneurship.* Chicago: University of Chicago Press.

Kitagawa, F. (2003). Universities and industry-science relationships: enhancing the regional knowledge economy? — A comparative perspective from Japan and the UK. Paper presented at the Regional Studies Association Conference on *Reinventing Regions in the Global Economy.* Pisa, Italy, 12–15 April 2003.

Kitagawa, F. (2005). Universities and industry-science relationships: Enhancing the regional knowledge economy? — A comparative perspective from Japan and the UK. Paper presented at the Regional Studies Association Conference on *Reinventing Regions in the Global Economy.* Pisa, Italy, 12–15 April 2003.

Klandt, H., & Szyperski, N. (1988). Similarities and differences between business founders and NTBF founders. In: Anglo German Foundation, *New technology based firms in Britain and Germany* (pp. 33–47). London: Anglo German Foundation.

Klevorick, A. K., Levin, R. C., Nelson, R. R., & Winter, S. G. (1995). On the sources and significance of inter-industry differences in technological opportunities. *Research Policy, 24*(2), 185–205.

Krugman, P. (1998). What's new about the new economic geography? *Oxford Review of Economic Policy, 14*, 7–17.

Lach, S. (2000). *Do R&D subsidies stimulate or displace private R&D? Evidence from Israel.* NBER Working Paper 7943. National Bureau of Economic Research, Cambridge, MA.

Link, A. N. (1998). The US display consortium: Analysis of a public/private partnership. *Industry and Innovation, 5*, 11–34.

Link, A. N., & Rees, J. (1990). Firm size, university based research, and the returns to R&D. *Small Business Economics, 2*, 25–32.

Los, B., & Verspagen, B. (2000). R&D spillovers and productivity: Evidence from U.S. manufacturing microdata. *Empirical Economics, 25*, 127–148.

Lotka, A. J. (1926). The frequency distribution of scientific productivity. *Journal of the Washington Academy of Sciences, 16*(6), 317–323.

Lynskey, M. J. (1999). The transfer of resources and competencies for developing technological capabilities: The case of Fujitsu-ICL. *Technology Analysis and Strategic Management, 11*(3), 317–336.

Lynskey, M. J. (2001). Technological distance, spatial distance and sources of knowledge: Japanese 'new entrants' in 'new' biotechnology. In: R. Burgelman & H. Chesbrough (Eds), *Comparative studies of technological evolution: Research on technological innovation, management and policy* (pp. 127–205). Oxford: JAI (Elsevier Science).

Lynskey, M. J. (2002). Introduction. In: M. J. Lynskey & S. Yonekura (Eds), *Entrepreneurship and organization: The role of the entrepreneur in organizational innovation.* Oxford: Oxford University Press.

Lynskey, M. J. (2004a). Determinants of innovative activity in Japanese technology-based start-up firms. *International Small Business Journal, 22*(2), 159–196.

Lynskey, M. J. (2004b). Bioentrepreneurship in Japan: Institutional transformation and the growth of bioventures. *Journal of Commercial Biotechnology, 11*(1), 9–31.

Lynskey, M. J. (2004c). Knowledge, finance and human capital: The role of social institutional variables on entrepreneurship in Japan. *Industry and Innovation, 11*(4), 373–405.

Lynskey, M. J. (2006a). The locus of corporate entrepreneurship: Kirin Brewery's diversification into biopharmaceuticals. *Business History Review, 80*(4), 689–723.

Lynskey, M. J. (2006b). Transformative technology and institutional transformation: coevolution of biotechnology venture firms and the institutional framework in Japan. *Research Policy, 35*(9), 1389–1422.

Mansfield, E. (1991). Academic research and industrial innovation. *Research Policy, 20*(1), 1–12.

Mansfield, E. (1995). Academic research underlying industrial innovations: Sources, characteristics and financing. *Review of Economics and Statistics, 77*(1), 55–64.

Mansfield, E. (2000). Intellectual property protection, direct investment and technology transfer: Germany, Japan and the USA. *International Journal of Technology Management, 19*, 3–21.

Mansfield, E., & Lee, J.-Y. (1996). The modern university: Contributor to industrial innovation and recipient of industrial R&D support. *Research Policy, 25*(7), 1047–1058.

Murakami, Y. (2007). Technology spillover from foreign-owned firms in Japanese manufacturing industry. *Journal of Asian Economics, 18*(2), 284–293.

Narin, F., & Breitzman, A. (1995). Inventive productivity. *Research Policy, 24*(4), 507–519.

Nelson, R. R. (1986). Institutions supporting technical advance in industry. *American Economic Review, 76*, 186–189.

Nelson, R. R. (1992). What is 'commercial' and what is 'public' about technology, and what should be? In: N. Rosenberg, R. Landau & D. C. Mowery (Eds), *Technology and the wealth of nations* (pp. 57–71). Stanford, CA: Stanford University Press.

Nelson, R. R. (Ed.) (1993). *National innovation systems: A comparative analysis.* Oxford: Oxford University Press.

Nooteboom, B. (1999). Innovation, learning and industrial organization. *Cambridge Journal of Economics, 23*(2), 127–150.

Odagiri, H., & Iwata, H. (1986). The impact of R&D on productivity increase in Japanese manufacturing companies. *Research Policy, 15*(1), 13–19.

Odagiri, H., & Kinukawa, S. (1997). The contributions and channels of inter-industry R&D spillovers: An estimation for Japanese high-tech industries. *Economic Systems Research, 9*, 127–142.

OECD/IMHE. (1999). *The response of higher education institutions to regional needs.* Paris: OECD.

Office of Technology Assessment (OTA). (1986). *Research Funding as an Investment: Can We Measure the Returns? A Technical Memorandum.* Washington, DC: Congress of the United States.

Piergiovanni, R., Santarelli, E., & Vivarelli, M. (1997). From which source do small firms derive their innovative inputs? Some evidence form Italian industry. *Review of Industrial Organization, 12*(2), 243–258.

Polanyi, M. (1958). *Personal knowledge: Towards a post-critical philosophy.* Chicago: University of Chicago Press.

Reynolds, P. D. (1997). Who starts new firms? Preliminary explorations of firms-in-gestation. *Small Business Economics, 9*(5), 449–462.

Roberts, E. B. (1991). *Entrepreneurs in high technology: Lessons from MIT and beyond.* New York: Oxford University Press.

Robinson, P. B., & Sexton, E. A. (1994). The effect of education and experience on self-employment success. *Journal of Business Venturing, 9*(2), 141–156.

Romijn, H., & Albaladejo, M. (2002). Determinants of innovation capability in small electronics and software firms in southeast England. *Research Policy, 31*(7), 1053–1067.

Rosenberg, N., & Nelson, R. (1994). American universities and technical advance in industry. *Research Policy, 23*(3), 323–348.

Sakakibara, K., Koga, T., Honjo, Y., & Kondo, K. (2000). Nihon ni okeru gijutsukei benchaa kigyo no keiei jittai to sougyou-sha ni kan suru chousa kenkyu [*Survey research on technology-based start-ups and their entrepreneurs in Japan*]. National Institute of Science and Technology Policy, Tokyo (in Japanese).

Sakakibara, M. (1997). Heterogeneity of firm capabilities and cooperative research and development: An empirical examination of motives. *Strategic Management Journal, 18*, 143–164.

Santoro, M. D., & Chakrabarti, A. K. (2002). Firm size and technology centrality in industry–university interactions. *Research Policy, 31*(7), 1163–1180.

Schartinger, D., Rammer, C., Fischer, M. M., & Fröhlich, J. (2002). Knowledge interactions between universities and industry in Austria: Sectoral patterns and determinants. *Research Policy, 31*(3), 303–328.

Scherer, F. M., & Huh, K. (1992). Top managers' education and R&D investment. *Research Policy, 21*(6), 507–511.

Stinchcombe, A. L. (1965). Social structures and organizations. In: J. G. March (Ed.), *Handbook of organizations* (pp. 142–193). Chicago: Rand McNally.

Stolpe, M. (2002). Determinants of knowledge diffusion as evidenced in patent data: The case of liquid crystal display technology. *Research Policy, 31*(7), 1181–1198.

Stuart, R. W., & Abetti, P. A. (1990). Impact of entrepreneurial and management experience on early performance. *Journal of Business Venturing, 5*(3), 151–162.

Suzuki, K. (1993). R&D spillovers and technology transfer among and within vertical keiretsu groups. *International Journal of Industrial Organization, 11*, 573–591.

Szulanski, G. (1996). Exploring internal stickiness: impediments to the transfer of best practice within the firm. *Strategic Management Journal, 17*(10), 27–43.

Teece, D. J. (1986). Profiting from technological innovation: Implications for integration, collaboration, licensing and public policy. *Research Policy, 15*(6), 285–305.

Teece, D. J. (1992). Strategies for capturing the financial benefits from technological innovation. In: N. Rosenberg, R. Landau & D. C. Mowery (Eds), *Technology and the wealth of nations* (pp. 175–205). Stanford, CA: Stanford University Press.

Teece, D. J., & Pisano, G. (1994). The dynamic capabilities of firms: An introduction. *Industrial and Corporate Change, 3*(3), 537–556.

Thomas, A. S., Litschert, R. J., & Ramaswamy, K. (1991). The performance impact of strategy-manager coalignment: An empirical examination. *Strategic Management Journal, 12*(7), 509–522.

Tyler, B. B., & Steensma, H. K. (1998). The effects of executives' experiences and perceptions on their assessment of potential technical alliances. *Strategic Management Journal, 19*(10), 939–965.

Van de Ven, A. H., Hudson, R., & Schroeder, D. M. (1984). Designing new business startups: Entrepreneurial, organizational and ecological considerations. *Journal of Management, 10*(1), 87–107.

Verona, G. (1999). A resource-based view of product development. *Academy of Management Review, 24*(1), 132–142.

Wally, S., & Baum, J. (1994). Personal and structural determinants of the pace of strategic decision making. *Academy of Management Journal, 37*(4), 932–956.

Westhead, P., & Storey, D. J. (1994). *An Assessment of firms located on and off science parks in the United Kingdom.* London: HMSO.

Wilbon, A. D. (2000). Executive technology education and firm performance. *Technology Management: Strategies and Applications, 5*(1), 103–109.

Zucker, L. G., & Darby, M. R. (1996). Star scientists and institutional transformation: patterns of invention and innovation in the formation of the biotechnology industry. *Proceedings of the National Academy of Science, 93*(November), 12709–12716.

Zucker, L. G., & Darby, M. R. (1998a). *Capturing technological opportunity via Japan's star scientists: Evidence from Japanese firms' biotech patents and products.* NBER Working Paper 6360. National Bureau of Economic Research, Cambridge MA.

Zucker, L. G., & Darby, M. R. (1998b). Intellectual capital and the birth of U.S. biotechnology enterprises. *American Economic Review, 88*(1), 290–306.

Zucker, L. G., & Darby, M. R. (1999). Star-scientist linkages to firms in APEC and European countries: Indicators of regional institutional differences affecting competitive advantage. *International Journal of Biotechnology, 1*(1), 119–131.

Zucker, L. G., Darby, M. R., & Armstrong, J. (1994). *Intellectual capital and the firm: The technology of geographically localized knowledge spillovers.* NBER Working Paper 4946, 1–59. National Bureau of Economic Research, Cambridge, MA.

Zucker, L. G., Darby, M. R., & Armstrong, J. (1998). Geographically localized knowledge: Spillovers or markets? *Economic Inquiry, 36*(1), 65–86.

Chapter 10

# The Development of Venture-Capital-Backed and Independent Companies: An Empirical Study Among Germany's Internet and E-Commerce Start-Ups

Stephan Golla, Martin Holi, Tobias Johann, Heinz Klandt and Lutz Kraft

## Introduction

The "New Economy" was the economic buzzword of the 1990s. Digitization and networking, accompanied disproportionally by an increasing efficiency of information and communication technology exchanges, served as the foundation for sustainable economic changes in the way business is conducted (Gersch & Goeke, 2004). The new Internet architecture and the economic transactions that are based on it became of increasing importance worldwide.

Innovative new ventures are in general considered as "fountains of youth" in any economy (Pleschak, 2000; Bygrave & Timmons, 1992). In particular, young technology companies were considered to play an important role in the beginning of the dot.com era. Our study examines the development of Internet and e-commerce start-ups in Germany over the period from 1990 to 2004. After a short description of the industry sector and its development, we will illustrate the differences in survival rates of venture-capital-backed and independent, Internet, and e-commerce start-ups.

## Courses of Development in the Internet and E-Commerce Sector

### The Industry Sector

The term e-commerce refers to commercial transactions that are contracted via an interactive electronic medium. The most prominent forms of today are business-to-business

New Technology Based Firms in the New Millennium, Volume VI
Edited by A. Groen, R. Oakey, P. van der Sijde and G. Cook

(B2B), business-to-consumer (B2C), business-to-government (B2G), and consumer-to-consumer (C2C). Recently, the importance of these kinds of transactions has risen dramatically. Germany, for example, has increased activity in the area of B2B, since more than 20% of German companies now distribute their products and services via the Internet. This percentage is higher than in the Unites States. Moreover, almost 50% of inputs to German companies are conducted via the Internet, and B2C-e-commerce in Germany reached volume of €4.7 billion in 2002. The most frequently traded products are books, clothes, shoes, compact disks, computer accessories, and travel services (Riehm, Orwat, & Petermann, 2002; Riehm, Orwat, & Petermann, 2003).

Internet-service-providers, also known as Internet-access-providers are providers of services that enable the customer to access the Internet. These companies finance themselves mainly by collecting fees for web hosting, FTP hosting, or other services. This group consists of providers, agencies, and specialized service-providers. The group of internet-technology-providers constitutes the beginning of the Internet-value-chain and comprises companies that create a technological infrastructure and develop software for online-systems.[1]

## Market Entries of the Internet and E-Commerce Companies

By the 1980s the Internet had been widely used by universities and research institutes. This was followed by privately run mail-boxes aimed at the generation of owners of personal computers that used the C64, Atari, or Amiga computers. But after the CERN Research Institute announced, in April 1993, that it would not claim any license or copyright-fees for the usage of the www-technology, and the first browser "Mosaic" was published,[2] and the commercial expansion of the Internet began.

The analyses presented in this chapter are based on an empirical inquiry into German Internet and e-commerce start-ups, conducted by the KfW Endowed Chair for Entrepreneurship. After a first round of data gathering in 2000 the data sample was regularly enlarged and updated. The relevant data for each start-up were extracted from economic databases as well as gathered by the analysis of websites and other online- and offline-sources. As part of the analysis we also checked if the survey companies were backed by venture capital. In July 2000, we registered e-start-up.org project, in total 12,585 active companies in the Internet and e-commerce sector.[3] From the basis of these data, we drew a subset consisting of young companies that entered the market later than 1990. At the last point of observation, in October 2004, this subset comprised 5700 start-ups.

Within the Internet industry individual lines of business show different clusters regarding the market entries. Table 1 highlights that initially the Internet-service- and Internet-technology-providers emerged. The e-commerce providers then developed over the period from 1998 to 2000. To support this funding we used a $\chi^2$ test and the corresponding statistic of residuals. This test examines the observed and expected frequencies per cell. Large

---

[1]For a detailed illustration of the segments we refer to the presentations at http://www.e-startup.org/ergebnis.htm.
[2]For a comprehensive illustration of the history see http://www.w3.org/History.html.
[3]www.e-start-up.org.

Table 1: Market entries of Internet and e-commerce start-ups structured along business models.

| Year | Business model | | | Total |
|------|-----------|------------------|-------------------|-----|
| | **E-commerce** | **Internet-service-provider** | **Internet-technology-provider** | ***n*** |
| 1990 | 8 | 66 | 6 | 80 |
| 1991 | 5 | 72 | 17 | 94 |
| 1992 | 17 | 107 | 19 | 143 |
| 1993 | 15 | 155 | 27 | 197 |
| 1994 | 53 | 278 | 37 | 368 |
| 1995 | 73 | 527 | 58 | 658 |
| 1996 | 123 | 736 | 87 | 946 |
| 1997 | 175 | 725 | 75 | 975 |
| 1998 | 359 | 579 | 108 | 1046 |
| 1999 | 406 | 403 | 86 | 895 |
| 2000 | 154 | 114 | 37 | 305 |
| 2001 | 13 | 8 | 2 | 23 |
| 2002 | 1 | 2 | 2 | 5 |
| 2003 | 0 | 0 | 1 | 1 |
| Sum | 1402 | 3772 | 562 | 5736 |
| $\chi^2$ | 635.6 | 546.8 | 36.8 | |
| p | <0.00 | <0.00 | <0.01 | |

*Source*: Own inquiry.

differences between the observed and expected value in a cell, measured with the help of the standardized residuals that quantify the deviation, make a high contribution to the $\chi^2$ value and thus to a significant result (Bühl & Zöfel, 2002). We compared the market entries of start-ups per year of one business model with those of the others. Thereby we can ascertain if a business model is over- or under-represented according to the trend expectations.

The $\chi^2$ statistic shows that in the period from 1993 to 1997 Internet-service-providers entered the market to a particularly high degree. Looking at the e-commerce sector, in comparison to the other two lines of business, it becomes obvious that e-commerce developed below average in the years from 1990 to 1997. This rate of development, however, increased rapidly from 1998 onward (Chart 1). The market entries of the years 1998–2000 show an above average growth of the e-commerce providers. This makes it very clear, that the development of the Internet and e-commerce industry was subject to a technological path dependency in which infrastructure provision needed to proceed Internet trading.

Chart 1 illustrates the development of the companies in the three areas of e-business. The different slopes of the curves show the observed differences in the trends. These results are congruent with the results of a study conducted in the United States. In the

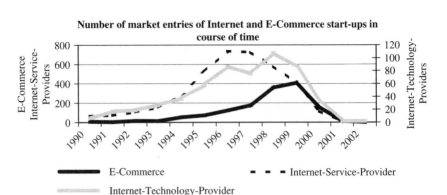

Chart 1:  Market entries of Internet and e-commerce companies. *Source*: Own inquiry.

United States the development of e-commerce companies was particularly strong in 1999. Internet-service-providers dominated the year 1995 and market entries of companies focussing on the Internet technology emerged most frequently in the years from 1992 to 1994 (Zacharakis, Shepherd, & Coombs, 2003). Zacharakis et al. (2003) however, only observed venture-capital-backed start-ups.

## Market Exits of the Internet and E-Commerce Companies

After having illustrated above, the sequence of market entries of Internet and e-commerce companies, this section examines market exits. The observation period comprises the years from 2000 to 2004, although the sources that are used have also been examined for earlier exits of the identified companies. In October 2004 the date of market exit was known for 1504 young companies. Table 2 shows the corresponding failure- or survival-rates respectively, distributed over the same three categories as chosen above.

In absolute terms the highest number of failures is accounted for by Internet-service-providers. In relation to the other lines of business, however, only 20% of the market participants failed, whereas the figure for e-commerce was 38%, while in the sector of Internet-technology-providers 36% disappeared from the market.

As in the analysis of the market entries, we examined the time periods for significant differences between the Internet released activities; in this case the $\chi^2$ test showed clear differences. In 2001, the group of e-commerce start-ups broke away from the trend and showed, with 243 market exits, a significant difference to the other lines (Table 3). It is interesting that the e-commerce sector displays a pattern of early exits since Table 1 revealed that it was the last group to experience strong market entries from 1998 to 1999. This trend of above-average market exits, however, began to decline in the subsequent year 2002, a trend mirrored by the other two sub-sectors. This might be evident that inefficient e-commerce providers disappeared rapidly from the market. In 2002 the level of failure in Internet-service providers peaked. With 414 market exits this is the climax of this sub-sector and at the same time the only point in time at which the failure-rate is significantly statistically higher than in the other two sub-sectors. The Internet-technology

Table 2: Survival rates of Internet and e-commerce start-ups.

| Status | Business model | | | | | | Total | % |
|---|---|---|---|---|---|---|---|---|
| | E-commerce | | Internet-service-providers | | Internet-technology-providers | | | |
| | *n* | *%* | *n* | *%* | *n* | *%* | | |
| Active | 872 | 62.2 | 3002 | 79.6 | 358 | 63.7 | 4232 | 73.8 |
| Inactive | 530 | 37.8 | 770 | 20.4 | 204 | 36.3 | 1504 | 26.2 |
| Sum | 1402 | 100.0 | 3772 | 100.0 | 562 | 100.0 | 5736 | 100.0 |

*Source*: Own inquiry.
$\chi^2 = 192.5$; $p < 0.00$.

Table 3: Market exits of Internet and e-commerce start-ups structured along business model.

| Year | Business model | | | Total |
|---|---|---|---|---|
| | E-commerce | Internet-service-provider | Internet-technology-provider | *n* |
| 1999 | 1 | 3 | 0 | 4 |
| 2000 | 14 | 26 | 8 | 48 |
| 2001 | 243 | 246 | 86 | 575 |
| 2002 | 209 | 414 | 77 | 700 |
| 2003 | 49 | 66 | 30 | 145 |
| 2004 | 14 | 15 | 3 | 32 |
| Sum | 530 | 770 | 204 | 1504 |
| $\chi^2$ | 23.4 | 37.1 | 12.7 | |
| $p$ | $<0.00$ | $<0.00$ | $<0.027$ | |

*Source*: Own inquiry.

providers already experienced most of the market exits in 2001 and 2002 (86 and 77 p.a., respectively), but these failure rates are in accordance with the general trend. A sharp decline in the number of failures is not registered until 2003, where 30 companies exit the market. Statistically, this value is however less significant. Interestingly the market exits paint a picture that is the reverse of the market entries. For example, e-commerce providers who were late entrants to the market in the late 1990s, were the first to exit the market. The pioneers of the Internet industry, the technology providers in contrast, stayed in the market for a relatively long time. These figures, nevertheless, allow only for limited conclusions regarding the different market exit barriers of the respective lines of business as the failure rates are inconsistent.

Table 4: Duration of the market activity of Internet and e-commerce start-up companies structured along business models.

| Business model | Duration of market activity in months | | | |
|---|---|---|---|---|
| | Average | Maximum | Minimum | Variance |
| E-commerce | 63 | 179 | 9 | 29 |
| Internet-service-providers | 87 | 179 | 4 | 29 |
| Internet-technology-providers | 79 | 167 | 10 | 33 |

*Source*: Own inquiry.
$\chi^2 = 472.6$; $p < 0.00$.

These figures of market exits show that the life expectancy of firms varies with respect to the sub-sector to a highly significant degree. While failed e-commerce providers were on average active in the market for 63 months, Internet-service providers stayed in the market for an average for 87 months, Internet-technology providers lasted an average for 79 months (Table 4).

## The Importance of the Venture Capital Financing for Internet and E-Commerce Start-Ups

*Venture Capital Investments*

The business ideas of innovative companies are often characterized by the potential for rapid growth, although such new ventures often lack the necessary resources. Particularly with regard to financing in the form of equity, venture capital companies are often seen as ideal partners that, beyond providing pure financing, they provide advice and assistance. The potential investee company thus undergoes a comprehensive selection process and after investment, receives additional support for its development which mainly included management support, the provision of wide networks of customers, suppliers, and further capital providers (Baeyens, Vanacker, & Manigart, 2006; Holi, Krafft, Golla, & Klandt, 2005; Schefczyk, 2000; Sapienza & Manigart, 1996). Ideally, this valuable contribution by the investor leads to substantial growth of the investment in company and sustainable competitive advantage.

In the analyzed data sample of this study 895 (15.4%) new ventures were backed by venture capital (Table 5). Measured in absolute terms the venture-capital-providers investment focus in the e-commerce sub-group of start-ups, of which 399 were venture-capital-backed. In relation to the proportion of firms per sub-sector, the Internet-technology providers took the lead with 280 financed companies, which account for nearly 50% of the total number of companies in the industry sub-sector.

Regarding these sub-sector firms, we could identify significant differences in entry points for venture capital investments. Statistical analysis shows that the venture capital firms became particularly involved with younger companies. In Table 6, the number of

Table 5: Venture capital investments in Internet and e-commerce start-ups.

| Status | Business model | | | | | | Total | % |
|---|---|---|---|---|---|---|---|---|
| | E-commerce | | Internet-service-providers | | Internet-technology-providers | | | |
| | *n* | *%* | *n* | *%* | *n* | *%* | | |
| VC-backed | 399 | 28.5 | 216 | 5.7 | 280 | 49.8 | 895 | 15.6 |
| Non-VC-backed | 1003 | 71.5 | 3556 | 94.3 | 282 | 50.2 | 4841 | 84.4 |
| Sum | 1402 | 100 | 3772 | 100 | 562 | 100 | 5736 | 100 |

*Source*: Own inquiry.
$\chi^2 = 955.1$; $p < 0.00$.

Table 6: Year of foundation of venture-capital-backed and non-venture-capital-backed Internet and e-commerce start-ups.

| Year of market entry | Internet and e-commerce start-ups | | | | Total | % |
|---|---|---|---|---|---|---|
| | With VC Investment | | Without VC Investment | | | |
| | *n* | *%* | *n* | *%* | | |
| 1990 | 11 | 1.2 | 69 | 1.4 | 80 | 1.4 |
| 1991 | 18 | 2.0 | 76 | 1.6 | 94 | 1.6 |
| 1992 | 18 | 2.0 | 125 | 2.6 | 143 | 2.5 |
| 1993 | 34 | 3.8 | 163 | 3.4 | 197 | 3.4 |
| 1994 | 41 | 4.6 | 327 | 6.8 | 368 | 6.4 |
| 1995 | 67 | 7.5 | 591 | 12.2 | 658 | 11.5 |
| 1996 | 96 | 10.7 | 850 | 17.6 | 946 | 16.5 |
| 1997 | 97 | 10.8 | 878 | 18.1 | 975 | 17.0 |
| 1998 | 173 | 19.3 | 873 | 18.0 | 1046 | 18.2 |
| 1999 | 245 | 27.4 | 650 | 13.4 | 895 | 15.6 |
| 2000 | 87 | 9.7 | 218 | 4.5 | 305 | 5.3 |
| 2001 | 6 | 0.7 | 17 | 0.4 | 23 | 0.4 |
| 2002 | 1 | 0.1 | 4 | 0.1 | 5 | 0.1 |
| 2003 | 1 | 0.1 | 0 | 0.0 | 1 | 0.0 |
| Sum | 895 | 100 | 4841 | 100 | 5736 | 100 |

*Source*: Own inquiry.
$\chi^2 = 208\ 7$; $p < 0.00$.

formations of non venture-capital-backed start-ups reached its maximum in 1997, while the formation of new ventures that raised equity capital reached a peak in 1999, although there was a sharp decline in 2000.

This analysis of firm formation data compared to whether they were venture-capital and non-venture-capital-backed start-ups makes it clear that external equity provided by venture was not especially advantageous to those firms receiving such investment. Venture capital providers reinforced their financial involvement by investing in younger start-ups, and by doing this, rather followed the trend instead of starting it.

## Closure of Venture-Capital-Backed Internet and E-Commerce Companies

Venture Capital providers focused on younger start-ups and financed half of the internet-technology providers active in the market. However, in absolute terms, the e-commerce companies received the highest number of investments. In our analysis of the closures we observed that, the youngest companies, closed first. Here the e-commerce start-ups dominated. Below we will analyse the failure rates of venture-capital-backed companies. Table 7 shows a significantly higher failure rate of venture-capital-backed start-ups. While the aggregate failure rate of all companies was 21.3%, the failure rate for companies with external equity financing was 53.1%. Of the 895 venture-capital-financed companies, only 420 were still active at the time of our latest observation in September 2004.

Comparing the venture-capital-backed start-ups in terms of sub-sectors does not result in significant differences in failure rates. Across-the-board we can say that about half of all financed companies, independent of their sub-sector origin, failed (Table 8).

We see that, in contrast to the common belief, venture capital positively influences the development of start-ups and the failure rates in this group of high-technology firms are especially, high. Thus, the question has to be raised whether venture capital companies behaved inefficiently in their investments or whether neither start-ups nor capital providers

Table 7: Failure rates of venture-capital-backed and non-venture-capital-backed Internet and e-commerce start-ups.

| Start-up status | Internet and e-commerce start-ups | | | | Total | % |
|---|---|---|---|---|---|---|
| | With VC investment | | Without VC investment | | | |
| | *n* | % | *n* | % | | |
| Active | 420 | 46.9 | 3812 | 78.7 | 4232 | 73.8 |
| Non-active | 475 | 53.1 | 1029 | 21.3 | 1504 | 26.2 |
| Sum | 895 | 100.0 | 4841 | 100.0 | 5736 | 100.0 |

*Source*: Own inquiry.
$\chi^2 = 395.2; p < 0.00.$

Table 8:  Failure rates of venture-capital-backed Internet and e-commerce start-ups structured along business models.

| Start-up status | VC financed start-ups per business model | | | | | | Total | % |
|---|---|---|---|---|---|---|---|---|
| | E-commerce | | Internet-service-providers | | Internet-technology-providers | | | |
| | *n* | *%* | *n* | *%* | *n* | *%* | | |
| Active | 183 | 45.9 | 109 | 50.5 | 128 | 45.7 | 420 | 46.9 |
| Non-active | 216 | 54.1 | 107 | 49.5 | 152 | 54.3 | 475 | 53.1 |
| Sum | 399 | 100.0 | 216 | 100.0 | 280 | 100.0 | 895 | 100.0 |

*Source*: Own inquiry.
$\chi^2 = 1.4$; $p < 0.48$.

could survive a negative macro-economic environment. In order to measure the influence of the venture capital financing on the longevity of the new ventures we availed ourselves of a survival analysis methodology. Furthermore, we examined the influence of the economic environment on the development of the start-ups. As an indicator, we used the devolution of the Nemax Technology All Share for the years from 1998 to 2004.

Regarding the length of survival, previously, we have presented the respective averages and standard deviations for failed companies in Table 4. For the analysis of all companies (i.e., the failed and surviving ones), we conducted a regression analysis according to the Cox proportional hazard model. With the help of the Cox regression we can ascertain whether a specific variable, in this case venture-capital-financing, influences the probability of survival of the start-ups. The method is related to the logistic regression and thus serves also as an instrument for prognosis. Coefficients of the function are estimated, whereupon the probability of survival is decreased by negative coefficients, and increased by positive ones.

The graph of Chart 2 shows the cumulated probabilities of survival of the start-ups over the course of time. Also, the relative duration of the market activities of the venture-capital-financed companies decreases more sharply than that of the comparison group. Table 9 shows the coefficients of the analysis. The double negative value of the logarithm of the likelihood-function (–2LL) is used as a measure of the quality of fit in the context of the Cox regression. It shows whether the introduction of the variable "VC financing" has any effect on the likelihood-function. The level of significance of the change in value is determined by the $\chi^2$ test (Tabachnick & Fidell, 2000). The Wald-statistic is also presented and used to evaluate the significant influence of the regression coefficient.

The analysis shows a significantly negative relationship between venture-capital-financing and the probability of survival for start-ups. However, the strength of this relationship is with an $R^2$ of 6%, which is relatively low. Thus, it can be assumed that venture capital involvement has only a small influence on the reduced life span of the financed companies. A possible objection that the life spans examined at the time of observation

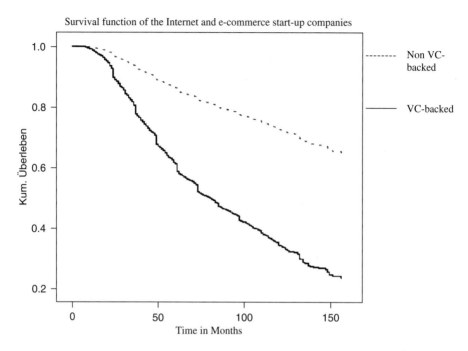

Chart 2: Probability of survival of venture-capital-backed and non-venture-capital-backed Internet and e-commerce start-ups. *Source*: Own inquiry.

Table 9: Results of the Cox's regression.

| | Variables in the equation | | | | | |
|---|---|---|---|---|---|---|
| | **B** | **SE** | **Wald** | **df** | **p** | **Exp(B)** |
| VC financing | 1.205 | 0.056 | 468,012 | 1 | 0.000 | 3337 |

*Source*: Own inquiry.
$\chi^2 = 192.85$; $p < 0.00$; and $R^2 = 6.6\%$.

were lower, due to the fact that venture-capital firms have focussed on financing younger companies (as illustrated in Table 6), does not lead to different results. We conducted the survival analysis also for younger companies that entered the market after 1997 and derived an explained percentage of variance by the venture-capital investment of a little more than 6%. The analyzed start-ups were divided into different size ranges, since it can be assumed that financed companies, because of the resource assignment, hired more employees and possibly generated higher turnovers (Krafft, 2006).[4] The Cox's regression, however, did not lead to any change in the negative influence a venture-capital investment had on the probability of survival, even when the size of the company was taken into con-

---

[4]For details see: http://www.e-start-up.org.

sideration. Thus we cannot assume that venture-capital firms cause non-viable companies to close, for example, by not granting them follow-up financing needed for an on-going development.

However, if significant differences concerning the survival duration between the companies exist, this might also be a result of negative external effects. A specific intervention, occurring at a certain point in time, might possibly affect all firms to the same extent. At the time of the negative effect, young venture-capital-backed companies have been active in the market for a shorter period of time than the other more established companies. This factor might explain the deviations of the Cox regression. In order to measure the impact of a possibly negative effect, we examined the following: the movements of the Nemax Technology All Share and the tread in closures of the observed companies. We point out that interpretations concerning causal relationships have to be treated cautiously. Nevertheless, the development of the stock exchange can provide interesting evidence for further screening-effects.

The boom of the stock exchange in the context of the new economy, that was first observable in the development of the NASDAQ, led to an enormous influx of capital. German technology shares experienced a tremendous boom. Venture Capital experienced records investments and fundraising. In 1999, 4420 start-ups were financed by members of the German Private Equity and Venture Capital Association (BVK). Expansion stage investments accounted for 41%, although 23% of the capital was invested in early stage companies. German financial institutions provided the venture-capital firms with 30% of their investment capital. They were followed in this order by American and British pension funds, which after having invested heavily in their home countries, searched for adequate returns abroad. The investments of insurance companies and industry accounted for 10% and private investors still contributed 8 %.[5] In the middle of 2000, more than 100 Internet and e-commerce companies of German origin had been listed at the Neuer Markt, also being complemented by quotations of foreign companies, for example, from Austria, the United Kingdom, or Switzerland. In previous years, these placings reached market on an average capitalization of about €100 million. Even when taking into account heavy-weight quotations such as Comdirect AG or the T-Online International AG, smaller placements remain with an average of €50 million.[6]

Retrenchment did not happen overnight. It was rather that the group of skeptics continuously grew, while the group of optimists shrunk. The first corrections in the market took place, however, on the hope that those were healthy consolidations. Additionally several items of company news enforced the negative trend. With the demise of the British Internet trader Boo.com, one of the most glamorous e-commerce companies disappeared from the market — even before it actually started. At the same time the first so-called "death lists" emerged which also announced bad news. In Germany a sensation was caused by the study of an auditing company that came to the conclusion that 8 out of a total of 56 analyzed Internet companies were steering towards liquidity shortages. As no names were published there was an empty space for speculation. Further pressure on the stock prices

---

[5]Börsen-Zeitung (2000), No. 138, p. 11.
[6]Neuer Markt per July 2000.

resulted from an announcement made by the service provider Gigabell right after its IPO in which the company stated that the targeted annual loss of DM 6 million (€3.1 m) would increase by three times. Gigabell had to admit flaws in its expectations concerning the market and its financial statements.[7] The result was insolvency. These kinds of announcements, in combination with other negative macro-economical indicators, put pressure on investors to search for possible risky positions in their portfolios, which they found in the shares and stocks of the Neuer Markt. They increasingly began to believe that any business model, which argued that a currently insane looking idea would always have a great future solely because of its innovative potential, was no longer valid.[8]

The result of strongly reduced company valuations was the burst of the stock market bubble. A possible relationship between this trend and the failure of young Internet and e-commerce companies is presented in the following analysis. Chart 3 shows the number of failed companies as well as the development of the stock index.

The trend presented in Chart 2 shows the quarterly averages but not the daily fluctuations, of the index. In fact, the Nemax Technology All Share index reached its maximum on March 10, 2000 with a value of 8559. Important for our study is the negative trend that starts in the first quarter of 2000. The subsequent closures of venture-capital-backed start-ups reached their maximum in the third quarter of 2001 with 75 companies closed. The total number of exits in 2001 was 225. The summit of market exits in general was reached in the third quarter of 2002 when 150 of a total of 548 non-venture-capital-backed companies disappeared from the market. In the following analysis we are testing whether the negative trend of the Nemax, as an indicator for a weak economical environment and a

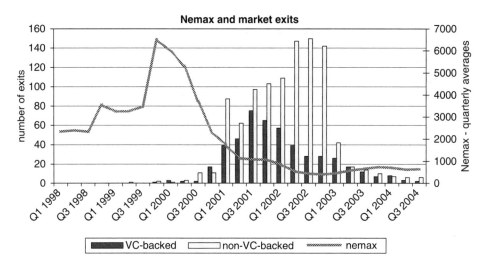

Chart 3: Development of market exits of Internet and e-commerce start-ups in comparison to the Nemax. *Source*: Wallstreet Online, Own inquiry.

---

[7]Börsen-Zeitung (2000), No. 134, p. 4.
[8]Börsen-Zeitung (2000), No. 76, p. 4.

deterioration of exit perspectives, provides any explanation for the failure of the young companies. Because of the low number of observation points, only few analytical methods are usable. The chosen regression with Newey–West (Newey & West, 1987) standard errors is the most suitable one because of its robustness against auto-correlation and heteroscedacity. However, the low number of observation points has to been seen critically (Greene, 2003). In our analysis we looked at the negative Nemax returns, i.e., a decreasing stock index as points of intervention. Hereby we did not choose the real value of the Nemax, but described the negative effect with dummy variables (negative Nemax trend = 1, positive Nemax trend = 0). In order to account for the varying number of companies in each group, we did not take the absolute number of market exits but the percentage of market exits within a group for calculation. The results of the time series analysis are presented in Tables 10 and 11. Both tables show a significant influence of the falling Nemax on the failure rate. The regression coefficient for start-ups not supported by venture capital is 1.58 and 3.57 for those that were venture-capital-backed.

It becomes obvious that the intervention of the negative effect is followed by high failure-rates of young Internet and e-commerce start-ups. For the purpose of interpretation, however, the expected effect is less remarkable than the differences between the venture-capital-backed

Table 10: Influence of the falling Nemax on non-venture-capital-backed start-ups.

| Variable | Coefficient | SE | *t*-statistic | Probability |
|---|---|---|---|---|
| Negative trend Nemax | 1.590583 | 0.558675 | 2.847062 | 0.0083 |
| $R^2$ | 0.458604 | Mean dependent variable | | 0.759179 |
| Log likelihood | −32.56959 | SD dependent variable | | 1.071701 |

Dependent variable: Market exits of non-VC-backed companies in %.
Method: Least squares.
Sample: 1997:4, 2004:3.
Included observations: 28.
Newey–West HAC standard errors and covariance (lag truncation=3).

Table 11: Influence of the falling Nemax on venture-capital-backed start-ups.

| Variable | Coefficient | SE | *t*-statistic | Probability |
|---|---|---|---|---|
| Negative trend Nemax | 3.733667 | 1.236379 | 3.019841 | 0.0055 |
| $R^2$ | 0.398275 | Mean dependent variable | | 1.903393 |
| Log likelihood | −57.47823 | SD dependent variable | | 2.474445 |

Dependent variable: Market exits of VC-backed companies in %.
Method: Least squares.
Sample: 1997:4, 2004:3.
Included observations: 28.
Newey–West HAC standard errors and covariance (lag truncation = 3).

and non-venture-capital-backed companies. The impact of the regression coefficient is clearly higher for the companies that were financed by venture capitalists. This group of young start-ups seems to be more strongly affected than the other companies in their specific industry sector. Chart 3 shows, furthermore, a delay in the market exits of not venture-capital-backed start-ups. Interpreting these results raises the question for potential causal relationships. Although the development of a stock index and of young companies is influenced by a variety of indicators, and certain relations exist even within the observed group of variables, we want to briefly discuss the potential explanations.

At the beginning, the first effects were observable within the group of venture-capital-backed companies. Young, innovative companies that raised equity capital pursued an aggressive growth strategy because of the high-return expectations of investors. The key issues were the market opening, brand building, and the fight for market share. Other objectives such as profitability or securing liquidity out of the cash flow were minor priorities. Financial resources were invested and after a certain "cash-burn-rate" a new financing round should support future growth. Many business models however, proved to be non-marketable in the long run. Venture capital providers had to "write-off" investments and several of the formerly, large number of investors exited the market. The opportunity of a profitable exit via the stock exchange was blocked. Young companies could not raise the necessary financial resources and exits followed. Of specific interest here, is our observation that this negative trend, not only affected venture-capital-backed start-ups, but also companies that did not receive venture-capital-financing. Although the effect is delayed and less strong, the entanglement of the rest of the industry becomes obvious. Besides the negative effects of a change in the market environment, the description of business relations between the surviving and failing companies increased the impact.

Particularly the venture capital and the capital raised by the issuing of shares, were justified by orders and sales transmitted to other companies in the Internet and e-commerce industry. Thus, companies not backed by venture capital depended on the development of the market and the capital in- and out-flows. In contrast to the venture-capital-backed companies that had to strive to reach certain milestones in corporate development due to contractual agreements, the group of non-venture-capital-backed companies could work adjusting their capacities accordingly. With their less aggressive growth-policy they were able to react more flexibly to the market changes. Their smaller company size allowed them to reduce costs through staff reductions or moving into cheaper offices. In the medium-term, numerous companies, however, could not elude from the negative industry trend and were also forced to close.

# Conclusion

This study has shown that the Internet and e-commerce industry has developed through technological cycles. First, the Internet-technology providers entered the market, then the Internet-service providers followed, and finally the e-commerce providers joined in. The analysis of market exits has painted an exact opposite picture. The e-commerce providers were the first to exit the market and the Internet-technology providers stayed active longest. Our analysis has shown that the provision of venture capital was not a decisive trigger for this industry sector, but rather that venture-capital firms became involved at a later stage in the market development by focusing on particularly young companies. In contrast to the common assumption that venture-capital-backed start-ups have a higher probability of survival due to the screening process, financial resources, and management support, we identified a significantly higher failure rate among venture-capital-financed companies. The environmental changes in the stock exchange from spring 2000 onwards had a negative impact on the survival rates of the start-ups. A slowly growing skepticism toward high-technology small-firm investment was enforced by spectacular bankruptcies and negative company data. Investors withdrew from the market. A downturn in the Nemax accelerated market exits of venture-capital-backed start-ups. However, start-up companies *without* venture capital financing could not elude their general market trend. Nonetheless, their flexibility and the adjustment of cost structures to the more difficult business environment enabled them to stay active in the market a little longer, but in the end many of the companies of this group succumbed.

# References

Anonymous (2007). *The internet history*, source: http://www.w3.org/History.html, per Dec 11, 2007.

Baeyens, K., Vanacker, T., & Manigart, S. (2006). Venture capitalists' selection process: The case of biotechnology proposals. *International Journal of Technology Management, 34*(1/2), 28–46.

Bühl, A., & Zöfel, P. (2002). *SPSS 11: Einführung in die moderne Datenanalyse unter Windows* (8th ed.). München: Pearson Studium.

Bygrave, W. D., & Timmons, J. A. (1992). *Venture capital at the crossroads*. Boston, MA: Harvard Business School Press.

Gersch, M., & Goeke, C. (2004). Entwicklungsstufen des E-Businesses. *Wisu-Das Wirtschaftsstudium, 33*(12), 1529–1534.

Greene, W. H. (2003). Econometric analysis (5th ed.). Upper Saddle River, NJ: Prentice-Hall.

Holi, M. T., Krafft, L., Golla, S., & Klandt, H. (2005). *A survey of the venture capital market in Germany from 1997–2003* (pp. 165–176). Jahrbuch Entrepreneurship, Berlin: Springer .

Krafft, L. (2006). *Entwicklung räumlicher Cluster: das Beispiel Internet- und E-Commerce-Gründungen in Deutschland* (1st ed.). Wiesbaden: Dt. Univ.-Verl.

Krafft, L. (2007). *E-start-up project*, source: http://www.e-startup.org/ergebnis.htm, per Dec 9, 2007.

Newey, W. K., & West, K. D. (1987). A simple, positive, semi-definite, heteroskedasticity and auto-correlation consistent covariance matrix. *Econometrica, 55*(3), 703–708.

Pleschak, F. (2000). Wachstum FuE-intensiver Unternehmen: Strategien, Probleme, Erfahrungen: Wissenschaftliche Konferenz am 7/8. November, Dresden.

Riehm, U., Orwat, C., & Petermann, T. (2002). Stand, Perspektiven und Folgen des E-Commerce.

Riehm, U., Orwat, C., & Petermann, T. (2003). E-Commerce in Deutschland, source: http://www.itas.fzk.de/deu/lit/2003/ riua03a_inhalt.htm, per Dec 12, 2007.

Sapienza, H. J., & Manigart, S. (1996). Venture capitalist governance and value added in four countries. *Journal of Business Venturing, 11*(6), 439–470.

Schefczyk, M. (2000). *Erfolgsstrategien deutscher Venture Capital-Gesellschaften: Analyse der Investitionsaktivitäten und des Beteiligungsmanagement von Venture Capital-Gesellschaften* (2nd ed.). Stuttgart: Schäffer-Poeschel.

Tabachnick, B. G., & Fidell, L. S. (2000). *Using multivariate statistics* (4th ed.). Boston, MA: Allyn and Bacon.

Zacharakis, A. L., Shepherd, D. A., & Coombs, J. E. (2003). The development of venture-capital-backed internet companies: An ecosystem perspective. *Journal of Business Venturing, 18*(2), 217–232.

Chapter 11

# The High-Technology Pecking Order in Spinoffs and Non-Spinoffs in the Irish Software Sector

Teresa Hogan and Elaine Hutson

## Introduction

Despite their increasing importance in innovation, employment creation and economic growth, there is a dearth of theory-driven research on the financing and capital structure of new technology-based firms (NTBFs).[1] Hogan and Hutson (2005a) advance the High-Technology Pecking Order Hypothesis (HTPOH) to explain the role of equity in the financing of NTBFs in the software product sector. The HTPOH posits that NTBFs exhibit a hierarchical pattern of financing that gives precedence to internal sources, but if external financing is required, equity is preferred to debt. This study investigates the extent to which the genesis of the NTBF affects its financing patterns?

The paper examines the capital structure and financing decisions of 117 Irish software product firms, divided into 3 sub-groups by genesis: industry spinoffs, university spinoffs and non-spinoffs. NTBFs are much more likely to 'spinoff' from existing organisations than the general population of start-ups. While spinoffs account for no more than 20% of start-ups (Bernardt, Kerste, & Meijaard, 2002; Moncada-Paternò-Castello, Tübke, Howells, & Carbone, 1999), about three-quarters of high-technology entrepreneurs set up in the same sector as their parent organisations (Cooper & Bruno, 1977; Oakey, 1995; Segal, Quince, & Wicksteed, 2000).

One might expect *a priori* that spinoffs are able to take advantage of the resource base provided by the 'parent' organisation, giving them a head start on non-spinoff firms. It is surprising, however, how little empirical evidence there is on the

---

[1] NTBFs are defined by Little (1977) as independent ventures less than 25 years old that supply a product or service based on the exploitation of an invention or technological innovation.

New Technology Based Firms in the New Millennium, Volume VI
Edited by A. Groen, R. Oakey, P. van der Sijde and G. Cook

performance of spinoffs versus non-spinoffs. Prior studies have tended to focus on types of spinoffs, in particular, university spinoffs. Findings from studies of university spinoffs can be compared with studies of the general population to get an overview of the impact of firm genesis on performance. Shane (2004), for example provides evidence from a number of countries attesting to the superior survival rate of university spinoffs. He finds that, in comparison with the general population of start-ups, university spinoffs in the US (Goldfarb & Henrekson, 2003) are more likely to go public, and that in the UK (Wright, Binks, Vohora, & Lockett, 2003) they are more likely to secure venture capital. With the exception of Lindholm-Dahlstrand (1997) and Koster (2004), very few comparative studies attempt to link variations in the performance of spinoffs and non-spinoffs to difference in firm characteristics. The current database offers a unique opportunity to compare the financial decision-making process in industry spin-offs, academic spinoffs and non-spinoffs.

The paper provides a breakdown of the sources of finance used by industry spinoffs, university spinoffs and non-spinoffs, separated into internal (savings, consulting revenues and retained earnings) and external (bank debt, venture capital, private investors and government grants). In total, 96 of the 117 respondents provided this information. The average figures for the full sample show a 50/50 divide between internal and external sources of finance. A mere 4% is sourced from banks, and almost 39% (28% from venture capital and 11% from private investors) is external equity. Overall, there is little difference in the pattern of financing found in industry spinoffs and non-spinoffs. Academic spinoffs, however, have a very different capital structure, being more dependent on external equity, and using considerably less of their own savings and retained profits, than both industry spinoffs and non-spinoffs.

In the second part of the study, four predictions of the HTPOH are examined in the context of the three sub-groupings. This analysis is based on a survey of the lead founders' perceptions of business risk, information asymmetries in bank and venture capital markets, the tax benefits of debt and the signalling potential of debt versus equity. Overall, we find that the founders perceive low tax benefits of debt and very high levels of business risk. They also perceive greater information asymmetries in debt than in private equity markets. Consistent with the findings of an atypical funding structure for academic spin-offs, their founders' views on two of the four financing issues differ from those of founders in the other two sub-groups. Academic spinoffs perceive higher levels of information asymmetry in debt markets, and higher levels of business risk, than both industry spinoffs and non-spinoffs, which may explain their greater use of external equity.

The paper is structured as follows. Section 2 discusses the spin-off literature, and Section 3 presents the HTPOH, as well as the testable implications. In Section 4, the sample characteristics are outlined, including summary information on spin-off activity and age structure. Section 5 presents the funding structure for the three sub-groups and their founders' perceptions of issues relating to capital structure choice. Section 6 summarises and concludes.

## Spinoffs

The genesis of new firms is complex and diverse, and this gives rise to widely differing firm characteristics. The term 'spinoff' was coined to signify that the technology basis of the new firm had its origins in the founder's 'mother' organisation (Roberts, 1968, p. 250). The terms 'mother', 'parent' and 'incubator' are used interchangeably to denote the "established organisation for which the entrepreneur had previously been working" (Cooper, 1971, p. 11). The definition of *spinoff* varies across studies. Most studies have tended to adopt a broad definition, whereby it is sufficient that the founders start a business in the same sector as the parent organisation. Others researchers require a legal tie between the parent and the spinoff organisation (Lindholm-Dahlstrand, 1997). Obviously, the definition employed will affect the rate off spinoff activity identified in a particular study. In this study a spinoff is defined, in broad terms, as a new firm formed by individuals who worked for the same parent organisation and/or where the core technology originated in the parent organisation (Smilor, Gibson, & Dietrich, 1990).

Firms can be 'spun off' from different kinds of parent organisation, and spinoff patterns tend to reflect a particular region's industrial, economic and institutional infrastructure. The NTBFs in Cooper's (1971) seminal study of the San Francisco area were predominantly spinoffs from local industry. In contrast, nearly all the spinoffs documented in Roberts' (1991) work had their origins in academic institutions in the Boston region, and in particular MIT. Outside the Boston region, however, industry spinoffs tend to outnumber academic spinoffs. Even in the Cambridge region, industry spinoffs outnumber academic spinoffs three to one (Segal, Quince, & Wicksteed, 2000).

Resource-based theory views the firm in terms of the resources it controls, particularly at start-up, and should therefore be useful in comparing the financing of spinoffs and non-spinoffs. Since firms have different start-up points (resource heterogeneity) that other firms may not be able to replicate (resource immobility), inherit in the theory is the causal relation between the quantity and quality of resources and firm performance. In other words, the genesis or history of the firm has important implications for subsequent performance. Viewed from this perspective, Garnsey (1998) predicts that spinoffs should outperform other NTBFs as a result of the resources that are available via their connections with the mother company.

Few researchers have undertaken in-depth studies of the performance of spinoffs that include a control group of non-spinoffs. Lindholm-Dahlstrand (1997) found that spinoffs grew significantly faster than non-spinoffs, but only after the 10th year in business. However, Lindholm-Dahlstrand found no link between growth and the variables measuring the relationship between the previous employer and the new firm, including competition and cooperation. Koster (2004) compared the early stage performance of spinouts, spinoffs and non-spinoffs in the US, and found that spinoffs (defined as firms that receive support from a third party company) develop their products, hire employees and generate income faster than other firms. There is, however, no study that investigates the effect of NTBF genesis on their financing.

## Theoretical Background and Testable Implications

Two competing theories from the finance literature explain the broad and diverse range of observed capital structures. The *static trade-off hypothesis* suggests that there is an 'optimal' capital structure for each firm, which trades off the tax benefits of debt against the increasing likelihood of financial distress as leverage rises. The *pecking order hypothesis* (POH) of Myers (1984) and Myers and Majluf (1984) posits that due to information asymmetries between firms and providers of finance, internal sources of funding are preferred over external, debt is the preferred source of external funding, and equity is issued only as a last resort. Extrapolating from the large body of empirical evidence on capital structure, it is clear that while each theory contributes useful insights to explain financing in large public firms, neither provides a complete explanation of observed capital structure across industries, countries and firms of different size and age (Brealey & Myers, 2000). Drawing on both theories, the HTPOH seeks to explain the role of the debt tax shield, business risk, information asymmetries and signalling in the capital structure of NTBFs.

### The Debt Tax Shield

Modigliani and Miller (1963) noted that the classical tax system provides a 'debt tax shield' because interest payments on debt are tax-deductible and dividends are not. This shield increases the firm's after-tax net cash flows, thus the levered firm is more valuable than the equivalent unlevered firm. The greater the marginal corporate tax rate and the higher the firm's earnings before interest and taxes (EBIT), the greater the benefit from the debt tax shield. The evidence relating to the value of the debt tax shield in large corporations is equivocal. Brealey and Myers (2000) conclude from an analysis of the evidence that a 'moderate tax advantage' applies to firms that are earning sufficient EBIT against which to claim the tax benefit. Highly profitable firms with few non-debt tax shields will benefit from leverage, while companies with large accumulated losses or other valuable tax shields may not benefit at all.

A number of researchers have found that small firms tend to be less profitable than larger firms (Ang, 1991, 1992; Day, Stoll, & Whaley, 1983; McConnell & Pettit, 1984; Michaelas, Chittenden, & Poutziouris, 1999; Van der Wijst, 1989), suggesting that the debt tax shield is relatively unimportant to new and small firms. Vos and Furlong (1998) found that the tax advantage of debt was particularly irrelevant in the early stages of firm development. This would particularly be the case for NTBFs, whose EBIT is substantially reduced by high research and development expense, reducing the tax benefits of debt.

There is no obvious reason why spinoffs and non-spinoffs should value the debt tax-shield differently. All NTBFs have high levels of research and development expense, and thus substantial debt tax shields. The study does not expect to find major differences between our three sub-groups on this issue.

### The Probability of Financial Distress: Business Risk

The static trade-off theory predicts that leverage is inversely related to business risk. Business risk is the variability of the expected future cash flows from the company's operations. High levels of business risk manifest as volatile EBIT, and such companies may find it difficult to support the large fixed interest costs that high levels of leverage involve. The firm's debt capacity therefore depends on costs associated with financial distress and the probability of becoming distressed. Research on large public firms indicates there is an inverse relation between optimal debt levels and business risk (Bradley, Jarrell, & Kim, 1984; Castanias, 1983).

There is a widely held perception that business risk is higher for NTBFs than for SMEs in general. The products of NTBFs are often untried, and are commonly subject to rapid obsolescence (Cooper, 1971). The limited empirical evidence on NTBF failure rates, however, is not consistent with this perception. In a review of research on the determinants of small firm failure, Storey (1994) found that sectoral differences in failure rates are relatively modest, and Storey and Tether (1998) reported that European NTBFs actually have lower failure rates than start-ups in other sectors.

A second approach to assessing likely levels of business risk relates to the extent of within-firm diversification. The less diversified the product and customer base, the greater the firm's exposure to variability in future income, and the riskier the firm. NTBFs tend to focus on developing a single product, which is often designed to meet the specific needs of one or a small number of customers (European Commission, 2000).

In terms of the three sub-groups, one might expect industry spinoffs to experience lower business risk when compared with non-spinoffs, given that they have access to a greater resource base through their connections with the mother company. However, close ties with the mother company might also limit the industry spinoff's potential to expand its customer base and diversify its product range. It is therefore difficult to predict whether industry spinoffs will have higher level of business risk than non-spinoffs.

Academic spinoffs, however, are likely to be less diversified than industry spinoffs, given that they commonly have links to a specific research project. It is also possible that academic spinoffs have higher business risk because the academic entrepreneurs are likely to have limited business experience (Franklin, Wright, & Lockett, 2001; Roberts, 1991), and need to make the transition from running not-for-profit research centres to commercially viable entities (Vohora, Wright, & Lockett, 2004). Their inexperience in business may make potential outside investors more wary of academic spinoffs due to a higher perceived risk of failure. These features suggest that academic entrepreneurs will face greater financing constraints, particularly in debt markets, than industry spinoffs and non-spinoffs. However, in a review of the cross-country evidence, Shane (2004) finds that university spinoffs have *lower* failure rates than the average population of start-ups. In the face of such contradictory evidence on the business risk of academic spinoffs versus other NTBFs, it is difficult to predict what the capital structure will look like and how financing decisions are made within sub-groups.

### Information Asymmetries and the Pecking Order

At the heart of the POH is the asymmetry of information between the company's management and 'uninformed' outside investors. This information asymmetry implies that a new issue of stock will trigger a reduction in the stock price, because investors assume that managers will issue stock only if they perceive it to be overvalued. The POH predicts that, in order to avoid this adverse signalling problem, managers will finance projects from retained earnings where possible. Once internal sources of finance are exhausted, managers will opt for debt because debt securities are less sensitive to news than equity. Under the POH, the firm's capital structure depends on both its profitability and its investment opportunities. It predicts, for example that a more profitable enterprise in a mature market will have a lower debt-to-equity ratio than a less profitable enterprise in the same market.

Several studies have shown that the POH holds for small privately held firms (Berggren, Olofsson, & Silver, 2000; Cosh & Hughes, 1994; Schulman, Cooper, & Brophy, 1993). The rationale for this pattern of financing, however, cannot be the same for SMEs as it is for large firms. The information asymmetries discussed in Myers (1984) and Myers and Majluf (1984) arise from the separation of ownership and control, and this is not a feature of most small businesses. Stanworth and Gray (1991) explain the preference for internal sources of finance in SMEs by pointing out that small firm debt markets suffer from information asymmetries that give rise to moral hazard and adverse selection. Since the repayments on debt financing are fixed, debt holders face an asymmetric payoff. They do not participate in the additional returns generated if the firm is successful, but they share in the losses if the firm fails. The owner-manager is the beneficiary if the firm is successful. In such cases, SME borrowers have an incentive to 'gamble with the bank's money' and pursue high-risk projects. Adverse selection arises if debt providers such as banks have difficulties in discriminating between 'good' and 'bad' investment projects, resulting in financing constraints for all small business. Several studies have confirmed that adverse selection is an issue for SMEs; potential lenders experience significant problems in assessing owner-managers' capabilities (Berger & Udell, 1998; Binks & Ennew, 1994; Chittenden, Hall, & Hutchinson, 1996; Cosh & Hughes, 1994; Michaelas, Chittenden, & Poutziouris, 1999; Stanworth & Gray, 1991).

### Information Asymmetries in NTBFs

The evidence from several countries suggests that, as for SMEs generally, internal funds are the preferred financing source for NTBFs (Bank of England, 1996; Giudici & Paleari, 2000; Lindholm-Dahlstrand & Cetindamar, 2000; Lumme, Kauranen, & Autio, 1994; Moore, 1994; Roberts, 1990, 1991; Tyebjee & Bruno, 1981). There is some evidence, however, that NTBFs are less likely to issue debt than other small businesses. Hyytinen and Pajarinen (2002) find a negative relation between technology intensity and debt. From the US and the UK there is evidence that debt is not the preferred source of outside funding at start-up (Brewer & Genay, 1994; Brewer, Genay, Jackson, & Worthington, 1997; Moore, 1994; Roberts, 1990, 1991) and on a continuing basis (Oakey, 1984; Roberts, 1990, 1991) for NTBFs.

NTBFs face serious information asymmetries in debt markets, even relative to the general population of SMEs (Bank of England, 1996, 2001; Berger & Udell, 1998; European Commission, 2003). High-technology investment projects are associated with greater 'technology uncertainty' than the average SME investment project; that is, banks do not understand high-technology businesses (Bank of England, 1996; Deakins & Hussain, 1993; European Commission, 2001; Oakey, 1984). For this reason, banks tend to avoid lending to NTBFs. Moral hazard is also a potentially serious problem in NTBFs, because monitoring research and development activity is particularly difficult for outsiders (Jordan, Lowe, & Taylor, 1998). Compounding these informational problems is that NTBFs tend to lack fixed assets to offer as collateral. Their assets tend to be highly firm specific and their value is dependent on specialised know-how. In addition, they are likely to be dominated by intangibles, which retain their value only as long as the firm is a going concern (Brealey & Myers, 2000; Myers, 1977).

Venture capitalists are best equipped to overcome these information asymmetries and moral hazard problems (Amit, Brander, & Zott, 1998; Gompers & Lerner, 2003). Their ongoing relationship with the firm allows them to closely monitor and advise managers, which ensures that the owner-managers' interests are aligned with their own (Sahlman, 1990), thereby reducing moral hazard. Information asymmetries are less likely because venture capital firms usually have in-depth knowledge of markets and technologies in specific fields (Gupta & Sapienza, 1992; Lindholm-Dahlstrand & Cetindamar, 2000; Norton & Tenenbaum, 1993; Ruhnka & Young, 1991).

*Information Asymmetries in NTBFs: Academic and Industry Spinoffs versus Non-Spinoffs*

Consistent with the predictions of HTPOH, Hogan and Hutson (2005a) found that NTBFs perceive greater information asymmetries in debt markets than in venture capital markets. Academic spinoffs may encounter higher levels of information asymmetries than industry spinoffs because of higher levels of technology uncertainty. The technologies introduced by academic entrepreneurs tend to be at an earlier stage of development since they are more likely to have their origins in basic research programmes. The founders of industry spinoffs may face lower levels of information asymmetries because their technologies are more established with direct or indirect links to existing products and services of parent organisations. In a review of the empirical evidence from the US, Shane (2004) concludes that university spinoffs are a key mechanism in the commercialisation of early stage inventions that would be too uncertain for established companies to adopt. As a result, academic entrepreneurs may face even greater information asymmetries in financial markets than other high-technology entrepreneurs.

# Data and Sample Characteristics

The analysis is based on a survey of the population of NTBFs in the software product sector in Ireland. The software sector is sub-divided into 'products' and 'services'. Software products refer to packaged software that is generally produced in large volumes for mass markets,[2] while software services include consulting, implementation, support services, operations management and training. Software product firms are defined as those primarily involved in the development and commercialisation of their own products.

The survey design is based on self-administered questionnaires using the tailored design method (Dillman, 1976, 2000). The survey was administered by mail and addressed to named CEOs. A covering letter requested that the surveys be completed by the founder or by the lead founder if a team had founded the company. Respondents were given the choice of completing either a paper or web-based questionnaire. The first follow-up contact was also by mail, and the second by telephone. The final contact was via e-mail, and it contained a hyperlink to the electronic version of the questionnaire. Completed questionnaires were received during April and May, 2002. At the end of 2001, there were

---

[2] This can be distinguished from 'bespoke' software, which is provided on a client-by-client basis.

Table 1:  Spinoffs in the software product sector.

|  |  | **Firms** | **%** |
|---|---|---|---|
| Academic spinoff |  | 11 | 9.4 |
| Industry spinoff |  |  |  |
|     Indigenous parent company | 32 |  |  |
|     Multinational parent company | 23 | 55 | 47.0 |
| New business |  | 45 | 38.5 |
| Family business |  | 6 | 5.1 |
|  |  | 117 | 100 |

Table 2:  Age characteristics of the sample firms (in years).

|  | **Academic spinoffs** | **Industry spinoffs** | **Non-spinoffs** | **Full sample** |
|---|---|---|---|---|
| Mean | 3.6 | 6 | 6 | 5.8 |
| Median | 3 | 5 | 4 | 4 |
| Min | 2 | 1 | 1 | 1 |
| Max | 9 | 27 | 19 | 27 |
| *n* | 11 | 55 | 51 | 117 |

257 indigenous software product SMEs in Ireland. The number of valid returns was 117, giving an impressive response rate of just under 46%.[3]

Table 1 shows that 56% of founders in this study link their origins to a parent organisation. This figure is somewhat lower than the average spinoff rate of 70% typically associated with NTBFs, but similar to rates reported for Sweden (Lindholm-Dahlstrand, 1997). As already noted, variations in definitions employed can lead to significant differences in the spinoff rate reported across studies. In addition, software development is a relatively mature technology sector and the start-up and development costs are comparatively low (Hogan & Hutson, 2005b; Oakey, 1995). Software product firms are five times as likely to spinoff from industry than from academia; 9% spinoff from universities and 47% spinoff from existing businesses. Very few firms in the sample (5%) are family businesses.

Table 2 summarises the data on company age. The youngest firm is 5 months old and the oldest is 27 years. For the full sample the average age is just under 6 years and the median age is 4 years. Academic spinoffs are on average younger than the rest of the sample, with a mean age of 3.6 years and a median age of 3, compared to an average of 6 years for industry spinoffs and non-spinoffs.

---

[3] Response rates of 10% and less are commonly reported in small business mail surveys (Curran & Blackburn, 2001).

# Results

Table 3 provides summary information on the sources of finance used to support current investment projects for the 96 firms in the sample that provided detailed funding information. These average figures for the full sample show a 50/50 divide between internal and external sources. A mere 4% of financing is sourced from banks, and the remaining outside finance (46% of the total financing requirement) is private equity and government grants. External sources of finance are more important for firms in the 2 to 9 year old age range, but are less in evidence for firms in the 10 plus age range. Retained earnings increase in importance for the older firms (10 years plus), for which it provides nearly half of financing requirements. Retained profits appear to replace outside finance, which comprises an average of only a quarter of the funding for these more established firms.

It is clear that the NTBFs in the software sector in Ireland are primarily self-financing at start-up; 73% of financing for the 12 firms under 2 years is sourced internally. Most of this funding is from the personal savings of the founders (43% of the total), but a substantial component is provided by cash flows from consulting services (27% of total funding). These findings are largely consistent with prior research on capital structure in NTBFs. In the US, Roberts (1991) found that bank finance did not feature at all as a funding source for high-technology start-ups, and private outside equity comprised 21% of total funding. However, the proportion of private equity in Irish software firms, at 39%, is much higher than for UK-based NTBFs reported by Moore (1994), who found that venture capitalists provide only 10% of funding. This may reflect the Irish sample frame that is restricted to NTBFs in the software product sector and investment portfolios of Irish venture capitalists are dominated by software companies (IVCA, 2006). The relative unimportance of bank loans amongst the older firms is consistent with the findings of Oakey (1984) that bank debt as a source of ongoing funding for NTBFs is negligible.

Table 4 reports the capital structure for spinoff and non-spinoff companies. The table clearly shows that while the capital structure of industry spinoff and non-spinoff firms is similar, the financing of academic spinoffs is quite different from either of the other two categories, which (apart from a higher proportion of financing from retained earnings for industry spinoffs) have remarkably similar capital structures. Both industry spinoffs and non-spinoffs source 47% of their funding externally, whereas 73% of academic spinoffs' financing comes from external source. Academic spinoffs finance a higher proportion of their investment requirement from private equity, government grants and venture capital. Industry spinoffs and non-spinoffs source much more of their finance from savings and retained earnings. Founders' savings account for only 4% of funding in academic spinoffs, compared to 13% and 18%, respectively, for industry spinoffs and non-spinoffs, and retained earnings comprise 3% of all funding in academic spinoffs versus 17% for the overall group.

These findings are consistent with our central hypothesis, which is the need to treat academic spinoffs as a separate group in relation to capital structure. The relatively insignificant role played by retained earnings in academic spinoffs suggests that they are more likely to be engaged in early stage inventions as predicted by Shane (2004), which are unlikely to generate substantial earnings. It may also be indicative of a relative lower

Table 3: Sources of financing for current investment in different stages in the lifecycle of software product firms.

| [1] Stages | [2] No. of firms | Internal sources of financing (%) | | | | [7] Bank loans | External sources of financing (%) | | | |
|---|---|---|---|---|---|---|---|---|---|---|
| | | [3] Savings | [4] Consulting revenues | [5] Retained earnings | [6] Total internal | | [8] Venture capital | [9] Private investors | [10] Govt. grants | [11] Total external |
| [A] Start-up <2 years | 12 | 43.0 | 27.0 | 2.5 | 72.5 | 0.0 | 13.0 | 10.0 | 4.5 | 27.5 |
| [B] Commercialisation 2–4 years | 46 | 10.0 | 13.5 | 8.5 | 32.0 | 3.0 | 38.0 | 18.5[a] | 8.5 | 68.0 |
| [C] Growth 5–9 years | 20 | 9.5 | 28.0 | 18.0 | 55.5 | 6.5 | 28.0 | 3.0 | 7.0 | 44.5 |
| [D] Mature >10 years | 18 | 10.0 | 20.0 | 46.0 | 76.0 | 5.0 | 11.0 | 5.0 | 3.0 | 24.0 |
| [E] Full sample | 96 | 14.0 | 19.0 | 17.0 | 50.0 | 4.0 | 28.0 | 11.0 | 7.0 | 50.0 |

[a]Funds from corporate investors featured as a source of finance for firms in the 2–4 year age band and for presentation purpose have been included with the figure for private investors for this group.

Table 4: Capital structure in academic and industry spinoffs, and non-spinoffs.

| Source of finance | Spinoffs | | Non-spinoffs | All firms |
|---|---|---|---|---|
| | **University** | **Corporate** | | |
| Savings | 4 | 13 | 17.5 | 14 |
| Consulting revenues | 20 | 18 | 20 | 19 |
| Retained earnings | 3 | 22 | 15.5 | 17 |
| Total internal | 27 | 53 | 53 | 50 |
| Banks | 3 | 6 | 3 | 4 |
| Venture capital | 36 | 25 | 29 | 28 |
| Private equity | 21 | 9 | 10 | 11 |
| Government grants | 13 | 7 | 5 | 7 |
| Total external | 73 | 47 | 47 | 50 |
| $n$ | 11 | 41 | 44 | 96 |

earning power, which from a resource base viewpoint would reflect a relative lack of knowledge of the commercial world. On a more positive note, academic spinoffs appear to be very successful in accessing external equity – venture capital and private capital – and government grants. In addition, academic spinoffs shows a strong ability to generate funding from consulting activities; 20% of their financing needs come from consulting revenues, which is about the same as the rest of the sample.

Interestingly, industry spinoffs derive a higher proportion of their funds from banks than the average for the sample firms. However, at 6% of total funding, bank financing is still the least important source of funding for industry spinoff companies. Nevertheless, the finding is consistent with the predictions of resource-based theory. Industry spinoffs also finance a higher proportion of their funding from retained profits, which is consistent with the higher levels of profitability and superior performance of these firms, relative to non-spinoffs, reported in the literature (Koster, 2004).

Overall, with the exception of academic spinoffs, the analysis shows that capital structure in software NTBFs is similar, regardless of genesis. The firms tend to give precedence to internal sources of finance, and if external financing is required, equity is preferred. Debt is almost absent in all of the sub-groups. Academic spinoffs appear to be unique among firms in that the standard pecking order is completely turned on its head: external equity dominates financing, followed by internal sources of funds, and then debt. However, it is worth noting that (as shown in Table 3) firms at the commercialisation stage of their development, software NTBFs generally demonstrate the same pattern of financing. Therefore, are the findings on academic spinoffs driven by the fact that many of them were at the commercialisation stage at the time of the survey?

In fact, 9 of the 11 academic spinoffs *were* in the commercialisation stage of their development cycle at the time of the survey, and they comprise 20% of all sample firms in this stage. Table 5 presents the sources of finance for academic spinoffs versus the full sample at this stage. It is clear from the table that the academic spinoffs' reliance on external equity

Table 5: Capital structure in academic spinoffs at the commercialisation stage.

| Source of finance | Commercialisation | |
|---|---|---|
| | **University spinoffs** | **Full sample** |
| Savings | 5.5 | 10 |
| Consulting revenues | 9 | 13.5 |
| Retained earnings | 2.5 | 8.5 |
| Total internal | 17 | 32 |
| Banks | 3 | 3 |
| Venture capital | 45 | 38 |
| Private equity | 26 | 18.5 |
| Government grants | 9 | 8.5 |
| Total external | 83 | 68 |
| *n* | 9 | 46 |

is not solely attributable to life cycle factors, because they are much more dependent on outside equity than other firms at the commercialisation stage; 71% of their funding requirement at the commercialisation stage comes from equity sources, compared to 56.5% for all firms in this stage. Although the number of observations is small, the results suggest that the dominance of equity over all other sources of funding may be a persistent feature of academic spinoffs.

## The Debt Tax Shield

The survey addressed the question of the importance of the debt tax shield by asking founders the extent to which they consider the difference in the tax treatment of retained earnings, interest and capital gains for shareholders when making financing decisions. Table 6 (row 4) shows that, consistent with the first prediction arising from the HTPOH, tax issues are clearly not a critical factor. Only 19% consider the difference in the tax treatment of retained earnings, interest and capital gains for shareholders to be important, and for 35% the issue is not important at all. As anticipated, there is little difference between industry spinoffs and non-spinoffs with regard to the value of the debt-tax shield; 14% of non-spinoffs and 22.3% of industry spinoffs consider differences in tax treatment important. Surprisingly, the founders of academic spinoffs appear to be more concerned about this issue; 27.3% consider the difference in the tax treatment of retained earnings, interest and capital gains to be important. Only 18% of academic founders do not consider these tax issues to be important compared to 40.7% of the founders of industry spinoffs and 32% of the founders of non-spinoffs.

These findings point to the presence of non-debt tax shields in the form of research and development expenses typical of software development firms. It may also reflect a unique feature of the Irish tax system. Ireland has for many decades operated a low-corporation

Table 6: The impact of taxation on the financing decision.

| Consider the difference in the tax treatment of retained earnings, interest and capital gains for shareholders | Not at all (%) | To some extent (%) | To a large extent (%) |
|---|---|---|---|
| Industry spinoffs ($n = 54$) | 40.7 | 37.0 | 22.3 |
| Non-spinoffs($n = 50$) | 32.0 | 54.0 | 14.0 |
| Academic spinoffs ($n = 11$) | 18.2 | 54.5 | 27.3 |
| NTBFs (full sample) | 34.8 | 46.1 | 19.1 |

Table 7: Founders' perception of the risk of firm failure.

| Even with adequate finance, the company has a 50% chance of failing | Agree (%) | Neither agree nor disagree (%) | Disagree (%) |
|---|---|---|---|
| 1. Industry spinoffs ($n = 54$) | 46.3 | 11.1 | 42.6 |
| 2. Non-spinoffs ($n = 51$) | 52.9 | 17.6 | 29.4 |
| 3. Academic spinoffs ($n = 11$) | 72.7 | 0.0 | 27.3 |
| 4. NTBFs (full sample, $n = 116$) | 51.7 | 12.9 | 35.3 |

tax regime and currently has the second lowest rate in the European Union. Originally designed to encourage foreign direct investment in traded manufacturing, all trading manufacturing and service activities now benefit from this low tax rate.

*Business Risk*

Table 7 presents the findings on founders' perceptions of business risk. Consistent with the second implication of the HTPOH, overall the founders perceive a very high level of business risk. In April/May 2002 respondents were quite pessimistic about the probability of survival of their businesses in that 52% believed that, even with adequate financing, the company had a 50% chance of failing, while only 35% disagreed with the statement. The founders of academic spinoffs were most pessimistic about their probability of survival: 72% of the founders of academic spinoffs believed that, even with adequate financing, the company had a 50% chance of failing. This may contribute an explanation for why academic spinoff entrepreneurs have a much lower proportion of their own savings invested in the firm, as reported in Table 4. If academic founders perceive a very high risk of failure, then they will be less likely to put their own money at risk.

Our findings on perceived business risk for academic spinoffs is inconsistent with Shane's (2004) finding that university spinoffs have lower failure rates than the average population of start-ups. It should be noted, however, that the academic spinoffs are on average younger than the other firms in the sample, and that the perceived probability of failure tends to decline with age (Hogan & Hutson, 2005b).

The founders of industry spinoffs are split between those that are confident about their chances of survival and those that are not: 46% believe that their firms have a 50% chance of failing, and 43% disagreed. Nevertheless, the founders of industry spinoffs are more optimistic about their chances of survival than the sample average.

## Information Asymmetries

Table 8 reports founders' perceptions of the bank-client relationship. Supporting the third prediction arising from the HTPOH (the extent to which founders perceive that banks understand their business), panel A shows strong evidence of severe information asymmetries in the market for bank finance. 58% of founders do not agree that banks understand their business, whereas only 9% of founders believe that banks understand them (row 4). This is consistent with findings from the Bank of England (1996), which found that few NTBF firms believed that banks understood their products or markets. If bank managers are unable to assess the technological basis for investment proposals, then information asymmetries will be severe and adverse selection will restrict the flow of debt funds to the technology sector. Consistent with the predictions, in relation to the different subgroups, academic spinoffs appear to experience the greatest levels of information asymmetries, followed by non-spinoffs and lastly industry spinoffs. None of the founders of the academic

Table 8: Founders' perceptions of bank finance.

| | Agree (%) | Neither agree nor disagree (%) | Disagree (%) |
|---|---|---|---|
| [A] Banks understand my business | | | |
| 1. Industry spinoffs ($n = 55$) | 12.7 | 36.4 | 50.9 |
| 2. Non-spinoffs ($n = 51$) | 7.8 | 23.5 | 68.6 |
| 3. Academic spinoffs ($n = 11$) | 0.0 | 54.5 | 45.5 |
| 4. NTBFs (full sample, $n = 117$) | 9.4 | 32.5 | 58.1 |
| [B] Banks are willing to provide a long-term loan to my company | | | |
| 5. Industry spinoffs ($n = 53$) | 18.9 | 34.0 | 47.2 |
| 6. Non-spinoffs (51) | 19.6 | 21.6 | 58.8 |
| 7. Academic spinoffs ($n = 11$) | 9.1 | 36.4 | 54.5 |
| 8. NTBFs (full sample, $n = 115$) | 18.3 | 28.7 | 53.0 |
| [C] Banks lend money to companies with cash/fixed assets | | | |
| 9. Industry spinoffs ($n = 52$) | 82.7 | 11.5 | 5.8 |
| 10. Non-spinoffs ($n = 49$) | 77.6 | 18.4 | 4.1 |
| 11. Academic spinoffs ($n = 10$) | 50.0 | 50.0 | 0.0 |
| 12. NTBFs (full sample, $n = 111$) | 77.5 | 18.0 | 4.5 |

spinoffs believe that banks understand their business, and this compares to 7.8% of the founders of non-spinoffs and 12.7% of the founders of industry spinoffs.

The perceived lack of understanding on the part of bankers is reflected in founders' perception of the willingness of banks to lend to software NTBFs (panel B of Table 8). Row 8 shows that only 18% of founders believe that banks would be willing to provide long-term loans to their companies, whereas 53% disagree with the statement. The founders of academic spinoffs perceive that banks are less willing to lend to them than other NTBF founders. Only 9% of the founders of academic spinoffs believe that banks are willing to provide long-term financing to their firms compare to a sample average of 18%.

Banks rely on collateral in order to mitigate adverse selection (Stiglitz & Weiss, 1981). But the assets of NTBFs, particularly in the software sector, tend to be intangible and based on scientific knowledge and intellectual property. The findings on this issue (panel C, row 12) show that 77.5% of founders believe that banks lend money to companies with fixed assets and/or cash. The founders' perceptions of bank-client lending conditions are consistent with the existence of high levels of information asymmetries. The founders of academic spinoffs appear to be less clear in relation to this issue than their counterparts from industry spinoffs and non-spinoffs. Although half of the academic founders agreed that banks lend to companies with assets, the other half neither agreed nor disagreed (row 11).

Overall, academic spinoffs clearly perceive a higher level of information asymmetries in debt markets than other spinoffs and non-spinoffs. This is consistent with the view that academic spinoffs experience greater technology uncertainty, because their technologies are more likely to evolve from basic research projects.

The survey respondents have a more positive perception of venture capital than bank finance, as shown in Table 9. One-fifth of software firm founders do not believe that venture capitalists understand their businesses (row 4), which is a much lower count for the equivalent statement relating to banking markets. 49% of software firm founders believe that venture capitalists understand their businesses (row 4), whilst only 9.4%

Table 9: Founders' perceptions of venture capital finance.

|  | Agree (%) | Neither agree nor disagree (%) | Disagree (%) |
|---|---|---|---|
| [A] Venture capitalists understand my business | | | |
| 1. Industry spinoffs ($n = 54$) | 55.6 | 29.6 | 14.8 |
| 2. Non-spinoffs ($n = 51$) | 41.2 | 35.3 | 23.5 |
| 3. Academic spinoffs ($n = 11$) | 54.5 | 18.2 | 27.3 |
| 4. NTBFs (full sample, $n = 116$) | 49.1 | 31.0 | 19.9 |
| [B] Venture capitalists invest in companies with cash/fixed assets | | | |
| 1. Industry spinoffs ($n = 51$) | 19.6 | 23.5 | 56.9 |
| 2. Non-spinoffs ($n = 49$) | 14.3 | 40.8 | 44.9 |
| 3. Academic spinoffs ($n = 9$) | 11.1 | 55.6 | 33.3 |
| 4. NTBFs (full sample, $n = 109$) | 18.4 | 33.9 | 47.7 |

believe that banks understand their businesses. There is little difference in the views of the founders of academic spinoffs, industry spinoffs and non-spinoffs in relation to this issue. However, it is worth comparing academic founders' perceptions of bank finance (Table 8, row 3) and venture capital finance. Over half (54%) of the founders of academic spinoffs believe that venture capitals understand their business and none of them believe that banks understand their business.

Panel B of Table 9 reports the views of respondents on the willingness of venture capitalists to invest in companies with cash/fixed assets. The perception in general is that, unlike for banks, the presence of fixed assets is not a prerequisite for venture capitalist involvement. In row 8, only a small minority of founders (18%) believe that venture capitalists invest in firms with fixed assets, while the remainder have no opinion (34%) or disagree with the statement (48%). There is little difference between the three groups with regard to this issue. However, it is noticeable that both the founders of non-spinoffs and academic spinoffs are more unsure about this issue than the industry spinoffs. Only 23% of the founders of industry spinoffs neither agreed nor disagreed that venture capitalists invest in companies with cash/or fixed assets, while the corresponding figure for the founders of academic spinoffs is 55.6% and 40.8% for the founders of non-spinoffs. This perhaps indicates a lack of understanding of the venture capital process, which is surprising given that 50% of these firms have obtained venture capital finance.

### Signalling

Table 10 shows that 70% of all founders believe that issuing equity sends a positive signal to external investors about the firm's future prospects. In contrast, only 21% believe that issuing debt sends a favourable signal, and a substantial 50% disagree that raising debt

Table 10: Founders' opinions on signalling the value of debt and equity.

| | Not at all (%) | To some extent (%) | To a large extent (%) |
|---|---|---|---|
| [A] Raising debt sends a favourable signal to lenders, investors, creditors and customers about the firm's future prospects | | | |
| 1. Industry spinoffs ($n = 53$) | 54.7 | 20.8 | 24.5 |
| 2. Non-spinoffs ($n = 50$) | 46.0 | 32.0 | 22.0 |
| 3. Academic spinoffs ($n = 11$) | 45.5 | 54.5 | 0.0 |
| 4. NTBFs (full sample, $n = 114$) | 50.0 | 28.9 | 21.1 |
| [B] Raising external equity sends a favourable signal to lenders, investors, creditors and customers about the firm's future prospects | | | |
| 1. Industry spinoffs ($n = 54$) | 9.3 | 11.1 | 79.6 |
| 2. Non-spinoffs ($n = 50$) | 10.0 | 32.0 | 58.0 |
| 3. Academic spinoffs ($n = 11$) | 0.0 | 27.3 | 72.7 |
| 4. NTBFs (full sample, $n = 115$) | 8.7 | 28.9 | 69.6 |

conveys a positive signal. The fact that founders understand the signalling value of equity investments demonstrates their positive attitude towards its use as a source of funding.

There is little difference in the perceptions of the three groups in relation to the signalling value of equity versus debt. However, it does appear that the academic spinoffs are even less convinced about the signalling value of debt than the others; none of the founders of academic spinoffs agree that raising debt is a positive signal compared to a sample average of 21%. This is consistent with their views on the prevalence of information asymmetries in bank markets reported in Table 8.

The contrasting findings on the perceptions of debt versus equity market asymmetries and signalling provides very strong support for the HTPOH prediction that NTBFs perceive greater asymmetries in bank relationships than in equity markets. These findings are consistent with the spirit of Myers' (1984) and Myers and Majluf's (1984) hypothesis that firms prefer to obtain external finance from sources associated with the least information asymmetry — in the case of NTBFs, equity rather than debt. It is also clear that academic spinoffs perceive greater levels of information asymmetries that non-spinoffs and industry-spinoffs. There is some evidence, consistent with the resource-based theory, that industry spinoffs experience lower information asymmetries in bank versus equity markets than non-spinoffs, although the difference between these two groups' views on this issue is small.

## Summary and Conclusions

Using survey responses for 117 private Irish software product firms, this study compares the capital structure and financing decisions of academic spinoffs, industry spinoffs and non-spinoffs. It finds very little difference between the capital structure of industry spinoffs and non-spinoffs NTBFs. Academic spinoffs, in contrast, are much more dependent on external equity than their NTBF counterparts, and much less dependent on internal sources, including the founders' savings and retained earnings. Academic spinoffs appear to be unique amongst firms in that the standard financing 'pecking order' is completely turned on its head: external equity dominates their capital structure, followed by internal sources of funds, and debt as a last resort. This heavy reliance on equity may, in part, reflect the impact of lifecycle factors on capital structure — the vast majority of the academic spinoffs were in the commercialisation stage of their development, and at this stage software firms generally have the same external equity-internal-debt capital structure. However, at 71% of total financing, the equity component (comprising venture capital and equity from private investors) in academic spinoffs at the commercialisation stage is much higher than the sample average of 56.5%. The dominance of external equity in capital structure appears to be a persistent feature of academic spinoffs.

Drawing on the resource-based theory of the firm and the rather scant evidence on comparative firm performance, we attempt to explain the dominance of equity in the capital structure of academic start-ups within the context of two of the four predictions of the HTPOH; one relating to business risk and the other, information asymmetries. Prior research suggests that academic spinoffs experience greater levels of technology uncertainty than other NTBFs because their products are at an earlier stage of development, implying greater information asymmetry in debt markets. The findings indicate that academic founders perceive higher levels of information asymmetries in debt markets than either industry spinoffs or non-spinoffs. None of the founders of academic spinoffs believe that banks understand their business, compared to a small number of founders of industry spinoffs and non-spinoffs. We argue that academic spinoffs would face higher levels of business risk because they are more likely to have an undiversified product base, and their founders are less likely than NTBF founders generally to have the business acumen to successfully develop their ideas. The founders of academic spinoffs were most pessimistic about their probability of survival: 72% believed that, even with adequate financing, the company had a 50% chance of failing, compared with a sample average of 52%.

The study sheds light on a facet of NTBF decision-making that has received very little prior academic attention. NTBF owner-managers have a good understanding of the effect of information asymmetries in equity and debt markets, and this appears to inform their choice of financing. The findings indicate that the HTPOH is also useful in exploring variations in financing decision in NTBFs of different genesis. Our finding that academic spinoffs have very different capital structure to industry spinoffs and non-spinoffs is a novel one. However, although the proportion of academic spinoffs in the sample is representative, the absolute number is small. Future research could test the HTPOH on larger samples of NTBFs. Another important topic for future work relates to the conflicting evidence on NTBF business risk. The strong findings relating to founders' perceptions of business risk are inconsistent with prior research that has found relatively low levels of NTBF failure rates. This suggests that higher levels of perceived business risk/uncertainty in NTBFs do not necessarily translate into higher failure rates. There is an urgent need for more wide-ranging, systematic studies of business risk in NTBFs, and also in SMEs in general.

In most countries there is increasing emphasis on universities' ability to become adept at exploiting their own science base and transferring their scientific knowledge to the private sector (Lockett & Wright, 2004). Academic spinoffs are increasingly viewed as important mechanisms for the transfer of this scientific knowledge. The study's findings that academic spinoffs are more dependent on equity due to higher perceived information asymmetries and business risk send a clear message to policymakers: university spinoffs are funded by equity and not by debt. Governments that support formal venture capital markets and informal investment markets will be facilitating increased participation in the development and commercialisation of knowledge intensive business ideas.

The other key difference between the academic spinoffs and their industry counterparts — the relatively insignificant role played by founders' savings — is possibly indicative of lower levels of commitment amongst academic entrepreneurs. As financiers understand, lower levels of personal investment are consistent with higher levels of perceived risk; in other words, academics are less likely to invest their own money in their businesses if they perceive they have a high chance of losing it. This raises the issue of providing appropriate financial instruments and incentives for high-risk investment projects derived from basic research. If these projects are financed by very high levels of external funding, in the form of equity and grants, academic founders may be tempted to gamble with investors' money and pursue ever high-risk projects. Harrison (2004) argues that many academic spinoffs are more like technology lifestyle companies than entrepreneurial ventures which suggests that they would be unable to provide adequate returns to equity investors. Clearly, the founders of academic spinoffs are unlikely to be a homogenous group in terms of expectations for the success, growth and performance of their businesses, and should not be viewed as panacea for Europe's commercialisation malaise. Nevertheless it is clear that new and creative solutions to financing university spinoffs may be required to provide academics with effective incentives to engage in spinoff activity.

# References

Amit, R., Brander, J., & Zott, C. (1998). Why do venture capital firms exist? Theory and Canadian evidence. *Journal of Business Venturing, 13*, 441–446.

Ang, J. S. (1991). Small business uniqueness and the theory of financial management. *Journal of Small Business Finance, 1*(1), 1–13.

Ang, J. S. (1992). On the theory of financing for privately held firms. *Journal of Small Business Finance, 1*(3), 185–203.

Bank of England. (1996). *The financing of technology-based small firms.* London.

Bank of England. (2001). *Financing of technology-based small firms.* London: Domestic Finance Division.

Berger, A. N., & Udell, G. F. (1998). The economics of small business finance: The role of private equity and debt markets in the finance growth cycle. *Journal of Banking and Finance, 22*(6–8), 613–673.

Berggren, B., Olofsson, C., & Silver, L. (2000). Control aversion and the search for external financing in Swedish SMEs. *Small Business Economics, 15*(3), 233–242.

Bernardt, Y., Kerste, R., & Meijaard, J. (2002). *Spin-off startups in the Netherlands: At first glance.* Zoeterm: E.I.M.

Binks, M., & Ennew, C. (1994). The provision of finance to small businesses: Does the banking relationship constrain performance? *Journal of Small Business Finance, 4*(1), 57–73.

Bradley, M., Jarrell, G. A., Kim, E. H. (1984). On the existence of optimal capital structure: Theory and evidence. *Journal of Finance, 39*(3), 857–878.

Brealey, R. A., & Myers, S. C. (2000). *Principles of corporate finance* (6th ed.). Boston: McGraw-Hill.

Brewer, E., & Genay, H. (1994). Funding small business through the SBIC program. *Federal Reserve Bank of Chicago Economic Perspectives, 18*, 22–34.

Brewer, E., Genay, H., Jackson, W. E., & Worthington, P. R. (1997). *The securities issue decision: Evidence from small business investment companies.* Working Paper. Federal Reserve Bank of Chicago, Chicago.

Castanias, R. (1983). Bankruptcy risk and optimal capital structure. *Journal of Finance, 38*(5), 1617–1635.

Chittenden, F., Hall, G., & Hutchinson, P. (1996). Small firm growth, access to capital markets and financial structure: Review of issues and an empirical investigation. *Small Business Economics, 8*(1), 59–67.

Cooper, A. C. (1971). *The founding of technology-based firms.* Milwaukee, WI: Centre for Venture Management CVM.

Cooper, A. C., & Bruno, A. V. (1977). Success among high-technology firms. *Business Horizons, 20*(2), 16–22.

Cosh, A., & Hughes, A. (1994). Size, financial structure and profitability: UK companies in the 1980s. In: A. Hughes & D. J. Storey (Eds), *Finance and the small firm*. London: Routledge.

Curran, J., & Blackburn, R. A. (2001). *Researching the small enterprise*. London: Sage.

Day, T. E., Stoll, H. R. & Whaley, R. E. (1983). *Taxes, financial policy and small business*. Lexington, Mass: Lexington Books.

Deakins, D., & Hussain, G. (1993). Overcoming the adverse selection problem: Evidence and policy implications from a study of bank managers on the importance of different criteria used in making a lending decision. In: F. Chittenden, M. Robertson & D. Watkins (Eds), *Small firms: Recession and recovery*. London: Paul Chapman.

Dillman, D. (1976). *Mail and telephone surveys*. New York: Wiley .

Dillman, D. (2000). *Mail and internet surveys* (2nd ed.). New York: Wiley .

European Commission. (2000). *European innovative enterprises: Lessons from the successful applications of research results to dynamic markets*. Innovation Papers, No. 5. Luxembourg: Office for Official Publications of the European Communities.

European Commission. (2001). *Innovation management: Building competitive skills in SMEs*. Innovation Papers, No. 8. Luxembourg: Office for Official Publications of the European Communities.

European Commission. (2003). *Green paper on entrepreneurship in Europe*. Luxembourg: Office for Official Publications of the European Communities.

Franklin, S. J., Wright, M., & Lockett, A. (2001). Academic and surrogate entrepreneurs in university-spin-out companies. *Journal of Technology Transfer*, *26*, 127–144.

Garnsey, E. (1998). A theory of the early growth of the firm. *Industrial and Corporate Change*, *7*(3), 523–556.

Giudici, G., & Paleari, S. (2000). The provision of finance to innovation: A survey conducted among Italian technology-based small firms. *Journal of Small Business Economics*, *14*(1), 37–53.

Goldfarb, B., & Henrekson, M. (2003). Bottom-up versus topdown policies towards the commercialization of university intellectual property. *Research Policy*, *32*(4), 639–658.

Gompers, P., & Lerner, J. (2003). Equity financing. In: Z. J. Acs & D. B. Audretsch (Eds), *Handbook of entrepreneurship research*. Netherlands: Kluwer Academic Publishers.

Gupta, A., & Sapienza, H. (1992). Determinants of venture capital firms' preference of in term of industry and geographical scope of their investment. *Journal of Business Venturing*, *7*, 347–362.

Harrison, R. T. (2004). Dynamics in academic spin-out companies: Entrepreneurial ventures or technology lifestyle businesses? Paper presented at the Gate2Growth Research Workshop. *Managing growth: The role of private equity*. IESE-Universidad de Navarra Barcelona, November.

Hogan, T., & Hutson, E. (2005a). Information asymmetry and capital structure in SMEs: New technology-based firms in the Irish software sector. *Financial Management Association Annual Meeting*, Chicago, 12th–15th October.

Hogan, T., & Hutson, E (2005b). Capital Structure in new technology-based firms: Evidence from the Irish software sector. *Global Finance Journal*, *15*(3), 369–387.

Hyytinen, A., & Pajarinen, M. (2002). *Financing of technology intensive small business: Some evidence from the ICT industry*. The Research Institute of the Finnish Economy Discussion paper No. 813.

Irish Venture Capital Association (IVCA). (2006). *The economic impact of venture capital in Ireland-2005*. Dublin Ireland: IVCA.

James, C., & Weir, P. (1993). Are banks different: Some evidence from the stock market. In L. D. H. Chew (Ed.), *The new corporate finance: Where theory meets practice*. New York: McGraw-Hill.

Jordan, J., Lowe, J., & Taylor, P. (1998). Strategy and financial policy in UK small firms. *Journal of Business Finance and Accounting*, *25*(1&2), 1–27.

Koster, J. (2004). *Spin-off firms and individual start-ups. Are they really different?* Paper presented at the 44th ERSA conference, Porto, 25–29 August.

Lindholm-Dahlstrand, A. (1997). Growth and inventiveness in technology-based spinoff firms. *Research Policy, 26*(3), 331–344.

Lindholm-Dahlstrand, A., & Cetindamar, A. (2000). The dynamics of innovation financing in Sweden. *Venture Capital, 2*(3), 203–221.

Little, A. D. (1977). *New technology-based firms in the United Kingdom and the Federal Republic of Germany.* London: Wilton House.

Lockett, A., & Wright, M. (2004). Resources, capabilities and the creation of university spin-out companies. Paper presented at the Gate2Growth Research Workshop. *Managing growth: The role of private equity,* IESE-Universidad de Navarra Barcelona, November.

Lumme, A., Kauranen, I., & Autio, E. (1994). The growth and funding mechanism of new technology-based firms: A comparative study between the United Kingdom and Finland. In: R. Oakey (Ed.), *New technology-based firms in the 1990s.* London: Paul Chapman.

McConnell, J. J., & Pettit, R. R. (1984). Applications of the modern theory of finance to small *business* firms. In: P. M. Horvitz & R. R. Pettit (Eds), *Small business finance* (Vol. 1). Greenwich, CT: JAI Press.

Michaelas, N., Chittenden, F., & Poutziouris, P. (1999). Financial policy and capital structure choice in UK SMEs: Empirical evidence from company panel data. *Small Business Economics, 12*(2), 113–130.

Modigliani, F., & Miller, M. (1963). Corporate income taxes and the cost of capital: A correction. *American Economic Review, 53*(3), 433–443.

Moncada-Paternò-Castello, P., Tübke, A., Howells, J., & Carbone, M. (1999). *The impact of corporate spin-offs on competitiveness and employment in the European Union: A first study.* Seville: Institute for Prospective Technological Studies (IPTS).

Moore, B. (1994). Financial constraints to the growth and development of small high technology firms. In: A. Hughes & D. J. Storey (Eds), *Finance and the small firm.* London: Routledge.

Myers, S. C. (1977). Determinants of corporate borrowing. *Journal of Financial Economics, 5,* 146–175.

Myers, S. C. (1984). The capital structure puzzle. *Journal of Finance, 39*(3), 575–592.

Myers, S. C., & Majluf, N. S. (1984). Corporate financing and investment decisions when firms have information that investors do not have. *Journal of Financial Economics, 13*(2), 187–221.

Norton, E., & Tenenbaum, B. H. (1993). Factors affecting the structure of venture capital deals. *Journal of Small Business Management, 30*(1), 20–30.

Oakey, R. P. (1984). *High technology small firms.* London: Frances Pinter.

Oakey, R. P. (1995). *High-technology new firms: Variable barriers to growth.* London: Paul Chapman.

Roberts, E. B. (1968). A basic study of innovators: How to keep and capitalize on their talents. *Research Management, XI*(4), 249–266.

Roberts, E. B. (1990). Initial capital for new technological enterprise. *IEEE Transactions on Engineering Management, 37*(2), 81–93.

Roberts, E. B. (1991). *Entrepreneurs in high technology; lessons from MIT and beyond.* Oxford: Oxford University Press.

Ruhnka, J. C., & Young, J. E. (1991). Some hypotheses about risk in venture capital investing. *Journal of Business Venturing, 6*(1), 115–133.

Sahlman, W. A. (1990). The structure and governance of venture capital organisations. *Journal of Financial Economics, 27,* 473–521.

Schulman, J., Cooper, R., & Borphy, D. (1993). Capital structure life cycle: Static or dynamic evolution? Proceedings of the International Conference on Establishment Surveys; Survey

Methods for Businesses, Farms, and Institutions June 27–30. American Statistical Association, Buffalo, NY.

Segal Quince Wicksteed. (2000). *The Cambridge phenomenon revisited*. Cambridge: Segal Quince Wicksteed.

Shane, S. (2004). *Academic entrepreneurship-university spinoffs and wealth creation*. Northampton: Edward Elgar.

Smilor, R. W., Gibson, D. V., & Dietrich, G. B. (1990). University spin-out companies: Technology start-ups from UT-Austin. *Journal of Business Venturing*, *5*(1), 63–67.

Stanworth, J., & Gray, C. (1991). *Bolton twenty years on: The small firm in the 1990s*. London: Chapman, on behalf of the Small Business Research Trust.

Stiglitz, J. E., & Weiss, A. (1981). Credit rationing in markets with imperfect information. *American Economic Review*, *71*(3), 383–410.

Storey, D. J. (1994). *Understanding the small business sector*. London: Routledge.

Storey, D. J., & Tether, B. S. (1998). New technology based firms in the European Union: An introduction. *Research Policy*, *26*(9), 933–946.

Tyebjee, T. T., & Bruno, A. V. (1981) Venture capital decision making: Preliminary results from three empirical studies. In: K. H. Vesper (Ed.), *Frontiers of entrepreneurship research* (pp. 281–320). Wellesley, Mass: Babson Center for Entrepreneurial Studies.

Van der Wijst, D. (1989). *Financial structure in small business: Theory, tests and applications*. Berlin: Springer-Verlag.

Vohora, A., Wright. M., & Lockett, A. (2004). Critical junctures in the development of university high-tech spin out. *Research Policy*, *33*(1), 147–175.

Vos, E., & Furlong, C. (1995). The agency advantage of debt over the lifecycle of the firm. *Entrepreneurial and Small Business Finance*, *5*(3), 193–211.

Wright, M., Binks, M., Vohora, A., & Lockett, A. (2003). *Annual UNICO_NUBS survey on university commercialisation activities: Financial year 2001*. Nottingham: NUBS.

Chapter 12

# The Role of Spin-Outs within University Research Commercialisation Activities: Case Studies from 10 UK Universities

Tim Minshall, Bill Wicksteed, Céline Druilhc, Andrea Kells, Michael Lynskey and Jelena Širaliova

## Introduction

In 2003, there was a concern among policymakers that spin-outs were being given undue prominence in consideration of the research commercialisation performance of UK Higher Education Institutes (HEIs) (Lambert, 2003). The aim of this research was to investigate what issues lay behind the data reported on spin-out activity by UK HEIs in the period 1998–2002.

The structure of this paper is as follows: Firstly, we place this research within the context of existing research on the commercialisation of university research. Secondly, we describe the approach taken for acquiring the evidence needed to address the research question. We then present and discuss the evidence captured through the pilot research. Finally, we draw our conclusions and then highlight areas of new research that build on the outputs of this project.

The research on this paper was presented at the 2005 High-Tech Small Firms conference, but has been updated to include references to recently published literature.

## Context

The UK has 168 HEIs that vary in size between student enrolments of over 30,000 down to just a few hundred.[1] External research income to HEIs ranges from over

---

[1] Higher Education Statistics Agency (http://www.hesa.ac.uk); not included in this above figure is the open university which is by far the largest HEI with over 150,000 students enrolled on its distance learning programmes (see also http://www.universitiesuk.ac.uk).

---

New Technology Based Firms in the New Millennium, Volume VI
Edited by A. Groen, R. Oakey, P. van der Sijde and G. Cook

£180 m$^2$ per annum for the top-tier institutions, down to zero for those that focus only on teaching activities.

### Emergence of the 'Third Mission' for UK HEIs

Commercialisation activities have long suffered from a poor image in the UK, particularly when compared to the US. Significant progress has been made since the late 1990s both in the volume of activities and in the implementation of structures and frameworks supporting research commercialisation. In 1985, the termination of the British Technology Group's monopoly on the ownership of intellectual property rights generated by academics provided universities with the right to exploit their own inventions. In 1993, the UK Government White Paper *Realising Our Potential: A Strategy for Science, Engineering and Technology*[3] reflected a growing policy interest in innovation from the science base, a theme developed steadily since then.

Before examining these developments, we need to place them in the context of the evolution of the higher education sector in the UK. Since the birth of the medieval university, the roles attributed to academic institutions have evolved according to two main perspectives on teaching and research:

- The 'classical university' generates and transmits knowledge through research conducted for its own sake, and teaching aiming to develop the full potential of students.
- The 'technical university' focus on training students with knowledge and skills that are useful for society and on creating knowledge of direct societal benefit (Druilhe, 2002; Martin & Etzkowitz, 2000).

In many respects, the two contrasting perceptions of the university's functions in society still underpin the current emphasis on a third mission for academic organisations. The evolving role of the university has been encapsulated in the metaphor of the 'Triple Helix', which by reference to the DNA double helix reflects the interdependent and convoluted relationships between three groups, industry, the university and government (Etzkowitz & Leydesdorff, 1997; Leydesdorff & Etzkowitz, 1998). The main thrust of the argument is the integration of a mission of economic development by universities, alongside their traditional activities of research and teaching.

Current developments have also been seen as the emergence of a new 'social context' between science, engineering, technology and the universities on the one hand, and society and the state on the other. The simple social contract that emerged in the 1950s drew on a dissemination model of innovation whereby publicly funded basic research flows to the economy through a linear process. The progressive awareness of the inadequacy of this model and the constraints on public funding for research lead to the suggestion that a new social contract should be drawn up. It would reflect the social accountability of scientists,

---

[2] This figure refers only to external research funding provided by industry, charities and the research councils. It excludes 'core' funding provided by the UK government, part of which is used to support research activities.

[3] "Realising Our Potential led to a complete overhaul of the organisation of government support for science and technology in the UK, including the Office of Science and Technology's move from the Cabinet Office to the Department of Trade and Industry (DTI) in 1995." (http://www.britishcouncil.org/science/gost/rop.htm).

engineers and technologists and the requirement for these disciplines to address social and economic needs (Guston & Keniston, 1994).

### Government Scheme for Third Mission Activities

Third mission activities are now taken to encompass a wide range of 'interaction' or 'collaboration' programmes that include both socially and commercially focused activities. Since 1998, the UK government has launched a number of funding schemes to support HEIs in developing their capacity to commercialise knowledge generated through research activities. The most important are summarised in Table 1.

### Metrics for Commercialisation Activities

With the support provided by funding schemes, such as those shown in Table 1, the UK HEIs have developed new central structures to manage commercialisation and collaborative activities, such as industrial liaison offices, entrepreneurship centres and policies to manage intellectual property rights. Research commercialisation activities have increased, whether through patenting/licensing, spin-outs or consulting.[4] The expenditure of public funds on supporting such activities has been liked to a desire to measure their impact.

Government has been keen to show that third stream funding activities have led to a marked increase in activity and that this has led to useful outcomes. One way of viewing the performance of third mission activities is to view universities in terms of inputs, outputs and outcomes (Livesey, Minshall, & Moultrie, 2006). Various output measures can be used including papers (to show volume of output), citations (to show quality of output) and various commercialisation indicators, such as invention disclosures, patents, licence deals, income from licences, income from consultancy, number of spin-outs, value of spin-outs, funding raised by spin-outs and many more. However, limiting metrics to the relatively easily measurable may result in other interactions between universities and businesses, which may be harder to measure but nonetheless very useful, being ignored.

Aside from giving the policy makers a sense of how much value for money is being derived from activities funded by the public purse, performance measurement has a direct impact upon HEI funding. The bulk of higher education innovation fund (HEIF) funding for universities is now being awarded on a formula-driven, rather than bid-for, basis. If HEIs can show that they have strong performance against key performance indicators, they will automatically receive on-going funding for their third mission activities.

The risk of using such a formula-driven approach is that it encourages HEIs to 'play the system' and may result in the channelling of resource into inappropriate activities. For example research on knowledge transfer in Germany shows that by simply encouraging universities to increase the numbers of spin-out ventures can lead to ideas being prematurely packaged into new ventures that have little chance of attracting funding and hence growing to make a positive contribution to the economy (Gill, Minshall, & Rigby, 2003).

---

[4] For data on university commercialisation activities (see Wright, Vohora, & Lockett, 2002, 2003).

Table 1: Example UK government funding streams to support 'third stream' activities.

| Start year | Initiative | Purpose | Details |
|---|---|---|---|
| 1998 | Higher Education Reach Out to Business and the Community (HEROBaC) | Funding to support activities to improve linkages between universities and their communities. | £20m per year allocated to provide funding for the establishment of activities, such as corporate liaison offices. |
| 1999 | University Challenge Fund (UCF) | Seed investments to help commercialisation of university intellectual property rights. | £45m was allocated in the first round of the competition in 1999, (with 15 seed funds being set up) and £15m in October 2001. Fifty-seven HEIs now have access to this funding. |
| 1999 | Science Enterprise Challenge (SEC) | Teaching of entrepreneurship to support the commercialisation of science and technology. | SEC provided £44.5m through two rounds of funding. There are now over 60 HEIs participating in SEC-funded activities.[11] |
| 2000 | Higher Education Innovation Fund (HEIF) | Single, long-term commitment to a stream of funding to 'support universities' potential to act as drivers of growth in the knowledge economy'. | HEIF was launched in 2000 to bring together a number of previously independently administered third stream funding sources. This was then extended (HEIF2) in 2004 with £185m awarded, and HEIF3 funding commenced in 2006. |
| 2000 | Cambridge-MIT Institute | A range of research projects and education activities to drive improvement in the UK's competitiveness, productivity and entrepreneurship. | £65m for a 5-year programme of activities. |

[11] Centres formed through this initiative now have their own network (UKSEC). More information available online at http://www.enterprise.ac.uk

### Too Many or Too Few Spin-Outs?

The economic boom of the late 1990s coupled with funding for innovation support mechanisms resulted in an upsurge in spin-out activity from the UK HEIs. In part this was driven by an implicit (and many cases explicit) belief that spinning-out ventures based around HEI-owned intellectual property could generate significant direct returns to the host HEI. Examples of the returns generated by spin-outs from Stanford and MIT were often used as an example of such.[5] During this buoyant period, commercialisation offices within the UK HEIs were strongly encouraged to create spin-outs.

However, the bursting of the Internet-driven economic bubble in 2000, coupled with closer examination of data on the US university spin-out activity, led to a realisation that the likelihood of spin-outs generating significant direct returns to the parent HEI was extremely remote. The Lambert Review (Lambert, 2003)[6] increased discussion of this issue by raising concern at a perceived over-focus on spin-out activities. Licensing of intellectual property (IP) to established firms, the report indicated, might be a more reliable route to getting ideas from university labs to industry application. This prompted further research and discussion that sought to reveal the role that spin-outs can usefully play within the commercialisation strategies of different types of HEI (see, e.g. BVCA, 2005; Williams, 2005).

### Licensing

Improved understanding of how difficult it can be to generate direct returns from spin-outs has increased the interest in licensing technologies to established firms. For some HEI technology transfer offices, their focus is to 'find the best way to get technology and expertise out there, by patenting or licensing or whatever route is appropriate'.[7] If a technology is readily licensable (i.e. does not need substantial additional resource applied to make it useable to an identified customer) then the inventor will be encouraged to take the licensing route. If it is clear that the idea does need additional development (and hence resource applied to it) then the spin-out route may be encouraged.

However, the licensing strategy for commercialisation also can be problematic. For example, examples from the US shows that universities which are over-aggressive in negotiating licences can harm their own efforts to raise other sources of funding from industry (FCO, 2003). The extent to which universities are able to form the types of relationships with industry required to develop a strong portfolio of licenses, which depends very much upon the university's perceived prestige. There are also the 'demand deficiency' issues

---

[5] The oft-cited figures are as follows: "If the companies founded by MIT graduates and faculty formed into an independent nation, the revenues produced by the companies would make that nation the 24th largest economy in the world. The 4,000 MIT-related companies employ 1.1 million people and have annual world sales of $232 billion" (BankBoston, 1997) (see also Koepp, 2002).

[6] One of the more enduring legacies of the Lambert Review was a set of model agreements setting out intellectual property rights when universities deal with industry, especially smaller firms (see http://www.innovation. gov.uk/lambertagreeements).

[7] Interview with UK university technology commercialisation director.

raised by the Lambert Review (i.e. highlighting the fact that while universities have made good efforts to increase their openness to industry, many companies do not yet have the capability to get best value from working with universities) (Lambert, 2003).

Research from the US is also showing some problems with the licensing business model. Universities have traditionally been able to access patented IP for research purposes on a fee-exempt basis. However, companies are increasingly reluctant to allow this as they are concerned that universities are not just seeking to develop new knowledge based on the IP, but will at some time of the future seek to exploit this knowledge commercially (Economist, 2005).

The UK HEIs that seek to commercialise the outputs of research went through a period of experimentation during 1998–2002. This experimentation took a strong lead from work funded by the Gatsby Charitable Foundation (see, e.g. projects reported in Wicksteed and Herriot (2000)) and was then fuelled by government initiatives that have allowed the HEIs to apply resource to existing and new activities to bring technologies to market. Inevitably, during this learning phase, government support for differing types of commercialisation activity was delivered through separate programmes. HEIs realised that initiatives which have been pump-primed through soft money need either (a) further external funding, (b) to generate their own funding and (c) to become centrally funded.

The government merged many of the previously disparate funding streams for HEI commercialisation activities under the HEIF. HEIF provides a long-term commitment from the government to support third mission activities with HEIs. These two factors, one internal the other external, encouraged HEIs to formulate strategies that provide them with a means to build a balanced portfolio of 'third stream' activities appropriate to their distinctive academic strengths, their particular regional context, and which are effective, affordable, sustainable and consistent with their mission.

## Methodology

The aim of the research reported in this paper was to gain a sense of what reality lay behind the data being published on university spin-outs and, therefore, what weight of interpretation should be put on these data. To address these issues, we implemented an approach that combined quantitative and qualitative methods.

The first phase of the project was to approach 10 UK HEIs to ask whether they would be prepared to collaborate in this work. The HEIs selected were as follows:

- The four universities with the largest research budgets — Cambridge, Imperial College London, Oxford and University College London (UCL).
- Three other large universities in major cities — Edinburgh, Newcastle and Southampton.
- Three universities with significantly smaller research budgets, reflecting in part their lack of medical research activities, but each with a high proportion of research funds coming from the UK industry — Cranfield, Loughborough and Strathclyde.

We then focused our data gathering narrowly onto spin-out companies. We defined spin-outs to be new commercial ventures based around university IP in which the university had an equity stake. We selected only spin-outs formed in the 5-year period from the beginning of 1998 to the end of 2002.

All the 10 universities generously agreed to help us with this work and we are most grateful to them for doing so. Each spent time explaining the context for their spin-out activity within the university's mission and its wider commercialisation activities, and in providing lists of companies that met our criteria. We have deliberately not sought to present any comparative analysis that identifies individual universities.[8]

Having obtained the lists of companies and such information (necessarily limited) that the commercialisation offices felt could be provided without breaching confidentiality, we then approached each company by mail and telephone to gather information from them covering:

- Age (year of incorporation)
- Originating department(s) within the university
- Area of activity (description and SIC (standard industrial classification) code(s))
- Size (number of employees)
- Financial history (equity investment received, revenues and valuation)
- Location (region, type of accommodation)
- On-going links with the university.

Despite our seeking only a limited range of information and undertaking as much secondary research as possible ourselves (i.e. web and news archive searches) to reduce the range of information requested, not all companies were willing to co-operate with the work. This we expected as (a) despite giving a confidentiality undertaking, we offered them no tangible benefit in return and (b) there are numerous surveys and research projects each year looking at university spin-outs and this is leading to a growing sense of 'research fatigue'.

To ensure that the replies we did obtain were not likely to give a false overall impression, we cross-checked with the university commercialisation teams whether the balance between non-respondents and respondents was, in their judgement, likely to give a fair overall picture. In the light of their responses, we made further efforts to obtain information from a small number of companies. Consequently we feel that the cautious generalisations offered in this paper should be reasonably free from bias.

## Results

This section draws together two strands of work: the review of spin-out activity and experience at the 10 universities; and findings from the data on individual companies provided by the technology transfer offices and by the spin-out companies themselves.

Descriptive data on the 10 universities are given in Table 2 in which we show full time equivalent (FTE) figures for academic staff and postgraduate research students, together with a breakdown of research funding. Most of these data come from the Higher Education Statistics Agency (HESA) and, for the sake of consistency, we show the most recent year for which comparative data are available for the period of our research. The penultimate

---

[8] Case studies describing the ten universities and their approach to supporting entrepreneurship have been published in Minshall and Wicksteed (2005).

Table 2:  Descriptive data on ten universities as of 2003.

| | Academic staff and research students[a] | | Research funding[a] | | | | | Commercialisation staff |
|---|---|---|---|---|---|---|---|---|
| | FTE academic staff | FTE PG research students | Total/£m | % from research councils | % from charities | % from UK industry | % Medical and life science[b] | FTE staff engaged in research commercialisation[d] |
| Universities with largest research budgets | | | | | | | | |
| Cambridge | 3620 | 4401 | 214 | 39.6 | 30.7 | 8.6 | 55[c] | 24 |
| Imperial | 2982 | 1824 | 210 | 30.7 | 31.3 | 13.4 | 67 | 25 |
| Oxford | 3463 | 3195 | 219 | 32.9 | 37.9 | 7.9 | 70 | 35 |
| UCL | 3494 | 2156 | 212 | 30.9 | 45.4 | 6.5 | 75 | 32 |
| Other large universities in major cities | | | | | | | | |
| Edinburgh | 2354 | 1434 | 120 | 33.4 | 28.1 | 6.1 | 60 | 7[e] |
| Newcastle | 1753 | 1353 | 79 | 24.5 | 26.3 | 7.9 | 50 | 8 |
| Southampton | 1930 | 1250 | 95 | 45.6 | 13.9 | 12.8 | 30 | 20 |
| Universities with smaller research budgets | | | | | | | | |
| Cranfield | 726 | 675 | 46 | 18.7 | 0.6 | 38.6 | Life science only (low %) | 4 |
| Loughborough | 930 | 1014 | 39 | 33 | 5.1 | 24 | None | 6 |
| Strathclyde | 1246 | 744 | 40 | 34.5 | 11.6 | 18 | Pharma only (low %) | 10[f] |

[a] Data from Higher Education Statistics Agency (www.hesa.ac.uk) for 2001–2002.
[b] Estimates obtained from interviews at end of 2003.
[c] Cambridge data do not include MRC-funded research, but spin-outs will be influenced by it as many senior researchers have dual appointments.
[d] Data from interviews at end of 2003.
[e] The total staffing of Edinburgh research and innovation Ltd was 44 in 2003.
[f] Total staffing of the research and consultancy services office was 25 in 2003.

column, giving an estimate of the proportion of research funding accounted for by the medical and life sciences, is less precise and comes from our interviews.

The figures in the final column, for numbers of staff employed to encourage and assist the commercialisation of research, also come from our interviews. They should be regarded as indicative rather definitive, as some staff (lawyers for instance) also provide expertise to other aspects of research services (e.g. research grants and contracts).

## Types of Spin-Outs

Perhaps the most crucial conclusion from our discussions with the university commercialisation offices is that any analysis of spin-outs which implicitly assumes that they are a generic class of new business is inherently flawed. From our data, three distinct categories of spin-out companies could be identified:[9]

- Spin-outs that are identifiable with high growth potential, even if there are considerable risks that the potential will not be realised.
- Spin-outs that are likely to be serious businesses in that they create employment and generate profits, but which may have limited or slower growth potential.
- Spin-outs that are legal vehicles for the commercial development of a technology which, in due course, is likely to be commercialised through the licence or sale of the IP.

## Number of Spin-Outs

A second key finding is that at some universities there were considerably more start-ups (i.e. companies originating from the university, but where the university has no claim on the IP) than spin-outs. Start-up activity is likely to depend on the relevant university policies (including those relating to IP) and the overall 'culture' of the university in relation to enterprise. Start-ups may well be difficult to identify, categorise and track systematically. They may, however, form a significant area of activity for a university's commercialisation office.

Moreover, the number of spin-outs will depend in part on university decisions on resource allocations to the commercialisation effort and subsequently on the commercialisation office's view on the priority that should be given to spin-out formation. Amongst the universities we covered there were significant differences on both these variables.

There are two key conclusions from these observations:

- The number of spin-outs should not be interpreted as a free standing indicator of relevance of the university's research to the commercial world.
- It should not be used uncritically as an indicator of the level of entrepreneurial enthusiasm amongst staff and other researchers.

Bearing those caveats in mind, Table 3 shows the key quantitative survey findings on spin-out activity and performance for the period 1998–2002; analysed by the three university groups as described in the methodology section.

---

[9] The issue of categorising spin-outs is topic of growing research interest (e.g. Clarysse, Wright, Lockett, Van de Velde, & Vohora, 2005; Druilhe & Garnsey, 2004; Nicolaou & Birley, 2003).

Table 3:  Summary data on spin-outs from three categories of universities.[12]

| Indicator | Average per institution for universities with largest research budgets | Average per institute for other large universities in major cities | Average per institution for universities with smaller research budgets[h] |
|---|---|---|---|
| Total number of spin-outs (1998–2002) | 24.8 | 12.0 | 12.5 |
| Life science+clinical[a] | | | |
| Number | 11.8 | 3.7 | 2.0 |
| % | 47 | 31 | 16 |
| Physical Sciences[a] | | | |
| Number | 10.0 | 7.0 | 10.0 |
| % | 40 | 58 | 80 |
| 10 or more employees[b] | | | |
| Number | 6.8 | 4.0 | 3.0 |
| % | 27 | 33 | 24 |
| £250k or more of revenue[c] | | | |
| Number | 4.3 | 2.3 | 4.5 |
| % | 17 | 19 | 36 |
| Equity financing[d] | | | |
| Number | 17.8 | 8.3 | 5.0 |
| % | 72 | 69 | 40 |

| | | | |
|---|---|---|---|
| Total raised/£k | 86,143 | 40,602 | 9356 |
| Average per spin-out with equity/£K | 4853 | 4872 | 1871 |
| Stayed in sub-region[e] | | | |
| Number | 17.3 | 10.3 | 10.5 |
| % | 70 | 86 | 84 |
| In university accommodation or incubator[f] | | | |
| Number | 6.0 | 5.0 | 8.5 |
| % | 24 | 42 | 68 |
| On-going links to parent university[g] | | | |
| Number | 16.3 | 6.0 | 8.0 |
| % | 66 | 50 | 64 |

[12] This table summarises information drawn from a combination of public sources, from the university commercialisation offices and from the spin-out companies themselves.

[a] Classified by founders' university department(s). Spin-outs from departments other than physical, life science or clinical are not included in this table.

[b] Most recent figures available at time of research (end of 2003).

[c] Most recent figures available at time of research (end of 2003).

[d] Over life of company from start-up to end of 2003.

[e] Top level of postcode of company is same as university.

[f] Company address is within university, or in related incubator facilities.

[g] These include: work with/sponsor students, academics on staff, use HEI facilities, collaborate on projects, fund project in HEI, IP pipeline agreement, staff secondment.

[h] Data on the Cranfield spin-outs is not included here as, at time of data gathering, spin-out activity was at the very early stages of formation. Inclusion within the averages given here would distort the averages.

### Characteristics of Spin-Outs

**Origin**    The first two rows in Table 3 show the numbers of companies that originate, respectively from researchers in the life/clinical sciences and the physical sciences. Together these account around 90% of total spin-outs, the remainder coming from the arts, social sciences and humanities. There is a clear difference between the three groups of universities in terms of the proportion of spin-outs coming from the life/clinical sciences — which is understandable given their share of the research budgets at Cambridge, Imperial, Oxford and UCL.

**Growth and Equity Finance**    Growth performance was considered in terms of both employment and revenue. There are shortcomings in both measures. Revenue depends crucially on the nature of the business as it masks considerable variations in value added, whereas employment can encompass widely different qualification requirements and salary levels. Assuming that there has been a fairly even level of start-ups over the 5-year period, the data shows that a reasonable proportion of spin-outs had reached a position of substance in terms of employment and/or revenue levels.

This is further borne out by the proportion of companies securing equity finance and the substantial average level of such investments. The figures in the last column, for universities with smaller research budgets, average the experience of Strathclyde University, which has a long history of involvement with research commercialisation, and Loughborough University whose experience is much more recent. Their lower levels of equity finance — both the proportion of companies obtaining finance and the average level obtained — probably reflect the relatively low proportion of companies from the life/clinical sciences, which typically need significant equity funding from the outset. Conversely the two universities have a relatively high proportion of companies achieving revenue of £250,000 or more; and again the absence of life science businesses may be part of the explanation.

**Linkages**    The proportion of companies that have stayed in the sub-region is an interesting indicator of contribution to local economic development and the relatively lower percentage for the universities with the largest research budgets is chiefly a reflection of the 'London' factor; both Oxford and Cambridge had retention rates similar to the other non-London universities. It should not be assumed that the similarly lower percentage (24%) of companies in university accommodation or a related incubator is also accounted for by the London institutions. The proportions in Cambridge, Imperial, Oxford and UCL were, in fact, very similar with one another.

On a more encouraging note, the final row of data shows that, despite a greater spatial separation from their spin-outs, these four universities achieved an above average performance in terms of on-going links (though there was considerable variation concealed within the average and it was not explained by the 'London' factor). In addition, although we could not quantify the effect, companies were able to use their links with the universities to tap into wider networks. For instance, they may be able to draw on alumni as sources of managers, finance and commercial connections. This alumni link was often strong in connection with the universities' business schools and could well become a relation of growing importance as universities invest greater effort in their alumni relationships. Business schools also provided a link to 'free' commercial resource in the form of MBA student projects.

## Qualifications to the Data

The ten commercialisation offices researched were spinning-out an average of three companies per year, and most of the interviewees thought that between three to five per year was a 'manageable' number. The actual spread in the number of spin-outs was from less than one per year up to nine per year. This again highlights the important fact that we are not dealing with a homogenous group.

Our data are also incomplete, because they relate to companies that had survived to the point at which our study was undertaken. We did, however, cross check this aspect and found that the average failure rates for spin-out companies across all the 10 universities were very low; that is under 10% compared to the average for high-tech firms of 60–70% (Garnsey & Heffernan, 2003).

Using data such as these to measure the performance of university commercialisation offices is not straightforward. Commercialisation offices can only take a spin-out company to a certain point of its commercial development, after which the spin-out's success depends on a multitude of other factors. In measuring their own performance, university commercialisation offices often see the attraction of external investment by the spin-outs as a useful measure and this is why we have show these figures.

We have not tabulated returns to the university from dividends or the sale of its equity. Although there were some of those and they were, of course, welcomed but such returns are regarded as unpredictable rarities, especially in the short- to medium-term. Equally, it would be wrong to record such benefits without recording other direct benefits from spin-outs including research commissions for academics and jobs for students. Indirect benefits also need to be factored in and they include fulfilling institutional ambitions to help the local community and economy, and helping to encourage positive attitudes to entrepreneurship amongst staff and students.

## When to go the Spin-Out Route

In response to the question we posed during our interviews: 'How do you decide when to form a spin-out?' The following points were given by the commercialization offices:

- For platform technologies.
- Where the inventors are very keen to commercialise the technology themselves.
- When the idea needs to attract substantial investment to develop IP relating to the technology for subsequent licensing.
- When the technology is not readily licensable.
- For a generic technology with many different applications.

## Notes of Caution from our Discussions

The importance to spin-out activity of the national policy framework should be kept firmly in mind. Mention was frequently made of the impact that the research assessment exercise (RAE) has on the priority given to commercialisation activities within the UK universities. Through specific resource allocations, the government's HEIF is presently seeking to redress the balance somewhat more in favour of knowledge transfer and application. However, although outside the timeframe of our research, some of the universities reported that spin-out formation had largely dried-up as a result of the fiscal changes in the July 2003 Finance Act.[10] Clearly academic engagement with spin-out activity is sensitive to the various policies and incentives.

Successful spin-outs consume a significant amount of staff time from the university commercialisation office. Continuing resources are also needed to ensure that the university's investment stakes in spin-outs are appropriately managed. Such management requires specific expertise, which may need to be drawn in from beyond the commercialisation offices. However, this should not be taken to imply that licensing is an 'easier route' — it was also noted that considerable amounts of staff time and effort are needed to develop and manage a good licensing agreement with an established business.

It is often asserted that life science spin-outs are expected to have a very long pay-back period, but this can also be true for complex physics-based technologies. Patient financial resources have to be available to fund the initial establishment and on-going development costs of the individual technologies and also to manage what may become a portfolio of linked technologies (even if patenting costs can be recovered from co-investors).

Involving academics with spin-outs is often viewed as one of the positive outcomes to be gained from supporting this type of activity, but there will be opportunity costs here too. Academics focusing time and effort on commercialisation activities may divert attention from their core activities of teaching and research. There can, moreover, be serious questions concerning conflicts of interest. These have till date raised much more concern in the USA than the UK; a reflection perhaps on the relative levels of both activity and litigiousness.

Taking into account companies founded before our study period, several of the universities we interviewed have had some really encouraging successes producing significant returns from sale of equity in their spin-outs. This was, however, a relatively rare occurrence and had, in a number of cases, been linked to the buoyant economic conditions immediately prior to the internet-fuelled speculative bubble bursting in 2000. It was emphasised in discussion that it can be up to 10 years before significant returns start to flow from spin-out activities.

Some universities, but by no means all, gave us estimates of the likely number of spin-outs in an average future year. Levels were determined in part by availability of resources in the commercialisation office, but individual academic enthusiasm was also an important factor in the choice of commercialisation route and most universities mentioned engagement with spin-outs (and start-ups) being part of their strategic commitment to the regional/sub-regional economy. It was noted, however, that target setting inevitably leads to behavioural change. It is, therefore, arguable that if targets are set for spin-outs then there need to be targets set for other IP routes as well if distortion is to be avoided.

The majority of commercialisation offices have established informal or formal links to a range of venture capital sources, which they see as appropriate. However, these relationships have not always been fraternal; when the situation was tight some follow-on financing

---

[10] Schedule 22 of the Finance Act 2003 sought to ensure that those who are awarded shares as part of their remuneration packages are liable for income tax and national insurance on such payments. This unintentionally made it more difficult for academic members of universities to take equity stakes in spin-outs. This, in turn, put a slowing effect on the number of spin-outs formed by some universities.

could only be obtained on draconian terms. Some of the links were 'first option to fund' arrangements (i.e. a fund is given the right to consider possible deals before other investors) with the financial partner typically making a significant up-front payment, and these seemed to have worked well.

Scotland has had a relatively long history of strong and reflective public sector support for commercialisation (and especially spin-outs). University efforts have been supported and complemented by publicly funded input from the Scottish Executive, Scottish Higher Education Funding Council (SHEFC) and the Royal Society of Edinburgh. An international enquiry into good practice in commercialisation led to a number of innovative initiatives from Scottish Enterprise. However, the overall long-term impact of publicly funded early stage support for start-ups generally and, specifically, university spin-outs is yet to be proven. Widespread publicly funded support is less developed in many parts of England than in Scotland, though most RDAs are now actively involved in addressing the topic. An example of regional support for enterprise in England can be seen in the introduction of the regional venture capital funds.

## Conclusions

Spin-outs, if not over-emphasised, fit very well with a number of other university aims — the enterprise agenda, local economic contribution, laying the potential for a long-term relationship with a research-focussed firm.

It is arguable that, for the period of this research, university spin-outs were given too high a profile in policy pronouncements. Because they were 'in fashion' spin-outs had been seen as a 'good thing'. While there is a strong case for moving towards a more cautious appreciation of their contribution, it would be unfortunate if the fashion pendulum were to swing back too far the other way. Direct financial benefits to universities may well only accrue in the long-term and the distribution of financial benefits may well be heavily skewed towards a few spin-outs. There are, however, as this report has instanced, a number of valuable positive spillovers to both regional and national economies that are likely to be felt more immediately.

Investment in university spin-outs involves a significant commitment from the university sector as, in the short-term, the costs they entail will exceed the financial returns. It is, therefore, important that there is an overall policy encouragement towards university spin-outs that reflects their full range of contributions and not just their financial impact.

## Further Work

Research is now underway that builds on the findings reported here to address the following questions:

- What role do partnerships with larger companies play in the success of university spin-outs? While there is research that examines the general issue of how start-up companies work with established ventures, the links between large-scale corporate involvement in a particular university and the performance of its spin-outs remains unaddressed.

• What are the emerging models of knowledge transfer with the UK HEIs? In particular, what structures are emerging that have a greater focus on the softer (i.e. 'people centric' (Allott, 2006)) aspects of knowledge transfer and how do they integrate with the more traditional structures for knowledge transfer?

## Acknowledgements

We are more grateful to the Gatsby Charitable Foundation for their financial support for this research; to the university commercialisation officers for the information and insights they provided and to the individual spin-out companies.

## References

Allott, S. (2006). *From science to growth: What exactly is the mechanism by which scientific research turns into economic growth*. Lecture delivered at Hughes Hall, Cambridge, 6th March 2006. Downloadable via http://www.trinamo.com/news/articles.htm

BankBoston. (1997). *The impact of innovation*. MIT: BankBoston.

BVCA. (2005). *Creating success from university spin-outs*. British Venture Capital Association, http://www.bcva.co.uk/publications/univspinout.pdf

Clarysse, B., Wright, M., Lockett, A., Van de Velde, E., & Vohora, A. (2005). Spinning out new ventures: A typology of incubation strategies from European research institutions. *Journal of Business Venturing, 20*, 183–216.

Druilhe, C. (2002). *The emergence and process of academic enterprise: Cases from the University of Cambridge*. PhD thesis, University of Cambridge, Judge Business School, UK.

Druilhe, C., & Garnsey, E. W. (2004). Do academic spin-outs differ and does it matter? *Journal of Technology Transfer, 29*, 269–285.

Economist. (2005). Scholars for dollars. *The Economist*, 9th December.

Etzkowitz, H., & Leydesdorff, L. (1997). *Universities and the global knowledge economy: A triple helix of university-industry-government*. London: Pinter.

FCO. (2003). *Key lessons for technology transfer offices: Viewpoints from Silicon Valley*. Science and Technology Section of British Consulate-General of San Francisco.

Garnsey, E., & Heffernan, P. (2003). *Growth setbacks in new firms*. Centre for Technology Management Working Series 2003/1.

Gill, D., Minshall, T. H. W., & Rigby, M. (2003). *Funding technology: Germany — Better by design*. London: Wardour Communications ISBN 0 9538239 2 X.

Guston, D. H., & Keniston, K. (Eds.) (1994). *The fragile contract: University science and the federal government*. Cambridge MA: MIT Press.

Koepp, R. (2002). *Clusters of creativity: Enduring lessons on innovation and entrepreneurship from Silicon Valley and Europe*. Chichester, UK: Wiley.

Lambert, R. (2003). *Lambert review of business-university collaboration: Final report*. HM Treasury, ww.lambertreview.org.uk

Leydesdorff, L., & Etzkowitz, H. (1998). Triple helix of innovation: Introduction. *Science and Public Policy*, *25*(6), 358–364.

Livesey, F., Minshall, T. H. W., & Moultrie, J. (2006). *Investigating the technology-based innovation gap for the United Kingdom: A report for the UK design council*. Cambridge: University of Cambridge Institute of Manufacturing, ISBN 1 902546 49 0.

Martin, B. R., & Etzkowitz, H. (2000). *The origin and evolution of the university species*. Sussex: Science and Technology Policy Research (SPRU), Electronic Working Paper Series (SEWP-59), Sussex University.

Minshall, T. H. W., & Wicksteed, W. (2005). *University spin-out companies: Starting to fill the evidence gap*. A report for the Gatsby Charitable Foundation (http://www.stjohns.co.uk/documents/usoreport.pdf).

Nicolaou, N., & Birley, S. (2003). Academic networks in a trichotomous categorisation of university spinouts. *Journal of Business Venturing*, *18*(3), 333–359.

Wicksteed, W., & Herriot, W. J. (2000). *Six case studies in technology transfer*. SQW Ltd, ISBN 0 9510202 3 4.

Williams, E. (2005). *Too few university spin-out companies*. Warwick: Warwick ventures discussion document http://www2.warwick.ac.uk/services/ventures

Wright, M., Vohora, A., & Lockett, A. (2002). *Annual UNICO-NUBS survey on university commercialisation activities: Financial year 2001*. UNICO: NUBS.

Wright, M., Vohora, A., & Lockett, A. (2003). *Annual UNICO-NUBS survey on university commercialisation activities: Financial Year 2002*. UNICO: NUBS.

Chapter 13

# Analysis of the Factors Leading to Success or Failure of Start-Up Companies in the Field of Micro- and Nanotechnology

Devang Shah, Malcolm Wilkinson and Kevin Yallup

## Introduction

In the UK there is now recognition that university research can be a valuable source of intellectual property (IP) on which new wealth-creating industries can be based. This recognition has led to a debate about, how best the IP can be developed, captured and transferred to the commercial world. The Lambert Report, published in December 2003 made many useful observations about the relative merits of licensing or spin-out models of technology commercialisation and the roles of university-based Technology Transfer Offices (TTOs) in stimulating or supporting these processes (Lambert Review of Business-University Collaboration, 2003).

Although the TTOs had come in for much criticism because of the apparent lack of success, we felt that another contributory factor was a significant lack of knowledge about the underlying factors leading to success or failure of the process of commercialisation. Following an initial surge of start-up activity, mainly funded by venture capitalists (VCs) in the 1990s, there has been a realisation that other models of commercialisation such as joint ventures or licensing and other sources of finance might give better chances of success.

Our research has focussed on a particular sector; micro- and nanotechnology (MNT). By combining our own practical experience in seven start-up companies and desk research based on over 50 others, we were hoping to gain real insight into the factors behind success or failure and hence provide a useful body of knowledge for investors and some best practice guides for entrepreneurs or TTOs charged with supporting the commercialisation process.

New Technology Based Firms in the New Millennium, Volume VI
Edited by A. Groen, R. Oakey, P. van der Sijde and G. Cook

## Methodology

The purpose of the data collection exercise was to gain first hand information on the foundation of and strategic options available to start-up companies within the MNT sector in the various phases of growth. Findings were then analysed and a set of success criteria were derived for different phases of the start-ups.

The MNT sector in the UK comprises around 80 or so start-ups. However, because of the relatively nascent nature of these start-ups, it is very difficult to find data for some of them. This reduced the target group to about 60. It was decided that for a target group of this size and nature, quantitative analysis alone would be inappropriate and would be unlikely to produce meaningful findings. Therefore, a combination of quantitative and qualitative approaches was used, with data collection by means of semi-structured interviews. The companies were divided into high-growth and low-growth groups; and then a detailed analysis of these few selected companies was performed.

Data on each organisation was collected through a variety of techniques including personal interviews and secondary data sources such as annual reports, websites, press reports, Companies House database research, conference proceedings and exhibition catalogues.

The first stage involved large-scale screening to identify MNT companies that had been formed in the last 12 years. Most of the start-ups were found to be less than 5 years old.

MNT areas included were:

- Bio-nanotechnology.
- Characterisation and metrology at the micro- and nanometre scales.
- Manufacturing scale fabrication of polymer and glass components, such as microfluidic devices.
- Nanomaterials (including nanocomposites and nanostructured materials).
- Nanoparticles.
- Silicon and polymer MEMS and microdevice fabrication.
- Microoptics.

Under this definition, there were about 60 companies in the UK. These were either autonomous start-ups or university spin-outs or sponsored by an existing firm. The data was validated on age of the company, business activity and origin of foundation. This data was later further divided into high-growth, low-growth and medium-growth start-ups. Also companies that had subsequently ceased trading were also included. Appendix lists the companies included in the study.

The quantitative data collected included:

- Age of the company.
- Number of employees.
- Source of seed funding.
- VC funding raised.
- Number of patents.
- Geographical location of the start-up.
- Composition of management board.
- Business model adopted.

## Business Models Adopted

A number of different businesses models were employed in MNT start-ups (Figure 1).

IP licensing and inhouse design was the emerging business model adopted by 60% of the start-ups. The IP licensing model has the advantages that it allows the MNT start-up company to avoid the expense of setting up manufacturing and sales channels — both expensive propositions. The way the IP licensing model works is that a company develops IP, then licences it to other companies for commercial application and finally collects a royalty on the use of the IP. The royalty revenue is then used to fund more IP creation.

## Performance Measures and Success Analysis

To identify the most successful companies the age of the company, the size of the company along with the venture capital raised were compared. These results were used to classify the start-ups in the categories of high growth and slow growth. A detailed qualitative analysis of a selection of high growth (eight start-ups), low growth (four start-ups), and three companies which had stopped trading was then conducted. This analysis resulted in a set of criteria that could lead to the success of a start-up venture (Figure 2).

The size of the bubble in the graph indicates the amount of the venture capital funding.

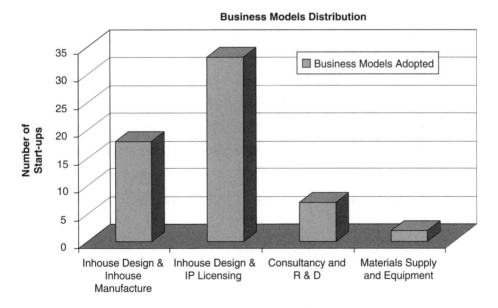

Figure 1: Business model adopted.

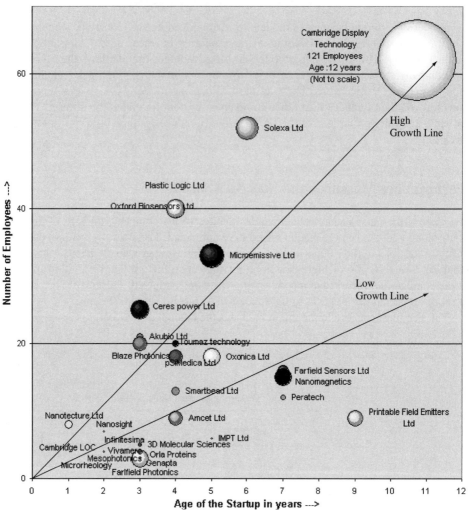

Figure 2:  Age versus number of employees versus venture capital raised.

## Success Criteria for the Start-Ups in Micro- and Nanotechnology

The graph below explains the trajectory that a start-up company normally follows after its inception (Figure 3).

The company starts with an initial capital investment and seed funding. Depending upon the funding needs, the company may secure additional loans or raise further venture capital funding. Hence, the start-up keeps on digging deep into the negative region. The company then starts generating initial revenue and then it reaches the first turning point i.e. Milestone 1. where the profit/loss trajectory changes its direction towards the positive.

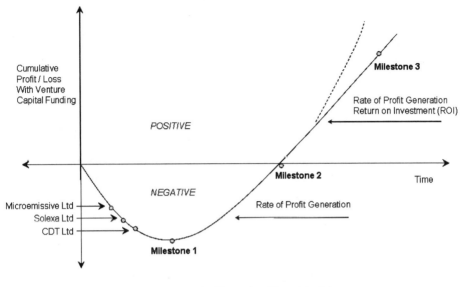

Milestone 1 :Change of direction / Generation of first substantial revenue
Milestone 2 :Break Even Point / Payback Phase starts
Milestone 3 :Growth Phase

Figure 3: Generic model of profit/loss.

Depending upon the rate of revenue generation (can be termed as profit generation for that period of time) the company reaches Milestone 2, which is the *most* significant milestone. This indicates that the company has reached the *break even point* and the payback phase starts.

After reaching the *break even* milestone, the company can concentrate on its growth. Milestone 3 is reached when the company starts to generate significant profits and is on its way to become a larger entity.

It was found that all of the high-growth start-ups in the MNT study were still unprofitable. This appears to be a typical characteristic of a high-technology start-up.

## Success Factors for MNT Start-Ups in the UK

Creating a new start-up requires a long and a complex process in order to transform an idea into a viable company.

The success of a start-up cannot be attributed to one single success factor. It is a combination of factors that are responsible for the success of the start-up.

The following are the success factors that were derived by observing the characteristics of the high-growth and slow-growth start-ups:

- Management of the start-up.
- Affiliation with a university.
- Adequate finance.

- Target market.
- Cluster environment.
- IP position.
- Strategic partners.

## *Management*

The management of the start-up as well as a strategy for the growth were found to be very important in performing strategic planning and generating a business model.

Commercial experience of the founders with strong target-market knowledge was found to be a very important factor in the *funding* as well as the *growth* phase of the start-up. Seventy percent of the high-growth case start-ups were headed by a non-academic commercial manager. The limited amount of time that an academic CEO could provide for the start-up was seen as a major impediment to the growth of the start-up.

For a company to pass the funding stage, they usually need to prove convincingly that they have a micro- or nanotechnology that has high market potential. But, taking that raw technology to a market is a different skill set than developing the technology in the first place. The commercial experience of the founders was found to be useful here.

The commercial experience of the founders also helped to target the right market for the technology. It was found that many companies that had created a nano-based technology with a target market in mind did not meet the needs of that target market. This oversight may be attributed to the lack of domain knowledge of the management team.

Another success factor observed was that of a well-balanced team — or at least having a plan to put one in place in the future in the case of a 'boot-strap' start-up.

There were two aspects to a well-balanced team that were perceived as important to a MNT start-up:

- The team needed to have the multi-disciplinary skill-sets that were required to accomplish the business plan goals. It was observed that some founding teams had all their members from the same academic discipline, but the product development required a multi-disciplinary team to achieve success. An example of this was a microarray company started by two geneticists. Their planned product required a significant amount of MEMS and electrical engineering design work but such knowledge was not present in the founding team.
- The other aspect of a well-balanced team was having senior people who came from the domains where the product was to be sold. For example, if a nano-based memory company was being formed, then having a founder who originated from the semiconductor memory industry would be essential. Without this input, the company would be in a danger of developing products that would not appeal to the marketplace due to lack of market knowledge. The company could be 'blind-sided' by an incumbent technology that could challenge the benefits of the new nano-based technology. Hence having a founding team member with contacts in the relevant business expertise helps facilitate both sourcing relationships and also generating first sales.

### Affiliation with a University

The links with the academic institute was another factor that was found to help the start-ups progress.

From the interviews, the following areas were found to have involvement by universities:

* Carrying out IP due diligence.
* Developing a professional group.
* Obtaining alternative sources of funding.
* Interfacing with financiers.

On the whole, it was also found that the founders had more involvement in formulating strategy and monitoring financial performance than the university. Many start-ups in nanotechnology get at least their initial IP from universities or government labs. Many universities have offices that focus on the commercialisation of their locally generated IP. The reputation of the university played a very important role in attracting venture capital investment. The reputation of the university was also an important variable that affected the licensing versus spin-out decision. Di Gregorio and Shane (2003) have empirically shown that intellectual eminence of universities attracted venture capital. It was seen that most of the high-growth start-ups were seen to be affiliated with the top academic institutions in the UK. The University of Cambridge has a strong reputation for spinning out ventures. High-growth start-ups such as Cambridge Display Technology Ltd, Solexa Ltd, Plastic Logic Ltd are spin-offs from Cambridge University.

### Adequate Finance

Most of the high-growth as well as slow-growth start-ups were not profitable. This was a common scenario for a high-tech start-up. The relative position of the company on the profit–loss curve gave a fair estimation of the progress and the growth of the company. Adequate finance has to be raised to see the company through this phase.

Even the top MNT start-ups in the UK were not yet profitable. The relative position of three start-ups has been marked on the graph in Figure 3. All of them were surviving on the venture capital funding raised by them to fund their growth.

A company that reached the first milestone could be said to be a revenue generating firm. However, only after the attainment of the second milestone, could the start-up be termed profitable.

The venture capital played an important role in the growth of the start-up. All except one of the high-growth companies had raised exceptionally high amounts of venture capital. The venture capital helped the company to fund its business plan.

The decision to fund the company using venture capital is a strategic one. It was found that venture capital was not appropriate for every start-up. Venture capital was most effective for the start-ups when the following conditions prevailed:

* A big market opportunity for the product.
* A defensible competitive advantage.

- Growth that demands external capital.
- A founding team was willing to bring external talent.
- A collective vision that was ambitious enough to build a large (usually global) company.

A team with strong commercial experiences addressing a large market opportunity was attractive to VC funders. A strategy that involved including 'luminaries' with the start-up company also proved to be attractive to the VCs.

Typically these luminaries were in the founding team or on one of the advisory boards. Frequently these luminaries were high-profile academics who had actually generated some of the IP that the company was based on.

Another success factor in obtaining funding from the VCs was a clear, concise, well thought-out and compelling business plan. A good business plant could show that the founders have thought about all the major issues they were likely to encounter in building their business. The critical components of a business plan focus on the issues that would enable the company to bring its products to market. A good business plan would also allow for efficient communication of the business idea to potential investors, which would become important in obtaining funding. The business plan would need to be comprehensive and cover all financial aspects, not just the technology. Technologist founders of start-ups were found to be not adept on key business issues such as manufacturing and sales channel strategies.

In the business plan another aspect that was linked to success was the executive summary. This section needs to convey key points across in a few words and must give a concise and comprehensive picture of what the company would do and how it would make money. Writing the executive summary was also found to be challenging for the found if he is a technologist, which is usually the case in MNT.

The founders of the start-ups were very receptive to government funding since it did not dilute the equity of the company. However, it could have the negative impact of altering the growth path of the company. Hence a company that was funded by government grants needed to take the precaution of accepting only those grants that were highly aligned with the company's interests. The start-up could have a risk of becoming a company that existed for the purpose of obtaining government grants and not developing a commercial application.

### Target Market

The term 'platform technologies' was mentioned frequently. The term meant that the technology would underlie many other new technologies and thereby derive revenue streams from many different applications and become a *de facto* standard.

However this could cause a lack of focus in a start-up company. Nanotechnology is associated with many platform technologies such as quantum dots, carbon nanotubes and nanowires each of which for biotechnology, information technology and other applications. The danger of not focusing on a particular application could be destructive for a start-up company. Market focussing is one aspect, which the VCs look for. It was found that most VCs would force a start-up with multiple divergent products to drop all but one.

Identifying a clear market space and market opportunity was much more difficult if the academic was developing a platform technology which could be used in many industries or products. One could argue that it would seem to be a greater market opportunity and indeed it would be if the academic was successful in developing the technology. However, in the initial phase of the start-up, the academic was faced with the problem of presenting an argument for support from a variety of possible sponsors.

It was found that selection of a particular market opportunity and matching that to particular sponsor's interest was critical. It was often found that the market was chosen upon serendipity or personal interest.

Most of the university-based start-ups were 'technology push' products rather than 'market pull' developments. In order for the start-up to attain high-growth levels it was important for it to have a market pull, which would facilitate immediate sales.

One of the main drivers of the companies researched was the perception that the MNT market was one of very significant untapped opportunities, combined with the ease of access to venture capital for MNT from 2000 to early 2001. This enabled most of the spin-offs to set up a manufacturing facility based purely around the founder's academic ideas rather than any market driven basis. Some of the more established companies had subsequently adjusted their product range to reflect expected market demand. It is important for the start-up to be 'market pull' which facilitates the growth of the company and eases the initial sales effort required.

### Cluster Environment

There was considerable empirical evidence that innovative activities tended indeed to cluster in specific geographic areas, at different levels of aggregation (Swann & Prevezer, 1998).

As in the US, innovative activities in MNT in UK too, tend to agglomerate into specific areas. The largest cluster of MNT companies was found in Cambridge. Location in a cluster helps the start-up in multiple ways including ready access to local talent, easy access to high-tech VCs, supportive infrastructure in place and assistance from the local university.

### IP Position

One key success factor was a strong IP position at the inception of the company with a plan to develop this asset over time. It was very common for the filer of a patent to be involved in the commercialisation of the technology. For example, Infinitesima Ltd was formed with IP from Bristol University and the professor who generated the IP, Dr Mervyn Milesis was still involved with the company. Similarly, Professor Richard Friend of University of Cambridge was still affiliated to Cambridge Display Technology Ltd. The most currently visible nanotech company in US, Nanosys (received €12.4 million in 2002, in series B financing), was formed by licensing IP. Nanosys' stated strategy is to 'build a dominant technology and IP estate through a combination of aggressive technology in-licensing, teaming with the world's leaders in academic nanoscience, internal technology development and patent filings'. Nanosys has licensed IP from the following universities to date: Columbia, Harvard, LBL, MIT, UCLA, UC Berekely and Hebrew University.

## *Strategic Partners*

Partnering with a larger corporation was generally beneficial for the start-ups. This stemmed from multiple specific benefits:

- It helped the start-up significantly in the funding context.
- Partnering gave the start-up access to manufacturing and sales channels, which would have been expensive for a start-up to develop.

An example of this was the partnership of Plastic Logic Ltd with larger firms like Seiko Epson Corporation, Dow Chemicals and Cambridge Display Technology Ltd. Plastic Logic was a leading developer of plastic electronics technology. Although the precise nature of their relationship was unknown, it was known from conversations with Plastic Logic that they were working very closely with Seiko Epson and Dow Chemicals. If Plastic Logic's technology was successful, they would have access to a large market via Seiko Epson's existing market position.

## Discussion: Problems Faced by the Start-Ups

The problems faced by start-ups in this study included:

- Lack of credibility with customers and investors.
- Inadequate funding.
- Tax law changes.
- Lack of focus.
- Understanding time to market.
- Lack of exist route.
- Trying to create a new market.

These factors will be examined in more detail below:

### *Lack of Credibility*

Universities could demonstrate the credibility of their spin-offs by:

- Presenting IP as a potential portfolio of products.
- Demonstrating proof of concept of technological assets.
- Clarifying the route to market and profitability.
- Being able to locate the venture off-campus.
- Implement mechanisms to attract surrogate entrepreneurs.

### *Inadequate Funding*

The development phase in MNT was found to be particularly expensive in nanotechnologies for a number of reasons, especially since they were based on physical science. Therefore the capital costs of setting up a research laboratory and development was very high.

An example to indicate the expenses involved could be a commonly used piece of equipment in nanotechnology, which is an atomic force microscope (AFM). The cost was found to be in the order of $100,000. There were many more pieces of this type of equipment required. Also many nanocompanies had shown interest in developing semiconductor like manufacturing facilities. A state-of-the-art semi-lab could cost several million pounds. Hence a lack of funding was a major obstacle to the growth of an MNT start-up. This differed from a dot.com company or a software company where the only capital costs involved were those of computers and inexpensive software development tools. Another key attribute of nanotechnology was the convergence of different areas of science. Consequently, most nanotechnology projects required a multi-disciplinary team. Hence, due to the diverse labour force involved, the cost of developing an IP in nanotechnology was high.

### Law Changes

A tax law that was passed in April 2002 in UK, made it difficult for academic to be rewarded with equity in university spin-outs. Any scientist, who was granted equity in the university spin-out was liable to pay a huge tax bill, irrespective of the current value of their equity stake or financial resources. Several Scottish universities had made formal decisions not to proceed with any further spin-outs until the matter is resolved. This tax change for university spin-outs was seen to be a major hindrance to the future creation of start-ups.

### Lack of Focus

Lack of focus was generally seen as a problem during the inception phase. There were greater chances of a lack of focus if the start-up was involved in developing a platform technology that could be used in many industries or products. Although it might seem a greater market opportunity, in the longer term it would hamper the *focus* of the start-up in the short term.

Another pitfall was looking for the wrong kind of funding. An example of this was if a nanocompany was too far away from launching a potential product (e.g. more than 5 years) then it should not approach VC investors. It should focus on government sources of funding when applicable.

### Time to Market

There were a number of pitfalls that were seen as MNT companies move into in the growth phase. One problem was making the transition from academic lab to commercial product. It was common for academic founders to underestimate the difficulty in commercialising a new technology. This was because it was much more difficult to produce material in high quantities at a certain level of quality and consistency than to demonstrate a process in a lab.

A prominent example of this was a nanoparticles company, Oxonica Ltd that took 5 years, rather than their planned 3 years, to bring their new material to market.

Lack of industry infrastructure was seen to be another factor detrimental to the growth of the MNT start-up. MNT start-ups were at the cutting edge of technology where there still does not exist a well-developed supply chain. Resources that other sector companies can take for granted such as — abundant technically trained workforce, manufacturing equipment, manufacturing services and design software — are all minimal or nonexistent for various nanotechnologies. Therefore, nanotech start-ups are forced to create more of their own infrastructure as they progress.

### Lack of an Exist Route

Very few MNT companies have had successful achieved exists to date, especially in nanotechnology. This is due to a combination of the state of MNT and the state of the economy. For this reason, it was difficult to establish 'best practice' regarding exits for MNT start-ups. There were a limited number of options observed:

- IPO
- Acquisition
- Merger
- Staying private

In the current market, an acquisition is seen to be the most likely option.

### Trying to Create a New Market

A common pitfall seen in MNT start-ups was failing to plan for the progress that a current incumbent technology could make during the time it took to develop a competing micro- or nano-based technology. The reason could be that in the nanotechnology area, there were already many technologies focussed on disrupting existing markets rather than creating new markets. An illustration of this pitfall was provided by the multiple initiatives in the nano-based memory emerging market. There were multiple start-ups as well as large company efforts in this area. In this market the current technology was semiconductor memory: DRAM, SRAM and flash memories. The nano-based memories are currently in the prototype phase. Hence to be competitive in any future market, the nano-based memory would have to out-perform the future generation of semiconductor memories.

## Conclusions

The aims of the study were:

- To analyse the start-up activity in the field of MNT in the UK.
- To study the various commercialisation modes of MNT, including university technology transfer mechanisms.
- To determine the various factors responsible for the success of a start-up in the field of MNT.
- To determine the various issues and problems encountered by the start-up companies.

The major findings from this study are:

- The majority of the start-ups in the MNT sector in the UK are university spin-offs. This is unlike the Internet start-ups that were concentrated with independent entrepreneurs. Most of the new university spin-offs were technology push — in some cases 'products looking for markets' with an element of chance as to whether the market would be interested.
- The attitude to venture capital was generally rather lukewarm and tinged with suspicion. This could possibly be a professional culture effect, with scientists typically suspicious of the financiers. One individual company felt that its failure was due to lack of understanding by the funders when taking key, long-term business decisions about which products to promote.
- Possibly the most critical factor in determining the success or failure of start-ups is the ability of the founder, the visionary, to pull together a management team which whole-heartedly supports his vision of the company's future and to obtain the long-term support of stake holders including capital providers, university backers and key employees. The founders of those companies with a demonstrable track record of success, such as Cambridge Display Technologies and Plastic Logic, were able to control this process, whereas Ilotron had failed because this aspect had been neglected.
- Even the companies with the best success records (Cambridge Display Technology) could not be characterised by market pull. One of the main drivers for the companies covered was the perception that the MNT market was one of very significant untapped opportunities, combined with the ease of access to venture capital for MNT during 2000 to early 2001.
- Venture capital providers do have a significant influence on the overall success. This is primarily because of the high level of initial investment required in an MNT start-up. It should be noted that having substantial long-term funding can also have it's drawbacks. It could allow the start-up to have a flawed business model for a long period of time.
- Spin-outs tend to come from a small number of top research institutions.
- There was a general feeling that, while academic support for start-ups had improved and moved away from the simple licensing of IP, there was still room for improvement. Specific areas found were: a better understanding of the value added by commercial companies, which was distinct from what could be generated in university environment, and clear guidelines on how academics should be handled. In most cases, universities viewed key individuals moving into commerce in strict 'win-lose' terms, which could in some cases result in total cessation of communication.
- Certain factors were seen as seriously detrimental to success. They included lack of credibility, lack of focus, lack of understanding of venture capital, changes in government policies and lack of funds.
- None of the start-ups studied were yet profitable. Even the most high-profile start-ups were struggling to generate profits. This could be seen in the cumulative profit-loss curve of Figure 3. The majority of the start-ups were still surviving on venture capital that they had raised.

# Appendix

## Companies Included in the Study

| No. | Name of the start-up/spin-off | Year established | Affiliated university |
|-----|-------------------------------|------------------|-----------------------|
| 1 | 3D Molecular Sciences Ltd | 2001 | Imperial College, University of Hertfordshire |
| 2 | Adaptive Screening | 2001 | Imperial College, University of Glasgow |
| 3 | Adelan | 1996 | Birmingham and Keele Universities |
| 4 | Advanced Optical Technology | 1999 | Independent |
| 5 | Advanced Technology Coatings Ltd | 1999 | Independent |
| 6 | Akubio Ltd | 2001 | University of Cambridge |
| 7 | Amcet Ltd | 2000 | University of Dundee |
| 8 | Blaze Photonics | 2001 | University of Bath |
| 9 | Cambridge Display Technology | 1992 | University of Cambridge |
| 10 | Cambridge Lab On A Chip Ltd | 2003 | University of Cambridge |
| 11 | Casect Ltd | 1999 | Imperial College |
| 12 | Ceres Power Ltd | 2001 | Imperial College |
| 13 | CVD Technologies Ltd | 2000 | University of Salford |
| 14 | Deltadot | 2000 | Imperial College |
| 15 | Durham Magneto Optics Ltd | 2002 | University of Durham |
| 16 | Epigem Ltd | 1995 | University of Durham |
| 17 | Farfield Sensors Ltd | 1997 | University of Durham |
| 18 | Farlfield Photonics Ltd | 2001 | Farfield Sensors/University of Durham |
| 19 | Genapta Ltd | 2001 | University of Cambridge |
| 20 | Gencoa Ltd | 1994 | Independent |
| 21 | IMPT Ltd | 1999 | Imperial College |
| 22 | Infinitesima Ltd | 2001 | Bristol University |
| 23 | Kelvin Nanotechnology Ltd | 1997 | University of Glasgow |
| 24 | Lein Applied Diagnostics | 2003 | UMIST |
| 25 | Mesophotonics | 2001 | University of Southampton/ BTG |
| 26 | Microemissive Ltd | 1999 | University of Edinburgh, Napier University |

*(Continued)*

(*Continued*)

| No. | Name of the start-up/spin-off | Year established | Affiliated university |
|-----|-------------------------------|------------------|------------------------|
| 27 | Microrheology Ltd | 2002 | University of Bristol |
| 28 | Microsaic | 1998 | Imperial College |
| 29 | Microstensil Ltd | 2003 | Heriot-Watt University |
| 30 | Microtest Matrices | 2002 | Imperial College |
| 31 | Molecular Photonics Ltd | 1995 | University of Durham |
| 32 | Molecular Profiles | 1997 | University of Nottingham |
| 33 | Molecular Vision | 2001 | Imperial College |
| 34 | Nanobiodesign Ltd | 2001 | Imperial College |
| 35 | Nanoco | 2001 | University of Manchester |
| 36 | Nanograph Ltd | 2003 | University of Nottingham |
| 37 | Nanomagnetics | 1997 | Bristol University |
| 38 | Nanosight Ltd | 2002 | Independent |
| 39 | Nanotecture Ltd | 2003 | Southampton University |
| 40 | Nitech Solutions Ltd | 2003 | Heriot-Watt University |
| 41 | Orla Proteins | 2001 | University of Newcastle |
| 42 | Oxford Biosensors Ltd | 2000 | University of Oxford |
| 43 | Oxford Gene Technology Ltd | 1995 | University of Oxford |
| 44 | Oxonica Ltd | 1999 | University of Oxford |
| 45 | Patterning Technologies | 1997 | Jetmask Limited |
| 46 | Peratech | 1997 | University Of Durham |
| 47 | Plastic Logic Ltd | 2000 | University of Cambridge |
| 48 | Printable Field Emitters Ltd | 1995 | Aston University/RAL |
| 49 | Psimedica Ltd | 2000 | Independent |
| 50 | Scalar Technologies Ltd | 1999 | University Of Edinburgh, Heriot-Watt University |
| 51 | Sensor Technology & Devices Ltd | 2000 | University of Ulster |
| 52 | Smartbead Ltd | 2000 | University of Cambridge/ Sentec Ltd |
| 53 | Softswitch Ltd | 2001 | Peratech Ltd and Wronz Inc. |
| 54 | Solexa Ltd | 1998 | University of Cambridge |
| 55 | Strathophase Ltd | 1999 | University of Southampton |
| 56 | Syrris Ltd | 2001 | Independent |
| 57 | TDL Sensors Ltd | 1999 | UMIST |
| 58 | Toumaz Technology | 2000 | Imperial College |
| 59 | Vivamer Ltd | 2002 | University of Cambridge |
| 60 | West Micro Technologies Ltd | 2003 | University of Birmingham |

# References

Di Gregorio, D., & Shane, D. (2003). Why do some universities generate more start-ups than others? *Research Policy, 32*(2), 209–227.

Lambert Review of Business-University Collaboration. (2003). Final report, Her Majesty's Stationery Office, UK.

Swann, G. M. P. & Prevezer, M. (1998). Conclusions. In: G. M. P. Swann, M. Pervezer & D. Stout (Eds), *The dynamics of industrial clustering: International comparisons in computing and biotechnology* (pp. 298–308). Oxford: Oxford University Press.

Chapter 14

# Drivers of Strategic Direction in High Technology Small Firms

Nicholas O'Regan, Abby Ghobadian and S Jaseem Ahmad

## Introduction

Previous studies have shown that small- and medium-sized manufacturing firms make a substantial contribution to national economies in terms of job and wealth creation (Daly & McCann, 1992; Schreyer, 1996). However, many smaller firms face unprecedented change arising from the increasingly competitive and changing environment in which they operate (Coopers and Lybrand, 1997; D'Aveni, 1994). Much of this competition often emanates from larger firms with greater resource capabilities. Firms of all sizes are increasingly turning to strategy as a means of achieving competitive advantage. Strategy research is mainly directed towards examining why firms differ in performance (Barnett & Burgelman, 1996; Schendel, 1996). Strategy has 'undergone, in the 1990s, a major shift in focus regarding the sources of sustainable competitive advantage: from industry to firm specific effects' (Spanos & Lioukas, 2001). This involves more than strategy formulation — it is about making choices based on competing alternatives and implementing the chosen direction using the organisational processes and systems (Shaw, Gupta, & Delery, 2002; Stopford, 2001). Other writers, such as Pettigrew and Fenton (2000), acknowledge that 'soft' aspects are an integral part of the evolutionary nature of strategy, and include cultural influences (Chakravarthy & Doz, 1992) and leadership (McNulty & Pettigrew, 1999).

The literature suggests there are two main perspectives that shape our understanding of strategy and strategic choices: the industrial organisation perspective (Connor, 1999; Nickerson, Hamilton, & Wada, 2001; Porter, 1985), and the resource-based view (Barney, 1995; Barney & Zajac, 1994; Miller & Shamsie, 1996; Peteraf, 1993; Wernerfelt, 1995). Whereas the industrial organisation view provides a straightforward assessment of industry structure, the resource-based view includes some of the more 'messy' areas of organisational development such as culture, leadership, skills and knowledge. Some authors doubt the ability of both these models to understand the modern competitive environment

New Technology Based Firms in the New Millennium, Volume VI
Edited by A. Groen, R. Oakey, P. van der Sijde and G. Cook
© 2008 Emerald Group Publishing Limited. All rights reserved.

(Courtney, Kirkland, & Viguerie, 1997; Markides, 1999). Arguably, this criticism arises from an inability to effectively 'fuse' both perspectives to achieve competitive advantage. This paper contends that a holistic approach, that acknowledges the strategic orientation of the firm, can be used to determine the activities that potentially lead to competitive advantage. The basis of this thinking is the provision of generic strategic choices to firms, each offering the 'key' to gaining, attaining or regaining sustainable competitive advantage.

To date, research has focussed on the examination and validation of two principal typologies: *Porter's Generic Strategies* (1980) and the Miles and Snow *Strategic Orientation Typology* (1978). *Porter's Generic Strategies* suggest that firms need to adopt a differentiation cost leadership or focus (target a niche segment) approach. Lee, Lim, Tan, and Wee (2001) question the applicability of Porter's generic strategies to small firms and suggest that they fail to consider resource constraints. They point out, for instance, that only the focus or niche strategy [concentrating on particular market segment(s)] seems applicable to small firms. Even this niche approach may come under attack from larger firms, and where small firms have free reign, it is largely due to the 'continued neglect or ignorance' of these niche segments by larger firms (Lee et al., 2001). As competition intensifies, however, it is only a matter of time before larger firms target 'profitable' niche markets. Lee et al. (2001) also question the applicability of cost leadership for small firms, arguing that it is doubtful if they have the necessary economies of scale to achieve competitive advantage based on cost leadership.

The Miles and Snow typology categorises firms into four main types: prospectors, defenders, enablers and reactors. While few criticisms exist in the literature of this typology, Hurst, Rush, and White (1989) and Parnell and Wright (1993) suggest that the two main categories: prospectors and defenders are not mutually exclusive. Parnell (1997) reviewed the various attempts at integrating both Porter's and Miles and Snow's typologies. His findings indicate that the major difference between these typologies relates to an ability to allow for a long-term viable combination strategy, which is only inherent in the Miles and Snow typology. In addition, each category of the Miles and Snow typology encompasses a holistic view of the operating environment. This, in effect, is a 'fusing' of strategy with the softer aspects of leadership and culture. Finally, the literature strongly argues that the Miles and Snow typology is particularly appropriate for use regarding small firms (Olson & Currie, 1992; Rugman & Verbeke, 1987). In addition, the authors were unable to find any empirical studies that cast doubt on the validity of this typology. Accordingly, this chapter focuses on the Miles and Snow typology.

An examination of the literature suggests the relationships depicted in Figure 1.

## Aims of the Research

The literature reveals substantial interest in the broad topic of business strategy and its subsequent performance and, in particular, the theoretical and empirical understanding of the link between strategy and performance (Ghobadian & O'Regan, 2000). Despite a common operating environment, some firms perform better than others. The reason for greater performance is attributed to the various stages of the strategic process from formulation to development (Mintzberg, 1990). While it is not clear what part of the strategic process triggers the increase in performance potential, it is contended that a key component in the

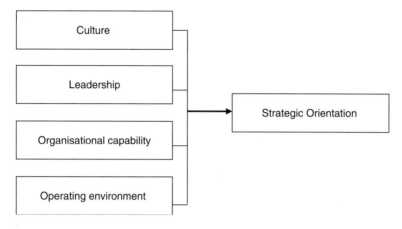

Figure 1: Strategic orientation framework.

response of small firms to their operating environment is based on strategic orientation (Hambrick, 1984). In this study, only 58% of firms indicated that they formulated a formal strategic plan. Since strategy is often associated with focus or direction in key operating areas (Ireland & Hitt, 1997), it is possible to deduce the strategic orientation of each firm from trends in behaviour and market outlook.

Much existing research focuses on large firms and provides a useful basis for examining strategic orientation in smaller firms. However, small firms differ from large firms in aspects such as competencies, ideals and resources (Jennings & Beaver, 1995; Wilkes & Dale, 1998). As an example, Beaver and Jennings (1996) refer to the strategic approach of small firms as adaptive (following a change in circumstances) and large firms as predictive (explicit policies followed to achieve a goal). Hannan and Freeman (1984) and Meyer and Zucker (1989), suggest that large firms can have unwieldy structures and complex procedures that hinder strategic change and give rise to complacency. By implication, smaller firms have greater flexibility. The following quotation encapsulates the variation caused by the differences in firm sizes and draws the conclusion that the transferability of applications is not advisable:

> *...a small business is not a 'little' large business; differences exist in structure, policy making procedures, utilisation of resources to the extent that application of large business concepts directly to the small business may border on the ridiculous* (Welsh & White, 1981).

Accordingly, the following hypotheses were formulated:

- The Miles and Snow generic strategies are applicable to HTSFs.
- The Miles and Snow strategic types are associated with different environmental types.
- The Miles and Snow strategic types place different emphases on the range of leadership styles.
- The Miles and Snow strategic types place different emphases on the range of culture types.
- The Miles and Snow strategic types have different organisational capabilities.

The paper begins with a brief overview of culture, leadership, organisational capability and operating environment followed by a description of the formulation of the constructs. In the following section strategic orientation is described and the literature reviewed. Next, the methodology is outlined, along with the conduct of the research. The penultimate section provides the analysis and its interpretation. Finally, conclusions are derived and their significance to managers of HTSF is considered.

## Culture

Culture is defined by Hofstede (1984) as 'the way things are done in the business', illustrating the firms' philosophy or character and distinguishing one organisation from another. Lounsbury and Glynn (2001) define culture as "an interpretive framework through which individuals make sense of their own behaviour, as well as the behaviour of collectivities in their society."

Organisational culture is often seen as the conduit through which top management can encourage the development and deployment of corporate strategy. Conversely, culture is often considered as a major obstacle in the implementation of new ideas, processes and systems (Morgan, 1989). The culture of any organisation relates to its values and beliefs, which are often influenced by various factors including the company's founder (Schein, 1983). The 'established organisation' tends to keep and build on the initial behaviour and values (Daft & Weick, 1984). This pattern can be recognised in many firms as founding members often stress personal beliefs, values and assumptions on a range of issues from the business strategy to the environment (Brown, 1995).

Research on culture and what comprises the various dimensions of culture is limited (Ashkanasy, Broadfoot, & Falkus, 2000). Indeed, Cooke and Szumal (2000) suggest that the determination of new initiatives by leaders to propagate controls results in a 'cultural bypass' and has an adverse impact on the motivation and loyalty of employees. The literature focuses on larger firms and suggests that corporate strategy is influenced by organisational culture (Barney, 1986).

In this context culture was operationalised based on the dimensions tested and validated by Wilderom and van den Berg (1997) regarding small firms. The culture styles used in this study were *external orientation, internal orientation, empowerment, intergroup orientation and human resources.*

## Leadership

Leadership is defined as "the art or process of influencing people so that they will strive willingly and enthusiastically toward the achievement of the group's mission" (Weihrich & Koontz, 1993). From a practical viewpoint, Bennis and Nanus (1985) suggest that the principle task of leadership is to ensure the effective deployment of a corporate strategy.

Miller and Shamsie (2001) state, "a growing body of literature has identified the significant impact that leader's characteristics can have on both strategic direction and overall organisational performance." Research to date, however, has often been contradictory.

"While the literature reflects no consensus regarding whether corporate leadership 'matters', there is little disagreement that the most powerful executive position is that of CEO" (Daily, McDougall, & Dalton, 2002). This is particularly true in the case of small firms where the CEO tends to 'occupy a position of unique influence, serving as the locus of control and decision-making'.

Begley and Boyd (1986) state that the role of the Chief Executive in the smaller firm is more significant as he/she is the controlling influence with regard to decisions and strategy. Chief Executives exert an influence on the firm that is significant and which may be either good or bad (Day & Lord, 1988), although Hambrick and Mason (1984) state that the environmental circumstances surrounding the firm dictate the leaders' actions to a large degree.

Wilderom and van den Berg (1997) derived, tested and validated four main leadership styles in an empirical study of small firms, namely, *transformational, transaction, human resources and laissez faire styles.* Accordingly, these constructs were used in this study in order to ensure external validity. Their validity was further tested by qualitative interviews with six Chief Executives of HTSFs, employers' representative bodies and in the pilot phase of the fieldwork.

### Organisational Capability

Organisational capabilities are defined by Chandler (1990) as a firm's collective physical facilities, the skills of its employees and the abilities and expertise of the top management layers. Organisational capabilities are commonly defined as a firm's capacity to deploy its assets, tangible or intangible, to perform a task or activity to improve performance (Amit & Schoemaker, 1993; Grant, 1991; Teece, Pisano, & Shuen, 1997). Examples include the capability to: offer excellent customer service, develop new products and innovate (Lorenzoni & Lipparini, 1999).

The importance of organisational capability is well-documented (Ramanujam, Venkatraman, & Camillus, 1986). Quelin (2000, p. 477) states, "more and more, the strategic management field is focusing on the role of competencies and resources that accumulate within a firm". He argues that each firm has a unique organisational capability based on its technological and organisational competencies. The literature suggests that an ability to build effective capabilities is a significant driver of performance (Teece et al., 1997). The literature, however, focuses largely upon organisational capabilities in large firms. Previous research has examined capabilities development (Henderson & Cockburn, 1994; McGrath, MacMillan, & Venkataraman, 1995; Teece et al., 1997), and cost reduction, higher quality and greater flexibility in manufacturing (Schroeder, Bates, & Junttila, 2002). This paper seeks to extend previous research by linking capabilities to strategic orientation. These constructs were operationalised by establishing a range of capabilities that drive competitive advantage during the focus group discussions and subsequent piloting of the questionnaire.

### Operating Environment

Managing directors face an increasingly dynamic, complex and unpredictable environment where technology, globalisation, knowledge and changing competitive approaches impact on overall performance (Asch & Salaman, 2002), Hitt, Ireland, Camp, and Sexton (2001).

The degree and complexity of the current changing environment is driving firms, both large and small, to seek new ways of conducting business to create wealth (Stopford, 2001). Nevertheless, it is imperative that change is handled carefully if firms are serious about achieving/retaining/regaining competitive advantage. These constructs were operationalised by establishing a range of attributes to describe the operating environment during the focus group discussions and subsequent piloting of the questionnaire.

### Strategic Orientation

All firms, even in a common industry grouping, do not respond to their operating environments in the same ways. For example, some firms may "anchor their reactions primarily to the behavior of other firms that are strategically similar to them" (Garcia-Pont & Nohria, 2002). Others may adopt a more independent stance based on different approaches. The responses to the operating environment can be categorised according to the strategic orientation of each firm.

Strategic orientation is concerned with the direction and thrust of the firm and is based on the perceptions, motivations and desires that precede and guide the strategy formulation and deployment processes (Miller, 1987). The usefulness of these typologies for senior managers lies in their predictive properties in establishing firm output and external market alignment (Gilad & Gilad, 1988). Taxonomies or typologies help "bring order to the complex set of inter-related phenomena by identifying recurring patterns of decisions which then provide a comprehensive, yet parsimonious, orientation to the study of strategy" (Slater & Olsen, 2000).

In order to test the applicability of generic strategies, the authors considered the literature on the Miles and Snow taxonomy and Porter's generic strategies. The authors chose the Miles and Snow typology since it focused on the "dynamic process of adjusting to environmental change and uncertainty" (Miles & Snow, 1978, p. 3), and took into consideration the trade-off between external and internal strategic factors (McKee, Varadarajan, & Pride, 1989). In any event, the literature suggests that the use of Porter's (1980) model of competitive strategy is not appropriate in the case of small firms (Rugman & Verbeke, 1987). They suggest that a focus strategy is the only real choice open to small firms. Accordingly, the element of choice is non-existent.

The Miles and Snow typology remains the main typology used (Conant, Mokwa, & Varadarajan, 1990), and has been tested extensively in a range of industries (Conant et al., 1990; Dvir, Segev, & Shenhar, 1993; James & Hatten, 1995; Ketchen, Thomas, & Snow, 1993; Miles &Snow, 1978; Shortell & Zajac, 1990; Zahra & Pearce, 1990). These studies suggest that the typology is sufficiently robust for analysing competencies and strategies of companies on a generic basis. The next section will consider the Miles and Snow typology in greater detail.

### The Miles and Snow Typology

The Miles and Snow typology focuses on the direction and influence given by managing directors and the top management team to the firm's strategic direction. It suggests that three fundamental issues need to be addressed by decision-makers in any firm: managing the firm's share of the market (the entrepreneurial problem), deploying solutions (the engineering problem) and, finally, structuring the firm to manage the processes outlined (the administrative problem). Miles and Snow's contention is that a pattern of the responses to these issues indicating the orientation of the firm can be detected. Accordingly, the Miles and Snow typology effectively considers the alignment of the firm's strategy with its external operating environment. Four types of organisation were identified, based on their approach to the changing operating environment: Prospectors, Analysers, Defenders and Reactors (see Table 1).

The literature suggests that a continuum of organisations exists dependant upon their action/reaction to the operating environment and the intensity of their strategic intent (at one end of the continuum firms will have robust strategies whereas at the other end firms will have a reactive response to environmental changes) (Miles & Snow, 1978).

Table 1: A Summary of the Miles and Snow generic strategy categories.

| Strategic orientation | Main focus | Traits |
| --- | --- | --- |
| Prospector | Entrepreneurial, innovation and new opportunities orientated. | External orientation, environment scanning. Maximise new opportunities. Innovation to meet market needs. Flexibility and freedom from constraining company rules and regulations. Welcome change and see their environment as 'uncertain'. |
| Defender | Defending existing market Targets a narrow market segment (may be a niche market). Uses variety of means to defend existing market | Narrow range of products/services Internal orientation, efficiency of existing operations Uses well-established ideas/methods and avoids unnecessary risk. Centralised control and a functional structure are common |
| Analyser | Hybrid of prospector and defender types | Operates well in both stable and dynamic markets. Thorough analysis. Uses efficiency and increased production in stable markets and innovates in dynamic markets |
| Reactor | Reacts to change | Short-term planning Reacts to others actions. Change inevitably presents some difficulties |

Miles and Snow contend that every organisation has a dominant trait resulting from the influence of its key decision-makers, and their perceived view of the operating environment. The choice of whether to be proactive or reactive will, to a large extent, follow from this view.

Each of the strategic orientation types represents specific relations with the firm's operating environment. For example prospectors welcome and thrive in innovative, dynamic environments by maximising new opportunities (Hambrick, 1983). They are likely to be the first to the marketplace and seek to exploit this advantage. Their main focus is on the end result that is facilitated by a tolerance of risk, an acceptance of change, empowerment and flexibility.

Defenders have a singular orientation as their managers "devote primary attention to improving the efficiency of their existing operations" (Miles & Snow, 1978, p. 29). The focus of 'defenders' is described as producing and distributing goods or services as efficiently as possible (Miles & Snow, 1978) and, at the same time, preserving a stable market niche. While they are happy to achieve change, they feel more comfortable with existing strategies (McDaniel & Kolari, 1987). In practice, defenders are likely to adopt a cost leadership approach and focus on efficiency and continuous improvement. This is likely to necessitate a high level of control. Defenders are likely to be heavily bureaucratic and unlikely to adopt a dynamic approach to change.

Analyser type firms comprise a mixture of both the prospector and defender traits. They operate in stable markets, routinely and efficiently. In unstable markets they monitor competitors for new ideas and try out the more promising ones. In other words, Miles and Snow's key supposition is that a firm's product and market lead to choices of how to compete (competitive advantage), to grow and attain functional support. Essentially, 'analysers' focus on efficiency and increased production when the market is stable and on innovation when the market is dynamic or uncertain (Slater & Narver, 1993).

Reactors are firms that adopt a laissez faire approach to their operating environment and are largely unprepared for any changes that arise. The main strategic goal of this category is 'survival'. Miles and Snow refer to the actions of 'reactors' as inconsistent, arising from a lack of clear goals and direction. Consequently, reactors are unlikely to be proactive and more likely to delay responding to the external environment until it is absolutely necessary. Conant et al. (1990) state that 'reactors' respond to the challenges of the market in an erratic manner. Essentially this is a management approach of the 'last resort' and could be categorised as continuous fire fighting.

Miles and Snow contend that the prospector, defender and analyser styles are capable of leading to competitive advantage within the industry. However, they caution that the reactor style is often a manifestation of a poorly aligned strategy and structure and therefore unlikely to lead to competitive advantage. The literature base suggests that the continuum ranges from prospector to defender (Doty et al., 1993), with no longer any place for reactors (Ketchen et al., 1993; Zahra & Pearce, 1990).

## Methodology

The sample on which the strategy was based consisted of 1000 small- and medium-sized firms in the UK electronics and engineering sectors. The reason for this choice was three-fold. Firstly, this approach acknowledged the contrasting product life cycles of the sectors. Generally, engineering organisations, operate in a mature market, whereas electronic firms operate in markets characterised by short product life cycles. Secondly, these sectors were chosen for their relative economic importance. Thirdly, there was a presence of a large number of small- and medium-sized firms within the two sectors. Small- and medium-sized firms were defined as having fewer than 250 employees. As there are nearly 15,000 electronic/engineering small- and medium-sized firms in the UK (DTI, 1996), it was decided to employ a random sampling methodology using a directory available from a reputable commercial firm. Manufacturing firms were chosen as their levels of fixed commitment and capital are higher when compared to service firms (Swartz & Iacobucci, 2000).

Based on an analysis of the Miles and Snow classification, each respondent was asked to indicate the Miles and Snow type classification that was the best fit to their firm. This technique is widely used in management studies (Davig, 1986; Snow & Hrebiniak, 1980), and is often used in studies of the Miles and Snow typology (Conant et al., 1990; James & Hatten, 1995; Shortell & Zajac, 1990).

We used managerial perceptions as they shape the strategic behaviour of the firm to a significant degree. This is consistent with the work of Chattopadhyay, Glick, Miller and Huber (1999) and Spanos and Lioukas (2001). Gioia and Chittipeddi (1991, p. 434) assert, "the C.E.O. is portrayed as someone who has primary responsibility for setting strategic directions and plans for the organisation, as well as responsibility for guiding actions that will realise those plans". In a review of the literature, Westphal and Frederickson (2001) found that top management has a significant impact on strategic direction and change. The literature accepts the validity of CEO or general managers self-typing of organisations' strategic configurations (Hillman & Keim, 2001).

The validity of the constructs used and their relevance was tested through the qualitative phase of the research. This involved in-depth interviews with six managing directors of HTSFs and discussions with employer representative bodies such as the Chamber of Commerce and the Confederation of British Industry. Furthermore, the survey instrument was tested and modified through the pilot phase of the fieldwork.

The procedures used to analyse the responses included the determination of the reliability of the instrument. Internal consistency was established using Cronbach's $\alpha$ and factor analysis. Cronbach's $\alpha$ was used to test the scale of reliability. Factor analysis was used to reveal the underlying themes and also used as a means of data reduction. The relationship between strategic orientation and strategy was examined using correlation analysis. We also correlated the strategic orientation categories with a range of performance indicators.

# Responses

Factors such as change in address, size and sector incompatibility reduced the effective size of the sample to 702. One hundred ninety four valid responses were received — a response rate of 27%. This is a satisfactory response for this type of research (Hart, 1987). The demographics of non-responding firms were compared with those of responding firms. No discernible differences were detected pointing to the absence of serious response bias. Furthermore, non-respondents were contacted to ascertain the reasons for non-response. These were analysed to determine whether or not the non-response was a source of potential bias. The reasons proffered for non-response did not reveal an underlying bias. In addition, early and late respondents were compared and no discernible differences were detected.

## Analysis

Each alternative answer to the questions was related to one of the four strategic types: analyser, defender, prospector and reactor. Prospectors and analysers represented 92% of the respondents (see Table 2).

The analysis indicates that 47.4% of the respondent firms perceive themselves as 'prospector' and 44.8% perceive themselves as belonging to the 'defender' style. Both styles accordingly account for over 92% of all firms in this sample. This is consistent with the findings of Miles and Snow (1978). The analysis indicates that only 5.2% of firms perceive themselves as 'analyser' type firms and a mere 2.6% of firms consider themselves to be 'reactor' type firms. This suggests that there are two main types of orientation with distinctive traits. An inference drawn from the analysis of this study, therefore, is that there is no room for the 'middle ground' or passiveness in the sectors studied. Interestingly, an analysis of the strategic orientation based on firm size indicates that the proportion of prospector firms decline in each category as the size band increases. This implies that as prospector type firms grow, their emphasis appears to change to become more 'defender' oriented as they seek to protect their market share. The analysis also indicates that the proportion of 'defenders' increase in each category as the size band increases — indicating that defending the market share is a high priority strategy. This finding provides another perspective to the previous work of Smith, Guthrie and Chen (1986), which suggests that larger firms tend to be 'prospectors' while smaller firms adopted the 'defender' type approach. Accordingly, *Hypothesis 1: The Miles and Snow generic strategies are applicable to HTSFs* is partially accepted.

### *Operating Environment*

Nine attributes were used to describe the operating environment of the firms. The results are depicted in Table 3.

The results of Table 3 indicate that a high proportion of prospector type firms perceive their environment to be 'dynamic' whereas defenders tended to perceive their environment as 'stable'. In addition, over half of all prospector type firms indicate that their products and

Table 2: Strategic orientation types.

| % Breakdown by orientation type (*N*=194) | | | | | | |
|---|---|---|---|---|---|---|
| Stated strategic type | No. of firms | % of firms | 1–19 | 20–49 | 50–99 | 100–249 |
| Prospector | 93 | 47.4 | 68.7 | 60.8 | 53.2 | 36.2 |
| Defender | 86 | 44.8 | 31.3 | 33.8 | 38.3 | 51.2 |
| Analyser | 10 | 5.2 | | 3.6 | 2.1 | 10.3 |
| Reactor | 5 | 2.6 | | 1.8 | 6.4 | 2.3 |
| Total | 194 | 100% | 100% | 100% | 100% | 100% |

processes are subject to technological change, over twice the percentage of defender type firms with similar perceptions. This finding is mirrored by the importance of a decreasing product life cycle. These findings are consistent with the descriptions of both prospectors and defenders provided by Miles and Snow. Accordingly, *Hypothesis 2: The Miles and Snow strategic types are associated with different environmental types* is accepted.

### Leadership

The emphasis placed on each of the four leadership styles derived by Wilderom and van den Berg is depicted in Table 4

The analysis of Table 4 indicates that prospector type firms place a greater emphasis on transformational and human resources styles of leadership, whereas defenders emphasise the transactional style to a greater extent.

This is consistent with the description of the Miles and Snow types depicted in Table 1. For example transformational and human resources styles of leadership emphasise flexibility and freedom from rules and regulations and welcome change. These are also attributes that are applicable to prospector type firms. On the other hand, transactional leadership styles emphasise centralised control and a functional structure. These attributes are also applicable to the defender type firms. Accordingly, *Hypothesis 3: The Miles and Snow strategic types have different emphases on the range of leadership styles* is accepted.

Table 3: Environment factors rated important/very important by each strategic type.

|  | Prospector | Defender | Analyser | Reactor |
|---|---|---|---|---|
| Stable environment | 29.3 | 48.3 | 20.0 | 40.0 |
| Dynamic environment | 60.8 | 21.8 | 50.0 | 40.0 |
| Subject to technological change in processes | 66.2 | 32.2 | 70.0 | 20.0 |
| Threat of substitutes | 43.5 | 32.5 | 70.0 | 60.0 |
| Threat of new firms | 19.6 | 24.1 | 50.0 | 40.0 |
| Threat from overseas firms | 53.3 | 37.1 | 30.0 | 80.0 |
| Technological change in products | 65.2 | 31.5 | 30.0 | 40.0 |
| Decreasing product cycle | 38.0 | 16.4 | – | 10.0 |
| Changing regulatory environment | 42.4 | 43.7 | 40.0 | 40.0 |

Table 4: Leadership styles rated important/very important by each strategic type.

|  | Prospector | Defender | Analyser | Reactor |
|---|---|---|---|---|
| Transformational | 34.8 | 14.9 | 10.0 | – |
| Transactional | 10.3 | 30.0 | 10.0 | 20.0 |
| Human resources | 35.9 | 15.9 | 20.0 | – |
| Laissez faire | 2.2 | 2.3 | – | – |

## Culture

The emphasis placed on each of the five culture styles derived by Wilderom and van den Berg is depicted in Table 5.

An analysis of Table 5 indicates that prospector type firms have a higher emphasis on all the leadership styles with the exception of internal orientation, compared with defender style firms. Defenders emphasise internal orientation leadership to a greater extent. These findings are consistent with the attributes of prospector and defender styles. Accordingly, *Hypothesis 4: The Miles and Snow strategic types have different emphases on the range of culture types* is accepted.

## Organisational Capability

The emphasis placed on eight attributes of organisational capability is depicted in Table 6.

The analysis of Table 6 suggests that prospector type firms compete by making rapid design changes and by effectively responding to swings in volume. On the other hand, defender type firms compete on price and have a lower emphasis on rapid design changes. This is consistent with the earlier finding that defender type firms perceive their operating environment to be stable rather than dynamic. Accordingly, *Hypothesis 5: The Miles and Snow strategic types have different organisational capabilities* is accepted.

Table 5:  Culture styles rated important/very important by each strategic type.

|                  | Prospectors | Defenders | Analysers | Reactors |
|------------------|-------------|-----------|-----------|----------|
| Intergroup       | 35.9        | 29.9      | 50.0      | –        |
| Empowerment      | 28.0        | 4.6       | –         | –        |
| External         | 35.0        | 11.5      | –         | –        |
| Human resources  | 47.8        | 17.2      | 20.0      | –        |
| Internal         | 19.7        | 36.1      | 20.0      | 20.0     |

Table 6: Organisational capability attributes rated important/very important by each strategic type.

|                      | Prospector | Defender | Analyser | Reactor |
|----------------------|------------|----------|----------|---------|
| Compete on price     | 66.3       | 86.7     | 60.0     | 100.0   |
| Rapid design changes | 79.3       | 60.9     | 70.0     | 100.0   |
| Responds to swings in volume | 65.2 | 50.6    | 60.0     | 60.0    |
| After sales          | 76.1       | 75.9     | 70.0     | 40.0    |
| Advertise and promote| 41.3       | 39.1     | 40.0     |         |
| Broad product range  | 52.2       | 48.3     | 60.0     |         |

## Discussion

Miles and Snow (1978) suggest that each strategic type in their firm typology has a role to play. They contend that prospectors generate the technological and product innovations that push an industry forward, whereas analysers rationalise some of those innovations for marketability and ease of manufacture. They also contend that defenders lower costs to facilitate mass consumption. Accordingly, the rationale for exploring the use of the Miles and Snow taxonomy is directly related to organisational performance.

In general, the literature findings indicate that the three main types — defenders, prospectors and analysers, perform well in most environments (Conant et al., 1990, Snow & Hrebiniak, 1980) whereas reactor styles tend to perform poorly relative to others. This study provides the following differences:

(a) The emphasis on, and the perceived performance of the small number of analyser types indicates a polarisation of strategic approaches by HTSFs in the two sectors examined.
(b) As firms represented in the study have been established for over 5 years, it is clear that the two main categorisations are prospectors and defenders. This implies that reactor types and to a lesser extent, analysers, has no longer appropriate categorisations for HTSFs similar to those examined.

The research findings indicate that the proportion of the prospector firms decreases as the size of the categories increase. For example, over 50% of all the firms employing less than 100 staff are prospector type firms, whereas this figure drops to 36% for firms employing 100–249 staff. On the other hand, less than 40% of all the firms employing under 100 staff are defenders, whereas over 50% of the firms employing 100–249 staff are also defenders.

This trend, if confirmed in future studies, has some profound implications for HTSFs managing directors and points to a decline in external orientation and an increasing emphasis on defending existing in markets. Given the dynamic business environment, firms ignore the search for new opportunities and markets at their peril.

It was also notable that few firms appeared in the analyser or reactor types, which could arguably be accounted for by the industrial sectors surveyed.

## The Practical Realities of the Findings

The study presents a number of findings that are of practical use to the HTSF Managers. Firstly, strategic orientation is a key determinant of competitive advantage and must be considered during the strategy formulation and deployment stages. The high proportion of the firms proclaiming to be 'prospectors' in the size categories (1–99) is encouraging and indicates an emphasis on external effectiveness rather than internal efficiency orientation that typifies the 'defender' style.

Secondly, the results show significant differences for both prospector and defender types as depicted in Figures 2 and 3.

Prospector type firms emphasise the external orientation and staff creativity characteristics of strategy, which are correlated with customer satisfaction and innovation.

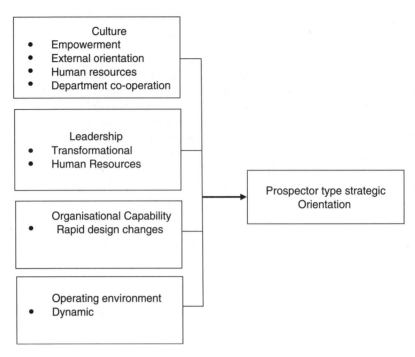

Figure 2:  Prospector type firms.

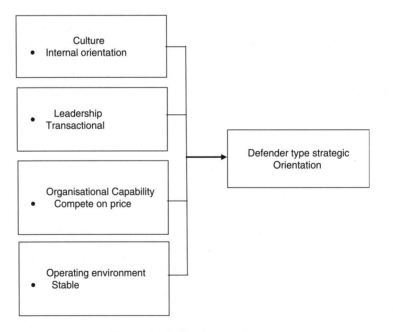

Figure 3:  Defender type firms.

On the other hand, defender type firms emphasise internal orientation and the control mechanisms of strategy, which are related to avoiding problem areas. This finding enables managers to identify the characteristics of strategy that are appropriate to their desired strategic orientation of the firm.

Defender type firms may wish to examine their rationale for emphasising external environment orientation to a lesser extent than other firms and conversely the reasons why they stress internal environment orientation. A summary of the results applicable to defender type firms is depicted in Figure 3.

Finally, there is a low emphasis on analyser and reactor type firms in this study. If this finding is replicated in future studies, then one can conclude that there is no room for these strategic orientation types — at least in the context of HTSFs.

## Limitations

This study has focussed on only two sector types: mature products and stable technology, products with short life cycles and changing technology respectively. Clearly these conclusions apply primarily to these sectors. Each sector was assumed to be internally homogeneous with no differences between sub-sectors. This assumption should be tested by future studies.

The main emphasis of this study relates to the two main strategic orientation types; prospector and defender. Any future research should consider a more in-depth approach. It would have been beneficial to augment the quantitative data with qualitative in-depth case studies or an ethnographic approach. Further testing should be carried out to confirm the relevance of these findings to practice and in particular its effective operationalisation.

## References

Amit, R., & Schoemaker, P. J. H. (1993). Strategic assets and organizational rents. *Strategic Management Journal, 14*(1), 33–46.

Asch, D., & Salaman, G. (2002). The challenge of change. *European Business Journal, 14*(3), 133–143.

Ashkanasy, N. M., Broadfoot, L. E., & Falkus, S. (2000). Questionnaire measures of organisational culture. In: N. M. Ashkanasy, C. P. M. Wilderom & M. F. Peterson (Eds), *Handbook of organisational culture and climate* (pp. 131–146). Thousand Oaks, CA: Sage Publications.

Barnett, W., & Burgelman, R. (1996). Evolutionary perspectives on strategy. *Strategic Management Journal, 17*, 5–19.

Barney, J (1995). Looking inside for competitive advantage. *Academy of Management Executive, 9*(4), 49–61.

Barney, J. B. (1986). Strategic factor markets: Expectations, luck and business strategy. *Management Science, 32*(10), 1231–1241.

Barney, J. B., & Zajac, E. J. (1994). Competitive organizational behavior: Towards an organizationally-based theory of competitive advantage. *Strategic Management Journal, 15*(8), 5–9.

Beaver, G., & Jennings, P. (1996). Managerial competence and competitive advantage in the small business: An alternative perspective. *Proceedings of 26th European Small Business Seminar* (pp. 81–97). Finland, Vaasa: University of Vaasa.

Begley, T. M., & Boyd, D. P. (1986). Executive and corporate correlates of financial performance in smaller firms. *Journal of Small Business Management, 24*(2), 8–15.

Bennis, W., & Nanus, B. (1985). *Leaders: The strategies for taking charge.* New York: Harper and Row.

Brown, A. D. (1995). *Organisational culture.* London: Pitman.

Chakravarthy, B. S., & Doz, Y. (1992). Strategy process research: Focusing on corporate renewal. *Strategic Management Journal, 13*(5), 5–14.

Chandler, A. D. (1990). *Scale and scope: The dynamics of industrial capitalism.* Cambridge, MA: Harvard University Press, Belknap Press.

Chattopadhyay, P., Glick, W., Miller, C. C., & Huber, G. (1999) Determinants of executive beliefs: Comparing functional conditioning and social influences. *Strategic Management Journal, 20*(8), 763–789.

Conant, J. S., Mokwa, M. P., & Varadarajan, P. R. (1990). Strategic types, distinctive marketing competencies and organizational performance: A multiple measures-based study. *Strategic Management Journal, 11*(5), 365–383.

Connor, T. (1999). Customer-led and market-orientated: A matter of balance. *Strategic Management Journal, 20,* 1157–1163.

Cooke, R. A., & Szumal, J. L. (2000). Using the organizational culture inventory to understand the operating cultures of organizations. In: N.M. Ashkanasy, C.P.M. Wilderom & M.F. Peterson, (Eds), *Handbook of organizational culture and climate.* Thousand Oaks, CA: Sage.

Coopers and Lybrand. (1997). *How to innovate with trust and passion.* London: Coopers and Lybrand.

Courtney, H., Kirkland, J., & Viguerie, P. (1997). Strategy under uncertainty. *Harvard Business Review, 75*(6), 67–79.

Daily, C. M., McDougall, C. J. G., & Dalton, D. R. (2002). Governance and strategic leadership in entrepreneurial firms. *Journal of Management, 28*(3), 387–412.

Daft, R. L., & Weick, K. E. (1984). Toward a model of organizations as interpretation systems. *Academy of Management Review, 9*(2), 284–295.

Daly, M., & McCann, A. (1992). How many small firms firms. *Employment Gazette.* February, 47–51.

D'Aveni, R. (1994). *Hypercompetition: Managing the dynamics of strategic manoeuvring.* New York: Free Press.

Davig, W. (1986). Business strategies in smaller manufacturing firms. *Journal of Small Business Management, 24*(1), 38–46.

Day, D. V., & Lord, R. G. (1988). Executive leadership and organisational performance: Suggestions for a new theory and methodology. *Journal of Management, 14*(3), 453–464.

Doty, D. H., Glick, W. H., & Huber, G. R. (1993). Fit, equifinality, and organizational effectiveness: A test of two configurational theories. *Academy of Management Journal, 36*(6), 1196–1250.

DTI. (1996). *Small firms in Britain report.* London: Department of Trade and Industry.

Dvir, D., Segev, E., & Shenhar, A. (1993). Technology's varying impact on the success of strategic business units within the Miles and Snow typology. *Strategic Management Journal, 14*(2), 155–162.

Garcia-Pont, C., & Nohria, N. (2002). Local versus global mimetism: The dynamics of alliance formation in the automobile industry. *Strategic Management Journal, 23*(4), 307–321.

Ghobadian, A., & O'Regan, N. (2000). Developing an exploratory model to determine the link between organizational culture, leadership style and contingency factors on the corporate strategy of manufacturing SMEs. *International Journal of Manufacturing Technology and Management*, *2*(1–7), 860–878.

Gilad, B., & Gilad, T. (1988). *The business intelligence system*. New York: AMACOM.

Gioia, D. A., & Chittipeddi, K. (1991). Sensemaking and sense giving in strategic change initiation. *Strategic Management Journal*, *12*(6), 433–448.

Grant, R. M. (1991). The resource-based theory of competitive advantage: Implications for strategy formulation. *California Management Review*, *33*(3), 114–136.

Hambrick, D. C. (1983). Some tests of the effectiveness and functional attributes of Miles and Snow's strategic types. *Academy of Management Journal*, *26*(1), 5–26.

Hambrick, D. C. (1984). Taxonomic approaches to studying strategy: Some conceptual and methodological issues. *Journal of Management*, *10*(1), 27–41.

Hambrick, D. C., & Mason, P. A. (1984). Upper echelons: The organisation as a reflection of its top managers. *Academy of Management Review*, *9*(1), 193–206.

Hannan, M. T., & Freeman, J. (1984). Structural inertia and organizational change. *American Sociological Review*, *49*(2), 149–164.

Hart, S. (1987). The use of the mail survey in 'incremental' market research. *Journal of Marketing Management*, *3*(1), 25–38.

Henderson, R., & Cockburn, I. (1994). Measuring competence? Exploring firm effects in pharmaceutical research. *Strategic Management Journal*, *15*(8), 63–84.

Hillman, A. J., & Keim, G. D. (2001). Shareholders, stakeholders and social issue. *Strategic Management Journal*, *22*(2), 125–139.

Hitt, M. A., Ireland, R. D., Camp, M. S., & Sexton, D. L. (2001). Guest editors' introduction to the special issue: Strategic entrepreneurship: Entrepreneurial strategies for wealth creation. *Strategic Management Journal*, *22*(6–7), 479–492.

Hofstede, G. (1984). *Culture's consequences: International differences in work-related values*. Beverly Hills, CA: Sage Publications.

Hurst, D., Rush, J., & White, R. (1989). Top management teams and organization renewal. *Strategic Management Journal*, *10*, 87–105.

Ireland, R. D., & Hitt, M. A. (1997). Performance strategies for high-growth entrepreneurial firms. *Frontiers of entrepreneurship research* (pp. 90–104). Wellesley, MA: Babson College.

James, W. L., & Hatten, K. J. (1995). Further evidence on the validity of the self-typing paragraph approach: Miles and Snow's strategic archetypes in banking. *Strategic Management Journal*, *16*(2), 161–168.

Jennings, P. L., & Beaver, G. (1995). The managerial dimension of small business failure. *Journal of Strategic Change*, *4*, 185–200.

Ketchen, D. J., Thomas, J. B., & Snow, C. C. (1993). Organizational configurations and performance: A comparison of theoretical approaches. *Academy of Management Journal*, *36*(6), 1278–1313.

Lee, K. S., Lim, G. H., Tan, S. J., & Wee, C. H. (2001). Generic marketing strategies for small and medium sized enterprises — Conceptual framework and examples from Asia. *Journal of Strategic Marketing*, *9*(2), 145–162.

Lorenzoni, G., & Lipparini, A. (1999). The leveraging of interfirm relationships as a distinctive organizational capability. *Strategic Management Journal*, *20*(4), 317–338.

Lounsbury, M., & Glynn, M. A. (2001). Cultural entrepreneurship: Stories, legitimacy and the acquisition of resources. *Strategic Management Journal*, *22*(6/7), 545–564.

Markides, C. C. (1999). A dynamic view of strategy. *Sloan Management Review*, *40*(3), 55–63.

McDaniel, S. W., & Kolari, J. W. (1987). Marketing strategy implications of the Miles and Snow strategic typology. *Journal of Marketing*, *51*(4), 19–30.

McGrath, R. G., MacMillan, I. C., & Venkataraman, S. (1995). Defining and developing competence: A strategic process paradigm. *Strategic Management Journal*, *16*(4), 251–275.

McKee, D. O., Varadarajan, P. R., & Pride, W. M. (1989). Strategic adaptability and firm performance: A market-contingent perspective. *Journal of Marketing*, *53*(6), 21–35.

McNulty, T., & Pettigrew, A. (1999). Strategists on the board. *Organization Studies*, *20*(1), 47–74.

Meyer, M. W., & Zucker, L. G. (1989). *Permanently failing organizations*. Newbury Park, CA: Sage Publications.

Miles, R. E., & Snow, C. C. (1978). *Organizational strategy, structure, and process*. New York: McGraw-Hill.

Miller, D. (1987). Strategy making and structure: Analysis and implications for performance. *Academy of Management Journal*, *30*(1), 7–32.

Miller, D., & Shamsie, J. (1996). The resource-based view of the firm in two environments: The Hollywood film studios from 1936 to 1965. *Academy of Management Journal*, *39*(3), 519–543.

Miller, D., & Shamsie, J. (2001). Learning across the CEO life cycle. *Strategic Management Journal*, *22*(8), 725–745.

Mintzberg, H. (1990). The design school: Reconsidering the basic premises of strategic management. *Strategic Management Journal*, *11*(3), 171–195.

Morgan, G. (1989). *Creative organization theory: A resource handbook*. London: Sage.

Nickerson, J. A., Hamilton, B. H., & Wada, T. (2001). Market position, resource profile, and governance: Linking Porter and Williamson in the context of international courier and small package services in Japan. *Strategic Management Journal*, *22*(3), 251–274.

Olson, S. F., & Currie, H. M. (1992). Female entrepreneurs: Personal value systems and business strategies in a male-dominated industry. *Journal of Small Business Management*, *30*(1), 49–57.

Parnell, J. A. (1997). New evidence in the generic strategy and business performance debate. *British Journal of Management*, *8*(2), 175–181.

Parnell, J. A., & Wright, P. (1993). Generic strategy and performance: An empirical test of the Miles and Snow typology. *British Journal of Management*, *4*(1), 29–36.

Peteraf, M. A. (1993). The cornerstone of competitive advantage: A resource-based view. *Strategic Management Journal*, *14*(3), 179–191.

Pettigrew A. M., & Fenton, E. M. (2000). *The innovating organization*. London: Sage Publications.

Porter, M. F. (1980). *Competitive strategy*. New York: The Free Press.

Porter, M. E. (1985). *Competitive advantage* (pp. 11–15). New York: The Free Press.

Quelin, B. (2000). Core competencies, R&D management and partnerships. *European Management Journal*, *18*(5), 476–487.

Ramanujam, V., Venkatraman, N., & Camillus, J. (1986). Multi-objective assessment of effectiveness of strategic planning: A discriminant analysis approach. *Academy of Management Journal*, *29*(2), 347–372.

Rugman, A. M., & Verbeke, A. (1987). Does competitive strategy work for small business? *Journal of Small Business and Entrepreneurship*, *5*(3), 45–50.

Schein, E. H. (1983). The role of the founder in creating organizational culture. *Organizational Dynamics*, *12*(1), 13–28.

Schendel, D. (1996). Evolutionary perspectives on strategy. *Strategic Management Journal*, *17*, 1–4.

Schreyer, P. (1996). *SMEs and employment creation*. Paris: OECD.

Schroeder, R. G., Bates, K. A., & Junttila, M. A. (2002). A resource-based view of manufacturing strategy and the relationship to manufacturing performance. *Strategic Management Journal*, *23*(2), 105–117.

Shaw, J. D., Gupta, N., & Delery, J. E. (2002). Pay dispersion and workforce performance: Moderating effects of incentives and interdependence. *Strategic Management Journal*, *23*(6), 491–512.

Shortell, S. M., & Zajac, E. J. (1990). Perceptual and archival measures of Miles and Snow's strategic types: A comprehensive assessment of reliability and validity. *Academy of Management Journal*, *33*(4), 817–832.

Slater, S. F., & Narver, J. C. (1993). Product-market strategy and performance: An analysis of the Miles and Snow strategy types. *European Journal of Marketing, 27*(10), 33–51.

Slater, S. F., & Olsen, E. M. (2000). Strategy type and performance: The influence of sales force management. *Strategic Management Journal, 21*(8), 813–829.

Smith, K. G., Guthrie, J. P., & Chen, M.-J. (1986). Miles and Snow's typology of strategy, organizational size and organizational performance. *Academy of Management Best Papers Proceeding*, 45–49.

Snow, C. C., & Hrebiniak, L. G. (1980). Strategy, distinctive competence, and organizational performance. *Administrative Science Quarterly, 25*(2), 317–336.

Spanos, Y. E., & Lioukas, S. (2001). An examination unto the causal logic of rent generation: Contrasting Porter's competitive strategy framework and the resource-based perspective. *Strategic Management Journal, 22*(10), 907–934.

Stopford, J. (2001). Should strategy makers become dream weavers? *Harvard Business Review, 79*(1), 165–169.

Swartz, T. A., & Iacobucci, D. (2000). *Handbook of services marketing and management.* Thousand Oaks, CA: Sage.

Teece, D. J., Pisano, G., & Shuen, A. (1997). Dynamic capabilities and strategic management. *Strategic Management Journal, 18*(7), 509–533.

Welsh, J., & White, J. (1981, July–August). A small business is not a little big business. *Harvard Business Review, 59*(4), 18–27.

Wernerfelt, B. (1995, March). The resource-based view of the firm: Ten years after. *Strategic Management Journal, 16*(3), 171–174.

Weihrich, H., & Koontz, H. (1993). *Management: A global perspective* (10th ed.). New York: McGraw-Hill, Inc.

Westphal, J. D., & Frederickson, J. W. (2001). Who directs strategic change? Director experience, the selection of New CEOs, and change in corporate strategy. *Strategic Management Journal, 22*(12), 1113–1138.

Wilderom, C., & van den Berg, P. (1997). *A test of the leadership-culture-performance model within a large Dutch financial organisation.* Working Paper no. 103952, Tilburg University.

Wilkes, N., & Dale, B. G. (1998). Attitudes to self-assessment and quality awards: A study in small and medium-sized companies. *Total Quality Management, 9*(8), 731–739.

Zahra, S. A., & Pearce, J. A. (1990). Research evidence on the Miles-Snow typology. *Journal of Management, 6*(4), 751–768.

Chapter 15

# Success Factors for High-Tech Start Ups: Views and Lessons of Israeli Experts

Schaul Chorev and Alistair Anderson

## Introduction

Beyond the widely acknowledged importance of new business, the role of young exporting high-tech business in Israel and many other small economies is seen as vital for economic growth. Israel is small and geographically isolated from the main markets, suffers from security difficulties, but fosters a culture, which promotes knowledge rich new technologies. Thus, new ventures with leading edge technologies and prospects of high growth and profitability offer a means to achieve the national goal of economical independence. Internationally however, the high-technology sector has recently suffered badly from the bursting of the dot.com bubble and the crash of the Nasdaq.

Prior to the collapse, the remarkable enthusiasm for new high-technology ventures led to quite unrealistic expectations about the profitability and sustainability of many of these new companies. A characteristic of companies formed during the overheated period was the elevation of ideas over substance and in particular, the lack of sound business practices. Nonetheless, the potential value of these high-technology companies is recognised and there is some evidence of their gradual re-emergence under difficult circumstances. To aid the sustainability of this re-emergence, this study addresses the issue of viable business models that could enhance the prospects of success. Such a model of best practices, if properly grounded in the experiences of both successful and unsuccessful entrepreneurs, may provide a template to guide the formation and operation of new and growing high-tech companies. The contribution of this paper is twofold, firstly to collate the experiences of practitioners and secondly, to synthesise these into a model that identifies factors critical for success, and factors that are important, but not deemed essential and the roles they play in shaping success.

Thus the study captures the implicit knowledge embedded in the experiences of entrepreneurs and others who are, or have been, engaged in the realities of high-tech venture

New Technology Based Firms in the New Millennium, Volume VI
Edited by A. Groen, R. Oakey, P. van der Sijde and G. Cook

creation. It categorises and synthesises this material and by analysis, establishes a practical model specifying the factors and their criteria seen to be critical for improving the success of high-technology new ventures. We developed a multi-stage study, consisting of multiple interviews of key players to develop a model, which was then tested and refined in a pilot and a final survey. The nature of this study thus provides empirical evidence regarding the factors deemed necessary for successful high-tech venturing in Israel. The paper begins by considering the role of high-tech ventures for economic growth generally and in Israel in particular. We then explain our methodology that builds upon the existing literature. Key factors and their roles are identified. From this, we present our initial findings as a tentative model which we operationalised in our pilot study. Our revised questionnaire was completed by some 80 experts and finally refined in a Delphi review. From these data we arrive at our final model.

## Defining High-Technology

Although defining high-technology industries has been the subject of debate (Oakey, Rothwell, & Cooper, 1988), a broad definition of a high-tech business is one whose business activities are heavily dependent upon innovation in science and technology (Medcof, 1999). The characteristics of high-tech include: heavier investment in R&D activities than the national average; employing a higher percentage of engineers and scientists among their staff; offering innovative and technologically advanced products; being dynamic in nature and having short product development cycles (Covin & Slevin, 1991; Oakey et al., 1988; Reeble, 1990).

## High-Tech in the Israeli Context

A number of authors have commented on the recent dramatic changes in the Israeli economy, (Azulay, Lerner, & Tishler, 2000; Dvir & Tishler, 1999; Israeli Ministry of Finance — Economic and Research Department, 2003b; Israeli Ministry of Finance-International Division, 2003a; Lerner & Avrahami, 1999). The main changes in Israel can be summarised as:

- The market has opened up to foreign competition and investments.
- Absorption of a considerable educated wave of immigration.
- Increase in government and private support in know–how infrastructure.
- Shrinkage of the defense industry.
- Education levels have continued to improve.
- Changing lifestyle now attracts many youngsters into computer science, electronics and IT fields.

High-tech is the major driver of the Israeli economy, emphasised by a growth rate that is the highest of all Israeli industrial sectors. During the first half of 2000, the high-tech growth rate was 12%, while the conventional industry growth rate was only 2%. High-tech contributes 75% of the growth in Israeli GNP and 36% of GNP (Israel Central Bureau of

Statistics (ICBS), 2001). At 3.5%, Israel has the greatest R&D expenditure in the world as a percentage of GDP (Traston, Sarusi, Kochavi, Zisapel, & Ayalon, 2002) and the highest number of start-ups in the world in relation to the population size.

A strong indicator of the substantial role of high-tech is the international comparison of venture capital investment. Figure 1 demonstrates that, internationally, Israel has the highest rate of VC investments, at 0.6% of GDP, in the high-tech sector. Remarkably, this is 50% higher than the US, three times higher than the UK and much greater than Germany or Japan.

As an indicator of the volume of investment in high-tech, Figure 2 indicates an apparent return of investor confidence in 2004.

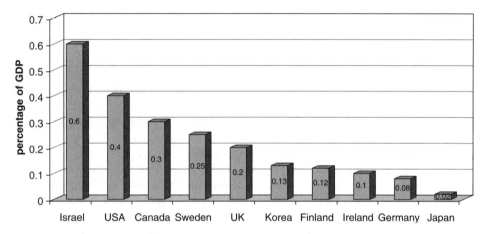

Figure 1: International Venture Capital Investment in high-tech as a percentage of GDP, 1999–2002. *Source*: Based on data from Israeli Export Institute.

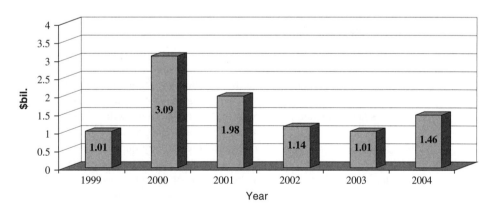

Figure 2: Capital raised by Israeli high-tech companies, 2000–2004. *Source*: Based on data from Israeli Venture Capital (IVC – Israel Venture Capital Research Center, 2004).

It is clear from the above that new high-tech firms play an important role in Israel. However, the nature of success, or even survival, is less obvious for these companies working at the leading edge of change. This is the issue addressed by this study. Based on the experience and the tacit knowledge of high-tech venture leaders, what are the critical factors for success?

### Research Methodology

The study employed a multiple stage methodology described below (Table 1).

The first phase of the study was a literature review with the objective of building a list of the topics, and their main parameters deemed as relevant for success of high-tech companies and high-tech start-ups; some are generic, whilst some are unique to Israel. After the literature review we employed an exploratory study. This exploration involved 14 in depth personal interviews with leading figures in the high-tech start-up community. The interviews were conducted with start-up managers who were involved in diverse fields of activity and at different life cycle stages, and also with investors.

Thereafter the provisional model was operationalised into a survey instrument. We applied it as a preliminary questionnaire pilot survey in face-to-face interviews with expert respondents from 12 diverse start-ups. This pilot was intended to refine our instrument; overcome any lack of clarity and ambiguity; establish reliability and discover missing issues. The questionnaire was tested for consistency (Cronbach's $\alpha$) and was modified in several steps to achieve the final questionnaire version.

The revised and final questionnaire included 42 questions and sub-questions and consisted of the 15 model topics. Each dimension was measured via a multiple set of questions. We also included many open-ended questions intended to tap into different types of responses to enquire about issues that could not be implemented in direct questions and to identify items that we had not anticipated. The final questionnaires were distributed through personal contacts and with the assistance of different organisations. The survey was completed by the CEOs or VPs of 70 high-technology start-up companies

Table 1: Multiple stage methodology.

| Step | Procedure | ⟶ Outcome |
|------|-----------|-----------|
| 1 | Literature Review | Identify the main topics and parameters influencing high-tech start-up success |
| 2 | Interviews and informal discussions | Expand literature findings with additional issues based on practical experience |
| 3 | Initial Model | Construct a preliminary questionnaire |
| 4 | Pilot Survey | Test Consistency and update the question |
| 5 | Final Questionnaire | Analysis of the open and closed questions |
| 6 | Final Model | Research summary, conclusion and recommendation |
| 7 | Model Validation | Endorsement of the model and its ranking |

and by 10 Venture Capitalists or consultants. Israel is a small country, so we treated it as one cluster so that the sample population for the interviews and questionnaires was selected from all over the country.

The data were first analysed qualitatively to investigate any unanticipated elements or patterns. This was followed by a statistical analysis of the findings, to establish a ranking of the topics and the major elements within each topic that were deemed critical and those seen as less important. From these data we developed a model. The final step was validation of the model by the Delphi method, where half of our respondents were asked to consider the model and rank it again. Using a panel of experts, the method proposes that the group will converge toward the 'best' response through this consensus process (Linstone & Turoff, 1975). The midpoint of responses is statistically categorized by the median score. Our response rate for the final stage was 40%, with a total of 16 verifying responses.

## Factors Affecting High-Tech Start-Up Success

In practice, most new ventures are better characterized by directed chaos than orderliness. However, to develop a conceptual viewpoint there is a need to establish a theoretical framework that articulates the formative dimensions of a new high-tech venture. Thus, the purpose of this section is to review the literature and to identify the conceptual categories considered important to new ventures. Cunningham (2000) asserts that more failures in high-tech can be attributed to business reasons than reasons associated with the technology. However, studies (Cooper, Gimeno-Gascon, & Woo, 1994; Dahlquist, Davidson, & Wilkund, 2000) suggest that there is no single dominant factor influencing the venture's destiny and that several dimensions shape the probability of success. Bell and McNamara (1991) describe the Bell–Mason model (as shown below) that identifies four major fields and includes twelve distinctive dimensions (three in each field) (Table 2).

Similarly, MacMillan, Zemann and Subbanarasimha (1987) identify four dimensions; the entrepreneur, the product, markets and finance. Kakati (2003), critical of the poor predictive power of existing models, adds two additional elements — resource-based capability and competitive strategy. Cooper et al. (1994) take a slightly different approach and specify four groups as predictors of new venture performance; general human capital, management know–how, industry-specific know–how and financial capital. Davidson and Klofsten (2003) describe a business platform of eight firm-level cornerstones; the business idea, the product, the market, the organisation, core group expertise, core group drive/motivation, customer

Table 2: The Bell–Mason dimensions for start-up assessment.

| Technology product | Marketing/sales | People | Finance/control |
|---|---|---|---|
| Technology/engineering (R&D) | Business Plan | CEO | Operations/control |
| Product | Marketing | Team | Finance-ability |
| Manufacturing | Sales | Board of Directors | Cash |

relations and other relations. They explain that the cornerstones can be divided into the development process (idea, product, market and organisation), key persons (founder, CEO, board of directors — expertise and motivation) and the flow of external resources (customer and other firm relations). The process emphasis in Davidson and Klofsten's (2003) work, which was tested on young high-tech ventures, seems to capture the inter-dynamic nature of the new venture creation rather better than a static list of elements. In summary, the literature indicates six distinctive domains of new high-tech ventures; entrepreneurship, strategy, marketing, technology and products, management, finance and control. To this the impact of the external environment must be added.

## The Role of Factors in High-Tech Success

The parameters described hereafter deal with the different domains influencing the success of high-tech start-ups, with a specific focus on the Israeli environment. We summarise the factors identified in a tentative theoretical model.

### *Strategy*

The strategy goal is to achieve an advantage for the organisation through the configuration of resources within a demanding environment and is, thus, the long-term direction and scope of the organisation (Johnson & Scholes, 2001). Two schools advocate different start-up strategies to gain competitive advantage; the formal strategy led by frameworks such as Porter's (1980) 'Five Forces' model, analysing the forces driving industry competition and the adaptive 'visionary' approach, proposed by Mintzberg (1994), whereby the organisation is run according to a mission, decisions are reached through learning and experience based on the intuition and creativity of the key personnel.

One of management's most critical strategic choices is whether to compete broadly across many geographic segments or, alternatively, to focus on a more limited set of geographic markets. Some researchers suggest a broad strategy for high growth markets and a focused strategy whilst penetrating a mature market. Others advocate focusing in the early stage of products. Several recent studies (Chandler & Hanks, 1994; Mahoney & Pandian, 1992) describe the importance of multiple strategies. Kakati (2003) argues that multiple strategies are the logical choice, provided the firm acquires multiple resources. However, since most small start-up ventures find it difficult to develop multiple resources to successfully implement broad strategies, the natural choice is to pursue a focus/customised strategy.

### *Marketing*

Gardner, Johnson, Moonkyu and Wilkinson (2000) identify unique characteristics of the high-tech market environment; an earlier stage of the industry life cycle, greater degree of turbulence, higher product differentiation, higher market growth rate, shorter expected life cycle, a visible future for technology, easier entry into the market, more diverse suppliers and a higher level of consumer involvement in purchase decisions. Recent developments in the marketing literature provide an interesting insight into the entrepreneurial process.

Market-driven capability, referred to as 'market orientation' is defined as a systemic process of tracking trends and recognising opportunities in the marketplace by utilising intelligence generation and information dissemination activities (Day, 1999; Jaworski & Kohli, 1993; Slater & Narver, 1999). Cooper (1994) identifies strong market orientation — a market driven and customer focused New Product Process — as a key success factor for new products. Market-oriented businesses usually seek to understand customers' expressed and latent needs and develop superior solutions to meet them (Kohli & Jaworski, 1990; Slater & Narver, 1995). Christensen and Bower (1996) claim that firms with a strong market orientation may however, over-emphasise current customer needs, possibly overlooking future products and growth opportunities; but other researchers, such as Slater and Narver (1998) disagree. Given the small size of Israel's domestic market, local firms typically need to penetrate foreign markets in order to succeed. Indeed, Frenkel, Reiss, Maital, Koschatzky, and Grupp (1994), Steinberg (1999) and Goldman (2001) all emphasise access to overseas markets as essential for the survival and success of a start-up enterprise.

There is also disagreement amongst scholars about the importance of market attractiveness. Nesheim (1997) holds that the target market should be large and rapidly expanding, so the venture should consider market size, intensity of competition, revenue (and margins) potential over 5 years and potential customers. Mishra, Kim, and Lee (1996) find that market growth and size are often most positively correlated with new product success. But, conversely, Stuart and Abetti (1987) find a strong negative correlation between success in young technological companies and market attractiveness. Their study shows that companies entering smaller and slowly growing markets were doing better than those in the larger, faster growing markets. This may be due to a lower level of competitiveness and the avoidance of head-on competition with large and strong organisations. Nonetheless, there is broad agreement that expertise in marketing activity and marketing effectiveness of the new product diffusion are critical for the success of new products (Cooper & Kleinschmidt, 1990; Gardner et al., 2000).

### Technology and Product

Great 'devices' are invented in the laboratory, but great 'products' are invented in the marketing department (Davidow, 1986). Cooper (1993) finds that the product must thus meet a market need. Cooper (1979, 1994) stresses the advantage of product uniqueness and superiority — products that are highly innovative and new to the market. Thus revolutionary breakthrough ideas are claimed to have a particular advantage; they are clearly differentiated and have high barriers for competitors. However, it is also harder to demonstrate market potential and to provide any evidence for sustainable profits (Christensen, 1997). Consequently the assessment of new 'yet to be born' product market potential is difficult. Indeed, market research may indicate little interest (potential) at this stage. Nonetheless, Perlmuter (2003) argues that leaders and managers have to understand the markets and their limits and should channel their creativity to solutions that provide the customer with the complete product.

Development of new technology (Berry, 1996), or being first to market Cooper (1979), does not determine success. The issue of what the market wants and needs thus requires a combination of marketing and technical skills. Moreover, the importance of buyer/seller relationships, particularly in improving the new product development process, is a growing area of concern and study (Birou & Fawcett, 1994). Many researchers support the notion that there is a need for strong links between the R&D department and other functional areas (Goupta, Raj, & Wilemon, 1986; Roberts, 1978, 1979; Von Hippel, 1978; Wind, 1981, 1982). Goupta and Wilemon (1990) describe the relationship between R&D and marketing as one aimed at successful product innovation. Young (1973) and Souder (1977, 1981) note that the failure to integrate R&D and marketing at an early stage of the innovation process, is one of the biggest contributors to new product failure.

## Management

High-tech is an evolutionary and fast moving environment and corporate survival depends upon successfully managing that evolution (Leonard-Barton, 1992). The pace of environmental change requires start-ups to be managed, not only by skilled managers, but also by a team capable of managing changing markets (Eisenhardt & Brown, 1998). Roure and Maidique (1986) demonstrate that founders of successful high-tech ventures tend to form larger, more complete teams. Thus a diversified management team, in which technological expertise coexists with business skills in other key areas such as marketing and finance, is recognized as a deciding factor for success in high-tech start-ups (Cooper, 1973; Roberts, 1968). High-performance new firms are rarely started by individuals; 80% are established by teams (Reynolds, 1993). Moreover, Chandler and Hanks (1998) and Roure and Keely (1990) find team completeness and previous joint experience to be strongly associated with firm performance.

## Finance

Most high-tech start-ups acquire seed funding then raise additional rounds of capital until exit or acquisition; most successful high-tech start-ups eventually become public or are procured by a larger company. Funding is thus the oxygen of start-ups. In Israel, Lerner and Avrahami (2002) note the ready availability of funds for new enterprise and that venture capital is a major source of funding. One recent difficulty commented upon was the reduction of government guarantees to new entrepreneurs. After the Nasdaq collapse in 2000 there was a substantial decrease in foreign investment in Israel, but by 2004 the uptrend returned to VC funds' inflow to the high-tech sector.

Several studies have reported important value added benefits provided by venture capitalists. These benefits include help in obtaining additional financing, improving investment decisions and providing non-financial assistance such as strategic planning and help in recruiting key executives (Gorman & Sahlman, 1989; Goupta & Sapienza, 1992; Hellman & Puri, 2001; MacMillan, Kulow, & Khoylian, 1989; Sapienza, 1992; Sapienza, Manigart, & Vermeir, 1996). But recent studies show that VCs are overconfident in their decision process and this negatively affects the accuracy of their decisions (Zacharakis & Shepherd, 2001). Moreover, Israeli VCs and their allies, the US investment bankers, claims Bainerman (2002), are solely concerned with quick exits and not with the once noble concept of building enterprises for the long-term and for the benefit of the entire country.

## External Environment

Specht (1993) classifies five main environmental factors affecting organisation formation;

- *Social*: Impact of networks, cultural acceptance.
- *Economy*: Capital availability, aggregate economic factors and unemployment.
- *Political*: Support of public or semi public agencies.
- *Infrastructure Development*: Several aspects such as the education system, the nature of the local labour market, incubator organisations, information accessibility and availability of premises.
- *Market Emergence*: Integrates concepts of niche emergence and technological innovation.

Perlmuter (2003) claims that the best solution for preserving high-tech competitiveness, is a strong education system providing broad knowledge. In Israel, the Defense Forces (IDF) has special education programs such as *Talpiot* and *Psagot*, to provide selected highly talented youngsters with a high-level technological education. Many high-tech start-ups include graduates of these programs and graduates of the IDF's special technology units. Moreover, some of the most successful high-tech start-ups stemmed from entrepreneurs formerly employed by the defense industry utilising knowledge acquired in those organisations.

## The Theoretical Model

The model in Figure 3 dubbed as 'the theoretical model' is based on the findings of the literature review. This model is later reshaped into the final research model after including the data collected from the in depth interviews' during the primary research. The major parameters of each topic were included in the research questionnaire and analysed in the findings of the empirical research.

The literature review identified some new areas as potentially having high importance. The Product and the Complete Solution emerged as separate issues closely related to Marketing and R&D. Other topics that have been emerged are the Networking and the importance of the Core Team, including the entrepreneurs/founders and the CEO, which is often one of the founders. The Core Team seems to have a crucial importance and hence is divided into two separate areas: Core Team Expertise and Core Team Commitment. The method of organisation is a managerial issue that can have an effect on the company culture and hence the attitudes and motivation of the employees. It has therefore been separated from other general managerial issues.

## The Empirical Research

The empirical study started with interviews of 14 recognised leaders of the high-tech community. The respondents made a number of observations that we captured to supplement

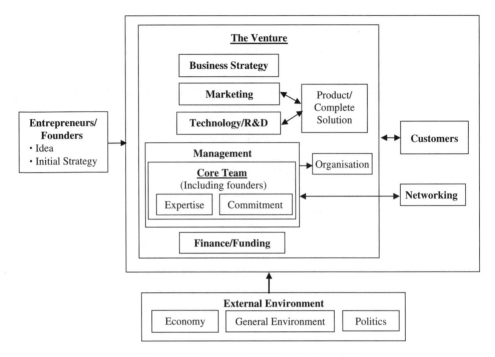

Figure 3: The expanded theoretical model.

the main issues revealed during the literature review and include in the final survey instrument. These are paraphrased below:

1. Strategy was emphasised as navigating the organisation. The business plan has to be clear and based on realistic market needs. A major fault in many start-ups is a focus on technology.

2. Core Team Expertise, diversified knowledge and harmony as they are essential for success. Very often start-ups are founded by young people who themselves lack management skills and experience but do not hesitate to hire suitable managers. At certain stages, where the start-up encounters gaps or lacks expertise, consultants can be useful.

3. Personnel should be selected very carefully. Almost every employee has a major effect on the accomplishments of the start-up.

4. The 'bubble' period created 'hot' funds that had to be invested urgently. Investors who were directors often lacked the competence to assist the start-up.

5. Most start-ups stem from engineers and scientists who often believe, erroneously, that a good product will sell. Marketing is not always seen as a profession and marketing departments are established very late (often too late). The 'professionals' should know the market; select the correct market niche, and continuously update the marketing strategy. Products that require market education should be avoided because of the lengthy and resource demanding process. Customer's needs should be well understood and their feedback implemented.

6. The product should provide a complete solution (if not sold to OEM) and has to meet real needs and provide good quality. Easy adaptation to different needs (markets and applications) is a big advantage.
7. R&D should take advantage of the unique technologies existing in Israel and the skilled workforce available in the market.
8. Strategic alliances with key customers, other companies or marketing organisations are often the key to success.
9. Funding has to be timed correctly, because of fluctuations in the economy.
10. Investors do not always add value, sometimes they become an obstacle.

## Ranking of Topics' Importance

In the questionnaire respondents were first asked (in part 1) to rank each of the 15 topics and its associated parameters on a Likert scale of 1–7, where 7 implies 'most important'. Respondents were also asked questions about details of the topics to identify any additional issues. Table 3 presents the findings of the ranking.

Table 3: Ranking of the importance of the topics.

|  | Mean | SD |  | Mean | SD |
| --- | --- | --- | --- | --- | --- |
| Idea | 5.89 | 1.240 | Strategy | 6.00 | 1.140 |
| Idea formulation | 5.87 | 1.390 | Mission statement | 5.30 | 1.555 |
| Idea meets customer needs | 6.27 | 1.136 | Industry analysis | 5.99 | 1.138 |
| Core team expertise | 6.13 | 1.018 | Strategy clarity | 5.09 | 1.487 |
| Team diversified | 5.95 | 1.142 | Strategy update | 5.82 | 1.295 |
| experience |  |  | Core team commitment | 6.47 | 0.936 |
| Team former experience | 5.04 | 1.490 | Core team association | 6.46 | 0.921 |
| Team leadership capacity | 6.32 | 1.183 | with goals |  |  |
| Consultants | 5.24 | 1.478 | Core team motivation | 6.58 | 0.919 |
| Investors' contribution | 4.64 | 1.450 | Marketing strategy | 6.17 | 1.088 |
| Organisation | 4.95 | 1.327 | Market expertise | 6.03 | 1.240 |
| Employee definition of | 5.08 | 1.238 | Marketing plan | 6.01 | 1.051 |
| responsibility domains |  |  | Marketing research | 5.08 | 1.457 |
| Few organisational levels | 5.19 | 1.368 | Market growth | 5.22 | 1.324 |
| Human relationship | 6.15 | 1.110 | New market standards | 4.78 | 1.533 |
| Customer needs | 6.15 | 1.167 | International market | 5.69 | 1.252 |
| Customer buying behavior | 6.16 | 1.126 | penetration |  |  |
| Feedback implementing | 6.15 | 1.167 | Market dynamics | 5.75 | 1.286 |
| Market receptivity | 6.11 | 1.173 | Patents registration | 5.36 | 1.751 |
| Continual sales | 5.53 | 1.588 | Perceived utility | 6.34 | 1.120 |

*(Continued)*

Table 3:  (*Continued*)

| | Mean | SD | | Mean | SD |
|---|---|---|---|---|---|
| Management in general | 6.05 | 1.250 | Distribution channels | 4.63 | 1.538 |
| Management style | 5.27 | 1.588 | Product positioning | 5.56 | 1.383 |
| Team solidarity | 5.99 | 1.204 | Marketing R&D | 5.96 | 1.265 |
| Employee development | 5.63 | 1.300 | relationship | | |
| Networking in general | 5.46 | 1.241 | Main market penetration | 5.92 | 1.285 |
| Complete solution | 5.36 | 1.485 | R&D capability | 5.95 | 1.038 |
| A gadget | 4.64 | 1.455 | Technological manpower | 5.78 | 1.141 |
| Complete product | 5.39 | 1.561 | availability | | |
| Cooperation in R&D | 5.31 | 1.528 | Defense technology and | 4.23 | 1.806 |
| Cooperation in | 5.71 | 1.426 | infrastructure | | |
| marketing | | | Development team | 5.95 | 1.161 |
| Funding type | 5.31 | 1.303 | Innovation level | 5.70 | 1.358 |
| Political situation | 4.34 | 1.553 | Technological | 5.34 | 1.353 |
| Political environment | 4.39 | 1.658 | breakthrough | | |
| Security situation | 4.26 | 1.708 | Easiness of adaptation | 5.55 | 1.341 |
| General environment | 4.96 | 1.219 | Product quality and | 6.12 | 1.256 |
| Military service | 4.45 | 1.730 | durability | | |
| Entrepreneurship | 4.85 | 1.387 | Product price | 5.71 | 1.346 |
| education | | | Time to market | 5.41 | 1.480 |
| Availability of skilled | 5.64 | 1.259 | Economy situation | 5.43 | 1.271 |
| workforce | | | Global economy | 5.63 | 1.340 |
| Government support | 4.89 | 1.420 | Domestic economy | 4.79 | 1.586 |
| Cultural and social | 5.18 | 1.325 | Availability of financial | 5.82 | 1.246 |
| norms | | | resources | | |

The data confirms that the list of 'important' topics was correct; no topic or parameter was ranked lower than 4.2. Perhaps the most revealing aspect of the data in this part was the high ranking placed on the team. Team commitment was ranked highest at 6.47 and team expertise was ranked 4th at 6.13. Other topics identified as highly important were marketing 6.17; customer relationships 6.15; core team expertise 6.13 and management 6.05. Strategy 6.0, R&D 5.95 and the idea 5.89 complete the list of the top eight topics, which formed the group of high effect factors on start-ups success. The remaining topics were ranked much lower and are perceived to belong to the second group, deemed to have a relatively lower impact.

We were interested to note that the complete solution was ranked as considerably less important than the human elements. Also funding type was not seen as critical. This may reflect the unique Israeli position in which the high involvement of VCs in high-tech start-ups generated disappointment because of the poor added value of the VCs. Both the general environment and the political situation were not highly rated, but the economic situation

was seen to have some importance. Thus, in many ways we see confirmation of the literature: a good team will be successful and that the actual product is less critical. Moreover,
the data suggests that a good team will succeed, even in poor economic, environmental and
political circumstances.

To obtain better discrimination between topics in part 2 of the survey the respondents
were asked to focus on the ranking of the topics. They were asked to classify the topics
into one of three groups, very important, important and less important and afterwards to
rank the topics within each group. We could thus establish an overall rating of 1 (the most
important topic) to 15 (lowest importance) for each of the topics. The final part of the study
involved asking half of the respondents to comment on the results of the general survey
(Delphi method).

Figure 4 is a summary of the rankings and compares the overall ranking in part 2 with
the outcome of the Delphi ranking. It demonstrates a broad trend towards agreement over
the relative importance of the different topics although some minor disagreements over the
relative ranking of the critical components are observed. The primary group that contains
eight topics deemed of highest importance and the seven topics of the secondary group
with a lower impact are clearly delineated. Both groups consist of the same topics identified in part 1 of the questionnaire. There are five topics that are ranked at the top. This
implies that all features associated with the core team (commitment and expertise), the
idea, strategy and marketing are considered critical for the new high-tech venture.
Customer relationship, management and R&D also belong to the high impact. Less important topics are networking, funding type, the economy, the complete product and the
organisation while the external factors of general environment and political situation are
ranked at the bottom (as in part 1) and apparently have the lowest influence on the fate of
the start-up.

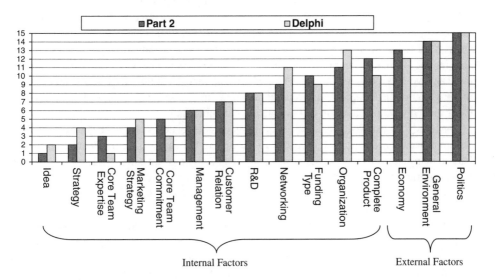

Figure 4: The respondents ranking of the topics.

In the ranking of part 2 and in the Delphi method, the idea and strategy were ranked much higher than in part 1. It seems possible that when forced to consider the relative importance of each topic, the respondents, recognised that without a good idea and a decent strategy to make it work, the other elements became secondary. In the first section, where respondents rated each topic individually, the importance of the team may have been prioritised on some sort of tacit assumption that the idea had been reasonable to begin with.

Although there were some differences in the scores attached to the ranking of the topics between companies defined as successful and those defined as unsuccessful or between the ranking of experts and the start-up community the overall positions in the rankings are very similar. The same conclusion was attained when the represented companies were divided into two groups, hardware companies (such as communication and electronic systems) and science and IT companies (Internet, software, life science, biotechnology). It manifests that most people involved in start-up activities have similar opinions about the level of importance of the different issues, some of it gained probably by similar real life experience.

## The Final Model Utilising the Research Results

The survey and Delphi results provide some confidence that the list of factors identified from the literature represent the factors deemed important by experienced practitioners. Moreover, the general agreement about the critical factors demonstrates their significance. This section elaborates on these findings by incorporating the responses to the open-ended questions.

The core team was identified as vital for success, thus both of the topics representing the core team — core team commitment and core team expertise —were placed at the top of the list. The two major factors relating to commitment — team motivation and association with the start-up goals — were emphasised. High importance was assigned to leadership capability and the diversity of team experience. This suggests that the core team is possibly more important than any other topic. Many respondents claimed that with a strong and committed team the start-up will succeed. The market may shift, the strategy could change, but ultimately people create success. Former experience was, surprisingly, ranked low. The investors' contribution was also evaluated as very low. This was probably an outcome of the general disappointment, commented upon in the interviews and open questions, about their investors' strategic or networking contribution.

The topic idea was also ranked very highly, as was the related subject, the necessity to meet customer needs, which appeared crucial to success in the market. Respondents commented that too many start-ups develop interesting products with innovative high-technology but with no real market need. Sometimes a breakthrough technology may introduce a product too early for the market. Examples cited included many products launched in 2000 and 2001 intended for the third generation of cellular communications.

Strategy was considered important, with an emphasis on future trend analysis and continuous updating. However, clear strategy at the outset and clear mission statement are not viewed as important. This was explained by noting how the dynamic situation of a typical start-up requires great flexibility in strategy formulation and adaptation. This data identified marketing as vital. Respondents allocated high importance to the perceived utility of a product comprehensive knowledge of the market, reliable marketing plan and the marketing and R&D relationship. Supporting distribution channels did not receive a high score nor was the idea of creating new markets with new standards. Respondents suggested that educating the market is too costly.

Management capability and the team solidarity within the enterprise were observed as important, particularly with reference to 'core team association with goals'. Nonetheless, no priority was given to a specific management style and it was argued that management style should adapt to each individual venture.

The relationship with customers was cited as a key driver of sales. Almost all parameters related to this topic are considered to have high priority. Personal acquaintance with the targeted customers, understanding the customer's buying behaviour, implementation of customers' feedback and market receptivity for the product were all noted. Only the parameter related to opportunities for continual sales was ranked with a somewhat lower importance. R&D was considered important, particularly in linking with the market. The quality of the R&D team and the product durability were seen as imperatives. Networking in marketing (to open doors into the target market niche) and finance (to assist future fund raising) are perceived as very valuable.

The issue of a complete product is somewhat complex and might have been misunderstood by some respondents. Although a complete solution was not ranked very highly, responses recognised that the market seeks a complete solution. A possible reason proposed was that many start-ups plan on selling directly to OEMs (Original Equipment Manufacturers), which market the complete product/solution and others plan marketing alliances as a solution to address market needs.

The economy is not seen as a main factor in success, but the availability of funds was seen as related to the global economical situation; funds should be raised when available and not when urgently needed. Most of the general environment parameters were ranked with low importance. However, many respondents noted that military service in Israel affects the capabilities of the young generation. Some of the skills gained during military service, such as improvisation skills were considered helpful in start-up regimes. Although the political situation and its parameters, the political environment and the security situation in Israel had amongst the lowest rankings, this may be a result of misconception. Some respondents noted that start-up leaders may lack awareness and understanding of the real-world behaviour, particularly when selling to large overseas organisation.

## The Final Model

Figure 5 depicts the final research model. The model highlights the topics (bold fonts within the figure) deemed to be critical for success (the group of topics with highest importance) and their key elements. As can be observed, the important topics namely, the idea; strategy; core team commitment; core team expertise; marketing; management; customer relations and R&D are relevant for start-ups in general. So although the data indicated that some factors were important in Israel these were not ranked very high. For example, team solidarity is perceived as very strong in Israel due to the influence of the military service and possibly provides a unique advantage to Israeli start-up ventures; availability of skilled work force — again a possible advantage for Israeli start-ups due to the high level of technological

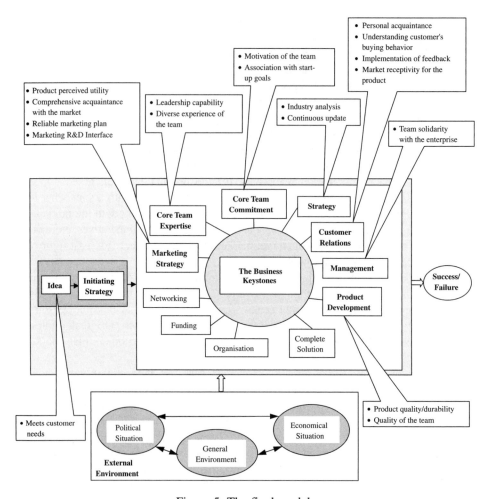

Figure 5: The final model.

education and the large influx of educated and skilled immigration from Russia during the 1990s. Penetration of the international market scored relatively high, but it is true for any start-up that has a limited domestic market. The global economy not only has a general influence on the willingness to buy new products in general and from small and distant start-up in particular, but also has a strong influence on the availability of Venture Capital funds that play a major role in financing Israeli high-tech start-ups.

## Conclusions

The attempt to establish a practical model of critical success factors for application by nascent, emergent and growing companies in the high-tech sector appears to have been successful. The data shows a high level of consistency and reliability and demonstrated two categories of topics; those of the highest importance and those ranked less critical. The first group included, the commitment of the core team, their expertise, the idea itself, strategy in general and marketing strategies; customer relationships, management and R&D capacity. Those less critical were seen as networking, type of funding, the economy, a complete product, organisation, the general environment and politics.

The research results clearly manifest some valuable aspects that should be considered by the start-up leaders:

- The value of the people. In the business world involving high-tech, where creative thinking and comprehensive understanding of the volatile markets are vital for success, the most important asset seems to be an excellent and motivated staff.
- A start-up suffers from limited resources. The creative minds of the engineers and the new opportunities arising almost daily are a dangerous combination. The ability to prioritize opportunities and to focus in terms of strategy, products and markets is crucial for success.
- Lack of resources often prevents developing a complete solution. In this case leveraging the strengths of others could be an optimal solution. Selling to OEMs that integrate the start-up product and/or using their networking in marketing and sales can be very beneficial. A strategy integrating partnership agreements can be very rewarding.
- The 'rush for gold' period is over and investment returned to utilise economic logic. The start-up should raise funds when possible and not wait until it is urgently needed.
- A start-up should strive to overcome local weaknesses. In Israel for example weaknesses were identified in management skills and international marketing.
- Don't be dogmatic, open eyes to new markets and opportunities.
- The external environment has a relatively low effect on success and should not be a barrier from entrepreneurial high-tech start-up activity.

We do not propose that the study represents an entirely inclusive picture of new venture performance because there are always variables that may have been omitted. It is suggested that the research model contains a more comprehensive approach than previously considered. Although the model has reliability and validity, detailed enhancement could improve its practical utility. Further research on larger and broader samples in different environments, cultures and industries may yield a model with broader applicability. The final model envisioned should have a multi-dimensional matrix specifying the detailed description of the necessary elements in each topic and the desired level of achievement depending on variables such as the different stages of the company life cycle, industry and geographic region.

Our model is derived from the extensive experience of many of the leading Israeli experts. In consequence, it is soundly grounded in experience and knowledge and should have a very practical utility. The application of the model may enable new firms to identify and assess their capacities and thus to change, modify, amend or to acquire capacity to improve success rates. Whilst the model is based on the Israeli environment and experience, many other countries geographically distant from their main markets share many of these characteristics, so the model may have general utility. The model is yet to be tested for causality, but could be adapted and expanded; hence it provides ample opportunities for future research.

# References

Azulay, I., Lerner, M., & Tishler, A. (2000). *Converting military technology through corporate entrepreneurship*. Tel-Aviv: The Israel Institute of Business Research.

Bainerman, J. (2002). *Broken promises – The rise and fall of Israel's technology based industries*. P.O.B. 387 Zichron Yaacov, Israel, 30900. (Unpublished).

Bell, G., & McNamara, J. (1991). *High-tech ventures — The guide for entrepreneurial success*. Reading, MA: Addison-Wesley.

Berry, M. M. J. (1996). Technical entrepreneurship, strategic awareness and corporate transformation in small high-tech firms. *Technovation, 16*(9), 487–498.

Birou, L. M., & Fawcett, S. E. (1994). Global supplier involvement in integrated product development: A comparison of U.S. and European practices. *International Journal of Physical Distribution and Logistics Management, 24*(5), 4–14.

Chandler, G. N., & Hanks, S. H. (1994). Market attractiveness resource-based capabilities, venture strategies, and venture performance. *Journal of Business Venturing, 9*(4), 331–349.

Chandler, G. N., & Hanks, S. H. (1998). An investigation of new venture teams in emerging businesses. In: P. D. Reynold, W.D. Bygrave & N. Carter, et al. (Eds), *Frontiers of entrepreneurship research*. Wellesley, MA: Babson College.

Christensen, C. M. (1997). *The innovator's dilemma: When technologies cause great firms to fail*. Boston: Harvard Business School Press.

Christensen, C. M., & Bower, J. L. (1996). Customer power, strategic investment, and the failure of leading firms. *Strategic Management Journal, 17*(3), 197–218.

Cooper, A. C., Gimeno-Gascon, F. J., & Woo, C. Y. (1994). Initial human and financial capital as predictors of new venture performance. *Journal of Business Venturing, 9*(5), 371–395.

Cooper, R. G. (1973). Technical entrepreneurship: What do we know? *R&D Management, 3*(2), 59–64.

Cooper, R. G. (1979). The dimension of industrial new product success and failure. *Journal of Marketing, 43*(3), 93–103.

Cooper, R. G. (1993). *Winning at new products: Accelerating the process from idea to launch*. Reading, MA: Addison-Wesley.

Cooper, R. G. (1994). New products: The factors that drive success. *International Marketing Review, 11*(1), 60–76.

Cooper, R. G., & Kleinschmidt, E. J. (1990). New product success factors: A comparison on "kills" versus successes and failures. *R&D Management, 20*(1), 47–63.

Covin, J. G., & Slevin, D. (1991). A conceptual model of entrepreneurship as firm behavior. *Entrepreneurship Theory and Practice, 16*(1), 7–25.

Cunningham, C. (2000). Technology diaspora: Israeli high-tech industry faces a modern day exodus. *Red Herring, Special Report on Israel, 82*, 252–257.

Dahlquist, J., Davidson, P., & Wilkund, J. (2000). Initial conditions as predictors of new venture performance: A replication and extension of the Cooper et al., study. *Enterprise and Innovation Management Studies, 1*(1), 1–17.

Davidow, W. (1986). *Marketing high-technology*. New York: The Free Press.

Davidson, P., & Klofsten, M. (2003). The business platform: Developing and instrument to gauge and to assist the development of young firms. *Journal of Small Business Management, 41*(1), 1–26.

Day, G. S. (1999). Creating a market-driven organisation. *Sloan Management Review, 41*(1), 11–22.

Dvir, D., & Tishler A. (1999). *The changing role of the defense industry in technological-industrial development in Israel*. Tel Aviv: The Israel Institute of Business Research (In Hebrew).

Eisenhardt, K. M., & Brown, S. L. (1998). Time pacing: Competing in markets that won't stand still. *Harvard Business Review*, *76*(2), 59–69.

Frenkel, A., Reiss, T., Maital, S., Koschatzky, K., & Grupp, H. (1994). Technometric evaluation and technology policy: The case of biodiagnostic kits. *Research Policy*, *23*(3), 281–292.

Gardner, D. M., Johnson, F., Moonkyu, L., & Wilkinson, I. (2000). A contingency approach to marketing high-technology products. *European Journal of Marketing*, *34*(9/10), 1053–1077.

Goldman, N. (2001). Israeli marketing: A work in progress. *Israeli High-Tech Investor*, February, 44–45.

Gorman, M., & Sahlman, W. A. (1989). What do venture capitalists do? *Journal of Business Venturing*, *4*(4), 231–248.

Goupta, A. K., Raj, S. P., & Wilemon, D. (1986). A model for studying R&D-marketing interface in the product innovation process. *Journal of Marketing*, *50*(2), 7–17.

Goupta, A. K., & Sapienza, H. J. (1992). Determinants of venture capital firms' preferences regarding the industry diversity and geographic scope of their investments. *Journal of Business Venturing*, *7*(5), 347–362.

Goupta, A. K., & Wilemon, D. (1990). Improving R&D/marketing relations. *R&D Management*, *20*(4), 277–289.

Hellman, T., & Puri, M. (2001). Venture capital and the professionalization of start-up firms: Empirical evidence. *Journal of Finance*, *57*(1),169–197.

Israel Central Bureau of Statistics (ICBS). (2001). *Annual report*. Jerusalem: Government Publishing House (In Hebrew).

Israeli Ministry of Finance — International Division. (2003a). *The Israeli economy at glance*. http://www.mof.gov.il/beinle/ie/glance_eco2003.htm

Israeli Ministry of Finance — Economic and Research Department. (2003b). *Economic outlook*. http://www.mof.gov.il/research_e/eo03_03/mainpage.htm

IVC – Israel Venture Capital Research Center. (2004). *Summary of Israeli high-tech company capital raising Q4 2004 and full year 2004*. http://www.ivc-online.com

Jaworski, B. J., & Kohli, A. K. (1993). Market orientation: Antecedents and consequences. *Journal of Marketing*, *57*(3), 53–70.

Johnson, G., & Scholes, K. (2001). *Exploring corporate strategy: Text and cases* (6th ed.) London: Prentice Hall.

Kakati, M. (2003). Success criteria in high-tech new ventures. *Technovation*, *23*(5), 447–457.

Kohli, A. K., & Jaworski, B. J. (1990). Market orientation: The construct, research propositions, and managerial implications. *Journal of Marketing*, *54*(2), 1–18.

Leonard-Barton, D. (1992). Core capabilities and core rigidness: A paradox in managing new product development. *Strategic Management Journal*, *13*(Summer Special Issue), 111–125.

Lerner, M., & Avrahami, Y. (1999). *Global entrepreneurship monitor: Israel executive report*. Tel-Aviv: Tel Aviv University.

Lerner, M., & Avrahami, Y. (2002). *Global entrepreneurship monitor: Israel executive report*. Tel-Aviv: Tel Aviv University.

Linstone, H., & Turoff, M. (1975). *The Delphi method*. Reading, MA: Addison-Wesley.

MacMillan, I. C., Kulow, D. M., & Khoylian, R. (1989). Venture capitalists' involvement in their investments: Extent and performance. *Journal of Business Venturing*, *4*(1), 27–47.

MacMillan, I. C., Zemann, L., & Subbanarasimha. (1987). Criteria distinguishing successful from unsuccessful ventures in the venture screening process. *Journal of Business Venturing*, *2*(2), 123–137.

Mahoney, J. T., & Pandian, J. R. (1992). The resource-based view within the conversation of strategic management. *Strategic Management Journal*, *13*, 363–380.

Medcof, J. W. (1999). Identifying 'Super-Technology' industries. *Research Technology Management*, *42*(1), 31–36.

Mintzberg, H. (1994). The rise and fall of strategic planning. *Harvard Business Review*, *72*(1), 107–114.

Mishra, M., Kim, D., & Lee, D. H. (1996). Factors affecting new product success: Cross-country comparisons. *Journal of Product Innovation Management*, *13*(6), 530–550.

Nesheim, J. (1997). *High-tech start-up*. Saratoga, CA: Nesheim.

Oakey, R., Rothwell, R., & Cooper, S. (1988). *The management of innovation in high-technology small firms—Innovation and regional development in Britain and the United States*. London: Pinter.

Perlmuter, D. (2003). How to maintain competitiveness in high-tech. *Haaretz Newspaper*, 20.10. 2003 (in Hebrew).

Porter, M. E. (1980). *Competitive strategy: Techniques for analyzing industries and competitors*. New York: The Free Press.

Reeble, D. (1990). High-technology industry. *Geography*, *75*, 361–364.

Reynolds, P. (1993). High performance entrepreneurship: What makes it different? In: N. C. Churchill & V. L. Lewis (Eds), *Frontiers of entrepreneurship research*. Wellesley, MA: Babson College.

Roberts, E. B. (1968). Entrepreneurship and technology: A basic study of innovators; how to keep and capitalize on their talents. *Research Management*, *11*(4), 249–266.

Roberts, E. B. (1978). What do we know about managing R&D. *Research Management*, *21*, 26–30.

Roberts, E. B. (1979). Stimulating technological innovation–organisational approaches. *Research Management*, *22*, 6–11.

Roure, J. B., & Keely, R. H. (1990). Predictors of success in new technology-based ventures. *Journal of Business Venturing*, *5*(4), 201–220.

Roure, J. B., & Maidique, M. A. (1986). Linking pre-funding factors and high-technology venture success: An exploratory study. *Journal of Business Venturing*, *1*(3), 295–306.

Sapienza, H. J. (1992). When do venture capitalists add value? *Journal of Business Venturing*, *7*(1), 9–27.

Sapienza, H. J., Manigart, S., & Vermeir, W. (1996). Venture capitalist governance and value added in four countries. *Journal of Business Venturing*, *11*(6), 439–469.

Slater, S. F., & Narver, J. C. (1995). Market orientation and the learning organisation. *Journal of Marketing*, *59*(3), 63–74.

Slater, S. F., & Narver, J. C. (1998). Customer-led and market-oriented: Let's not confuse the two. *Strategic Management Journal*, *19*(10), 1001–1006.

Slater, S. F., & Narver, J. C. (1999). Market-oriented is more than being customer-led. *Strategic Management Journal*, *20*(12), 1165–1168.

Souder, W. E. (1977). *An exploratory study of the coordinated mechanism between R&D and marketing as an influence on the innovation process*. Final Report to the National Science Foundation, University of Pittsburgh, School of Engineering, Pittsburg, PA.

Souder, W. E. (1981). Disharmony between R&D and marketing. *Industrial Marketing Management*, *10*(1), 67–73.

Specht, P. H. (1993). Munificence and carrying capacity of the environment and organisation formation. *Entrepreneurship Theory and Practice*, *17*(2), 77–86.

Steinberg, J. (1999). Taking the long view. *Israel high-tech Investor*, *5*, 18–19.

Stuart, R., & Abetti, P. A. (1987). Start-up venture: Towards the prediction of initial success. *Journal of Business Venturing*, *2*(3), 215–230.

Traston, I., Sarusi, Y., Kochavi, D., Zisapel, J., & Ayalon, E. (2002). *The technology industry as a growth lever*. Working paper for the Herzeliya Conference, December 2002.

Von Hippel, E. A. (1978). Users as innovators. *Technology Review, 80*, 30–39.

Wind, Y. (1981). Marketing and other business functions. In: J. N. Sheth (Ed.), *Research in marketing* (Vol. V). Greenwich, CT: JAI Press.

Wind, Y. (1982). *Product policy: Concepts, methods and strategy.* New York: Addison-Wesley.

Young, H. C. (1973). *Product development setting, information exchange and marketing-R&D coupling.* Ph.D. dissertation. Northwestern University, Chicago, IL.

Zacharakis, A. L., & Shepherd, D. A. (2001). The nature of information and overconfidence on venture capitalists' decision making. *Journal of Business Venturing, 16*(4), 311–332.